THE AMERICAN CIVIL WAR

A VISUAL ENCYCLOPEDIA

THE AMERICAN CIVIL WAR

A VISUAL ENCYCLOPEDIA

Edited by Angus Konstam

PRC

This edition first published in 2001 by
PRC Publishing Ltd,
8–10 Blenheim Court, Brewery Road, London N7 9NY

A member of the Chrysalis Group plc

ISBN 1 85648 608 7

Printed and bound in China

The Publisher and Editor would like to thank all
those who have contributed to this book:

writing—Michael Sharpe, George Grant, Michael Swift,
Ian Westwell, Judith Millidge,

photo research—Simon Forty, Terry Forshaw,
Louise Daubeny, Julie Brown, Teddy Neville

design—Heather Moore

The photographs are credited at the end of the book.

Preface

Encyclopedias are primarily concerned with facts, and this work provides them in abundance. It brings together information on all aspects of the Civil War, from the troops, leaders, battles, and campaigns which dominated the conflict, to a study of the political events which spawned the conflict. It includes a description of the weapons used by the combatants, including ships, artillery, and mines as well as the more mundane arsenal used by the rival armies. The work also provides numerous concise biographical entries about military commanders, politicians, and other leading figures, providing a wonderful reference tool. It also includes unit information, details of fortifications, and an analysis of the tactics and technology which helped shape the course of the war.

The bulk of the encyclopedia contains details of the battles and campaigns fought during the war, presented in a unique way; informative yet easy to follow. Campaigns, battles and the rival protagonists are linked in a sweeping and comprehensive view of the war. The work has been carefully constructed and cross-referenced in an Index at the back, so that the reader will be transported on a journey of exploration far beyond the confines of the usual history book.

Page 2: The Union's 96th Pennsylvania Infantry Regiment lined up for inspection at a camp near Washington, 1861.

Right: A powder monkey on board the Union warship *New Hampshire* off the South Carolina coast. "Powder monkeys" were young boys who brought powder charges to the gun crews. The Federal navy was always more powerful than that of the South and was able to blockade the Southern states effectively.

Abolitionists

For most of the war years Abolitionists represented the radical wing of Unionist sentiment rather than the mainstream. Although there was considerable public support for the total abolition of slavery in New England, it was by no means generally shared elsewhere in the North, in the Union Army, or in the administration. The North went to war to preserve the Union not to free the slaves. It was only as the practical necessities of total war became clearer, and the need for a wholesale restructuring of the Southern way of life in its aftermath apparent, that Lincoln's own position and that of his government shifted toward support for abolition. While welcoming this development, many within the Abolitionist movement continued to press for more radical changes, such as granting the vote to African-Americans, and they remained critical of what they saw as half measures and backsliding during Reconstruction.

Both Pennsylvania Quakers and, not surprisingly, African-Americans themselves had been expressing opposition to slavery as far back as the seventeenth century, but the organized movement for abolition developed in the late eighteenth and early nineteenth centuries. When the American Anti-Slavery Society was founded in 1833, it grouped more than a thousand Abolitionist societies organized on a regional, state, or city basis, along with women's groups, youth, and college groups and denominational religious bodies. Drawing intellectual inspiration from the aspirations of the American Revolution and the ethics of Protestant evangelism, the movement brought together white activists such as William Lloyd Garrison, Wendell

Phillips, John Brown, Julia Ward Howe, and Harriet Beecher Stowe, alongside leading African-American figures such as Frederick Douglass and Sojourner Truth. Journals and countless pamphlets were published, innumerable public meetings were held, funds were raised to assist fugitive slaves, and political figures were lobbied. In 1835 alone the American Anti-Slavery Society mailed over a million tracts, many of them to the South. In alliance with more mainstream Northern figures, Abolitionists played a key part in the Congressional disputes between pro and anti-slavery interests that dominated political debate in the first half of the nineteenth century and culminated in Southern secession and civil war. These focused repeatedly on two interrelated issues: the status of both free and fugitive blacks in the North, and the admission of new states to the Union. In 1819, with the "Missouri Compromise," and again in 1850 new states were admitted in such a way that the Union was preserved through concessions to both pro and anti-

The Abolitionists John W. Whittier (Left), William L. Garrison (Top), and Julia Ward Howe (Above) were all leaders of the anti-slavery movement during the decades preceding the war. William Lloyd Garrison, in particular, was a persuasive Abolitionist, using his Boston newspaper *The Liberator* as a platform for his views.

Above: Sergeant Major Christian A. Fleetwood of the 5th Colored Regiment, 18th Division, XVIII Corps after receiving a Congressional medal of honor for his action during the engagement at Chaffin Farm, near Richmond, VA, on September 29, 1864.

Below: The sinking of CSS *Alabama*, after her engagement with the USS *Kearsage*. Many of the survivors escaped capture as they were rescued by onlookers.

slavery interests that ultimately increased bitterness on both sides rather than resolving the issue. The failure of the Clay compromise of 1850 paved the way for the first violent conflict between pro-slavery agitators and "Free Soilers" that followed in the new territories of Kansas and Nebraska in 1854. The strengthened Fugitive Slave Act of 1850, though largely ineffective, radicalized sentiment on both sides. Although John Brown's militant actions were out of step with the mainstream of the Abolitionist movement, his execution following the failed uprising at Harper's Ferry in October 1859 electrified sentiment nationwide and helped set the stage for the approaching conflict.

Adams, Charles Francis (1807–86)

The son of President John Quincy Adams, Charles Francis Adams was Lincoln's envoy to London from 1861. A subtle diplomat, he aimed to prevent international recognition of the Confederate states and thus garner foreign financial support for the Union. His success played a vital part in the Northern victory.

African-Americans in the civil war

Despite resistance from the Lincoln administration in the early years of the war and widespread prejudice, many men from the African-American community in the North enlisted into the U.S. Army or Navy, while large numbers of women volunteered or were enlisted as nurses.

In the South, enforced black labor—both on the plantations and in munitions factories and foundries—was, of course, vital to the war effort. The widely feared general slave uprising never occurred, but historians have documented numerous minor individual acts of resistance and non-cooperation that no doubt weakened aspects of the Confederate economy. Once Union forces approached any district, work in the fields and houses virtually ceased and a flood of runaways, called "contrabands," sought refuge in Union lines. At first some pro-slavery officers allowed slaveholders to cross Union lines and reclaim their "property," but the outrage from Abolitionists and internationally damaging publicity forced a change of policy.

As the war progressed the sheer numbers of refugees caused major logistical problems, and conditions in the camps set up for them were often poor. Some found work in the hospitals and kitchens of army camps, or building trenches, while others were employed as paid laborers in liberated areas. After 1863 increasing numbers were recruited into the Union Army. With the issuing of the Emancipation Proclamation—effective from January 1, 1863—it became clear that a Union victory would mean the end of slavery, a promise that was fulfilled two years later when, on January 31, 1865, Congress passed the Thirteenth Amendment.

CSS *Alabama*

Built in England, the *Alabama*, commanded by Captain Ralph Semmes, narrowly escaped being impounded by the British authorities, leaving Liverpool in late July 1862. On August 20, she rendezvoused with her support ship off the Azores, and was loaded with supplies and munitions. In September she destroyed several Union whalers off the Azores, and other merchant ships as she crossed the Atlantic, before heading into the Caribbean, then on into the Gulf of Mexico. She sank the gunboat USS *Hatteras* off Galveston, then escaped pursuit to reach Brazil, attacking several ships en-route.

By May 1864 she was back in the North Atlantic, destroying several more Union merchantmen before putting into the French port of Cherbourg for repairs on June 11. Within two days the USS *Kearsage* was off the harbor, and Semmes sailed out to give battle. On June 19, the ships began a duel in view of thousands of spectators on the shore. The Union ship proved the more powerful, and after an hour the *Alabama* was battered into submission and sank. Most of her crew escaped capture due to the intervention of neutral vessels, and Semmes was brought to safety in Britain, where he received a hero's welcome. During her cruise the *Alabama* destroyed shipping valued at over $4.5 million, making her the most successful commerce raider of the war.

Dimensions: 230 feet x 32 feet x 20 feet
Armor: Unarmored
Armament: Seven smoothbores and one rifled gun
Commissioned: August 20, 1862

Alabama

Secession on January 11, 1861, following a vote of 61 to 39, made Alabama the fourth state to join the Confederacy. Alabama's loyalties remained divided, however, and the strong pro-Unionist sentiments that prevailed in Northern Alabama made the Confederate victory there more tenuous than in many of the seceding states. It was in Montgomery, Alabama that representatives from the seceding states met on February 4, 1861, to establish the constitution and government of the CSA, and who was to be President.

Together with Augusta and Atlanta, Alabama was an industrial center for the South for the duration of the war. The last Confederate forces in Alabama surrendered on May 4, 1865.

CSS *Albermarle*

Built in a cornfield near Plymouth, on North Carolina's Roanoake River, the *Albermarle* was laid down in April 1863 and ready for action a year later. Although her sister, the *Neuse*, never saw action, the CSS *Albermarle* had a brief but spectacular naval career. On April 19, 1864, she attacked a Union squadron in Albermarle Sound off Plymouth sinking the USS *Southfield*. On May 5 she was damaged in another engagement with Union warships in the Roanoake River, and withdrew up the river for repairs. On October 28 she was sunk at her moorings by a Union torpedo boat. The CSS *Neuse* ran aground at Kinston on her voyage down the Neuse River to attack New Bern. She was

repaired, but was destroyed on March 9, 1865, to prevent her capture.

Dimensions: 152 feet x 34 feet x 9 feet
Armor: Six-inch iron, with wood backing
Armament: Two rifled guns
Commissioned: April 1864

Allatoona Pass, Battle of, 1864

After Confederate General John B. Hood abandoned Atlanta to Union Major General William T. Sherman on September 1864, Hood moved his Army of Tennessee north to cut off Sherman's supply lines. From October 2–6 the Confederates tore up the railroad near Allatoona, but on October 5 a Union brigade from Atlanta, led by Brigadier General John M. Corse, reached Allatoona. Confederate Major General Samuel G. French's approaching division attacked the Unionists' positions at sunset, forcing Corse's men back into the earthen fort of Allatoona Pass. Despite repeated Confederate attacks, in which the

Above and Below Right: Like the other defensive battlefields chosen by General Joseph Johnson, Allatoona Pass presented formidable topographic obstacles to the attacking Union army. The Pass was part of the route of the Western & Atlantic Railroad that stretched from Chatanooga to Atlanta. This rail link served as a major supply artery for General Sherman.

Above Right: A Union steam launch fitted with a spar torpedo and a small howitzer. The torpedo (effectively a mine) was extended beyond the bow of the craft, and detonated by contact. A vessel of this type destroyed the CSS *Albermarle* in late 1864.

Confederates lost 799 men out of 1,900 and the Unionists 706 out of 2,000, the Unionists held out through the night and French, running out of ammunition and fearing Unionist reinforcements, was forced to retire and join Hood's main force.

Ammunition

ARTILLERY

The ammunition available to gunners during the Civil War came in a variety of forms, the use of which depended on the type of gun, the role it was playing in battle, the nature of the target, and its range. Generally, the ammunition available consisted of solid shot, shell, and case. The latter category consisted of shrapnel (also known as spherical case) and various types of canister.

Solid shot was the traditional iron cannon ball fired by smoothbore artillery, or the more conical streamlined type fired from rifled artillery. It was ideal for smashing hard targets such as bridges or buildings, or

was fired against dense bodies of troops. Shells contained an explosive charge that would split the round's iron casing, sending out large fragments of metal capable of demolishing buildings and damaging troops behind defenses. Spherical case, or shrapnel, was primarily directed against troops in the open. Typically, it consisted of an outer casing that contained within it a small "bursting" charge and a number of musketball-sized projectiles, which were designed to shower the target.

Canister was a close-range antipersonnel round of potentially murderous impact. It consisted of a number of shots placed in a tin canister. For example, a 12-pounder canister round was filled with 27 small cast-iron shot. The canister was designed to split apart shortly after leaving the muzzle, spraying out its contents in a manner similar to that of a shotgun. Although musket balls were the usual component of canister, in emergency the rounds might contain any bits and pieces of suitable scrap metal, such as nails. Canister was probably

the weapon in the artilleryman's armory most feared by troops.

SMALL ARMS

A bewildering array of small-arms ammunition was used during the Civil War, but there were essentially two types of cartridge, devices that consisted of both a round and an explosive gunpowder charge to propel the round down the barrel and toward its target. Although the traditional lead musketball was still used, there was increasing use of a fairly recent development, the Minié ball, which was invented by a French officer and formally adopted by the U.S. Army in 1852.

The Minié, which was widely copied by other ammunition manufacturers, successfully attempted to improved the range and accuracy of a round. Old musketballs never quite "gripped" the rifling inside a barrel when fired, and to overcome this Minié developed a conical bullet that expanded in the barrel when fired to create a better fit. This was achieved by fitting an iron or wooden plug into the hollowed out base of the bullet. Detonation of the cartridge, which could be of paper, linen, animal skin, copper, or brass, pushed the plug deeper into the hollowed out section of the bullet, thereby increasing its diameter slightly and producing the better fit.

Cartridges also developed rapidly during the Civil War. The chief change was from those made from items such as linen or paper to those constructed from metal. The crucial benefit of metal was that it was far less prone to water or moisture damage, so the likelihood of a misfire was greatly reduced.

Generally, however, metal cartridges were far more commonly used in certain Northern small arms as the South lacked the engineering facilities to produce such rounds.

Anaconda Plan

The initial Union military strategy of the war, the Anaconda Plan was the brainchild of General Winfield Scott, the general-in-chief of the U.S. Army. Scott's ambitious plan was so named because it called for a snake-like encirclement and strangulation of the Confederacy. President Lincoln at first embraced the plan, imagining that it would result in a fast end to the rebellion and reestablishment of the authority of the Federal government. In the execution of the plan, Generals Scott and McClellan decided in May 1861 that Union forces should out-flank Confederate troop concentrations in Virginia with a decisive thrust down the Mississippi River and a naval blockade of Confederate ports. Lincoln disagreed and decided that Union armies should advance

simultaneously into Virginia and Tennessee. After First Bull Run, the initiative was lost and the Anaconda Plan was superseded. Scott, who was thought to be too old for his command, retired in October 1861.

Anderson, Robert (1805–71)

Anderson had the dubious distinction of holding Fort Sumter on April 12, 1861,

Left: Ammunition schooners were commonly used to transport munitions to Union forces whose supply bases were anchored on the Atlantic seaboard.

Below: General Winfield Scott's Anaconda Plan summarized in a single cartoon. The term effectively summed up the strategic goal of strangling the Confederacy by means of a maritime blockade.

when Southern batteries fired the first shot of the Civil War. Besieged and cut off from reinforcements or resupply since Christmas, Anderson was forced to surrender the fort to his former pupil, Pierre Beauregard.

Andersonville, Georgia

Officially known as Camp Sumter, Andersonville in Georgia was the South's largest prisoner of war camp. Built in early 1864 to contain large numbers of Union prisoners who were previously held in and around Richmond, Andersonville was considered a more secure location with a more reliable food supply. However, in the fourteen months of the camp's existence, 13,000 of the 45,000 Union prisoners held there died of disease, malnutrition, poor sanitation, or exposure. The Swiss commandant of Andersonville was the only man to be executed for war crimes following the Confederate surrender.

Antietam Campaign

Following its defeat at the battle of Second Bull Run on August 29, 1862, the Union Army of Virginia withdrew to Washington. On September 2, 1862, Major General George B. McClellan was given command of all the defenses of Washington, consolidating the Armies of the Potomac and Virginia. On September 4, General Robert E. Lee's Army of Northern Virginia crossed the Potomac River and entered Maryland. Lee's plan was to take the offensive into the North while he had the strategic advantage. He believed that the presence of a Confederate army in Maryland would encourage supporters of the South within that state and help recruiting, possibly even gaining Maryland for the Confederacy. There were also political reasons for a Southern offensive, both in Maryland and in Kentucky, where General Braxton Bragg was leading an invasion. A great Confederate success might lead to

recognition by the European powers and possible military aid.

Having crossed the Potomac, Lee divided his army, sending Jackson with six divisions to capture the Union garrison at Harper's Ferry, while Longstreet's corps led a general advance towards Hagerstown. These arrangements were all laid out in the infamous "Special Order 191." Lee may have been taking a sizeable risk dividing his army so, but he believed that the Union forces would be slow to react and he thought the risk worth bearing. In fact, the Union armies had left Washington on September 5, and on September 12 they entered Frederick, Maryland, previously Lee's center of operations. Here, either by accident or design, Union troops found a copy of "Special Order 191" and, realizing its significance, it reached McClellan quickly. At this point McClellan had an exact idea of Lee's dispositions and intentions and had the opportunity to destroy the Army of North Virginia piece by piece.

By the evening of September 13 Lee had been informed that McClellan was completely aware of his intentions and ordered a withdrawal south of the Potomac. He also ordered Longstreet's corps to support Daniel H. Hill's division, which was covering the passes to the right of the Confederate advance around South Mountain.

The Union forces advanced against Hill's South Mountain position on September 14, and three separate engagements took place, the Battles of Crampton's Gap, Fox's Gap, and Turner's Gap. The aim of the attack was to force the passes and place the Union army between Jackson's corps at Harper's Ferry and Longstreet's position. Thanks to D. H. Hill's delaying action at South Mountain, the Union forces were unable to break through on the 14th. This, along with Jackson's taking of Harper's Ferry on the 15th, meant that Lee was able to concentrate his army once again, and the immediate danger for the Confederates was past. Lee then elected to stand and fight at Sharpsburg Creek rather than retire across the Potomac. On September 17, 1862, the Battle of Antietam took place, the bloodiest single day of the Civil War, yet by the end of it the Confederate position still held and they were able to withdraw across the Potomac River on the 18th and 19th, with the Union Army of the Potomac offering no effective pursuit.

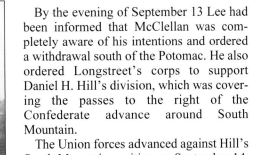

Left: Andersonville Prison Camp in southern Georgia was used to house over 45,000 Union prisoners. The lack of care and appalling conditions in the prison were exacerbated by the callous mentality of the prison commandant.

Below: President Lincoln holding a meeting with General McClellan and his staff on the battlefield of Antietam. McLellan proved to be the first of several commanders of the Union Army of the Potomac who was fired for incompetence.

The Charge across the Burnside Bridge - Antietam - 1 P.M. Sept 17th 1862 - Forbes -

Antietam, Battle of, 1862

Following his successes forcing the Unionists back from Richmond and out of Virginia earlier in the year, on September 4, 1862, General Robert E. Lee led his Confederate Army of Northern Virginia across the Potomac River into Union territory for the first time in the war, threatening Maryland and Pennsylvania. He was tracked by Major General George B. McClellan's Army of the Potomac, incorporating the remnants of the Army of Virginia. McClellan held the numerical advantage (approximately 80–85,000 troops to Lee's 40–50,000) and was gifted the added advantage of being forewarned of the Confederates' plans when a copy of Lee's operational orders fell into his hands.

On September 9 Lee sent Major General Thomas J. Jackson's corps back across the Potomac to capture Harper's Ferry in order to secure his line of retreat (if required). Harper's Ferry was surrendered on September 15. Jackson left a division under Major General Ambrose P. Hill to secure the fort, and regrouped on the afternoon of

the 16th with Lee, who had established his army by the town of Sharpsburg. McClellan had first encountered advance Confederate forces on September 14. They had held up his advance long enough to allow Lee to concentrate his forces defensively along Antietam Creek two miles west of Sharpsburg. On the morning of September 17 McClellan attacked Lee's main army. At dawn Major General Joseph Hooker led the Unionist attack on Jackson's corps to the north, on the Confederate's left wing. A Confederate counter-attack led by Major General John B. Hood stabilized the line but the Unionists continued to attack in waves, first Major General Joseph Mansfield's corps joined battle, then the corps commanded by Major General Edwin V. Sumner, pushing the Confederates back until they reached the Sunken Lane held by a Confederate division under Major General D. H. Hill. Here, the devastating fire

Right: The Battle of Antietam (called Sharpsburg by the Confederates).

Left: A contemporary sketch showing the charge across the "Burnside Bridge" over Antietam Creek by Union troops from General Burnside's IX Corps.

Below Left: The bridge photographed after the battle, seen from the Confederate (west) bank of Antietam Creek.

Below: Another view of the Lower Bridge, viewed from the same position as the sketch on page 14.

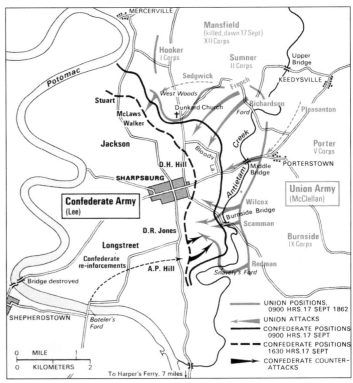

of Hill's well-concealed troops halted the Unionist advance. Nearly half the Unionist total losses of the battle were here, at what came to be called "Bloody Lane," and when the Confederate artillery arrived at 1:00pm, the battle on the northern flank petered out.

Major General James Longstreet's corps held the Confederate's right flank to the south, along Antietam Creek. The Unionist commander, Major General Burnside, struggled at first to cross the creek via a heavily defended bridge, but by 1:00pm his corps was across, and although he delayed his general advance until 3:00pm, his attack drove Longstreet's forces back to the outskirts of Sharpsburg. The battle was turned when A. P. Hill's division arrived after a 17-mile forced march from Harper's Ferry and drove the Federal's left flank back to Antietam Creek. The two exhausted armies

Left and Below: In the bloodiest single day of the war, the casualties from both sides at Antietam amounted to 22,726 men dead, wounded, or missing. This meant than one soldier in four became a casualty. These photographs by Mathew Brady shocked the American public when they were exhibited.

ceased battle at nightfall, and held their positions. It had been the bloodiest day of the Civil War. The Unionists suffered 12,400 casualties, with over 2,000 killed; the Confederates counted 10–14,000 casualties, with an estimated 1,500–2,500 killed. McLellan and Lee avoided further conflict the next day, and Lee withdrew on the night of September 18 back across the Potomac.

The battle (known by the Confederates as the Battle of Sharpsburg) effectively signaled the end of Confederate hopes of winning international recognition through bringing the war to Union territory, and on October 5, McClellan took his forces across the Potomac back into Confederate Virginia.

Appomattox, Virginia

On April 9, 1865, Lee surrendered to Grant at Appomattox Court House. Cut off on his way to meet up with Joseph E. Johnston, Lee found himself outnumbered by five to one and trapped with his 30,000 men between Appomattox Station and Appomattox Court House. The surrender itself took place in the living room of a man named Wilmer McLean, who, ironically, had moved to Appomattox to get away from the Civil War in Manassas. While Lee's surrender and the parole of the Army of Northern Virginia at Appomattox did not technically signify the end of the war, the Confederates' last hopes of victory died there.

Above and Left: The Appomattox River, flowing west through Virginia from Petersburg, was the backdrop for the final week of conflict between Lee and Grant. The inevitable end came on April 9, 1865, when Lee surrendered his army at Appomattox Court House (left).

Appomattox Campaign

The Appomattox Campaign is generally held to have started on March 25, 1865, when General Robert E. Lee sought to break General Ulysses S. Grant's ever-tightening stranglehold at Petersburg by attacking the Union position at Fort Stedman. The assault failed, and when Grant counterattacked a week later at Five Forks, on April 1–2, the thin Confederate line snapped, and Lee's skeleton forces abandoned Richmond and Petersburg on April 3, 1865. From this point onward the Confederate Army of Northern Virginia became involved in a race against Grant's Army of the Potomac. Lee had the advantage of a headstart and, initially, seemed relieved to be out of the breastworks and entrenchments around Petersburg. He headed for Amelia Junction, where he expected to find supplies and then to march along the route of the Danville & Richmond Railroad and join up with General Joseph E. Johnston's forces, which were retiring northward into North Carolina.

On reaching Amelia Court House on April 4, Lee found that the long-awaited supplies had not arrived. He had little option but to halt his army's march, well aware that Grant's troops were perilously close behind. He waited for a day at Amelia Court House, sending out forage parties all the time to try and provide for his men. However, the surrounding countryside had been stripped bare to provide for the defense of Petersburg and very few provisions were found.

The Army of Northern Virginia left Amelia Court House on the 5th but found that their delay had allowed Union cavalry and infantry to overtake them and entrench themselves on the route of the Confederate march. Lee was unwilling to attack a strong Union position and instead decided to strike out westward and follow the South Side Railroad, aiming to resupply his troops at Farmville. Due to a lack of food and sleep, the retreat became increasingly ragged, with numerous Confederate soldiers falling out of the line of march.

On April 6 the rearguard of the Army of Northern Virginia, two corps under Anderson and Ewell, was cut off from the rest of the army by Sheridan's cavalry at Sayler's Creek. Supporting Union infantry quickly destroyed these forces, causing Confederate losses of over 8,000 men. The remainder of Lee's ever-dwindling army reached Farmville on April 7, narrowly ahead of the pursuing Union forces, who had to be held back by the cavalry while the infantry moved out of the town.

Lee now decided to follow the Richmond to Lynchburg stage road, hoping to make it to Appomattox Station where he could receive rations and, again, follow the railroad. However, unknown to him, three

Union infantry corps and Sheridan's cavalry had already crossed the Appomattox River and were making their way to Appomattox Station ahead of him.

The Army of Northern Virginia reached Appottamox on the 8th, only to find that the Union forces had beaten them to it. After an attempt by Major General John B. Gordon's corps on the morning of the 9th to push back the Union forces had failed, Lee found his army trapped between two strong Union forces and had no choice but to ask Grant for terms, thus effectively ending the American Civil War.

CSS *Arkansas*

The *Arkansas* was laid down in Memphis, Tennessee, in early 1862, and when the city

Left: The swampy terrain surrounding the Appomattox River provided an obstacle to both sides during the brief final campaign of Lee and Grant.

Below Left: The key to Grant's success was logistics, and riverside depots such as this ensured the Union army remained in adequate supply as it fought its way inland.

Below: The CSS *Arkansas* was completed up the Yazoo River, then steamed through the Union fleet to reach the comparative safety of Vicksburg.

faced capture the *Arkansas* was towed to safety. She was completed on the Yazoo River. On July 15, 1862, the CSS *Arkansas* steamed down the Yazoo to attack the Union fleet. On July 15 she skirmished with Union gunboats, then continued into the Mississippi River. She ran through the Union fleet above Vicksburg and reached the safety of the city. On July 22 she repulsed an attack by the gunboat USS *Queen of the West* before being ordered downstream to bombard Baton Rouge. On August 6 she was attacked by the ironclad USS *Essex*. Her engines failed, and the Confederate ironclad was run aground and destroyed by her crew.

Dimensions: 145 feet x 34 feet x 11 feet
Armor: Two inches, with wood backing
Armament: Two rifled and four smooth-bore guns
Commissioned: May 26, 1862

Arkansas

Seceding on May 6, 1861, Arkansas was a slave-holding Southern state that joined the Confederacy on May 18, 1861.

On January 19, 1864, the pro-Union Constitutional Convention of Arkansas passed an anti-slavery measure that made the state eligible for return to the Union, and Lincoln was quick to propose an

election there the very next day. Despite this, the last Confederate forces in Arkansas, under the command of Brigadier General M. Jeff Thomson, did not surrender until May 1865.

Arkansas River

Following the fall of Vicksburg the Union forces turned their attention to the control of Arkansas. Fort Hindman, a Union fort on the Arkansas River, had already fallen to Rear Admiral D. D. Porter when Major General Frederick Steele was sent to Helena to take over control of Union forces in the region. Steele was quick to recognize that the security of Missouri and northern Arkansas from future rebel incursions rested on the control of the Arkansas River.

Armies

From 1776 on, American armies were based around citizen soldiers, where a small professional core was augmented by volunteers (or conscripts) raised from the civilian population. This was never more apparent than during the Civil War. To European military observers the campaigns of the early years of the war seemed to resemble fighting between two untrained mobs, as both armies lacked the polish found in Europe's professional standing armies. Despite their appearance, by the middle of the war both sides fielded veteran armies, tested in some the bloodiest conflicts fought on American soil. The total number of dead was probably in excess of 600,000, and fighting often took place in heavily wooded terrain which would have destroyed the cohesiveness of even European armies.

Although a string of initial Confederate victories gave the Southerners an aura of superiority, their success lay more in superior leadership than in any innate martial ability. Union soldiers were equally committed and eager for victory.

The volunteers of both sides were unprepared for the horrors of war. The lessons of the first year of war showed that there would be no quick end to the conflict, and an increasing professionalism was soon to be found in the ranks of both armies. American citizen soldiers were far more independent-minded than soldiers in professional standing armies, and therefore the maintenance of discipline in both Union and Confederate armies was a problem. Looting, drunkenness, desertion, and theft were commonplace, and after 1861, military justice was usually swift and harsh. One Union soldier wrote home to his mother claiming, "I have seen more wickedness and unblushing sin since my connection with the army than I ever dreamed of before."

Union forces were generally better fed and supplied than Confederate ones, and were able to forage, as they usually fought on Southern soil. Both sides suffered from disease in equal measure, and poor hygiene and a lack of sanitation meant that more soldiers died from disease than from the enemy. Lice were a constant irritation, and the opportunities to wash clothes and bodies were rare. Given the privations of the field, it was expected that soldiers from rural backgrounds would be better prepared than those from the cities. There may have been some truth in this, and it may in part explain the apparent superiority of

Left: Lincoln and his main military men. At the back, from left to right: Farragut, Sherman, Meade, Grant, Hooker, Sheridan; seated, Lincoln and Hancock.

Below: While the majority of Confederate soldiers came from a rural background, most Union soldiers in the eastern theater were raised in an urban environment, and were ill-prepared for the rigors of campaigning. This view depicts the Union Volunteer Refreshment Salon in Philadelphia, PA.

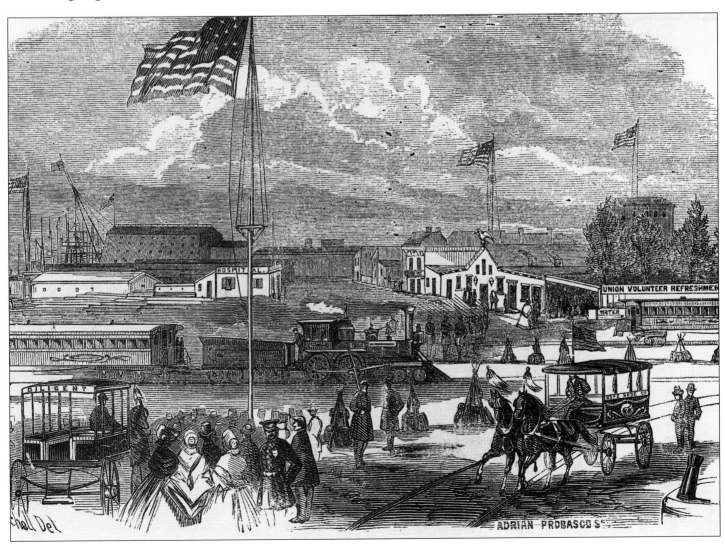

Southern soldiers over their largely urban opponents during the first years of the war. Contemporaries reported that after a year of active campaigning, it was impossible to tell the city dweller from the farm-boy or the regular soldier from the conscript or volunteer.

Apart from the rigors of campaign life, active service also served to strengthen bonds between men in the same unit. These bonds of comradeship were forged through shared dangers in battle, an experience which changed the perceptions of everyone who survived the ordeal. Soldiers reported fear before a battle, and depression afterward—a "survivor's guilt." The process also created battle-hardened soldiers out of

Above and Right: Discipline in both armies became increasingly severe as the war progressed. Punishments in the field (Above) and exposure to action turned raw recruits into hardened veterans such as this Union soldier (Right).

Far Right: The Union Army of the Potomac fought its campaigns in enemy territory, and consequently an enormous effort was made to keep the army supplied.

raw recruits, and turned the citizen soldiers of both armies into experienced combat veterans.

Armies, Organization of

The armies that fought in the Civil War were the strategic elements of maneuver, whose commanders could decide the fate of a theater, or the course of the war, in a single day. In the eastern theater, the Union Army of the Potomac and the Confederate Army of Northern Virginia served as the principal forces. In addition, a secondary Confederate army was stationed in Virginia's Shenandoah Valley, while the Union Army created smaller secondary armies at will during the war. These smaller armies fought in distinct independent areas of operation, such as in the Shenandoah, or along the James River. In the west, the situation was more complicated. While the principal Confederate army remained the Army of the Tennessee throughout the war, several Union armies fought against it. The principal Union force was also called the Army of the Tennessee, but it was supported by secondary formations—the Army of the Ohio and the Army of the Cumberland. On occasions these armies cooperated, but they were also capable of fighting independently. Secondary armies—such as the Trans-Mississippi Army—were also created for special independent operations beyond the Mississippi or in other areas beyond the effective control of the main forces in the theater.

Typically, an army would consist of two or more army corps, a supporting cavalry formation, and sometimes its own reserve park of artillery. In addition, an extensive staff, signals units, engineers, a logistical department, topographical experts, and an intelligence-gathering network supported the commanding general. The leading army staff members supporting the army commander included an adjutant general (a chief of staff), who was responsible for the army's movements, administration, appointments, and intelligence. An inspector general was responsible for the army's discipline and training, and was supported by a provost marshal, his staff (military police), and a judge advocate, to organize court-martial proceedings when required. The quartermaster general oversaw supply and transportation for the army, and his subsistence and ordnance staff contained subsections that dealt with medicine, pay, post, and rail and wagon transport. Each staff was also accompanied by couriers to relay orders down the chain of command. These couriers remained the main form of

communication in Civil War armies. Later in the war, or when an army had been stationary for some time, couriers were augmented by field telegraph lines or a system of signal stations (which used "wig-wag" flags or lever signals). Given the sometimes difficult country in which armies had to fight (such as the Wilderness in Virginia), couriers were also used to maintain links and a steady flow of information between the army commander and his subordinate units. This supply and transmission of information, and the efficiency of a general's staff, were vital to the success of the army. In many cases (and especially in the Union army), poor staff work and a lack of experience greatly limited the effectiveness of the army. In some cases, when armies grew extremely large, these problems of communication and control became increasingly acute.

Above: Union deserters were frequently executed in the field by members of their own unit.

Right: A wagon train carrying supplies for the Union army photographed as it entered the city of Petersburg soon after its capture.

Far Right: Scenes of an army encampment, home to tens of thousands of American volunteers of both sides for four bloody years.

Armor, Naval

Confederate experiments showed that two sheets of two-inch armored plate, backed by at least a foot of timber, were needed to withstand enemy fire. This became the standard armored protection for Confederate ironclads during the war. In the North, the hulls of Union monitors were all but submerged, and protection was concentrated on the turret. The turret of the USS *Monitor* had eight layers of one-inch plate, while her hull sides were protected by over four inches of armor. This configuration was repeated on most Union ironclads. Upper decks were rarely armored, although the pilot house was protected. In the South, if plate was unavailable, iron rails were used as a substitute. As the war progressed, iron became increasingly scarce, and several half-completed ironclads were abandoned due to a lack of armor. Although armored warships first appeared in Europe, ironclads received their baptism of fire in the Civil War.

Army of Northern Virginia (Confederate)

During the first year of the war, the Confederate army raised to defend Virginia in the eastern theater was confusingly known as the Army of the Potomac, which served as the boundary between Virginia and Maryland. In 1862, the Union's own Army of the Potomac launched its new offensive up the Peninsula from Fort Monroe through Wlliamsburg and Yorktown towards Richmond. On June 27, 1862, the Confederate defenders had already fought the Union, forcing the invaders to halt. President Davis renamed the army defending Richmond the Army of Northern Virginia, and appointed General Robert E. Lee to command it. It was already

Above and Right: The battle between the USS *Monitor* and the CSS *Virginia* (ex-*Merrimac*) on March 9, 1862 (Right) proved a turning point in naval warfare. Although neither vessel was sunk in this first battle between two ironclads, this photograph (Above) of the damaged turret of the *Monitor* taken after the battle bears testimony to the ferocity of the fighting.

battle-hardened, and during the campaign known as the Seven Days' Battles which followed, it proved its superiority over its Union opponents. Although it lacked the corps organization which had recently been adopted by the Union, it was divided into two "proto-corps" under General Thomas "Stonewall" Jackson and General John B. Magruder. Jackson commanded four divisions, while Magruder commanded seven. In addition, the army contained a reserve of artillery, and an un-brigaded cavalry force led by General J. E. B. Stuart, plus a few independent formations. Lee stripped the commands of both his subordinates down to three divisions each, and used them as independent elements of maneuver. He kept the remaining five divisions under his command. This seemingly inflexible system worked superbly, and the Army of the Potomac was consistently outmaneuvered and outfought. Within a week, the Union army was in retreat, and was withdrawn back to Washington.

During the Antietam Campaign which followed, Lee divided his army into two corps, one of four divisions commanded by Jackson, and the other of five divisions, which he gave to General James Longstreet. Stuart still controlled Lee's cavalry. By the end of the year, the two corps were officially given the designations of I Army Corps (Longstreet) and II Army Corps (Jackson). Unlike the corps formations of their Union opponents, these formations were larger, and by 1863, the Confederate army corps in the Army of Northern Virginia were twice the size of those used by the Union. The III Army Corps was added to the army in 1863, commanded by General Ambrose P. Hill, and following Jackson's death in May 1863, II Army Corps was given to General Richard Ewell. The loss of Jackson was a severe blow to the army, as Lee lost the only subordinate commander in whom he had complete faith.

Following the army's defeat at Gettysburg in July 1863, the Army of Northern Virginia was on the defensive. Apart from the creation of a Cavalry Corps under Stuart, the organization of the army remained the same through the bloody battles of attrition of 1864. Following the Petersburg Campaign and the abandonment of Richmond in April 1865, the army retreated as far as Appomattox, where Robert E. Lee surrendered the remains of his army to General Grant. Throughout the war, the army remained the most tenacious, best led, and most experienced formation in the Confederate army.

Army of the Cumberland (Union)

The army was formed in mid-1862 in Nashville from elements of the Army of the Ohio, and consisted of three proto-corps. Under General William S. Rosecrans it received its baptism at Murfreesboro (December 1863), then renewed the offensive in mid-1863, chasing the Confederate Army of the Tennessee as far south as Chattanooga. Following the battles of Chickamauga and Lookout Mountain (1863), Rosecrans was replaced by General George Thomas. His three corps (IV, XIV, and XX) were augmented by a Cavalry Corps, and formed part of General Sherman's Army during the campaign for Atlanta and beyond.

Army of the Gulf

Several small armies were formed during the campaigns along the Mississippi River and its tributaries. The Department of the Gulf was formed during the occupation of New Orleans in April 1862 under General Nathaniel Banks. Although not officially an army, it was sometimes called so in contemporary accounts. In 1864 it combined with the Department of Arkansas, commanded by General Frederick Steele, to conduct operations up the Red River, to conquer upper Louisiana and lower Arkansas (the "Trans-Mississippi region"). The expedition was an unmitigated disaster, and Banks' troops took no further active role in the war.

Opposite Page: Every army staff, such as Sherman's "Grand Army" (Top right, photographed during the Atlanta campaign) contained extensive support units, administering the supply of the army (Center right) and its welfare (Below right).

Below Left and Right: Visiting the monument to "Stonewall" Jackson, placed where he fell, May 2, 1863. After his death Ewell took over command of Confederate II Army Corps.

Army of the James (Union)

In 1864 Grant envisaged a diversion against Richmond while the main armies campaigned in Northern Virginia. Consequently, in April 1864 the Army of the James was founded using X and XVIII Army Corps, supported by the 10th Cavalry Division. Both corps were deactivated in December 1864, and the troops transferred to other formations, and the army was reformed using XXIV and XXV Army Corps, the latter being a "colored" formation. Commanded by General Benjamin Butler, the Army of the James performed badly during the Bermuda Hundred Campaign (1864), and also during the fighting around Petersburg (1864–65).

Army of the Ohio (Union)

General Don Carlos Buell's Department of the Ohio was formed around Louisville, Kentucky, during December 1861. Although Buell planned to use his five divisions to advance on Nashville, Tennessee, inertia prevented any offensive until after General Grant captured Fort Donelson in January 1862. Buell advanced to support Grant's flank, occupying Nashville in February, his force now officially designated the Army of the Ohio. By March he had 50,000 troops around Nashville. When Grant moved his command to Shiloh, Buell was ordered to join him. At the Battle of Shiloh (April 6–7, 1862), Buell arrived on the second day of the battle with four dicvisions, saving Grant's army. The Army of the Ohio's forces consisted of the divisions of McCook (2nd), Nelson (4th), Crittenden

(5th), and Wood (6th)—a total force of 17,918 men.

For the remainder of the year the Army of the Ohio campaigned in Tennessee before being sent to eastern Kentucky to hold off a Confederate offensive. Following Buell's victory at Perryville (October 8, 1862) the army became an occupation force, and Buell was removed from its command. By early 1864 the army consisted of a single corps (XXIII Army Corps), and was commanded by General John Schofield during the Atlanta campaign, where it formed part of Sherman's army. It was used to counter the surprise Confederate advance in Tennessee, and fought off General Hood's army at the battles of Franklin (November 30) and Nashville (December 15), with heavy casualties. The decimated army remained in Tennessee for the remainder of the war.

Right, Below Right and Overleaf: The Army of the Potomac was a vast machine. These photos of camp life depict a field post office (Overleaf), a park for supply wagons (Right), and a regimental camp (Below Right). By 1864, the army was the largest gathering of soldiers in America, a force of over 120,000 men.

Below: The city of Atlanta became the focal point for the final decisive campaign in the western theater. Like Chattanooga the year before, it was a strategic objective as it served as a major rail junction and supply base. Following the fight for the city between the Confederate Army of the Tennessee and three Union armies during the summer of 1864, Atlanta was left in ruins.

Army of the Potomac (Union)

Following its defeat at the First Battle of Bull Run (July 21, 1861), the Union army fell back to Washington. General George B. McClellan was appointed to command the army, which was redesignated the Army of the Potomac in October 1861. McClellan did an excellent job of converting this army into an effective force, which had grown to 155,000 men.

In March 1862 he divided his command into army corps, and in April six corps were transferred by sea to Fort Monroe, Virginia. During the Peninsular Campaign which followed, McClellan with 105,000 men advanced as far as the outskirts of Richmond. During the Seven Days' Battles (June 26–July 1) he was outfought by the Confederates commanded by General Robert E. Lee. The army consisted of II Corps (Sumner), III Corps (Heintzelman), V Corps (Porter), and VI Corps (Franklin). I Corps (McDowell) remained in northern Virginia, screening Washington. Heintzelman's forces were later temporarily assigned to General Pope's command (the Army of Virginia).

By August the Army of the Potomac was back in Washington, and Franklin and Heintzelman's corps assisted Pope during the Second Bull Run Campaign. By September, when Lee launched his

Left: Army of the Potomac field post office.

invasion of Maryland, McClellan screened Washington with three corps while he pursued Lee with six more (84,000 men). At the Battle of Antietam (September 17, 1862), McClellan commanded forces composed of I Corps (Hooker), II Corps (Sumner), V Corps (Porter), VI Corps (Franklin), IX Corps (Burnside), and XII Corps (Mansfield), but he failed to defeat Lee. He was duly fired in November 1862, and replaced by General Ambrose Burnside, who in December launched an attack on the Confederates at Fredericksburg (December 13). The result was a bloody repulse, and Lincoln fired Burnside too, appointing General Joseph Hooker to command the army. "Fighting Joe" revitalized the dispirited army, and in May 1862 the six corps under his command participated in the Battle of Chancellorsville (May 2–3, 1863). It ended in another defeat, and Hooker was replaced by General George Meade.

The army's first victory came at Gettysburg (July 1–3, 1863). Meade had 85,000 men under his command at the battle—I Corps (Reynolds), II Corps (Hancock), III Corps (Sickles), V Corps (Sykes), VI Corps (Sedgewick), XI Corps (Howard), XII Corps (Slocum), and the Cavalry Corps (Pleasanton).

The army was expanded during the winter of 1863–64, and although Meade remained in command, General Ulysses S. Grant was given overall command of all Union forces, and campaigned alongside Meade. In effect, he became the army's new commander. Grant led the army through a series of battles of attrition during the summer of 1863, until by June 1864 his troops had crossed the James River and stood in front of Petersburg. During the lengthy siege which followed, the Confederates were bled dry, and by April the siege was over as Lee was forced to abandon Petersburg and Richmond. The end came when Grant forced Lee to surrender on April 9, 1865, ending the Army of the Potomac's four years of chequered history.

THE AMERICAN CIVIL WAR: A VISUAL ENCYCLOPEDIA

Army of the Tennessee (Confederate)

The first Confederate army in the western theater was named the Army of the Mississippi, but following its defeat at Shiloh (April 6–7, 1862), the force was reformed around Corinth, Mississippi. General Braxton Bragg was given command of the army, which moved to Chattanooga, Tennessee, and was renamed the Army of the Tennessee. Bragg's army participated in a campaign to liberate Kentucky, but after a minor setback at Perryville in October, Bragg retreated to Knoxville, Tennessee. His force of 35,000 men was divided into General Polk's corps (two divisions), and General Hardee's corps (three divisions). In addition, General Wheeler commanded four brigades of cavalry.

When General Rosecrans advanced into eastern Tennessee in late 1862, Bragg was defeated by Rosecrans at Murfreesbro (December 31–January 2). For the next six months both armies remained inactive in central Tennessee. Finally, in June 1863, Rosecrans launched an offensive which forced Bragg to retreat to Chattanooga, Tennessee, which was evacuated in September. Rosecrans pursued Bragg, but reinforced by Longstreet's corps from Virginia, Bragg turned and fought. At the Battle of Chickamauga (September 19–20, 1863), Bragg won a costly victory, losing 18,500 of his 66,000 men in the battle. At Chickamauga, Bragg divided his army into two wings, commanded by Generals Leonidas Polk and James Longstreet. Polk's right wing contained three corps; his own of one division, Hill's corps (two divisions), and Walker's corps (two divisions). Longstreet commanded Buckner's corps (three divisions) and Hood's corps (three divisions). In addition, Bragg's army contained two small cavalry corps, under

General Joseph Wheeler (two divisions), and General Nathan Forrest (two divisions).

Rosecrans withdrew into Chattanooga, where his army was besieged by the Army of the Tennessee for two months before Grant arrived and broke the siege. Grant cleared the Confederates off Lookout Mountain and Missionary Ridge (November 24–25, 1863), forcing Bragg to retreat southward into Georgia. Bragg was replaced by Joseph E. Johnston, an expert in defensive warfare, and the army prepared for a fresh wave of Union attacks towards Atlanta in the spring.

In March 1864 General Sherman's 98,000 men drove south, and although Johnston held up his advance several times, he was eventually forced back to Atlanta. During the Atlanta campaign the Army of the Tennessee mustered 62,000 men, divided into three army corps—Hardee's corps (four divisions), Hood's corps (three divisions), and Polk's corps (three divisions) were supported by Wheeler's cavalry corps (four small divisions). During a series of battles around the city in July 1864, Johnston was defeated, and his army lost a third of its strength. He was replaced by General John B. Hood, who planned an invasion of Tennessee to divert Sherman. His campaign was a disaster, and the Army of the Tennessee was virtually destroyed in two battles at Franklin and Nashville. The remnants gathered in North Carolina, and Johnston was reappointed as their commander. On March 18, 1865, he was defeated at the Battle of Bentonville, and the Army of the Tennessee finally surrendered a month later.

Army of the Tennessee (Union)

General Ulysses S. Grant commanded 20,000 men, as part of General Halleck's Department of the Missouri. In February 1862 his troops captured Forts Henry and Donelson, forcing the Confederates to abandon Kentucky. Reinforced by another 28,000 men, his force was designated the Army of the Tennessee in late February. The army was transported down the Tennessee River, arriving near Shiloh on March 11. Grant's 48,000 men were divided into six divisions, under McClernand (1st), W. H. L. Wallace (2nd), Lew Wallace (3rd), Hurlbut (4th), Sherman (5th), and

Prentiss (6th). Grant was attacked at Shiloh (April 6–7, 1862) but repulsed the attack.

The army then moved west to campaign on the Mississippi around Memphis. Grant's attempts to take the city of Vicksburg from the rear proved fruitless until he was able to bypass the city in March and April 1863, landing his army south of Vicksburg. His force consisted of 41,000 in three army corps under McClernand (XIII), Sherman (XV), and McPherson (XVII). After surrounding

Vicksburg, the city was besieged. It surrendered on July 14, 1863.

After four months of campaigning in Mississippi, the army was sent to Chattanooga in November, where Grant coordinated the attacks which relieved the city. In 1864, while Grant assumed the supreme Union command, the army was given to General McPherson. During the Atlanta campaign his three corps (XV, XVI, and XVII) led the advance into Atlanta, then participated in Sherman's

Above: Grant cleared the Confederate Army of the Tennessee off Lookout Mountain and Missionary Ridge on November 24–25, 1863, forcing Bragg to retreat southward into Georgia.

Opposite Page: Lieutenant General Joseph E. Johnston (Left), commanded the Confederate Army of the Tennessee during the early part of the Atlanta campaign, while General Ulysses S. Grant (Right) rose from command of the Union Army of the Tennessee to head the entire Union army. During 1864–65, Grant led from the field, attaching his HQ to that of General Meade, commander of the Army of the Potomac.

March to the Sea. The army ended the war in North Carolina.

Army of the Valley (Confederate)

Raised to defend the Shenandoah Valley, this army was commanded by General Thomas "Stonewall" Jackson. During the spring of 1862, although his small army was always outnumbered, he inflicted a string of defeats on his opponents that prevented any further Union incursions into the valley for two years.

General Jubal Early was sent to the valley in June 1864, and his 21,000-man corps of five infantry and two cavalry divisions was renamed the Army of the Valley. In the battles of Winchester and Cedar Creek (1864), Early was defeated, and by October the Shenandoah was in Union hands.

Left: Defensive positions around Atlanta.

Pages 38–39: This photograph of a Union ammunition supply depot in late 1864 shows thousands of roundshot, shells, and mortar rounds, a fraction of the ordnance fired against the Confederate defenses of Petersburg.

THE AMERICAN CIVIL WAR: A VISUAL ENCYCLOPEDIA

Artillery

During the Civil War, the artillery of both sides was classified in several ways—by the weight of the projectile it fired, the bore of its barrel, or by the degree of ease of mobility of the piece.

The most commonly used type of artillery was known as "field." Such ordnance was light, easy to move, and was the type most commonly found in the front line of battle. The second category was termed "heavy" and had two main subdivisions. Siege artillery, large weapons that were still mobile enough to keep to keep pace with an army, was deployed to destroy enemy forts. Coastal artillery, as the name suggests, was primarily used in coastal fortifications to protect ports from naval attack. These were massive pieces that could only moved with great difficulty.

Such ordnance, whether field or heavy, was further subdivided into types reflecting the trajectory of the missile fired. Guns, the most common, fired rounds on a flat trajectory out to long range. Howitzers, which tended to be lighter than guns and with shorter barrels, usually fired heavier rounds than guns to medium ranges, and tended to have a rising-falling trajectory. The final category was the mortar, which had a very short barrel and fired large rounds over short distances with a steeply rising and plunging trajectory.

Artillery was also classified according to whether its barrel had been rifled or was of the smoothbore type. The latter was more common at the outbreak of the war, but rifled artillery became increasingly significant because the spin imparted by the barrel's internal grooving produced greater power, range, and accuracy.

Finally, artillery was either breech- or muzzle-loading. Breech-loading was a recent innovation and most artillery seen in action was of the muzzle-loading type. The various weapons were manufactured in a variety of metals. Generally, smaller pieces of smoothbore artillery were cast in bronze (brass), while rifled pieces were manufactured in wrought or cast iron. Bronze was used to produce some rifled pieces but experience soon revealed that the metal was too weak and the rifling quickly deteriorated.

Artillerymen could call on a wide range of ammunition depending on the task in hand. "Solid" shot was the traditional solid cannonball or the more streamlined version fired by rifled pieces. "Shells" were similar to both types of solid shot but filled with an explosive charge. Both solid shot and shells could be used against "hard" targets, such as buildings, or troop formations. The final category was "caseshot," generally used against troops. It was subdivided into shrapnel (spherical case), grapeshot, and canister.

Guns were usually able to fire most or all of the ammunition types, while howitzers used only shell or caseshot. Mortars were capable of firing just shell and shrapnel. The decision on which type of round to use depended on the nature of the target and its distance. For example, canister (small balls) was most effective against troops in the open less than a few hundred yards from the artillery piece.

All of the artillery used in the Civil War lacked any recoil mechanism and had to be retargeted after every round. It was this rather than the time taken to reload that often decided an artillery piece's rate of fire. With regard to accuracy, this was often a matter of skill and judgment as artillerymen lacked effective gunsights or devices to accurately plot the distance to a potential target. Nevertheless, artillery was the greatest killer of troops in action during the conflict, and responsible for battering many forts into submission.

Below and Bottom: Union siege guns in emplacements. Dahlgren smoothbores (Below) and Parrott rifles (Bottom) were extensively used during the Siege of Petersburg.

This Page: A Confederate fortification (Above) containing antiquated smoothbore guns; one of numerous earthworks defending the Confederate coast. When artillery was unavailable, "quaker" or dummy guns (Left) were constructed to give the enemy the impression that positions were well fortified. The photograph below shows a selection of Confederate smoothbored field guns.

THE AMERICAN CIVIL WAR: A VISUAL ENCYCLOPEDIA

manufacturers, both American and foreign, including Armstrong, James, Parrott, and Whitworth. However, the most common were the three-inch Ordnance, which had a wrought-iron barrel, and the ten-pounder Parrott, which had a barrel of cast iron strengthened by a band of wrought iron circling the breech area. The U.S. government took delivery of some 590 Parrotts and 925 of the three-inch Ordnance. The barrels of these weapons weighed 899 and 820 pounds respectively, and had effective ranges at five degrees of elevation of 1,900 and 1,830 yards. These figures compared favorably with those of the standard

Opposite Page: Three Union siege guns—a massive Columbiad smoothbore (Top), a heavy mortar (Center) and a Parrott rifled gun (Below)—part of the siege train around Petersburg.

Left and Below: A Union siege mortar (Left) used to bombard Petersburg, while regular artillery (Below) covered the Union siegeworks.

RIFLED

Rifled artillery, guns that had grooves cut inside their barrels, had one great advantage over smoothbore weapons—it was much more accurate. This was partly a result of the reduction of "windage," the difference between the diameter of the bore and that of the projectile. In smoothbores windage was greater to allow for rust, fouling, and expansion of the round. This gap, therefore, reduced accuracy and also velocity, as much of the charge's power was lost due to windage. As rifled pieces had considerably less windage, they were able to shoot out to greater ranges with more accuracy, and at the same time required a much smaller charge to do so. However, one disadvantage with rifled pieces was that they used semi-fixed ammunition—the explosive charge and missile were loaded individually. Consequently, smoothbores had a generally higher rate fire. The barrels of rifled pieces were made from iron unlike smoothbores, which tended to be of bronze (brass) construction.

Most rifled artillery used in the Civil War was of the muzzle-loading variety, although some breech-loaders did see service. The latter came from two British manufacturers, Armstrong and Whitworth, and were the most accurate guns to see action. Both were twelve-pounders, and both comfortably outranged comparable smoothbore and rifled pieces. At five degrees of elevation, the Whitworth had an effective range of 2,800 yards and the Armstrong 2,100 yards. The South's Army of Northern Virginia was equipped with a battery of Whitworths.

Rifled muzzle-loading field guns, designated by either weight of shot or caliber, were produced by a range of

twelve-pounder Napoleon—1,227 pounds and 1,619 yards.

Rifling was also applied to much heavier guns. Indeed, the Civil War saw the decline of smoothbore siege guns, because the long-range rifled types had greater penetrative power, particularly against brick and stone forts. A number of older smoothbore types were rifled, chiefly twenty-four, thirty-two, and forty-two-pounders, but purpose-built rifled weapons became the norm. Among the manufacturers were Blakely, Brooke, and Parrott. The thirty-pounder Parrott had a range of some 2,200 yards at five degrees of elevation and was capable of penetrating around eighteen inches of brick.

Some of the largest coastal guns were rifled. This group of weapons contained the largest pieces of the war; among the manufacturers of rifled types were Armstrong, Blakely, Parrott, and Whitworth. The largest of these muzzle-loaders was the monster 300-pounder Parrott with a barrel weighing 26,500 pounds, an effective range of 2,500

yards at ten degrees, and fired a projectile weighing between 230 and 250 pounds.

SMOOTHBORES

With regard to field artillery, both sides went into battle with considerable numbers of the M1841 six-pounder, a weapon with an effective range of some 1,500 yards at five degrees of elevation. However, the M1841 was quickly supplanted by the most famous artillery piece of the war, the M1857 Napoleon twelve-pounder. Its importance can be gauged by the fact that the U.S. Army ordered 1,127 of them during the war and the South manufactured or bought around 500 more. Some Southern Napoleons had barrels made from iron that were reinforced in the breech area. The Napoleon, which was lighter and had a shorter barrel than an earlier twelve-pounder, had a bronze barrel weighing 1,227 pounds, had an effective range of some 2,000 yards, and an average crew of seven could fire two rounds per minute.

Other field artillery pieces commonly used in the war included a range of howitzers. These tended to have shorter barrels than standard field pieces, and came in a range of sizes, although the most common were twelve, twenty-four, and thirty-two-pounders. The M1841 howitzer had a range of 1,322 yards at five degrees of elevation, and a barrel weighing 1,318 pounds. The Union also made use of a number of twelve-pounder mountain howitzers, which could be moved by mule. The barrel of such a weapon would weigh 220 pounds and the range was around 900 yards.

There was also a wide range of smoothbore siege guns, although these tended to decline in importance as rifled artillery types were more effective at penetrating brick and stone defenses. These came in a range of weights and calibers. The twenty-four-pounder M1839, for example, had a range of up to 2,000 yards at five degrees of elevation and had an iron barrel weighing 5,790 pounds.

Beyond the reasonably mobile siege guns was a variety of very large pieces, known as coastal artillery. These were so heavy that they were essentially "fixed" in position and could only be move with difficulty. Although some were rifled or breech-loaders, a considerable number were muzzle-loading smoothbores. Among them was the largest artillery piece to see service. This was the Rodman twenty-inch. The barrel alone weighed 117,000 pounds and its 1,080-pound round had an effective range of 3.5 miles at twenty-five degrees of elevation. Other guns in this category were a range known as Columbiads, which had calibers of eight to fifteen inches.

The final type of smoothbore artillery was the mortar, a weapon with a stubby barrel designed to deliver plunging fire at close range against fortifications and their

garrisons. Some of these were small enough to be moved easily, but others were so large as to be restricted to siege operations or coastal defense. Most mortars were manufactured in iron, and these came in a variety of sizes. For example, the Union deployed mortars in calibers of eight to thirteen inches. The latter, of which ninety were supplied, had a barrel weighing 17,120 pounds and could lob a 220-pound shell out to 4,325 yards at forty-five degrees of elevation. Crews for mortars tended to vary between three and five men.

SIEGE

Although virtually any ordnance could be used to prosecute a siege, it was really the job of the type of heavy artillery classified as either siege or garrison. These were generally the heaviest weapons that could be moved comfortable by road or rail. Perhaps the heaviest to be moved by road on its own carriage was the Model 1839, a smoothbore with a barrel weighing some 5,790 pounds.

Three types of artillery were available for siege works—standard guns fired over a flat trajectory over the longest ranges; howitzers, generally lighter and smaller, fired heavier rounds over a higher trajectory to medium distances; and mortars, which delivered larger rounds in a plunging trajectory over short distances. Generally, siege guns were either rifled or smoothbore. Rifled weapons rapidly proved decisive against stone and brick structures due to their greater penetrative power, but were less effective against earth fortifications, which absorbed much of their force. Nevertheless, many older smoothbore weapons were retrospectively rifled for siege work. Guns could be either muzzle- or breech-loading, although the greater majority in the war initially fell into the latter category. Howitzers and mortars were smoothbore weapons. In all cases a wide range of types were used on a regular basis. For example the Union purchased mortars of eight-inch, ten-inch, and thirteen-inch caliber during the Civil War.

A variety of rounds could be fired but solid shot, explosive shell, and spherical case, usually known as shrapnel, were most effective at neutralizing defenses and their garrisons. Smoothbore siege artillery also fired red-hot shot, which could prove effective against wooden building or insufficiently protected ammunition dumps.

Above Left: A siege mortar and its crew in a temporary field emplacement. Confederate mortar batteries such as this helped to defend the upper reaches of the Mississippi River.

Left: A park of Union siege mortars. Northern armaments production meant that Union forces were guaranteed an abundant supply of weaponry of all types during the last years of the war.

COASTAL

Artillery pieces that fell into the category of coastal artillery were the largest weapons to see action in the Civil War. Their primary purpose was to protect coastlines and ports from naval attack, although they were also used inland to protect important cities, not least Washington D.C. Because of their huge size, coastal artillery pieces tended to be "fixed" in position and were not easily moved. Their chief targets were likely to be enemy warships, floating batteries, and siege works. Typically, coastal artillery barrels were made from iron and many of the more modern designs had a distinctive hooped appearance, getting bigger toward the breech end to cope with the large charges they used.

Coastal artillery came in a variety of types, both smoothbore and rifled, muzzle-loading and breech-loading. The main manufacturers were both American and foreign, including Armstrong, Blakely, Parrott, Rodman, and Whitworth. Older-style guns were often termed Columbiads and tended to have a bore of equal distance throughout the barrel, although the barrel was much thicker at the breech end. Columbiads came in a range of calibers, from eight-inch to fifteen-inch. The latter had a barrel weighing 15,000 pounds and could fire a 350-pound round out to 5,730 yards at twenty-eight degrees of elevation.

One of the chief problems with these large guns was that they were prone to bursting due to the enormous gas pressures that built up in the barrel when their charges were fired. The problem was reduced somewhat by a new method of casting developed by Rodman, who perfected a technique to improve the quality of the iron used in barrel manufacture and also developed a type of gunpowder that did not produce as sudden a buildup of gas pressure.

UNITS

Before the war, the U.S. Army operated 163 field guns and howitzers. During the war this force was augmented by volunteer artillery regiments. Regiments rarely operated as a single unit, but rather individual batteries were attached to infantry formations. As the war progressed, the Army of the Potomac created an artillery reserve, controlled directly by the army commander.

The regular artillery regiment consisted of between eight and twelve batteries (companies). A battery consisted of six guns, divided into three sections. In addition, six ammunition caissons were attached to the battery. The total paper strength of an artillery battery was 122 privates, fourteen

Right: Pennsylvania's Keystone Independent Battery Light Artillery posed in firing position, equipped with twelve-pounder smoothbore guns deployed with the limbers and ammunition caissons behind the guns.

NCOs, and two officers, who were commanded by a captain. Union volunteer units followed the establishment of the regular army, but each regiment usually consisted of twelve batteries, each of six guns and 144 men. Unit designations contained the regimental name and an identifying letter (A–L). For example, at the Battle of Gettysburg (July 1–3, 1863), the Union V Corps included Batteries D and I, 5th U.S. Artillery (regulars), and Battery C, 1st New York Light Artillery (volunteers).

In the Confederate army, in most cases the battery was the highest level of artillery organization and was named after its commander or given some other distinctive name (e.g. Hampden's Virginia Battery). Originally, each battery was similar to those of the regular U.S. Army and contained six guns, but after October 1862, the batteries were reduced to four guns, in two sections. Otherwise, these units were similar to their Union counterparts.

Assassination of President Lincoln

At approximately 8:30pm on April 14, 1865, President Abraham Lincoln, his wife, and their entourage, arrived at Ford's Theater on Tenth Street in Washington, D.C., to attend a performance of the play *Our American Cousin*. The presidential couple, along with Clara Harris and her fiancée, Major Henry Rathbone, took their places in the theater's state box, located at balcony level, stage left. A police bodyguard, John Parker, was posted outside, but he abandoned his post prior to 10:00pm. At 10:15pm, John Wilkes Booth entered the box by its back door and shot the President in the back of the head.

A 27-year-old Shakespearian actor, John Wilkes Booth was the younger brother of the more successful fellow actor, Edwin Booth, and the son of the eccentric, Junius Brutus Booth, also a famous Shakespearian actor. A Northerner, but a Confederate sympathizer, the younger Booth had earlier concocted an elaborate plan to kidnap Lincoln and take him to Richmond. His conspiracy grew to include Samuel Arnold, Michael O'Laughlen, John Surratt, Lewis Powell (aka Lewis Paine or Payne), George Atzerodt, and David Herold as well as John Surratt's mother, who ran the boarding house where the conspirators met. The kidnapping was supposed to have occurred on March 17, 1865, but could not when the President changed his plans that day. After General Robert E. Lee surrendered to General Ulysses S. Grant at Appomattox, Booth decided to assassinate Lincoln instead of kidnapping him. He learned on the morning of April 14 that Lincoln would be attending the play at Ford's Theater that evening, so he and his coconspirators hatched a scheme wherein Booth would kill Lincoln, Atzerodt would assassinate Vice President Andrew Johnson at his home, and Powell and Herold would kill Secretary of State William Seward. They hoped that the United States government would be thrown into chaos by these simultaneous assassinations.

Booth entered the front of Ford's Theater at about 10:07pm and went to the state box armed with a derringer and a knife. Parker, the bodyguard, was gone, so Booth opened the door to the box and shot Lincoln in the back of the head at near point-blank range. In an ensuing struggle Booth stabbed Rathbone in the arm. Booth then jumped approximately eleven feet to the stage below, where he broke his left fibula above the ankle. From the stage, he shouted "*Sic Semper Tyrannis*" (Latin for "As always to tyrants") and hobbled out the back of the theater where he had previously arranged

Above Left: A sketch of the interior of Ford's Theater shows the state box in which President Lincoln was assassinated.

Above and Right: General Sherman (Right) entered Atlanta after a campaign of successive assaults against well-entrenched Confederate positions (Above), built to defend the city. (See page 50.)

(See page 50.)

for a young boy to be waiting with his horse. Meanwhile, Atzerodt made no attempt to kill Johnson, and Powell stabbed Seward but failed to kill him.

Lincoln, unconscious but still breathing, was taken across Tenth Street to the home of tailor William Peterson, where he was placed on a bed and treated by doctors through the night. He died at 7:22pm on the morning of April 15 without regaining consciousness. Vice President Johnson was sworn in as the new president later in the day.

Meanwhile, at about 4:00am on April 15, Booth and Herold arrived at the home of Dr. Samuel Mudd in Maryland, where the doctor set Booth's broken leg. On April 26, Union troops pursuing them caught up with the two conspirators hiding in a barn at a farm near Port Royal, Virginia. Herold gave up, but Booth did not, so the barn was set on fire. Booth was then shot and killed by Sergeant Boston Corbett, who was under orders *not* to shoot. Booth's detailed diary was found on his body.

The coconspirators were arrested, tried, and convicted by a military tribunal. Mrs. Surratt, Powell, Atzerodt, and Herold were all hanged, while O'Laughlen and Arnold, as well as Dr. Mudd, were given life sentences. O'Laughlen died in prison in 1867, but Dr. Mudd and Arnold were pardoned by President Johnson in 1869. Mudd is now believed to have been innocent of the assassination conspiracy. John Surratt, who had left the conspiracy before April 14, escaped to Europe, but was captured and tried. The jury deadlocked and he was released.

Of the three surviving occupants of the box, Mrs. Lincoln and Major Rathbone both went insane. Miss Harris, who later became Mrs. Rathbone, was murdered by her insane husband.

Atlanta, Georgia

The land-locked city of Atlanta was one of the South's most important industrial centers, and as such was targeted by Sherman's "total war" campaign of 1864.

The Battle of Atlanta began on July 20, 1864. First Joseph Johnston and then General John B. Hood struggled to defend the city, but on the night of August 31 Hood was forced to leave to avoid entrapment. Sherman marched in on September 2, evicting Atlanta's citizens from their homes. When he marched out on November 15 he left the city in flames—Sherman's treatment of Atlanta so demoralized Governor Brown of Georgia that he immediately exempted his Georgian militia from the obligation to serve the Confederates.

Atlanta Campaign

Following the decisive Union victory at the battle of Chattanooga in November 1863, the Confederate commander, Braxton Bragg, had resigned and his position was taken by one of the Confederacy's most experienced generals, Joseph E. Johnston, whose Army of the Tennessee consisted of around 65,000 men. Opposing him was William Sherman, appointed in the spring of 1864 to command the Military Division of the Mississippi, which consisted of George H. Thomas' Army of the Cumberland, James B. McPherson's Army of the Tennessee, and John Schofield's Army of the Ohio, a total of about 100,000 men.

Sherman's task was to take the city of Atlanta, in part of Grant's great offensive of 1864. This would deprive the Confederacy of their second most important city, along with its irreplaceable industrial capacity. Sherman was also to destroy Johnston's army and disrupt the Confederate war effort as much as humanly possible.

On May 7, 1864, Sherman's forces set off to confront Johnston's positions around Dalton. General Thomas moved to attack Johnston's entrenchments around the city, while Major General Schofield moved south through Varnell and the Crow Valley from the Tennessee-Georgia border. General McPherson also began to move from his position and crossed the valley through Villanow to Snake Creek Gap.

From here it was planned that he should move on the town of Resaca. Both Thomas and Schofield had been ordered to advance slowly to give McPherson time to get to Snake Gap. After a brief encounter with Confederates stationed at Tunnel Hill on May 7, Thomas began the Battle of Rocky Face with attacks at Dug and Mill Creek Gaps on May 8.

On May 10 Sherman decided to move the bulk of his forces south in support of the Army of the Tennessee. Faced with a larger force in his rear, Johnston pulled back. Although Johnston managed to hold his lines against a numerically superior Union force during the Battle of Resaca, afterward he was compelled to withdraw yet again.

The next major encounter between the two forces took place on May 18–19 around Cassville. Johnston had planned to counterattack Sherman from his strong defensive position, but, Hood was caught out of position and unable to time his attack correctly, thus forcing Johnston into a further withdrawal on the evening of the 19th

Sherman found that the new Confederate position in the Allatoona Pass was too strong for him to break, so, once again, he attempted a flanking maneuver to turn Johnston out of his position, approaching Dallas from the west. This resulted in a action at Dallas on May 25–27, when Johnston was forced to retire and take up another position at Kennesaw Mountain.

On June 18 the Confederate forces held a position from Kennesaw Mountain to Peter Kolb's farm. The Union line was less than a mile west. Sherman realized that a frontal assault on this entrenched position would be very costly for his troops and decided to try another flanking movement.

Appreciating this, Hood attacked Hooker's XX Corps in the vicinity of Kolb's (or Culp's) Farm on June 22. This assault halted Sherman's flanking movement but proved to be very costly in terms of Confederate casualties.

Following his repulse, Sherman decided to try and take Johnston's position frontally, and for five days the Union Army organized for the forthcoming attack. On Monday, June 27, 1864, Sherman launched his troops forward in the Battle of Kennesaw Mountain. This proved to be a major defeat for the attackers, with around 2,000 men lost compared to under 300 on the Confederate side.

Following this failed attack, Sherman once more resorted to his flanking tactics and Johnston was compelled to pull further back toward Atlanta.

Right: Bald Hill proved a focal point for the fighting during the decisive battle around Atlanta. It was followed by Sherman's March to the Sea, where his troops destroyed everything in their path.

THE AMERICAN CIVIL WAR: A VISUAL ENCYCLOPEDIA

Once Kennesaw Mountain had been subdued, Sherman resumed his advance towards Atlanta. On July 7, in response to repeated requests from Johnston for more men, President Davis informed Johnston of his decision not to send any additional troops. Skirmishing continued across a wide front, mostly to the north and west of Atlanta over the next few days. Braxton Bragg arrived to investigate the conduct of his successor, failing to stop Sherman's advance. On July 17, Davis relieved Johnston of command, giving it to Hood, a decision of which Sherman greatly approved.

Hood's instinct was to try and stop Sherman through a series of offensives, the first of which was at Peachtree Creek on July 20, 1864. Although successful at first, the battle ended with Confederate losses of over 5,000 men compared to Union casualties of only 2,000.

Two days later, on July 22, Hood once again attacked. The Battle of Atlanta was a devastating blow to the Confederate Army, with estimated casualties as high as to a quarter of the 40,000 men engaged. Union losses were far less significant, though General McPherson was killed.

On July 28, Hood tried the same tactic at Ezra Church with similar results—his aggressive tactics were causing the Confederate defenders of Atlanta to hemorrhage men at an alarming rate. For the next month Sherman and Hood would use cavalry to fight skirmishes around the city.

In late August 1864, Sherman decided to defeat the Confederates by completely severing their supply lines to the south of the city. He moved six of his seven divisions to the west of Atlanta, advancing to the rear of the Confederate positions and cutting off their supply lines. Hood, not realizing this, had sent Hardee south to protect these lines and lost contact with him on August 31.

Unable to reestablish communication with Hardee and with a significant Union force at his rear, Hood had no options but to abandon the city. Since Sherman had cut off his line of transportation, Hood had to blow up the munitions that could not be carried. Sherman felt the explosion in Jonesboro, fifteen miles south of Atlanta. General Henry Slocum's XX Corps received the surrender from Atlanta mayor James Calhoun on September 2, 1864.

CSS *Atlanta*

This ironclad was built by converting the hull of the iron British blockade runner *Fingal,* and was based in Savannah, guarding the seaward approaches to the city. She was a notoriously uncomfortable and underpowered vessel, but Commander Webb CSN elected to use her to attack the vessels blockading the port. On June 17, 1863 she engaged the monitors USS *Weehawken* and USS *Nahant* in Wassaw Sound, where they guarded the southeastern approaches to the Savannah Delta. During the brief engagement the CSS *Atlanta* ran aground and was unable to return the fire of the powerful Union vessels. After fifteen minutes of heavy pounding, Webb was forced to surrender his vessel. She subsequently served as part of the Union blockading squadron off the Georgia coast.

Dimensions: 165 feet x 35 feet x 11.5 feet
Armor: Four inches, with wood backing
Armament: Four rifled guns
Commissioned: September 1862

Above Right: The advance on and Battle of Atlanta.

Below and Right: Confederate field fortifications built around Atlanta helped to offset the numerical superiority of Sherman's Union army.

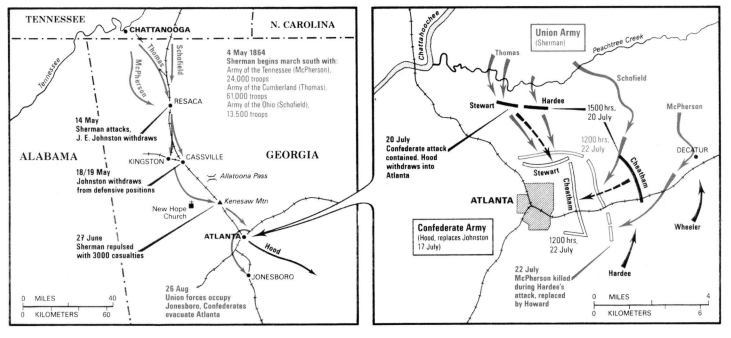

Balloons

The Union made the greatest—if still limited—use of ground-tethered hydrogen-filled observation balloons during the conflict, particularly after Colonel Thaddeus Lowe became the Army of the Potomac's Chief of Army Aeronautics. By January 1862 the short-lived unit, ultimately an offshoot of the Signal Corps, numbered some seven balloons. The winding gear and hydrogen-generating equipment for these was bulky, difficult to move and operate, although the problem of movement was lessened when they were placed on river-boats.

Nevertheless, Lowe and his men made scores of ascents during the Peninsular Campaign in 1862, identifying Southern dispositions and troop movements around the area of operations, although not always correctly. Messages were conveyed to the ground by telegraph, small colored balloons in daylight, flares at night, or simply written down and dropped. Sketches were also made and photographs occasionally taken. Despite seeing action at Chancellorsville, the Balloon Corps was disbanded shortly after Lowe resigned on May 8, 1863, following disagreements with General Joseph Hooker.

In contrast, the South had just a single balloon, which operated out of Richmond. It was made from silk dresses contributed by wealthy women, but saw little use as the Confederacy had only a limited capacity to generate hydrogen. It was deployed tethered to a locomotive or riverboat, but the boat eventually ran aground. Both it and the balloon were captured by Union forces.

THE AMERICAN CIVIL WAR: A VISUAL ENCYCLOPEDIA

Right: Balloon barges such as this were used by the Union forces on the James River to keep the Confederate forces around Richmond under observation.

Opposite Page, Above: A Union balloon detachment.

Opposite Page, Below: As it marches through Baltimore, Maryland, the 6th Massachusetts Regiment is forced to defend itself from a pro-Confederate mob.

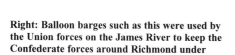

Ball's Bluff, Virginia, Battle of, 1861

Following the Union disaster at the first Battle of Bull Run, Major General George B. McClellan's task was to build up the Army of the Potomac in preparation for an attack on Confederate territory. On October 21, 1861, 2,000 Union troops under Brigadier General Charles P. Stone, led by U.S. Senator Colonel Edward D. Baker, attempted to cross the Potomac River at Harrison's Landing. Their aim was a reconnaissance mission to take the high ground of Ball's Bluff near Leesburg on the Virginian shore. The attack was badly coordinated and 1,600 Confederates led by Brigadier General Nathan G. Evans drove the Unionists over the bluff and into the river, where many drowned. The Unionists lost 921 men, including Baker, to Confederate losses of 149, and the debacle led to the creation of the influential Unionist Congressional Joint Committee on the Conduct of the War.

Baltimore, Maryland

When Maryland declared for the Union after the taking of Fort Sumter, the allegiances of Baltimore, rife with secession

supporters and famed for its "mob" politics, remained uncertain.

On April 19, 1861, an encounter between the rioting citizens of Baltimore and the 6th Massachusetts Regiment left twelve civilians dead, and the Mayor of Baltimore retaliated by severing all transport and communication links through the city, cutting off Washington from the North. He, the Chief of Police, and other prominent citizens were consequently imprisoned—Baltimore, however, remained a hotbed of unrest and insurrection. In May, 1864, Abraham Lincoln was also reelected in a Republican convention at Baltimore.

Banks, Nathaniel P. (1816–94)

Banks was a career politician, a Republican who served in both the Massachusetts and Federal legislature. A strong advocate of peace while governor of Massachusetts (1858–61), he nevertheless volunteered for the war in 1861, and Lincoln appointed him major general of volunteers. Banks had no military training.

He was outclassed and outwitted by "Stonewall" Jackson in the Shenandoah Valley in 1862, but later besieged Port Hudson on the Mississippi in Louisiana as part of the Red River Campaign. When the port surrendered in July 1863, Banks earned the Thanks of Congress. His tactical failures in 1864 prompted his resignation.

Barnard, George N. (1819–1902)

Photographer George Barnard worked for Matthew Brady's studio but left in 1863, unhappy with Brady assuming the credit for the work of his staff. He became official photographer of the U.S. Army's Engineer Division in 1864, producing memorable images of Sherman's devastating March to the Sea.

Barton, Clarissa H. (1821–1912)

A remarkable and redoubtable woman, Clara Barton was the outstanding Union battlefield nurse. Known as the "Angel of the Battlefield," she served in field hospitals at Second Bull Run, Antietam, Fredricksburg, Battery Wagner, the

Above Right: General Nathaniel Banks.

Right: Clara Barton.

Opposite Page, Above and Below: Two portraits of General Beauregard. He commanded the troops who began the war by firing on Fort Sumter, then went on to command the Confederate army which defeated the Union at the First Battle of Bull Run (1862). He returned to Charleston to organize the defense of the city for much of the war until he was called upon to defend the Virginian city of Petersburg.

Wilderness, and the Richmond-Petersburg siege. She not only nursed the wounded and dying, but also traced identification records for the missing and dead. More than any other person, she proved to the northern military establishment that women could serve competently and bravely in the field. After the war she worked in military hospitals abroad and established the U.S. branch of the Red Cross in 1881, becoming its first president.

Baton Rouge, Louisiana

Baton Rouge was used by the Union as a base and as a decoy in the early stages of the campaign for Vicksburg. In February 1863, in the days when the fortress town of Vicksburg still appeared impregnable, Major General Nathaniel P. Banks prepared an advance on Fort Hudson using Baton Rouge as his base—a move condemned by contemporary observers as ill-thought-out.

In April 1863, when Grant's attempts on Vicksburg were truly in earnest, he sent Colonel Benjamin H. Grierson to Baton Rouge in an attempt to distract attention from his own activities. Grierson's sixteen-day, 600-mile ride of plunder and destruction took him from La Grange, Tennessee, to Baton Rouge by May 3, 1863—Vicksburg, however, did not fall until July 4.

Beauregard, Pierre G. T. (1818–93)

A debonair Creole from Louisiana, Beauregard was one of the eight Confederate full generals and served in almost every theater of the war. A highly skilled artillerist, he ordered the first shots of the war at Fort Sumter.

Like many of the Civil War generals, Beauregard was a graduate of West Point and a veteran of the Mexican-American War. He was briefly superintendent of West Point for a record five days, January 23–28, 1861, when he resigned from the U.S. Army after the secession from the Union of his home state, Louisiana. He was commissioned brigadier general in the Confederate army.

Hailed throughout the South as the "hero of Fort Sumter" after he forced its Union garrison to surrender, Beauregard was charged with assembling the hastily recruited Confederate army at Richmond, prior to the battle of First Bull Run in July 1861. He commanded 35,000 men who moved north to defend Virginia, and Beauregard massed them in a meandering eight-mile-long line along one bank of Bull Run Creek near a railroad center called Manassas Junction. Reinforced by Joe Johnston's army, Beauregard led the Confederacy to its first victory and was promoted to full general. He swiftly fell out with Jefferson Davis; the ambitious and strong-willed Beauregard was convinced that he should have marched on Washington, whereas Davis advocated caution, instead sending Beauregard west to Tennessee as Albert Sidney Johnston's second-in-command.

With the Union threatening to split the Confederacy by capturing Tennessee, Beauregard worked with Braxton Bragg to concentrate the Confederate forces to join Johnston at Corinth, Misissippi. He drafted the battle plans for the Battle of Shiloh in 1862, basing his ideas on Napoleon's plan for Waterloo. It was a flawed idea: methods of warfare had changed in the intervening fifty years and the Confederates were defeated after two days' hard fighting. Johnston was killed on the first day and Beauregard, "Old Bory," assumed command. In the following weeks he surrendered western Tennessee, further angering Jefferson Davis. When Beauregard went on sick leave without seeking permission, an act bordering on insubordination, Davis replaced him with Bragg.

Two months later, Beauregard returned to command the southern coast from North Carolina to the tip of Florida, retaining his post for over eighteen months and defending the port of Charleston. He went north to North Carolina and southern Virginia while Lee tackled Grant's forces north of Richmond.

Having defeated Ben Butler's army at Drewery's Bluff, Beauregard continued to serve under Lee. He commanded a sorry force of boys and old men at Petersburg in June 1864, where he managed to withstand the assaults of Union troops until Lee's arrival. He assumed overall command of the West, just as Sherman began his devastating March to the Sea across Georgia. Lacking troops, Beauregard struggled to oppose him. During the final days of the war he was second in command to Joseph Johnston in North Carolina.

A capable combat commander, Beauregard often showed sound strategic sense, but his habit of questioning orders was a serious flaw in a high-ranking officer.

Beecher, Henry Ward (1813–87)

Born in Litchfield, Connecticut, Beecher was one of a number of prominent Protestant preachers who denounced slavery. Following his education at Amhurst College, Massachusetts, he preached at Indianapolis before becoming, in 1847, the first pastor at the Plymouth Congregational Church in Brooklyn, New York. Having supported the Free Soil party in 1852, he supported the pro-abolition Republican candidates in the presidential elections of 1856 and 1860. When war broke out, he was active in raising and equipping a volunteer regiment. During the war, smuggled rifles to the pro-abolitionists in the south became known as "Beecher's Bibles." Beecher was the brother of the author Harriet Beecher Stowe, who wrote, in 1852, the novel *Uncle Tom's Cabin*, the book that did so much to raise public awareness of the plight of the slaves.

Belmont, Battle of, 1861

In early November 1861 the Unionists decided on a series of attacks on the Confederate line in western Kentucky. Brigadier General Ulysses S. Grant took 3,000 men down the Mississippi on river steamers protected by the gunboats *Lexington* and *Tyler*, to raid Confederate positions at Belmont, Missouri, where a chain blocked the river. On November 7 Grant landed his forces and attacked the garrison at Belmont, driving off the defenders for the loss of approximately 600 men on each side in the first major battle of the western theater. Although Major General Leonidas Polk, in command of the main Confederate forces across the river at Columbus, sent 10,000 troops to cut Grant's men off from their transports, the Unionists managed to reach their boats and escape.

Benham, Henry Washington (1813–84)

In May 1861 Benham was appointed chief engineer in the Department of the Ohio. In June 1862. as brigadier general, he led his troops to a catastrophic defeat at Secessionville, near Charleston Harbor, when poor planning meant that Confederate troops beat back the more numerous Northerners.

Benjamin, Judah Philip (1811–84)

A talented Confederate politician, and a close advisor of Jefferson Davis, Benjamin was a Democrat who advocated secession

Left: Judah P. Benjamin.

Right: The Battle of Bentonville, North Carolina, 1865 (see page 60).

from the Union. Military disasters beset his short time as Secretary of War, and these defeats, coupled with anti-Semitism and resentment of his influence with Davis, provoked criticism. His espousal of employing slaves as soldiers also damaged his popularity.

Bentonville, Battle of, 1865

Once Major General William T. Sherman had marched through Georgia and taken Savannah in December 1864, his next goal was to drive his combined army of 60,000 men north through the Carolinas, destroying further Confederate resources and their remaining forces in the east. General Joseph E. Johnston, who was appointed commander of Confederate forces in the Carolinas in February 1865, had the job of stopping him with the remainder of the Army of Tennessee. Sherman's objective was Goldsboro in North Carolina, a strategically important railroad junction, and Johnston concentrated his 20,000-strong force nearby, digging in at Bentonville in an attempt to halt the advance. It was here that the major battle of the campaign took place. On March 19 Union Major General Henry W. Slocum's corps on Sherman's

left wing first encountered the entrenched Confederate defenses. Johnston attacked midafternoon, pushing back Slocum's troops, but his breakthrough was halted by a Union counterattack and, as the fighting died down at nightfall, the Unionists had managed to hold their line. Overnight, Johnston regrouped his forces into a defensive V-formation, and although the Unionist line was reinforced by the arrival of Sherman's right wing, led by Major General Oliver O. Howard, the fighting the next day was inconclusive. On the 21st the battle was renewed, and in the afternoon a Union division led by Major General Joseph Mower moved around the Confederate lines to attack Johnston's rear, although the division was later forced back. During the night Johnston withdrew from the battlefield, having lost 3,092 men compared to Union losses of 1,646, and Sherman was able to continue his march largely unopposed. On April 26 Johnston formally surrendered his army to Sherman and the Civil War was virtually over.

Black troops

Like the wider issue of emancipation, the question of employing free blacks and

escaped slaves in the Union Army involved the Republican administration in a gradual, and at times reluctant, accommodation with both the realities of a total war and the large numbers of individual African-Americans who were ready and willing to serve.

Although African-Americans had fought during the Revolution and in the War of 1812, racist prejudices ran deep in many parts of the army, and the remarks of General Thomas G. Stevenson in the Sea Islands in 1863, that he "would rather have the Union forces defeated than win with Negro troops," were an outspoken expression of quite widely held views—black troops had to fight Union prejudice as well as rebel bullets. Indeed, the Abolitionist General David Hunter was obliged to disband the regiment of some 800 black soldiers he had organized in South Georgia in May and June 1862. That same month, however, Secretary of War Stanton authorized Brigadier General Rufus Saxton to "arm, uniform and equip, and receive into the service of the United States such numbers of volunteers of African descent as you may deem expedient, not exceeding 5,000."

A small unit from this regiment, the 1st South Carolina Volunteers, saw action in November 1862, in which, according to

Above: Black recruits marching up Beekman Street, New York City.

Left: A squad of Negro troops in the Army of the Potomac. By the end of the war over 200,000 African-Americans served the Union cause.

their commanding officer, they "fought with astonishing coolness and bravery." The enlistment of African-Americans into the Union army and navy was finally explicitly permitted in the Emancipation Proclamation of New Year's Day 1863.

Despite such reports, white officers tended to deploy their growing numbers of black troops more for heavy fatigue duties such as fortification construction than for actual fighting. When they did see action, African-American regiments fought with valor and distinction, notable at such battles as Milliken's Bend, Port Hudson, Fort Wagner, and Nashville. On June 7, 1863, two newly recruited black regiments formed most of the garrison that fought desperately to repel a Confederate attack on the post at Milliken's Bend on the Mississippi above Vicksburg, prompting assistant Secretary of War Dana to comment that their bravery had "completely revolutionized the sentiment of the army" toward black troops.

The South was outraged at the arming of blacks, and there is no doubt that many who were captured faced summary execution or sale into slavery. At Fort Pillow, for example, several hundred black captives were massacred. More generally the Confederate administration refused to consider exchanging black prisoners, bringing a halt to the whole system of prisoner exchanges.

At the same time, black soldiers faced official discrimination within the Union Army. In 1863 African-American troops were paid $10 per month less a $3 clothing allowance, while other soldiers got $13 plus a $3.50 clothing allowance. It was only after the black soldiers of the 54th and 55th Massachusetts Regiments had refused all pay for many months that salaries were finally equalized. Throughout the Civil War as a whole, despite the prejudice and hostility they encountered, some 180,000 African-Americans served in the U.S. Army, and a further 25,000 in the U.S. Navy, making a vast contribution to the Union victory.

Blockade

When Abraham Lincoln used the term "blockade" in his proclamation of April 19, 1861, he made a serious political blunder. A country in rebellion can "close its own ports," but a "blockade" is only conducted against the ports of an enemy power. The declaration of a blockade was, therefore, both premature and gave legitimacy to the "rebellion" of the Southern states. At the start of the war, the U.S. Navy was too small to enforce a blockade at all, but by late 1861, blockading squadrons of wooden vessels lay off all the major southern ports, which were closed to all shipping, both Confederate and neutral. The Navy's aim was to cut off the South from commerce, and to prevent the import of war supplies. This would eventually lead to a collapse of the Southern economy, and the ability of her forces to wage war.

Although the south (and foreign merchants) employed "blockade runners" to slip through the cordon of Union warships, this practice became increasingly risky as the war progressed. By war's end, the handful of ships in the Union blockading squadrons had increased from less than ten to over 300, and by 1865, blockade-running had almost ceased. As the principal Southern ports were captured or their blockaders became too numerous, smaller Southern ports were used by the blockade runners, until they, too, were lost or sealed off. Although the Union Navy scored some spectacular successes during the war, her greatest achievement was the slow economic strangulation of the Confederacy.

Blockade runners

Commercial traffic from Southern ports was disrupted by an ever-strengthening Union blockade, from late 1861 onward, forcing Confederate and neutral ships to try to slip through the cordon of enemy vessels. These "blockade runners" carried

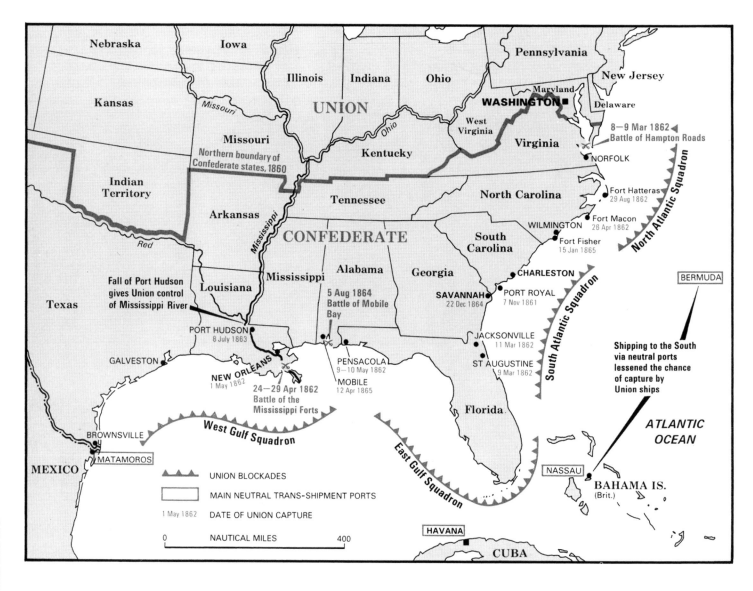

Nebraska **Iowa** **Pennsylvania**

Illinois **Indiana** **Ohio** **New Jersey**

Kansas **Maryland** **Delaware**
WASHINGTON

UNION *Ohio* **West** 8—9 Mar 1862
Virginia Battle of Hampton Roads

Missouri *Missouri* **Kentucky** **Virginia** **NORFOLK**
Northern boundary of
Confederate states, 1860

Indian **North Carolina** Fort Hatteras
Territory 29 Aug 1862
North Atlantic Squadron

Arkansas Fort Macon
26 Apr 1862
Tennessee **South** WILMINGTON
CONFEDERATE **Carolina** Fort Fisher
15 Jan 1865

BERMUDA

Fall of Port Hudson **Mississippi** **Alabama** **Georgia** **CHARLESTON**
gives Union control **Louisiana** SAVANNAH PORT ROYAL
of Mississippi River 5 Aug 1864 22 Dec 1864 7 Nov 1861
Battle of Mobile
Texas Bay JACKSONVILLE Shipping to the South
PORT HUDSON 11 Mar 1862 via neutral ports
8 July 1863 South Atlantic Squadron lessened the chance
GALVESTON PENSACOLA ST AUGUSTINE of capture by
NEW ORLEANS 9—10 May 1862 9 Mar 1862 Union ships
1 May 1862 MOBILE
24—29 Apr 1862 12 Apr 1865 **ATLANTIC**
Battle of the **Florida** **OCEAN**
Mississippi Forts

West Gulf Squadron NASSAU
BROWNSVILLE
MEXICO MATAMOROS East Gulf Squadron **BAHAMA IS.**
(Brit.)

UNION BLOCKADES

MAIN NEUTRAL TRANS-SHIPMENT PORTS

1 May 1862 DATE OF UNION CAPTURE

0 NAUTICAL MILES 400 HAVANA

CUBA

cotton, tobacco and other exports to Europe, Cuba, Bermuda, or the Bahamas, then returned with imports of foreign goods and military supplies. Nassau in the Bahamas, Havana, and Bermuda became havens for blockade runners, and acted as bases for vessels attempting to run the Union blockade. As the war progressed and the risks increased, the profits from blockade running also increased, and although many blockade runners were captured, the commercial incentives outweighed the risks. By 1864, the Confederate authorities demanded that half of all goods imported by blockade runners were of a military nature, helping support the Confederate war effort in its final year.

The majority of blockade runners were usually fast steam vessels, although small sailing craft were also used early in the war. In Britain, ships were specially constructed for the role, where speed, a sleek hull, a shallow draft, and a low silhouette improved the vessel's chances of survival. Anthracite coal was also favored, as it was virtually smokeless. These vessels were also painted gray or light blue as a form of

camouflage. Blockade running was often timed to coincide with favorable weather conditions or lunar cycles. An increasing number of blockade runners were lost as the war progressed, and over 1,500 were captured by the end of the war.

Blockading squadrons, Union

The Union Navy was charged with patrolling 3,550 miles of Confederate coastline, stretching from the Potomac River to the Rio Grande. As well as the principal Southern ports (Galveston, New Orleans, Mobile, Pensacola, Savannah, Charleston, Wilmington, and Norfolk), this coast was studded with numerous rivers, inlets and coastal waterways, making it difficult to maintain an effective blockade. The coastline was divided into four areas. The North Atlantic Blockading Squadron (based at Norfolk) was responsible for the waters of Virginia and North Carolina. South Carolina, Georgia, and the Atlantic coastline of Florida were the responsibility of the South Atlantic Blockading Squadron based at Port Royal. The East Gulf

Above: The blockade of the Confederacy by the U.S. Navy, and the major naval actions of the war.

Right: Confederate blockade runners had to run through the cordon of Union warships such as the screw frigate USS *Minnesota* (see photograph pages 64–65). The majority of blockade runners such as these pictured in Liverpool in England (Above Right) and St. George's Harbour, Bermuda (Right), were therefore sleek, fast side-wheel steamers, capable of outpacing Union warships.

Blockading Squadron (operating from Key West) controlled the waters east of Pensacola, including the Florida Straits, while the remainder of the Confederate coastline was patrolled by the West Gulf Blockading Squadron, whose base was first Key West, then New Orleans.

Blue Ridge Mountains

Together with the Allegheny mountain range to the west, the Blue Ridge Mountains define the Shenandoah Valley, down which Jackson led his remarkable offensive in summer 1862. Masterfully turning the very geography of the Blue Ridge Mountains to his own advantage, he managed to control and occupy Union forces 50,000 strong with his mere 17,000 men.

The valley between the Blue Mountains and the Allegheny range—of which the Confederates did not lose control until the fall of 1864—provided an invaluable "corridor of invasion" leading straight to Washington D.C.

Bocock, Thomas Stanley (1815–91)

A Virginia lawyer, Bocock served as a congressman during the antebellum years. After the secession of the Confederate states, he was elected Speaker of the Confederate Congress in February 1862. It was not an easy job, as the Confederate Congress was notoriously unruly; the members disliked each other, and they seemed united against the president.

Booth, John Wilkes (1838–65)

John Wilkes Booth was both an actor himself and the brother of the tragic actor Edwin Booth. A sympathizer of the Confederate states, he was to achieve notoriety as the assassin of President Lincoln in Ford's Theater, Washington, on April 14, 1865, as part of a pro-Confederacy conspiracy. During the assassination, Booth broke a leg while leaping onto the stage shouting "*Sic semper tyrannis!*" ("Thus always to tyrants!"—the state motto of Virginia; in another version he is supposed to have shouted, "The South shall be free!"). Despite his injury, he was able to evade immediate capture and escaped to Virginia but was discovered and killed on April 26, 1865; four fellow conspirators were hung.

Right: The U.S. Navy's screw frigate *Minnesota*.

THE AMERICAN CIVIL WAR: A VISUAL ENCYCLOPEDIA

Brady, Mathew (1823–96)

Photographer Mathew Brady (and his assistants) were responsible for some of the most memorable images of the Civil War. *The New York Times* said of his 1862 exhibition "The Dead of Antietam": "If he has not brought bodies and laid them in our door yards—he has done something very like it." In spite of his work—or, rather, because of the cost of it—Brady died in poverty in a New York almshouse.

Bragg, Braxton (1817–76)

The career and personality of Braxton Bragg are surrounded by controversy. He is either regarded as completely incompetent or, more generously, unlucky, or as a brave officer and skilled strategist. He certainly lacked interpersonal skills and quarreled with almost every middle- or high-ranking commander in the Army of Tennessee,

Right: Mass for N. Y. State Militia.

Opposite Page: Another well-known Brady photograph—Federals resting after taking Petersburg, Virginia, in 1865. In the assault on June 18, 1864, 1st Maine lost 604 men in just 20 minutes, about two-thirds of the 900 present for duty that day.

Below: Brady (in top hat) stands next to General Samuel P. Heintzelman, Arlington 1862.

General Robert E. Lee (Left), in Richmond after the war. He proved the most capable of all Confederate field commanders. The same could not be said of Braxton Bragg (Above) whose indecisiveness during the battles around Chattanooga led to Confederate defeat in the western theater.

although he was admired by Jefferson Davis. He was a harsh disciplinarian and exceptionally unpopular with his men.

Bragg graduated from West Point in 1837 and was an artillery officer until 1856, serving in the Mexican War. He returned to duty in 1861 as a brigadier general, and was posted to Pensacola, Florida, to organize a new brigade of troops. In 1862 he joined the desperate Confederate effort to defend Tennessee against the Union. Bragg commanded a corps at Shiloh under Albert Sidney Johnston and in June that year became a full general, and commander of the Army of Mississippi.

In December 1862 he hit the Union hard at Chickamauga, but for some unaccountable reason failed to follow up his advantage, enraging his officers. He favored frontal attacks and demonstrated a failure to adjust to the ebb and flow of battlefield conditions, a fatal flaw in a general. "I am convinced," said Longstreet of Bragg, "that nothing but the hand of God can help us as long as we have our present commander." There were calls for Bragg's dismissal, but Davis ignored them.

After the disastrous defeat at Missionary Ridge in 1864, Bragg resigned his command to become military advisor to Davis in Richmond.

Brandy Station, Battle of, 1863

The Battle of Brandy Station was the biggest cavalry engagement of the war. On June 3, 1863, Confederate General Robert E. Lee entered the Shenandoah Valley with the Army of Northern Virginia to invade the North. Major General J. E. B. Stuart's 10,000-strong cavalry corps was to screen Lee's advance but the Unionist Major General Alfred Pleasanton surprised Stuart with his 11,000 cavalry from the Army of the Potomac on June 9, as the Confederate cavalry was being reviewed at Brandy Station. Although Stuart eventually drove off Pleasanton with the help of a Confederate infantry division, during the fighting the Unionist cavalry matched the Confederates for the first time in the war.

Above: J. E. B. Stuart.

Right: Brigadier George A. Custer (left) pictured with his superior, General Pleasanton (right). Custer proved to be a capable and energetic cavalry commander, and helped to overcome the superiority in leadership which Confederate cavalry enjoyed during the first years of the war.

THE AMERICAN CIVIL WAR: A VISUAL ENCYCLOPEDIA

Bridges

During the Civil War, the U.S. Army's Corps of Engineers developed a reputation for the fast and efficient construction of both pontoon bridges across rivers and military trestles across canyons and gullies. The latter were used by infantry, cavalry, and wheeled vehicles, as well as by military railroads. Inspecting a 400-foot railroad bridge constructed across Potomac Creek in nine days, Abraham Lincoln commented, "Loaded trains are running every hour, and upon my word it consists of nothing but beanpoles and cornstalks."

In support of the Union attack on Fredericksburg, Virginia, in December 1862, Union engineer troops laid six pontoon bridges across the Rappahannock River under devastating fire from Confederate sharpshooters. The 2,170-foot pontoon bridge, which Union engineers laid across the James River in June 1864 as the Army of the Potomac approached Petersburg, Virginia, was the longest floating bridge erected before World War II.

Five important battles also took their names from bridges that played a role in the strategic thinking that led to the battle. For example, when Major General Earl Van Dorn's Confederate Army of West Tennessee retreated from Corinth in October 1862, Union generals William S. Rosecrans, Stephen A. Hurlbut, and Edward O. C. Ord cornered the Confederate force on the Hatchie River, but because of Hatchie's Bridge (also referred to as Davis Bridge) at Matamora, the Confederates escaped capture or destruction. In December 1862, Union Brigadier General John G. Foster defeated a brigade under Confederate Brigadier General Thomas Clingman by taking Goldsborough Bridge in Wayne County, North Carolina, thus preventing a Confederate escape.

During General Grant's operations against Vicksburg in 1863, the Big Black River Bridge was such a decisive structure. Retiring from their defeat at Champion Hill, the Confederates reached Big Black River Bridge on the night of May 16–17. Lieutenant General John C. Pemberton ordered Brigadier General John S. Bowen, with three brigades, to man the fortifications on the east bank of the river and stop the Union pursuit. Three divisions of Major General John A. McClernand's XIIIth Army Corps overwhelmed the defenses and

Below and Right: In a country criss-crossed by innumerable rivers and creeks, rail and road bridges (Below) were vital to the prosecution of the war. Where no crossings existed, temporary pontoon bridges (Right) were constructed.

the Confederate troops began to withdraw across the Big Black River on both the railroad bridge and the steamboat dock that had been rigged as a floating bridge. As they crossed, the Confederates set fire to the bridges, but Union forces captured approximately 1,800 troops, sealing Vicksburg's fate.

In March 1865, during operations on the St. Mark's River in Florida, Union General John Newton's force was on a search and destroy mission against Confederate troops that had attacked Cedar Keys and Fort Myers. They attempted to cross the river at Natural Bridge, but Confederate General Sam Jones was able to prevent this and force the Union troops to withdraw from an untenable position. It was one of the last Confederate victories of the war.

In the final days of the war, during the Appomattox Campaign of April 1865, Confederate cavalry fought stubbornly to secure the Appomattox River bridges, and having crossed them, to burn them. On April 7, General Longstreet's rearguard attempted to set fire to the High Bridge and a wagon bridge, but their failure to burn the latter allowed Union forces to cross in pursuit of General Lee's army. Failure to destroy this bridge enabled Union forces to catch up with the Confederates at Farmville. By now, the war was effectively over.

Right: Without temporary pontoon bridges, Union forces would have been unable to come to grips with the Confederate army in Virginia.

Below Right: A pontoon on its wagon traveling base.

Below: In places such as Fredericksburg, Virginia where the bridges over the Rappahannock River had been destroyed by the Confederates, the Army of the Potomac used pontoon bridges to create its own river crossings.

Brigades, Organization of

The basic battlefield "building block" during the Civil War was the infantry brigade. A formation which contained from two to six infantry regiments, the typical brigade contained about 1,500–3,000 men, and sometimes had an artillery unit attached to it. While most brigades tended to gain or lose regiments as the war progressed, a few retained the same units throughout the conflict. These brigades tended to have an "ésprit de corps" which was absent in other less stable formations. The two best-known examples of these were the Confederate "Stonewall Brigade" and the Union's "Iron Brigade".

Perhaps the most famous brigade in the Union army, the Iron Brigade was formed during the summer of 1861 from four regiments: the 2nd, 6th, and 7th Wisconsin, and the 19th Indiana. A battery of regular army artillery was also attached to the formation, and a year later a fifth regiment (24th Michigan) was added. In mid-1862 the Iron Brigade mustered 2,800 men, but by the Battle of Antietam (September 17, 1862) only 800 remained. Reinforcements brought the formation nearly up to strength, and at the Battle of Gettysburg (July 1–3, 1863) it contained 1,883 men. By the end of the battle the brigade contained less than 700 men, having being decimated for the second time in its career. These losses could not be sustained, and while the original regiments were either dissolved or amalgamated, fresh units took their place.

Although the name of the brigade continued, these new units lacked the unique spirit of the original units.

Typically, while the regimental commander was responsible for maintaining the battlefield effectiveness of his own unit, the brigade commander had to unite the regiments in his command into an effective fighting force. The position was held by a brigadier general or a senior colonel, and as the strength of an infantry regiment could dwindle to a third or less of its original strength during the campaign, the brigade was the basic tactical unit on the battlefield. Often the regiments under the brigade command came from the same state, or at least from the same general area (e.g. New England or the near Midwest). As the war progressed, and regimental strengths diminished, the number of regiments in a brigade was often increased, in order to maintain an approximate strength for the brigade. Generally, Union brigades tended to be larger than their Confederate counterparts, which contained an average of four or five regiments per brigade throughout the war. This meant that Confederate brigades became progressively weaker in numbers. By the time it surrendered at Appomattox in April 1865, the Stonewall Brigade mustered less than 200 men.

In battle, the brigade would ideally form up in two lines, each containing half its regiments. In attack or defense the second line was able to support the first line if it was hard pressed, or could exploit tactical opportunities presented to the brigade by the enemy. If required, it could also cover the retreat of the leading regiments.

Britain during the war, Role of

The British government was anxious to remain neutral in the conflict, aiming to profit from trade with both sides and balancing historical antipathy towards the Yankees with widespread public hostility to slavery. Despite southern hopes that the cotton embargo would pressure the British into conceding diplomatic recognition and even intervening on their behalf, in reality the British government was only prepared to recognize the South if it won the war.

Nevertheless, government sympathy allowed the South to use British dockyards to supply numerous blockade runners and even several important armed cruisers. The "*Trent* crisis" of December 1861, when the Union Navy seized two Southern delegates bound for Europe from a British steamer on the high seas, briefly threatened direct conflict before Lincoln agreed to their release.

Right: Queen Victoria pictured in *Punch*.

Far Right: Admiral Franklin Buchanan.

Below Right: Governor Joseph E. Brown.

Below: High casualties saw brigades change composition many times during the war. This is a view of the Battle of Spotsylvania which lasted for twelve days of bitter fighting, May 8–19, 1864.

"NEW CROWNS FOR OLD ONES!"

Brown, John (1800–59)

Brown was the abolitionist who seized the arsenal at Harper's Ferry in 1859 in an attempt to establish a base for freed slaves. Colonel Robert E. Lee retook the town after a short battle and Brown was later hanged. Hailed as a martyr, he became the subject of a popular song.

Brown, Joseph Emerson (1821–94)

Brown was governor of Georgia during the Civil War. His extreme right wing views were evidently popular as he was reelected three times, but his independent stance conflicted with Jefferson Davis's efforts to centralize Confederate government. Brown regarded Davis as a tyrant, imposing his will on the rights of the states.

Buchanan, Franklin (1800–74)

Franklin Buchanan enjoyed a distinguished naval career before the Civil War. He was the first superintendent of the U.S. Naval Academy at Annapolis (1845–47), an institution that was almost his sole creation. He served in the Mexican-American War and accompanied Matthew Perry on his ground-breaking expedition to Japan in 1852.

Buchanan was convinced that Maryland would secede from the Union in 1861, so in April he resigned his naval commission. This was an act that he would later regret; Maryland remained within the Union and Buchanan tried to rejoin the Federal navy. His application was rejected, so he offered his services to the Confederacy.

At Hampton Roads in 1862, Buchanan commanded the CSS *Virginia*, an ironclad ship salvaged by the Confederacy from the scuttled USS *Merrimac*. Desperate to break the stranglehold of the North over southern ports, the Confederacy intended to use their new ironclad to crush the wooden ships of the Union blockade. Hampton Roads was the first naval battle between ships of the industrial age, but it ended in stalemate. The *Virginia*, facing the new Union ironclad, the USS *Monitor*, was unable to disperse the northern fleet, although two Union frigates (*Cumberland* and *Congress*) were sunk.

Buchanan was promoted to admiral and served mainly as a senior officer for the rest of the war. In 1864 he took on Union ships in Mobile Bay with the ironclad ram *Tennessee* after most of the ships in his squadron had been disabled or captured.

Buell, Don Carlos (1818–98)

A West Point graduate, Buell fought in the Mexican-American War and was promoted to brigadier general at the start of the Civil War. He commanded the Army of the Ohio and reinforced Grant's campaign through Tennessee and Kentucky in 1862. He proved to be capable and efficient, capturing Nashville and then moving to reinforce Grant at Shiloh. His arrival was timely, and saved the day for the embattled Union forces. Six months later, in October 1862, he failed to follow up the retreating enemy after a fierce but inconclusive battle at Perryville, and was removed from command.

First Bull Run/Manassas Campaign

The Battle of First Bull Run, otherwise known as First Manassas, was the first significant encounter of the Civil War and the Confederacy's first victory in the field. In the summer of 1861 both sides were busy forming armies of newly recruited officers and men, principally in the area of northeastern Virginia. Here the commanders in the field for the Confederacy were Brigadier General P. G. T. Beauregard and General J. E. Johnston, and on the Union side Brigadier General I. McDowell and Major General R. Patterson. Beauregard

Above and Right: General Don Carlos Buell led the Union Army of the Ohio during the initial campaigns in the western theater. Although an efficient senior officer, he lacked the aggressive qualities which saw men like Grant and Sherman rise to prominence. His lack of decisiveness eventually cost him his field command.

Opposite Page, Above: During the first months of the war, the Confederates used dummy "quaker" guns to make their defenses along the Potomac River appear more impressive than they really were.

Opposite Page, Below: Bull Run Creek, the site of the first major battle of the war.

was positioned at Manassas Junction, while Johnston was originally located at Harper's Ferry, though he withdrew from there to Winchester, considering the position to be strategically unimportant. Patterson held his force opposite Johnston's, and moved forward when he withdrew from Harper's Ferry. Meanwhile, McDowell was busy organizing his troops around Washington.

At the end of June McDowell put forward his plan for the coming campaign that he felt sure would win the war for the North. He proposed an attack on Beauregard's force at Manassas Junction, with Patterson occupying Johnston's force in the Shenandoah Valley so that the two Confederate armies could not join together. He also did not intend to frontally attack Beauregard's army, but to move around his eastern flank and strike westward, cutting him off from Richmond. On July 16 McDowell's army began its march on Manassas Junction. Beauregard found out about this through Southern sympathizers the same evening and ordered his forward outposts to fall back. On the 17th, he requested that Johnston's army be transferred to support him at Manassas. Johnston received his orders on the morning of the 18th and immediately began moving his men by railroad to Manassas Junction. Patterson's force, which was supposed to be preventing Johnston from any such maneuver, was completely fooled into believing that Johnston's force was still in position by a cavalry screen set up by J. E. B. Stuart.

On July 18 McDowell's army reached Centerville. He first attempted to move toward the Confederate right flank, but his troops were checked at Blackburn's Ford. He then spent the next two days scouting the Southern left flank. This delay enabled Johnston to transfer more and more of his men from Winchester.

On the morning of July 21, McDowell sent his attack columns in a long march north toward Sudley Springs Ford. This route took the Federals around the Confederate left. To distract them, McDowell ordered a diversionary attack where the Warrenton Turnpike crossed Bull Run at the Stone Bridge. The Confederate troops managed to check McDowell's main advance with some difficulty, retiring in disorder to Henry Hill where the line stabilized. The fighting continued throughout the afternoon until fresh Confederate troops arrived on the Union right flank and the Union forces broke and started to withdraw, at first in an orderly manner and increasingly in a rout. The

Right: Typical terrain around Bull Run Creek.

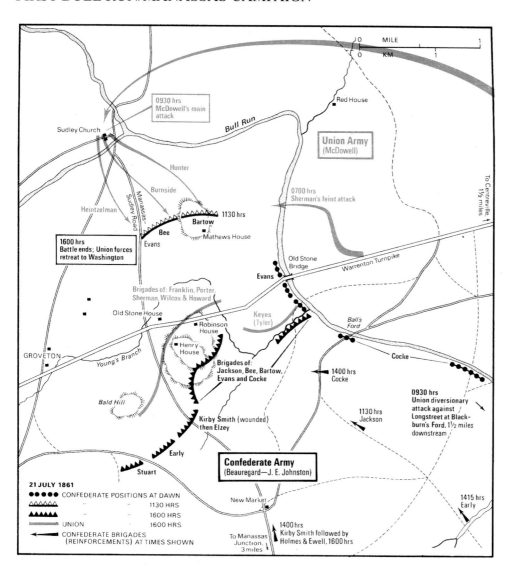

0930 hrs
McDowell's main
attack

Sudley Church

Bull Run

Red House

Hunter

Union Army
(McDowell)

Burnside

0700 hrs
Sherman's feint attack

Heintzelman

Manassas–Sudley Road

1130 hrs

Bartow

Bee

Mathews House

Evans

1600 hrs
Battle ends; Union forces
retreat to Washington

Old Stone
Bridge

Evans

Warrenton Turnpike

To Centreville,
1½ miles

Brigades of: Franklin, Porter,
Sherman, Wilcox & Howard

Old Stone House

Keyes
(Tyler)

Ball's
Ford

Robinson
House

Henry
House

Cocke

GROVETON

Young's Branch

Brigades of:
Jackson, Bee, Bartow,
Evans and Cocke

1400 hrs
Cocke

Bald Hill

1130 hrs
Jackson

0930 hrs
Union diversionary
attack against
Longstreet at Black-
burn's Ford, 1½ miles
downstream

Kirby Smith (wounded)
then Elzey

Confederate Army
(Beauregard—J. E. Johnston)

Early

Stuart

1415 hrs
Early

21 JULY 1861

●●●●● CONFEDERATE POSITIONS AT DAWN
△△△△△ " " 1130 HRS
▲▲▲▲▲ " " 1600 HRS
▬▬▬▬ UNION " 1600 HRS
◄─── CONFEDERATE BRIGADES
(REINFORCEMENTS) AT TIMES SHOWN

New Market

1400 hrs
Kirby Smith followed by
Holmes & Ewell, 1600 hrs

To Manassas
Junction,
3 miles

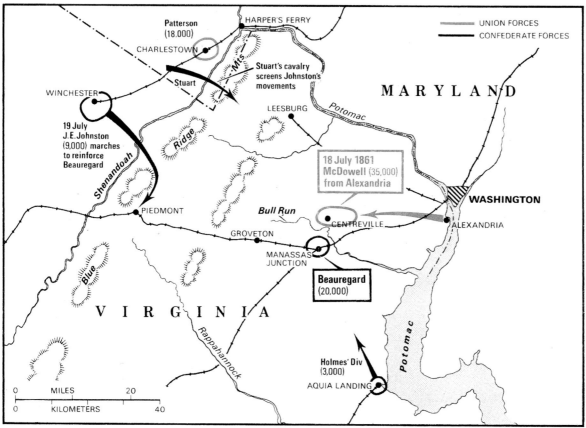

Patterson
(18,000)

HARPER'S FERRY

UNION FORCES
CONFEDERATE FORCES

CHARLESTOWN

Stuart's cavalry
screens Johnston's
movements

Stuart

M A R Y L A N D

WINCHESTER

LEESBURG

Potomac

19 July
J.E.Johnston
(9,000) marches
to reinforce
Beauregard

Blue Ridge

18 July 1861
McDowell (35,000)
from Alexandria

Shenandoah

PIEDMONT

Bull Run

WASHINGTON

GROVETON

CENTREVILLE

ALEXANDRIA

MANASSAS
JUNCTION

Blue

Beauregard
(20,000)

V I R G I N I A

Rappahannock

Potomac

Holmes' Div
(3,000)

0   MILES   20

AQUIA LANDING

0   KILOMETERS   40

This Page: Maps show-
ing the prelude to the
battle and the first Battle
of Bull Run.

Right: The Battle of Bull
Run saw the creation of
the legend of "Stonewall"
Jackson, and the end of
Union hopes to crush the
"rebellion" quickly and
easily. Union forces were
launched in a flank
attack on the
Confederate position,
but after initial success,
they were held. A
subsequent Confederate
counterattack (Above
Right) led to the rout of
the Union army, who
were pursued back over
Bull Run Creek as far
as their defensive
positions around Fairfax
Court House (Below
Right).

Confederate forces were too tired to offer a pursuit and by July 22 the defeated Union army was back behind the defenses of Washington.

THE BATTLE

When the Unionists and Confederates slid into war in spring 1861, the Unionists began to raise their army around Washington. In July a 35,000-strong Unionist force, under the command of Major General Irvin McDowell, advanced towards Confederate northern Virginia. The objective was to take the strategically important railway junction at Manassas, and advance towards Richmond. The Confederate forces barring the way was split into two—General Joseph E. Johnston's 12,000 troops defending the route into Virginia to the northwest through the Shenandoah Valley and Major General Pierre G. T. Beauregard positioned at Manassas Junction with his 22,000-strong army—but crucially they were linked by the Manassas Gap Railroad. Beauregard set up his forces on the south side of Bull Run Creek, about three miles north of Manassas Junction railway station. The original Unionist plan had entailed Johnston's Confederates in the Shenandoah Valley being pinned down by a force led by Major General Robert Patterson but by the time McDowell neared Beauregard's positions Patterson had withdrawn his forces to Harpers Ferry. The first skirmishes between McDowell's and Beauregard's forces took place along the creek on July 18 but the main attack did not take place until July 21, allowing time for Johnston to bring his forces by rail on the 19th to swell the defending Confederate army to over 30,000.

Both sides intended to attack. The Unionist movement started at 2:00am and did not reach the creek until several hours later, three brigades under Brigadier General Daniel Tyler reaching the stone bridge crossing the creek at 5:00am, and

Right and Below Right: Several contemporary depictions of the battle captured the confused nature of the fighting. In reality the battle was a contest of wills between two largely untrained armies.

Below: The stone bridge over the creek (photographed after the battle) was the site of the initial Union attack by General Tyler's division, and later served as a crossing point for much of the routed Union army.

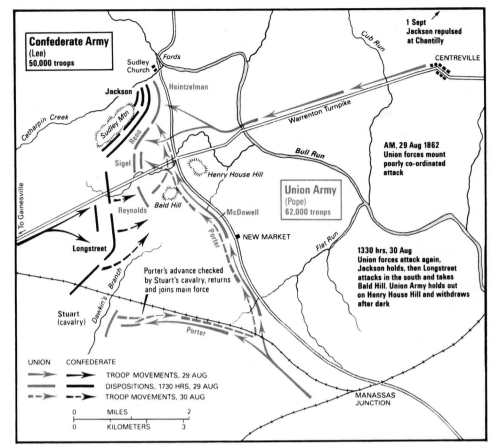

Confederate Army
(Lee)
50,000 troops

1 Sept
Jackson repulsed
at Chantilly

CENTREVILLE

Cub Run

Sudley
Church

Fords

Jackson

Heintzelman

Catharpin Creek

Sudley Mtn.

Reno

Warrenton Turnpike

Sigel

Bull Run

Henry House Hill

Union Army
(Pope)
62,000 troops

AM, 29 Aug 1862
Union forces mount
poorly co-ordinated
attack

To Gainesville

Reynolds

Bald Hill

McDowell

Longstreet

NEW MARKET

Porter

Flat Run

1330 hrs, 30 Aug
Union forces attack again,
Jackson holds, then Longstreet
attacks in the south and takes
Bald Hill. Union Army holds out
on Henry House Hill and withdraws
after dark

Dawkin's Branch

Porter's advance checked
by Stuart's cavalry, returns
and joins main force

Stuart
(cavalry)

Porter

UNION   CONFEDERATE

→ ▬▶ TROOP MOVEMENTS, 29 AUG
━ ━▶ DISPOSITIONS, 1730 HRS, 29 AUG
- -▶ ╺ ╺▶ TROOP MOVEMENTS, 30 AUG

MANASSAS
JUNCTION

0   MILES   2
0   KILOMETERS   3

the planned main attack of two divisions under Brigadier Generals David Hunter and Samuel P. Heintzelman crossing the creek at Sudley Springs after 9:00am on the Confederates' left flank. To stabilize his line, Beauregard was forced to call off his attack, Colonel Nathan G. Evans holding the bridge against Tyler then turning to help the brigades of Brigadier General Barnard Bee and Brigadier General Francis S. Bartow repel Hunter's and Heintzelman's flanking assault from the north.

However, the Unionists kept the momentum of the attack going when Tyler managed to cross the creek at a ford near the stone bridge, and the Confederate line in the northwest was driven back to Henry House Hill. Here the Confederate Brigadier General Thomas J. Jackson had established his brigade and the retreating Confederate forces were exhorted by Bee to rally round him—"There stands Jackson like a stone wall"— coining the subsequent nickname "Stonewall" Jackson.

Realizing that the main battle was taking place northwest of the Confederate HQ, Beauregard and Johnston rode to Henry House Hill to prepare the Confederate line. The Unionists attacked at 1:00pm, five brigades charging up the hill supported by artillery, but the Confederate line held firm, repulsing a series of attacks through the afternoon. By 4:00pm the exhausted Unionist troops were becoming increasingly disorganized, and the arrival of Confederate reinforcements allowed Beauregard to launch an attack. The now

demoralized Unionists fled from the battlefield, but the Confederates were too exhausted themselves to pursue them. Although the battle was to have no lasting strategic significance, and losses were low (the Unionists suffering nearly 3,000 killed, wounded, or captured; the Confederates losing nearly 2,000), compared to later battles fought by much more experienced and battle-hardened troops, the victory was a boost to Confederate confidence.

Second Bull Run/Manassas Campaign

Scene of the first major engagement of the war, in July 1861, Bull Run (Manassas) again became the focus of attention the following year. The failure of McClellan's attack on Richmond prompted Lincoln to order the withdrawal of the Army of the Potomac from the peninsula to the vicinity of Washington. On June 26, 1862, a "western" general, John Pope, received command of the newly created Federal Army of Virginia. It was formed by the consolidation of the commands of McDowell, Banks, and Fremont (the Federal commands that Jackson had beaten during his Shenandoah Valley Campaign) to cover McClellan's movement and protect Washington.

By July 12, Pope's army had moved south to a point from where it could threaten Richmond's access to the Shenandoah Valley. Although McClellan's withdrawing forces were still perceived to be a potential threat to Richmond, Lee felt Pope

now represented the more immediate threat and sent reinforcements to Jackson with orders to "suppress" the Army of Virginia.

On August 3, McClellan was ordered to evacuate the Peninsula, thus removing the dual threat to the Lee's troops and allowing him the opportunity to concentrate on Pope exclusively. The opposing armies maneuvered through mid-August, and by August 22 were facing each other across the Rappahannock River near Sulphur Springs, Virginia.

At this point, Lee cunningly split his forces and on two separate occasions sent raiders around Pope's unsecured flanks to cut his supply lines. The second raid succeeded in neutralizing Bristoe Station and Manassas Station and destroyed Federal supplies distributed over almost a square mile.

Pope now hurried his command to Manassas hoping to smash Jackson's isolated wing, only to discover that he had taken up positions on the year-old battlefield of First Manassas. Despite furious Federal attacks during August 29, Jackson held his position and the following day was relieved by Longstreet who routed the Federal army from the field in the late afternoon. As well as the loss of a large cache of arms and equipment, Pope's defeat at the Second Bull Run cost the Federals dear and allowed the Confederacy an opportunity to threaten Washington.

THE BATTLE
In June 1862 Major General John Pope was appointed commander of the newly formed Union Army of Virginia, and in July advanced into Confederate Virginia. The Confederate General Robert E. Lee, although engaged with Major General George B. McClellan in the Peninsular Campaign, released Major General Thomas J. Jackson with 11–12,000 men to counter the threat. On August 13 a further ten of Lee's brigades, commanded by Major General James Longstreet, joined Jackson in the reorganized Army of Northern Virginia. Lee's aim was for Jackson to take his corps on a march round Pope's flank, cutting off his supply lines, at which point Lee and Longstreet would rejoin him to defeat Pope before McClellan's slow-moving army could combine the Unionist forces. Covering fifty-four miles in two days Jackson's forces cut the Unionists' railroad on

August 27 and ransacked their supply depot at Manassas ·Junction, before taking up defensive positions near the old battlefield of Bull Run.

Pope, now with a combined force of 60–70,000 troops, moved against Jackson, expecting him to retreat, but was surprised to encounter Jackson's forces on August 29 dug in along the line of an unfinished railroad. Frontal attacks by the Unionists failed to dislodge Jackson and, most crucially, Pope's intended encirclement of Jackson using McDowell's and Porter's corps was stymied by an unexpected clash with Jackson's skirmishers, leaving the way open for Longstreet's corps of 25–30,000 men to advance and take position undetected facing the undefended left flank of Pope's forces.

Pope resumed his attacks on Jackson's line the next day, August 30, and Lee and Longstreet waited while the Unionists exhausted themselves. By 4:00pm Jackson could hold out no longer, and Longstreet's hidden artillery launched a barrage which tore through the Unionist line. Longstreet's troops then charged and drove the Unionists back to Henry House Hill, whence they conducted a fighting retreat into the next day. Despite his losses (the Confederates suffered approximately 9,000 casualties; the Unionists 14–16,000), Lee's forces were in Unionist territory, in Maryland, within days.

Burnside, Ambrose Everett (1824–81)

Burnside was a graduate of West Point, a former soldier and arms manufacturer. An easy-going, courageous man, he was naturally hesitant and indecisive, and bold actions were simply not his style. This proved to be his chief failure as a commander. "Few men," wrote one Massachusetts colonel, "have risen so high upon so slight a foundation as [Burnside] . . . He is equally remembered for his imposing whiskers, which have become immortalized as "sideburns."

Burnside commanded a brigade at First Bull Run in 1861, and in 1862 he was responsible for the creation of the first amphibious force in the United States. He led an amphibious landing on the North Carolina coast, capturing Roanoake Island and destroying a couple of small Confederate fleets. At Antietam Burnside commanded IX Corps, McClellan's left wing. Burnside's failure to capture a well-defended bridge over Antietam creek (later known as "Burnside Bridge") limited the Union victory.

Nevertheless, Lincoln promoted him to command the Army of the Potomac in place of McClellan. Burnside sought to exploit the Union victory at Antietam by capturing Fredericksburg, but it was here in December 1862, that he suffered his most spectacular defeat. He ordered fourteen ill-advised frontal assaults on well-entrenched Confederate infantry positions on Marye's Heights that resulted in 9,000 Union dead.

After a year in Ohio, Burnside returned to command IX Corps in the spring of 1864, but the bloody fiasco of "the Crater" when miners blew up a tunnel under Confederate lines at the siege of Petersburg, ended Burnside's career.

Butler, Benjamin (1818–93)

Butler was a controversial politician and mediocre general. Although he promised slave owners in Maryland that troops would protect them if their slaves rose up against them, once in command of Fort Monroe, Virginia, in 1861, he reversed this decision. Slaves who arrived at the frontier were declared "contraband of war" and allowed to cross to the north rather than being returned to their Southern owners.

Butler was a Massachusetts politician who owed his military rank entirely to his exalted connections rather than any military talent. He commanded the troops who occupied Baltimore in 1861, and was then promoted to major general at Fort Monroe. In May 1862 Butler became military governor of the recently conquered New Orleans and acquired a reputation as a martinet. He executed a man suspected of

desecrating the American flag, and confiscated the property of citizens who refused to swear allegiance to the Union. "I was always a friend of Southern rights, but an enemy of Southern wrongs," he said. However, his administration was suspected of corruption; Butler first acquired the nickname "Spoons" for allegedly pocketing silverware, and was later known as "Beast Butler" because of his repressive regime. He was recalled in December 1862 after difficulties with foreign consuls over confiscated property.

Butler became commander of the Army of the James in Virginia in November 1863, and in 1864 failed to penetrate Confederate defenses of Richmond and Petersburg. He was relieved of his command in January 1865 after the failure of an expedition against Fort Fisher, North Carolina.

Far Left: General Ambrose E. Burnside and his staff, pictured in late 1862. He proved to be one of the worst of a series of incompetent Union commanders.

Left: General Benjamin Butler was one of the most controversial commanders in the Union Army. The lack of compassion he showed for Southerners under his protection in New Orleans led to his nickname of "Beast Butler." His lack of ability as a military administrator was matched by his ineffectiveness as a field commander.

Below: Butler (seated far left) seen on a postwar committee.

Cabinet, Confederate

There was only one presidential administration from the formation of the Confederate States of America in 1861 to its dissolution in 1865, hence only one cabinet. Jefferson Davis was inaugurated as the President of the Provisional Confederate Government on February 18, 1861, and as President of the Permanent Government of the Confederate States of America on February 22, 1862. His vice president in both presidential roles was Alexander H. Stephens.

As with the United States Executive Branch prior to the addition of the Department of the Interior in 1849, the Confederate Executive Branch consisted of six executive branches, and these exactly paralleled those of the United States government. Of the six appointed in February 1861, two cabinet secretaries remained until the Confederate States of America was dissolved at the last cabinet meeting, held in Washington, Georgia, on May 4, 1865. The two who served for the entire four years were Secretary of the Navy Stephen Mallory and Postmaster General John Reagan.

The Confederate States of America would have two treasury secretaries, four secretaries of state, five attorneys general, and six secretaries of war. One man, Judah Philip Benjamin, would hold three of these

Southern politicians: Jefferson C. Davis pictured as a young Senator (Left) and Robert Toombs, the first Confederate Secretary of State who came from Georgia (Right).

portfolios at various times through the short history of the Confederate States of America. The last Secretary of War was John Cabell Breckinridge, who had served as Vice President of the United States from 1857 to 1861, and who had come in third in the race for President of the United States in 1860.

The first Confederate Secretary of State, Robert Toombs, served for five months, being succeeded by R. M. T. Hunter, who held the office from July 1861 through January 1862. William M. Brown was the Confederate Secretary of State for six weeks until the portfolio was assumed by Judah Benjamin, who was in the post from March 18, 1862, to May 4, 1865.

Judah Benjamin had been the first Attorney General of the Confederacy, serving from February 1861 to September 1861, when he became Secretary of War. Wade Keyes took over the portfolio from Benjamin and served for two months before passing it to Thomas Bragg. Bragg was in office for four months and was succeeded by the longest-serving Confederate Attorney General, Thomas Watts, who held the post from March 1862 through

September 1863. Wade Keyes returned to the job for three months before handing the reins to George Davis on January 2, 1864. Davis would remain through April 1865.

The two Secretaries of the Confederate Treasury were Christopher Memminger, who served through July 1864 and George Trenholm, who held the post through April 1865.

The post of Secretary of War was the one which changed the most often, going to military officers on three occasions. Leroy Pope Walker was in office through a cabinet shake-up in September 1861, when Judah Benjamin moved over to take the job for six months. Brigadier General George Randolph succeeded Benjamin, who moved to the State Department in March 1862. Randolph's successor, Major General Gustavus Smith, held the post for a mere four days in November 1862 before the portfolio passed to James Seddon, who held the post until February 1865. The last Confederate Secretary of War was former United States' Vice President, now Confederate Major General, John Cabell Breckinridge. His term coincided with the last four months of the Confederacy.

The most trusted and perhaps the most famous of the Confederate cabinet members, Louisiana's Judah Benjamin began his political career in 1852, when he became the first Jew to be elected to the United States Senate. Here, he formed a close friendship with Jefferson Davis, who was a senator from Mississippi. Benjamin resigned from the Senate in February 1861 when Louisiana seceded from the Union, to become Attorney General. Known variously as "Jeff Davis's Pet Jew" and "the Brains of the Confederacy," Benjamin was considered to have been perhaps the best lawyer in the South. When he became Secretary of State in 1862, Benjamin focused his attention on obtaining diplomatic recognition of the Confederate States of America as a legitimate nation.

When the war ended and members of the Confederacy were subject to arrest, Benjamin slipped through Union lines in western Florida and escaped to Havana. By August 1865, he had arrived in England, where he became an advisor to Queen Victoria. He would not set foot in North America again for seventeen years.

Cabinet, Union

The Civil War essentially coincided with the first term of President Abraham Lincoln. It began six weeks after his first inauguration on March 4, 1861, and ended less than five weeks after his second on March 4, 1865. In 1861, the Vice President's role in the Executive Branch was a great deal more peripheral than it would become in the late twentieth century. Lincoln's first term Vice President was Hannibal Hamlin, and Andrew Johnson was sworn into that office on March 4, 1865, five weeks before he succeeded Lincoln as President.

Originally the United States Executive Branch consisted of just five executive departments, but with the addition of the Department of the Navy in 1798 and the Department of the Interior in 1849, the President's Cabinet had grown to include seven secretaries by Lincoln's time. Of the seven appointed in March 1861, only two cabinet secretaries remained throughout Lincoln's entire tenure in the White House. These were Secretary of State William H. Seward and Secretary of the Navy Gideon Welles. Both men would also remain in their offices through the end of President Johnson's term in 1869.

Lincoln's first Secretary of the Treasury was Salmon P. Chase, who served until 1864. He was succeeded by William P. Fessenden, and shortly thereafter by Hugh McCulloch, who would remain in President Johnson's cabinet until 1869.

Secretary of War Simon Cameron was succeeded in 1862 by Edwin M. Stanton, who retained that post through the end of the war. He remained in the Johnson cabinet until 1867.

Lincoln's first Attorney General was Edward Bates. He was replaced in 1864 by James Speed, who would go on to serve President Johnson until 1866.

For most of President Lincoln's first term, Montgomery Blair would serve as Postmaster General. He was replaced in 1864 by William Dennison, who served in that role under President Johnson until 1866.

Secretary of the Interior Caleb B. Smith was succeeded in 1863 by John P. Usher, who left office shortly after Andrew Johnson became president.

Of the Lincoln cabinet, Seward and Chase were arguably the most visible and historically important. Seward was a serious contender for the Republican presidential nomination in 1860 that went to Lincoln, but he campaigned hard for Lincoln after losing the nomination. Because of this and his prominence in the Party, he was given the top cabinet post, and he was seen as a political asset to the Lincoln administration, as well as to that of Andrew Johnson. During the Fort Sumter crisis of 1861, he sought to avert war by reinforcing Union sentiment in the South. Seward is also well known for having engineered the purchase of Alaska from Russia in 1867 for two cents an acre.

Chase was an early member of the Republican Party and was elected as governor of Ohio in 1855. Like Seward, he was a contender for the Republican presidential nomination in 1860, but having lost, he ran for the United States Senate and won. When Lincoln appointed him to the cabinet, Chase resigned his Senate seat and served as Secretary of the Treasury until July 1864. In this role, Chase was the key player in arranging financing for the war effort and in establishing the National Banking System in 1863. Because of his less compromising views on slavery, Chase was always at odds with the more moderate Lincoln, who eased Chase out in 1864. However, when Supreme Court Chief Justice Roger Taney died in October 1864, Lincoln gave the job to Chase. In this post,

President Lincoln pictured with his War Cabinet (Below), including the white-bearded Gideon Welles, Secretary of the Navy, and Edwin M. Stanton, the Secretary of War. Lincoln took a keen interest in his armies, and paid several visits of inspection to the Army of the Potomac in the field (Right). In this photograph, taken at Antietam in September 1862, he is seen consulting with General Lew Wallace.

Chase presided over the impeachment of Andrew Johnson, as well as many issues related to the war, Reconstruction, and government finance. He was briefly considered as a possible presidential candidate in 1868.

Campaigns

For some time after it was concluded, the American Civil War was the largest and bloodiest war the world had known in terms of the number of combatants, which ran into millions, and the number of them that became casualties. It also saw the involvement, for the first time, of an entire population and economy—a term later defined as "total war." The scale of the war is reflected in the number of engagements that were fought. For the period 1861 and 1865, in all the theaters of the war, some 6,500 separate land and sea engagements have been identified. Collectively these engagements usually formed part of longer campaigns, the most important of which are discussed separately under the headings listed below. The strategies of the Union and Confederacy were based on such campaigns, each of which had a significant objective; the capture, dominance or destruction of an important military stronghold, railhead, port or transportation hub, population center, manufacturing base or else a geographical feature such as a river or valley. The main campaigns were:

Campaigns in Missouri and Arkansas

The only fighting of note in Missouri took place in August 1861. This was the Battle of Wilson's Creek, near Springfield, fought by Confederate troops under Maj. Gen. Stirling Price and Union forces led by Brigadier General Nathanial Lyon and

Right: An outpost of the Army of the Potomac.

Below Right: Carolinian pickets flee in the face of Federal troops.

Below: The main areas of fighting and the main campaigns of the Civil War.

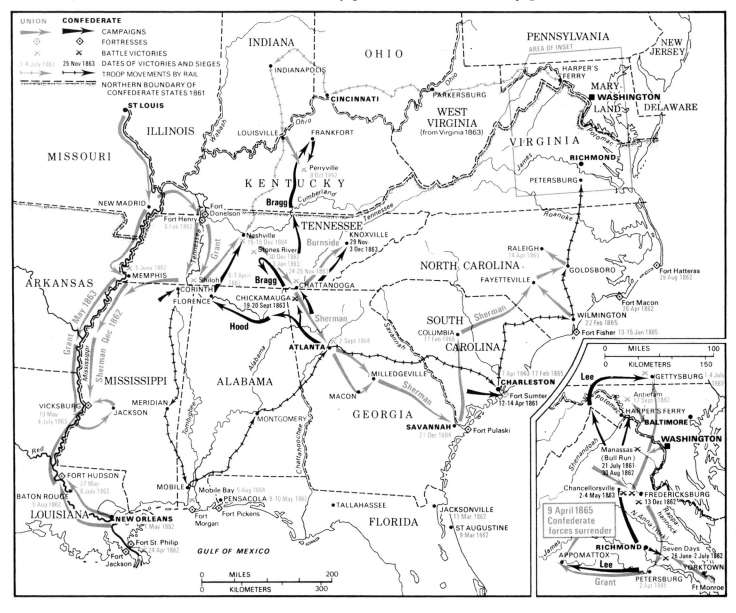

Brigadier General Ben McCulloch. The battle was won for the Confederacy, and Lyon was killed. It was followed by the Battle of Pea Ridge, in the northwest corner of Arkansas, on March 6–8, 1862. Here the Unionists, commanded by Brigadier General Samuel R. Curtis, decisively defeated Confederates, led by Major General Earl van Dorn, and established Union control of the state for the remainder of the war.

Campaigns in the Far West

The year 1862 witnessed important developments in the far southwest. Confederate successes in 1861 had given them control of the southern part of the territory of New Mexico, and the conquered area then became the Confederate Territory of Arizona, with a representative in the Confederate Congress. In January 1862, Brigadier General Henry Sibley, with a force of about 3,700 Confederates, launched a movement up the Rio Grande from Fort Bliss against a Union command at Fort Craig of about 3,800 men under Colonel Edward Canby. Sibley's immediate objective was the conquest of New Mexico, but his ultimate goal was California. The forces clashed in the Battle of Valverde on February 21, the Confederates winning the day, and Sibley moved on to Albuquerque. But Sibley's situation soon became precarious owing to lack of supplies and the prospective reinforcement of Canby's command. On April 14 Sibley evacuated Albuquerque and headed for Fort Bliss where he arrived early in May. The threatened approach of further Union reinforcements from California caused him to continue his retreat to San Antonio, with a force greatly depleted by battle, hunger, illness, and exhaustion.

Canada, Part played in the war

During the early nineteenth century, "Canada" as we know it today did not exist. British North America consisted of a collection of British colonies, with the population centered mainly in English-speaking Upper Canada (roughly analogous to today's southern Ontario), French-speaking Lower Canada (roughly analogous to today's southern Quebec), and in the English-speaking Maritime Provinces of Nova Scotia, New Brunswick, and Prince Edward Island.

As events in the United States were pushing that nation toward the Civil War, a low-level civil war of sorts was already going on north of the border in British North America. This came to a head in the rebellions of 1837, and in 1848 Britain finally granted a measure of home rule. By the time that the United States split in two in 1861, the people of British North America

were moving in the opposite direction—that is, toward the idea of a "confederation" of disparate colonies into a unified federal entity. This would culminate in the British North America Act of 1867, that brought the five listed colonies into the new Dominion of Canada as provinces.

In the meantime, despite efforts by both sides in the Civil War, Britain and the subject components of the British Empire remained technically neutral, although anti-American sentiment ran high, and there was a fear that the United States would attempt to invade and occupy its northern neighbor. The British, in North America and Britain, were tacitly pro-Confederate because of the long animosity growing out of the wars of 1776 and 1812, and demands by some American politicians that portions of British North America should be annexed by force.

At the same time, the United States was angered by the British willingness to give asylum and sanctuary to Confederates who appeared in neutral Canadian territory.

The actual Civil War was fought far from Canada's border, so direct Anglo-Canadian involvement was restricted to a series of relatively small-scale incidents. The first of these was what was called "the *Trent* Affair." On November 8, 1861, the USS *San Jacinto*, contrary to international maritime law, stopped the British mail packet *Trent* sailing from Havana to England and arrested two Confederate diplomats and their secretaries who were on a diplomatic mission to England. They were imprisoned in Boston and the British government demanded their release because they were taken from a neutral ship. The atmosphere became so heated that there was talk of war between the United States and Britain. London announced that it would defend its colonies with all its power and sent 14,000 officers and men as reinforcements. The release of the prisoners a month later dissipated the tension considerably.

Two years later, however, a group of Confederates seized the American ship *Chesapeake* making a run between New York and Portland, Maine, taking it to British territorial waters near New Brunswick and Nova Scotia where they hoped to sell the ship's cargo. The Confederates had violated British neutrality, as would the U.S. Navy, when it came north to recapture the *Chesapeake*.

In October 1864, a group of Confederate agents, dressed in civilian clothes, robbed three banks in the village of St. Albans,

Right: Captain Raphael Semmes, captain of the CSS *Alabama*, standing by his ship's 110-pounder while at Capetown, South Africa in August 1863.

Vermont, killing one person before escaping across the border with $200,000. The British arrested them in Montreal and returned the money. President Lincoln personally canceled a U.S. Army operation aimed at pursuing the Confederates into Canada.

Perhaps the most blatant violation of neutrality on the part of the British was the building of warships in Britain for the Confederate Navy. Among these was the raider CSS *Alabama*, which was the scourge of the North Atlantic until she was sunk by the U.S. Navy in 1864. The Americans claimed compensation from Britain and it was suggested that Britain cede some Canadian territory as a reparation. The issue was finally submitted to arbitration in 1871, and a Geneva tribunal awarded the United States $15.5 million in gold (but no territory) in 1872.

Carbines

Carbines were mostly associated with cavalrymen, who needed a weapon shorter than the traditional musket or rifled musket that would give them firepower when fighting dismounted. On average the carbines found in the Civil War had a length of around thirty-eight inches, while the commonest rifled musket of the conflict, the M1861 Springfield, measured 55¾ inches. Equally, carbines weighed less than the heavier infantry weapons.

There were two types of carbine to be found in use during the conflict—breech-loaders, which were either single-shot or repeating weapons, and the single-shot muzzle-loader. In general, Union troops had far greater access to the former category, while the South relied on the single-shot types because the Confederacy's arms manufacturers were not able to produce the more complex breech-loaders (or their

ammunition) in any great quantities. Ammunition for carbines came in several forms, most common was the linen cartridge, which self-consumed when fired. Other carbines, such as the Burnside, used metallic cartridges, often of brass. Rounds were also smaller than those used in rifled muskets and potentially less damaging, although still sufficient to case serious wounds.

Probably more than thirty different types of carbine saw some service during the Civil War. The U.S. government often contracted private manufacturers to produce them, and chief among these was the M1859 Sharps breech-loader, which was the U.S. Army's first widely used carbine, and the Spencer, which was a repeater with a seven-shot magazine. Various other companies, such as Starr and Gwyn & Campbell, also supplied the North with carbines similar to the Sharps model, but in far lesser quantities—for example, just 25,603 from Starr and 9,342 from Gwyn & Campbell compared to more than 80,000 of the M1859 Sharps.

The South's access to modern carbines was much more limited. Many breech-

Right: The Sharps carbine was the most successful cavalry weapon of the war—easily reloaded in the saddle, powerful, accurate, and reliable. Confederate troopers used captured Sharps whenever possible.

Below and Far Right: Cavalry carbines were the weapon of choice for cavalrymen, who for the most part avoided dashing cavalry charges for the more effective but less spectacular role as highly mobile foot soldiers. The variant of the Sharps Carbine pictured below could be reloaded by a cavalryman lying prone. Other innovative carbines such as the Henry Repeating Carbine gave Union cavalry a firepower which the Confederates were unable to match. One Confederate soldier called the Henry "that tarnation Yankee rifle they load on Sunday and shoot all week."

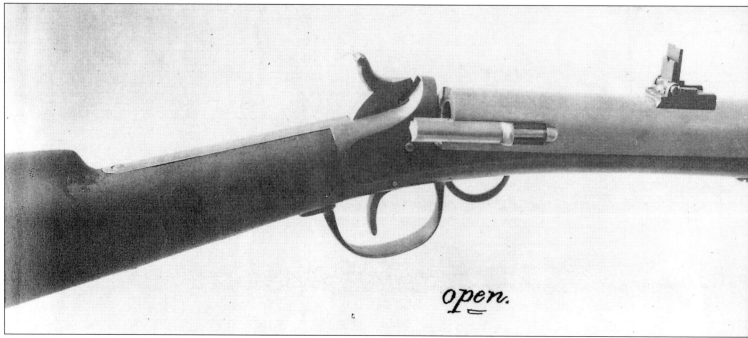

open.

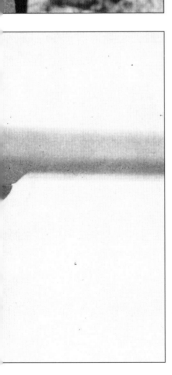

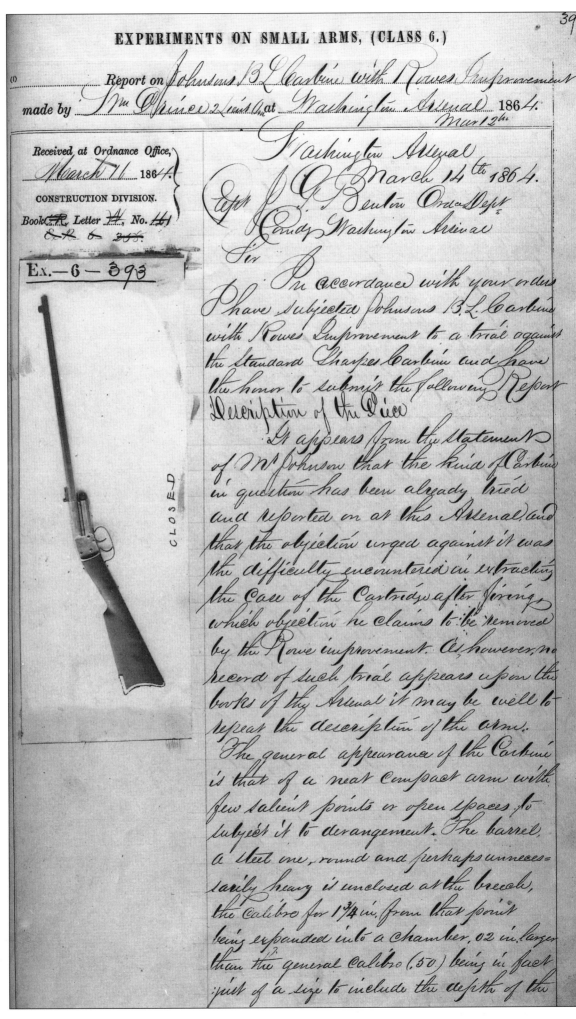

EXPERIMENTS ON SMALL ARMS, (CLASS 6.)

(1) Report on *Johnsons B L Carbine with Rowes Improvement*

made by *Wm Prince 2 Lieut* at *Washington Arsenal* 1864.
Mar 12th

Received at Ordnance Office,

March 11 1864.

CONSTRUCTION DIVISION.

Book *C R* Letter *H*, No. *161*
S R 6 366

Ex.—6—393

CLOSED

Washington Arsenal

March 14th 1864.

Capt J G Benton Ord Dept

Comdg Washington Arsenal

Sir

In accordance with your orders I have subjected Johnsons B.L. Carbine with Rowes Improvement to a trial against the standard Sharps Carbine and have the honor to submit the following Report.

Description of the Piece

It appears from the statement of Mr Johnson that the kind of Carbine in question has been already tried and reported on at this Arsenal, and that the objection urged against it was the difficulty encountered in extracting the Case of the Cartridge after firing, which objection he claims to be removed by the Rowe improvement. As, however, no record of such trial appears upon the books of the Arsenal it may be well to repeat the description of the arm.

The general appearance of the Carbine is that of a neat compact arm with few salient points or open spaces to subject it to derangement. The barrel, a steel one, round and perhaps unnecessarily heavy is enclosed at the breech, the calibre for 1¾ in from that point being expanded into a chamber, .02 in larger than the general Calibre (.50) being in fact just of a size to include the depth of the

loaders were captured from Union forces, but home-manufactured ones were less common and generally inferior. For example, a copy of the Northern Sharps appeared as the "Richmond Sharps" but initially suffered from production problems. Only 5,200 were ever made. Other Southern breech-loaders, such as the .52-caliber Tarpley, the Morse, and the Perry or Maynard, appeared in even smaller numbers. The Southern cavalry, therefore, relied on muzzle-loading carbines, either produced by the Confederacy's own arms manufacturers or imported from abroad, often Britain, and copied locally. Among the former were a number of designs that were simply cutdown versions of existing rifled muskets, including some 2,800 carbines based on the M1855 rifled musket produced by the Richmond Armory. Among the imports were copies of the British P1856 "East India Pattern" carbine, which in 1863 became the standard issue weapon for Southern cavalry.

The carbine gave the cavalrymen of both sides a degree of firepower, which was primarily used for defensive purposes. However, the effectiveness of the carbine was restricted by its limited range, which was a product of its shorter barrel and generally lighter charge. Some carbines were sighted up to several hundred yards—the Sharps could reach 800 yards and the Spencer 1,000 yards. However, effective ranges were considerably lower at between 400 and 500 yards. In battle, accurate aimed fire was most effective at between 150 and 200 yards.

HENRY

The Henry was capable of a greater rate of fire than any other breech-loader of the period, yet was ordered in comparatively small numbers by the U.S. government—a mere 1,731 were issued through official channels—although considerably more were bought by ordinary soldiers. Estimates suggest that around 10,000 were purchased in such a way. Those in the front line quickly recognized that the Henry had several valuable attributes on the battlefield, and anecdotes indicate that potential purchasers were willing to spend several times their monthly salary to secure the weapon.

There were several reasons for its popularity. The Henry could be reloaded without the firer having to stand and it could carry a large number of rounds in its magazine that made rapid fire possible without time-consuming reloading. A skilled operator could empty the full magazine in around eleven seconds, although reloading took somewhat longer. The magazine ran underneath the weapon's barrel and could be persuaded with fifteen brass cartridges of .44 caliber. The rifle itself weighed a little under ten pounds and had a short twenty-four-inch

barrel. The weapon was fired by way of a lever positioned on the trigger guard, which ejected a spent cartridge and replaced it with a ready-to-use round.

Despite its limited deployment during the Civil War, the Henry was destined to have a long-term significance as it is considered the blueprint for the Winchester repeating rifle that was to gain fame in the opening of the West in the latter part of the century.

SHARPS

The M1859 Sharps single-shot breech-loader, which was primarily used by the Union, appeared as both a rifle and a carbine, the latter designed as a shorter weapon for use by cavalry units were it found greatest favor. The rifle version had a length of forty-seven inches, while the carbine model measured thirty-nine inches. Both were of .52 caliber and fired a linen cartridge, which combusted during firing and therefore did not have to be extracted before another cartridge was inserted, unlike carbines that used metallic cartridge. A later version, the M1863, was virtually identical to the original weapon, except for iron barrel bands, trigger guards, and butt plates rather than brass.

Many claims were made for the Sharps. Certainly it was more accurate than many muzzle-loading weapons, particularly in the hands of first-rate sharpshooters, who could hit a chosen target at around 700 yards. However, a good muzzle-loading rifle in skilled hands could also do this. The Sharps also suffered one particular failing—despite its fairly robust and simple firing mechanism, it leaked hot gases during firing, thereby reducing the power of the bullet and discomforting the user. However, the Sharps did have two distinct advantages. First, its rate of fire was around three times as great as a breech-loading rifle. Second, it could be loaded much more easily while the firer was prone.

The carbine version of this privately manufactured weapon saw most action with the cavalry, with the U.S. government purchasing some 80,000 carbines compared to just over 9,000 of the longer rifle model. Many Sharps were also bought by individual units or their state governments in the North, while the smaller numbers manufactured by the South were generally found to be inferior.

SPENCER

The Spencer was produced in both cutdown carbine and longer rifle models, and became the most coveted breech-loaders to see service. The U.S. government purchased some 94,000 carbines and 12,000 rifles while others were bought by individuals, units, and state governments. The carbine version, when entered service from 1863 onward, weighed a little more than nine pounds unloaded and was just thirty-nine inches long. Its popularity was

partly explained by its reliability, robustness, and unmatched rate of fire. Spencer himself was able to fire 21 rounds a minute during an evaluation by the U.S. Navy. However, the carbines effective range was between 300 and 400 yards.

The Spencer represented a generational shift in firearms, chiefly because its round comprised a ball of .52 caliber fixed into a copper cartridge. These self-continued cartridges, which included both detonator and charge and were therefore less prone to water or moisture damage, were loaded into a spring-fed magazine tube that led from the rear of the stock to the breech. Each time the hammer was cocked and the trigger guard pushed forward, the spent cartridge was ejected to be replaced by an unused round. Fully loaded the Sharps carried eight rounds (seven in the magazine and one in the firing chamber. Initial objections concerning the time taken to

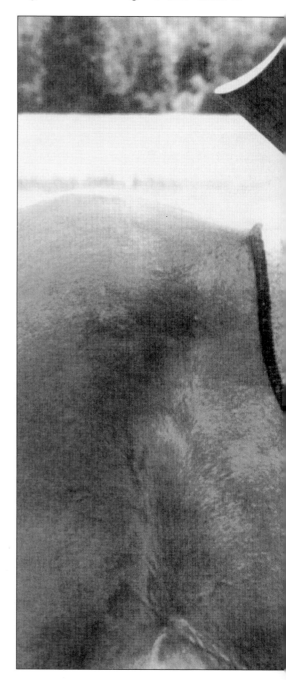

THE AMERICAN CIVIL WAR: A VISUAL ENCYCLOPEDIA

Right: The Sharps carbine was powerful, accurate, and almost "soldier-proof," and was extremely common toward the end of the war.

Below: The carbine remained strapped to the trooper when he was mounted, but a gimble on the saddle provided support to keep the weapon from flopping around during non-combat operations.

101

fully load the weapon were overcome by the development of a cartridge box, which held a number of tubes each containing seven cartridges. Each tube could be loaded into the magazine in one reasonably easy action in a matter of ten seconds.

Spencers were almost unknown among Southern forces. Those that were used were often taken on the battlefield, but the South did not have the facilities to manufacture the cartridges. Once the captured rounds had been fired, the weapon was effectively useless unless replacement ammunition could be found from the same source.

Carolina Sounds, Blockade of the (1861–65)

In late August 1861 a Union expedition siezed Hatteras Inlet in the Outer Banks of North Carolina. By gaining access to the protected waterways of the Carolina Sounds and the rivers which flowed into them, the Union was able to threaten large parts of the state. In February 1862, Union forces captured Roanoake Island, driving the Confederate gunboat fleet in the area north to Elizabeth City, where it was destroyed. During the Spring, New Berne and Beaufort fell to the Union, bottling any remaining Confederate naval forces in North Carolina's rivers. This blockade continued for another two years, while the Confederates built forces to contest Union control of the Sounds. Despite the construction of ironclads such as the CSS *Albermarle*, the Confederates were unable to regain control of the internal waterways, and the Union blockade remained in place until the end of the war.

Carpetbaggers

During the Reconstruction period that followed the Civil War, the U.S. Army forces occupying the states of the former Confederate States of America introduced restrictive laws that prevented many former southern business people from a role in the Southern economy. At the same time, this provided an opening for Northern opportunists to go into the South with half-baked business schemes, many of which were simply ill-conceived, but some of which were designed specifically to cheat Southerners—both white and black. Since these people often carried their belongings in the carpet-covered suitcases popular at the time, they were called "Carpetbaggers."

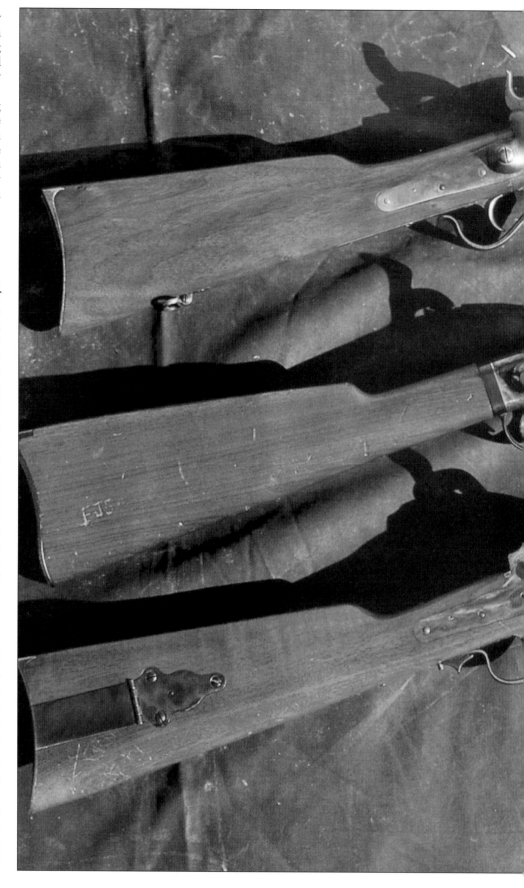

Above Right: Three very common cavalry carbines (from the top): Sharps, Smith, and Spencer. Each had its virtues, but the Spencer was the first really successful American repeating rifle in military service. All sorts of other weapons were used, including shotguns, full-length muskets, and single-shot muzzle-loading carbines, but these were the preferred weapons of most cavalry troopers.

THE AMERICAN CIVIL WAR: A VISUAL ENCYCLOPEDIA

The term applied to Northern politicians, as well as "financial adventurers," who were accused of going South to use the newly enfranchised freed slaves as a means of obtaining office or profit. The epithet later came to refer to any unwelcome stranger coming to exploit or dominate a region against the wishes of some or all of its inhabitants.

Casualties

The Civil War was the second bloodiest conflict in American history, exceeded in combat deaths and total casualties only by American losses in World War II—and then only barely. Indeed, some estimates make the Civil War bloodier than World War II for America. Based on conservative estimates, for every ten Americans who were casualties in World War II, there were nine killed or wounded in the Civil War. As a proportion of total population,

the Civil War was easily the bloodiest in American history. In World War II, seven percent of the mobilized forces (or less than one percent of the total population) wound up as casualties. In the Civil War, between a quarter and a third of the mobilized forces (or about three percent of the total population) wound up as casualties.

The American Civil War was the bloodiest conflict of its duration to occur anywhere in the world in the century between Waterloo (1815) and the beginning of World War I (1914), and the probably bloodiest ever to be fought in the Western Hemisphere.

According to recent United States Department of Defense calculations based on a thorough review of all historic records, 2,213,363 persons served in Union uniform. Of these, 2,128,948 served in the U.S. Army and the balance in the U.S. Navy and Marine Corps. The U.S. Army lost 138,154 soldiers killed in combat, plus another

During the American Civil War approximately half a million men of both sides lost their lives in action or through disease, while a similar number of soldiers were wounded. This made it the most costly conflict in American history until World War II.

221,374 dead from other causes including disease, accidents, and deaths of prisoners of war. There were 280,040 persons wounded in action who did not die of their wounds. However, many of these were missing arms and/or legs.

The total casualties for the U.S. Navy and Marine Corps were 6,824, including 2,260 killed in action. The total number of casualties of 646,392 translates as three persons for every ten in uniform. The

Above: Negro soldiers disinterring the dead on the battleground of Cold Harbor after the end of the war

Left: The majority of war casualties died through disease and poor medical care rather than from enemy fire. In the South, the high death rate amongst amputees (Above Left) and prisoners of war (Above Right) was due in part to a lack of basic medical resources.

Union side alone lost more than twice the personnel lost by the United States in World War I.

Precise data for the Confederate forces is lacking. Although there was an effort made to keep accurate tallies during 1861 and 1862, the information for later years of the war can be based only on estimates.

Estimates of the number of persons serving in the Confederate Army and Navy range from 750,000 to more than one million. Casualty estimates range from 335,000 to 485,000, including roughly 200,000 killed in action. At the time that General Robert E. Lee surrendered the

Army of Northern Virginia in April 1865, that force, the largest intact in the Confederate Army, numbered fewer than 10,000 soldiers.

Causes of the war

In the simplest terms, the American Civil War was the result of regional differences pushed to the bloodiest of extremes. Regional competition became nationalism. The North saw the United States as a single nation, while the South saw it as a collection of sovereign states. The North imagined Federal, or national, law as omnipotent, while the south insisted on the rights of the states being preeminent.

During the early nineteenth century, the United States had been growing more and more divided, both politically and culturally. The agrarian South saw the national government as being dominated by the Northern industrialists. The North looked to the South as a market for its manufactured goods, but it was often cheaper for the South to purchase the goods abroad, so the

Federal government put tariffs on imported goods that could be manufactured in the North. In 1832, when South Carolina refused to collect tariffs, Federal troops were sent in.

Disagreements between the North and South, as well as with the West, grew increasingly heated, especially after 1850. The strain on the national economy caused by the panics of 1837 and 1857 only served to exaggerate the differences.

The issue of slavery, which became the signature issue of the Civil War, was only one of many on which the North and South differed. Indeed, Lincoln had not been elected in 1860 with a promise of freeing the slaves. When the war began, his goal was preservation of the Union, not abolition of slavery. Even after the war began, he used a promise not to interfere with slavery as an inducement to persuade the Confederacy to rejoin the Union. For its part, the Confederate States of America banned the importation of slaves in 1861, and had enacted a measure emancipating its slaves before the war came to a close.

By 1861, North and South had evolved as distinctly different and separate nations. By assuming that it represented the politically correct point of view for the entire United States, the North sought to dominate the South. The South, which did not have the capability or desire to dominate the North, declared itself separate from the North. Thus began the conflict which the North insisted on calling "the Civil War," while the South fought what it called "the War for Southern Independence."

Cavalry, Confederate

During the first three years of the war the Confederate Cavalry enjoyed a marked superiority over the Union troopers. In general terms, as the South was a rural economy, its population was used to riding from childhood, and several Southern states were prized for the quality of the horses they produced. Southern society was also dominated by a horse-conscious aristocracy, who provided the leaders which used this resource to its best advantage. Confederate cavalrymen widely regarded themselves as the best of the troops in the army, and at least in the early years of the war, recruits came equipped with their own horses, which they were accustomed to riding. They were certainly better horsemen than the troopers of the Union cavalry, who had often never ridden a horse on a regular basis before enlisting in the army. Another advantage was that the war was usually fought on Confederate soil, and most cavalry regiments were able to find fodder for their horses and had an intimate knowledge of the terrain, while the enemy cavalry were forced to rely on bad maps and inadequate supplies. As a consequence, under Confederate cavalry leaders such as J. E. B. Stuart, Nathan Forrest, Wade Hampton, and "Fighting Joe" Wheeler, Confederate cavalry formations were capable of extraordinary feats during raids behind enemy lines, or on extensive independent operations.

Their main use was to serve as the "eyes and ears" of the army, scouting ahead of it,

screening it from enemy cavalry scouts, and raiding the Union's supply lines. Unlike the Union cavalry, who considered themselves first and foremost mounted infantry, Confederate cavalrymen preferred to fight on horseback. Unable to match the firepower which the repeating carbines gave to Union cavalry forces, the Confederates concentrated on these conventional uses for their cavalry arm. By contrast, the Union cavalry developed into an effective and fast-moving force capable of fighting infantry formations. By 1864, superiority in numbers meant that the Confederates were increasingly hard put to counter the large mounted formations fielded by the enemy.

While similar to the organization of Union cavalry regiments, Confederate units had ten troops, divided into five squadrons. Their units also contained fewer officers and NCOs, but an increased complement of farriers or blacksmiths, to ensure the mobility of the unit would not be impeded during independent operations.

A typical Confederate cavalry troop mustered a paper strength of 76 men, and was commanded by a captain. A further 20 troopers were added to the complement in late 1862, but by that stage, all Confederate units were seriously under strength, so the increase never took place. While the original strength for a regiment was laid down

Confederate cavalry were often used to raid enemy supply lines (Far Left). Under leaders such as Colonel Ashby (Above) and Lieutenant General Wade Hampton (Left), Confederate horsemen proved superior to their Union counterparts for much of the war.

Above: The 1863 Quantrill Raid on Lawrence is depicted here from the sketch by Union cavalryman Sherman Enderton. Fueled by harsh treatment of civilians by the Union general, Thomas Ewing, who commanded the Missouri and lower Kansas area, the raid heralded a lawless period where it was difficult to tell the difference between irregular or guerilla activity and criminality.

Right: Union cavalry—Sheridan's troops attack Lee's rearguard at Sayler's Creek on April 6, 1865. By this stage of the war, early Union cavalry weaknesses had been all but sorted out.

Opposite Page, Above: The 1st Virginia Cavalry at a halt during the Antietam Campaign, from a pencil and wash drawing by Alfred R. Ward.

Opposite Page, Below: Early cavalry action— Tomkins charges into the town of Fairfax, June 1, 1861.

as being 755 men, by mid-1863 the average unit contained less than 600 men, and probably had horses for only two out of three troopers. In the summer of 1864 the 7th Tennessee Regiment had less than 400 men and 200 horses left when it took part in General Nathan Bedford Forrest's campaigns in Tennessee.

Cavalry, Union

In April 1861 there were only eight mounted cavalry troops in the entire U.S. Army. Recent developments in weaponry and tactics altered the role of cavalry. No longer capable of mounted charges against formed infantry, the role of cavalry was primarily one of reconnaissance. In this capacity, cavalry played a vital part in the conduct of the war, and as the war progressed, the Union cavalry arm gained in experience and ability. It took approximately two years to train a cavalry mount, and while the Confederates began the war with an ample supply of quality horses, the Union had to breed their mounts specially for service in the army.

The basic cavalry unit was the regiment. In the prewar regular army, a cavalry regiment consisted of three battalions, each

containing two squadrons of two troops (companies) each. In reality, the only regiment the army possessed had only two active battalions, as the third battalion lacked horses. Volunteer and State Militia cavalry units were created during the war; a total of 258 cavalry regiments, plus 170 independent cavalry troops, which were usually employed by individual states to guard important communication and supply centers. A volunteer cavalry

regiment consisted of between four and six squadrons, each of two troops of eighty horsemen. Each troop was commanded by a captain, assisted by two lieutenants and several NCOs. The regimental staff of a cavalry regiment contained a colonel, a lieutenant colonel, three majors, musicians, and an administrative staff, including a chaplain and a surgeon. The battalion system was adopted to mirror the regular cavalry organization, but it was abandoned in July 1862. A cavalry regiment of twelve troops (six squadrons) had a full paper strength of 1,278 troopers. By October 1862, the regimental band had been dispensed with, and remaining battalion staffs (from the earlier organizations) were used to form the staff of new regiments. In addition, the number of troopers in each troop were increased, giving a full paper strength of seventy-eight privates, eight support staff, sixteen NCOs, and three officers. On campaign, formations were much weaker, with regiments having an average strength of under 400 riders and mounts.

In battle, a cavalry regiment would usually form into a series of two lines, each containing five or six troops. Mounted cavalry charges were considered impractical, so cavalry most frequently operated as "mounted infantry," where the fast-firing carbines issued to Union troopers gave them an edge over their Southern counterparts. As the war progressed, and Union cavalry became increasingly proficient, their commanders became more confident of countering Confederate cavalry in mounted engagements. At the start of the war, cavalry operated as individual regiments attached to larger formations

Above and Left: Given superior weapons and capable commanders such as Custer, the standard of Union cavalry improved as the war progressed.

Right: Union cavalry corps based in the Shenandoah Valley (Above) or in central Virginia (Below) played a decisive part in the course of the war.

(e.g. divisions). During 1861–62, these were combined into brigade-sized formations, then cavalry divisions. By 1863, whole cavalry corps were being employed by both sides. By 1865, the Union armies in both the eastern and western theaters were using corps-sized cavalry formations as flying columns, penetrating deep into the Confederate heartland on destructive campaigns designed to destroy the Southern infrastructure.

Cavalry Corps, Organization of

For the first few years of the war, cavalry were used in a supporting role to the infantry, scouting and occasionally launching raids on enemy supply lines. By 1863, both the Army of the Potomac and the Army of Northern Virginia created Cavalry Corps, capable of operating as powerful and fast-moving strategic combat formations in their own right. For the Union, the Cavalry Division which accompanied the army in 1862 was expanded into a corps, and its divisional commander (General Alfred Pleasanton) was promoted to command the force of almost 12,000 horsemen in three divisions, supported by horse artillery. For the Confederates, their

"proto-corps" of cavalry was commanded by General J. E. B. Stuart, whose failure to screen Lee's army was a major contributing factor to the Confederate defeat at Gettysburg (1863). By 1864, it became a proper corps of three small divisions, each of two or three brigades. In the West, the Union Army of the Cumberland contained a cavalry corps during the Chickamauga Campaign (1863). It was commanded by General Robert Mitchell. General Joe Wheeler commanded a small Confederate "proto-corps" of two cavalry divisions.

During the Atlanta Campaign (1864) both sides used their cavalry corps as a strategic force, each trying to outflank or block the positions held by the main armies. Following the dashing cavalry moves by both Stuart and the Union General Phil Sheridan in the east, cavalry was relegated to a secondary role, and the armies engaged in a war of attrition around Petersburg.

Cedar Creek, Battle of, 1864

In the the Confederate campaign up the Shenandoah Valley of summer 1864, Lieutenant General Jubal Early threatened Washington. In August General Philip H.

Sheridan was appointed commander of Washington's defensive forces by General Ulysses S. Grant, with orders to destroy Early's Army of the Valley. Sheridan concentrated his Army of Shenandoah at Harper's Ferry.

After twice being defeated—at Opequon Creek on September 19 and Fisher's Hill on September 22—Early launched a surprise counterattack with his 21,000 men on October 19 at Cedar Creek, while Sheridan was absent. Although two Union corps were at first routed, when Sheridan arrived he rallied his 32,000-strong force and, despite 5,665 casualties compared to 2,910 Confederates, drove Early's forces south out of the valley.

Chamberlain, Joshua Lawrence (1841–96)

One of the more unusual Union commanders of the Civil War, Colonel Joshua L. Chamberlain was originally a professor of rhetoric and modern languages at Bowdoin College until 1862. While the

college believed that he had taken leave of absence to study in Europe, Chamberlain in fact joined the Union forces. Commander of the 20th Maine at Gettysburg in July 1863, his troops defended successfully the Union forces' left flank; after the defense, he ordered his troops to fix bayonets and advance, forcing the surprised Alabamians on the Confederate right flank to surrender. This engagement was known as Little Round Top and earned Chamberlain the Medal of Honor. He was the officer in charge of the surrender ceremony at Gettysburg.

Champions Hill, Battle of, 1863

Major General Ulysses S. Grant's Army of the Tennessee's advanced against the strategically important Confederate fortress at Vicksburg on the eastern bank of the Mississippi in 1862–63. As the advance neared its goal, the Confederate commander of the fortress, Lieutenant General John C. Pemberton, realized that he had to halt Grant before he was cut off at the fortress. Pemberton's 23,000-strong force met the Unionists at Champions Hill on the morning of May 16. Although Pemberton was

Above: The headquarters of the 1st Brigade (Pennington's) of 3rd Division's Cavalry Corps near Winchester, Virginia, February 23, 1865.

Below: The view from Little Round Top, the site of Colonel Chamberlain's successful stand during the Battle of Gettysburg.

established in a strong position east of the Big Black River and achieved some success early in the battle, once Grant arrived mid-morning and ordered his forces to attack, the Unionists prevailed. By midafternoon Pemberton was forced through his heavy losses (3,800 casualties compared to Union losses of 2,500 out of 32,000 men) to fall back behind prepared defenses at Vicksburg on May 19. These came under siege from Grant and would fall on July 4.

Chancellorsville Campaign

Following Burnside's defeat at Fredericksburg on December 13, 1862, and the subsequent debacle of the "mud march" in early 1863, Ambrose Burnside was removed from his position in command of the Army of the Potomac and replaced by the ambitious Major General Joseph Hooker on January 25, 1863. Within weeks, Hooker's able administrative skills restored the health and morale of his troops.

The immediate problem for the Union was that, following the Battle of Fredericksburg, Lee's Army of Northern Virginia occupied a strong defensive position around the town, holding the Union army away from the Richmond road. Hooker wanted to drive Lee away from his entrenched position and overwhelm him with his superior numbers.

So, in April 1863 Union Major General Joseph Hooker led the 130,000-strong Army of the Potomac against General Robert E. Lee's Army of Northern Virginia, established across the Rappahanock River at Fredericksburg, Virginia. His plan was to himself lead a third of his army in a great "Turning Movement" around Lee's flank; meanwhile Sedgwick, with about another third of the Army of the Potomac, was to drive across the Rappahannock in a diversionary attack, holding Lee in his position, the final third of the army was to be held in reserve, ready to exploit whichever of the two attacks was the more successful.

On April 27 the Union forces began crossing the Rappahannock, and by April 29 Hooker had over 40,000 men upriver, while a sizeable detachment of Sedgwick's force was also on Lee's side. Realizing from cavalry reconnaissance that Hooker's flanking movement was the more serious threat, Lee boldly left 10,000 men under Early to man the Fredericksburg defenses and marched with the rest of the army to confront Hooker. Surprised by Lee's bold-

General "Fighting Joe" Hooker (Right) replaced General Burnside as commander of the Army of the Potomac after the Union defeat at Marye's Heights above Fredericksburg (Far Right). At Chancellorsville, Hooker's troops centered their defense around Chancellor House (Below), at the crossroads of Plank Road and the Turnpike. The house served as Hooker's headquarters during the battle.

Below Right: Map of the battle of Chancellorsville.

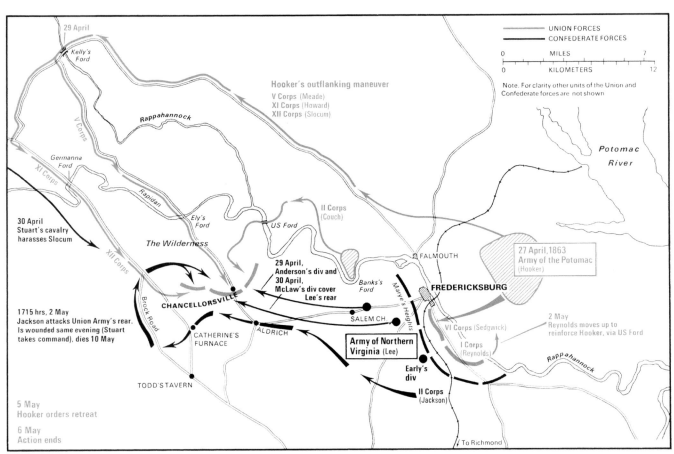

ness, Hooker pulled his advance forces back to defensive positions within the Wilderness.

THE BATTLE

Hooker intended to encircle Lee and three corps were despatched to outflank the Confederates upriver at Kelly's Ford while a further three corps under Major General John Sedgwick tied down Lee's forces at Fredericksburg. Hooker's remaining troops were to hold the river upstream near Fredericksburg, crossing to join the force marching down. By April 30 Hooker had crossed the river with four corps and reached an area of scrub known as the "Wilderness" near Chancellorsville, ten miles west of Fredericksburg. To divert the Confederates' attention, Sedgwick took his troops across the river on April 29–30, detaching one of his corps to join Hooker at Chancellorsville. Lee realized Sedgwick's advance was a feint and, although heavily outnumbered, took the gamble of splitting his forces. He left a reinforced division of 10,000 men under Major General Jubal Early to hold Sedgwick's 47,000 troops at Fredericksburg; the remainder of his force —some 40–50,000 men—was to take the battle to Hooker's 70–80,000-strong force, waiting at Chancellorsville.

On April 29 Major General Richard H. Anderson had already dug in four miles short of Chancellorsville with a division of Confederates, when Lee's main force headed to join them on the night of the 30th. The next day Hooker sent an advance party through the Wilderness but on encountering Confederate skirmishers retreated to defensive positions in the thick woods around Chancellorsville. Lee, outnumbered, received information that the Unionists' right flank held by Major General Oliver O. Howard's corps was open to attack from the west and decided to split his forces in two yet again.

Lee remained to face Hooker at Chancellorsville with 12–15,000 men, while Lieutenant General Thomas J. Jackson left on the morning of May 2 to take the remainder of the army (25–30,000 men) on a nine-mile march round the Unionists' right flank. During the day, while Lee moved troops and sporadically fired on the Unionist line, Hooker received news of the Confederates' movements but intepreted them as a retreat. Between 5:00pm and 6:00pm Jackson had organized his troops in the Wilderness, then unleashed his surprise attack on Howard's corps, which was driven back. Fighting continued until nightfall, at which point the Unionists had established a defensive line nearer Chancellorsville, Hooker compressing his army into a V-shape. During the night the Confederates were dealt a serious blow when Jackson was mistakenly fired on and wounded by his own troops while

reconnoitering the battlefield. He died eight days later.

On the morning of May 3 Lee and Major General J. E. B. Stuart, newly appointed to lead the attack, renewed the Confederate attack on the Unionist salient, supported by massed artillery. The intense fighting lasted much of the day and by the afternoon the Unionists began to pull back. Lee was able to detach a division to stop Sedgwick who was advancing towards Chancellorsville, forcing him to retreat back across the Rappahannock after the Battle of Salem Church on May 4.

The next night, Hooker also took his army back across the river. Overall, the Unionists had suffered 17,000 casualties compared to 13,000 Confederate casualties. Confederate morale was high after the battle; the Unionists were no nearer threatening the Confederate capital Richmond than at the start of the war.

Charleston, South Carolina

Confederates took over Charleston following the secession of South Carolina, and it was from there that the first shot of the war was fired when Edmund Ruffin opened fire on Fort Sumter on April 12, 1861.

Defended by Fort Moultrie, Fort Johnston, and Fort Sumter, the city became a center for blockade runners in 1863 when

Below: "Stonewall" Jackson died of wounds sustained at Chancellorsville.

Right and Bottom Right: The abortive Union attack on Charleston in April 1862 was repulsed at Secessionville. For the remainder of the war, the city was subjected to a rain of Union shells (Right), but the defenders' ironclads (Below Right) and fortifications protected the city until December 1864.

the Union attempted to starve the Confederacy into submission.

Charleston was finally evacuated in January 1865, when the fall of Columbia to Sherman's "total war" campaign left it vulnerable. One of Lee's first decisions as General in Chief, the evacuation of Charleston was carried out largely without Federal knowledge—when Union troops marched in they found the city ablaze.

Charleston, Attacks on (1861–65)

Following the fall of Fort Sumter on April 14, 1861, increasing numbers of Union warships joined the blockade of the Southern port. Although the defenders braced themselves for an attack they saw as imminent, no attack came for a year.

In April 1862 General Hunter landed troops and attacked Charleston from the south. He was defeated at Secessionville in June, and any further plans for land attacks were abandoned. By January 1863 the defenders could draw on the support of a small ironclad squadron. On January 31, the CSS *Palmetto State* and the CSS *Chicora* attacked the blockading squadron, who escaped a disaster by lifting the blockade for a few days until Union ironclads were sent to the port, together with other powerful wooden warships

By April, Admiral Dupont had nine ironclad warships at his disposal, including his flagship USS *New Ironsides*, and the double-turreted monitor USS *Keokuk*. On April 7, 1863, Admiral Dupont attacked Fort Sumter with these ironclads. When the leading monitor USS *Weehawken* encountered a defensive field of mines, the attackers halted. Both fort and the warships exchanged fire for several hours before the Union squadron withdrew.

Although the fort was battered, it survived the ordeal, but several of the Union ironclads were badly damaged. Dupont's flagship, the USS *New Ironsides* narrowly avoided being blown up by a submerged mine during the attack. Although she lay directly over the submerged torpedo, it failed to explode. The Confederate ironclads were held in reserve during the attack, but they were never called into action.

Dupot was replaced by Admiral Dahlgren, who avoided another direct naval attack, and the blockade of Charleston became a stalemate. During the summer and autumn of 1863, Union forces captured parts of Morris Island, including Fort Wagner. This allowed siege guns to shell Charleston and Fort Sumter, a bombardment which continued intermittently for over a year.

In December 1864, General Sherman's army bypassed Charleston, cutting it off from the rest of the Confederacy, and on February 17, 1865, the city was abandoned. Dahlgren's forces entered the port the following day.

Charleston, Defense of

As the principal Confederate port on the Atlantic coast, Charleston boasted the best coastal defenses in the South. Following the Confederate capture of Fort Sumter in April 1861, the defenders struggled to protect the port against a Union attack which seemed inevitable.

By late 1862 these defenses were in place. A string of fortifications to the north and south of Charleston Harbor faced to seaward, including Fort Wagner and Fort Moultrie. Secondary batteries on James Island provided overlapping fire with smaller island and shoreline fortifications behind Fort Sumter. Some seventy-six large-caliber guns covered the main entrance to the port, while smaller weapons protected the fortifications themselves from direct attack. Supporting batteries covered the city itself, from the "Battery" on the southern tip of the city, past Castle Pinckney and Fort Ripley in the center of the harbor, to the batteries on James Island and Mount Pleasant; these protected the outer reaches of the harbor, including Fort Sumter. Rows of underwater obstructions constricted the harbor entrance, while torpedoes (mines) were sown off Morris Island and Sullivan's Island.

In addition to static defenses, the Confederates maintained a powerful fleet of ironclad warships. The *Chicora*, *Palmetto State*, and *Charleston* all maintained offensive patrols just behind the entrance, supported by numerous wooden gunboats and torpedo boats.

Although Morris Island fell to the Union during 1863, these defenses remained intact, preventing the capture of the city from naval or amphibious assault. Charleston eventually fell to the army of General Sherman in February 1865.

Chase, Salmon Portland (1808-73)

A distinguished radical statesman, Chase was Federal Secretary of the Treasury 1861–64. He issued the first paper currency not backed by gold, known as "greenbacks." Chase resigned from the cabinet in 1864 because he regarded Lincoln's anti-slavery position as too moderate, but was appointed chief Justice of the Supreme Court later that year.

Right: The ruins of Charleston after the fighting. This is Meeting Street showing the ruins of the Theater, Circular Church, the Mills House, and St. Michael's Church in the distance.

Chickamauga and Chatanooga Campaign

In summer 1863 the situation was bleak for the Confederacy, Lee had been driven back from Gettysburg, Vicksburg had been captured, and in Tennessee General William S. Rosecrans' Army of the Cumberland, almost 60,000 strong, was poised to attack General Braxton Bragg's 43,000 Confederates dug in twenty miles to the southwest defending the road to Chattanooga. The Confederate authorities decided to reinforce Bragg by stripping a large proportion of the other Confederate armies, to that end Lieutenant General James B. Longstreet was sent west with two divisions.

Following his successful campaigns around Tullahoma, Rosecrans forced the Confederates to withdraw into Chattanooga. There Bragg dug in again, guarding the Tennessee River crossings northeast of the city, where he expected Rosecrans to attack. But early in September the Union forces crossed the Tennessee well below Chattanooga and again Bragg had to withdraw southward to Layfayette, Georgia, where he received the reinforcements sent from the east.

Using these men he attempted to take the fight to Rosecrans' Army of the Cumberland, initially attempting to destroy his forces in detail before these two armies finally met at the Battle of Chickamauga on September 18–19, 1863. On the first day the fighting was fairly even, though the Union troops were pushed back by the superior Confederate numbers. On the second day Rosecrans' line seemed to be holding against Bragg's attacks until, through his own mistaken orders, a gap opened in the Federal ranks and Longstreet's men took full advantage of the opportunity, routing

most of the Union army. General George H. Thomas took command of the few Union troops still organized and held off repeated Confederate assaults until the close of day. This defeat forced the Union troops to retreat into Chattanooga and allowed the pursuing Confederates to occupy Missionary Ridge, Lookout Mountain, and Chattanooga Valley, effectively blockading the city and the Union Army of the Cumberland trapped within it.

Realizing that Rosecrans' forces had to be relieved, the Union authorities ordered reinforcements sent in to the theater. General Hooker came from Virginia late in October with 20,000 men and General Sherman brought in 16,000 more from Mississippi in mid-November. Thomas replaced Rosecrans as head of Army of the

Cumberland and General Ulysses S. Grant assumed overall command.

At the end of October the situation began to change for the Union. First a supply line was forced through to Chattanooga on the 28th; then, in a series of engagements around the town in late November, the Confederates were pushed out of some of their prepared positions. Finally, on November 25, 1863, Grant launched a coordinated assault on the Confederate positions, with Hooker on the left and Sherman on the right. With Hooker's attack stalled, Grant called on Thomas' troops to assault the base of Missionary Ridge. Not only did they achieve this, they also succeeding in driving the Confederates from the top of the hill, compromising the whole position and forcing the line backwards. That night Bragg withdrew his forces into Georgia.

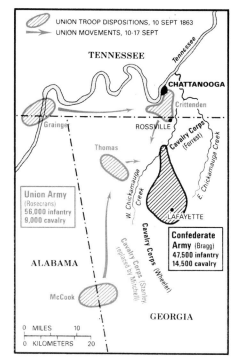

THE AMERICAN CIVIL WAR: A VISUAL ENCYCLOPEDIA

The battle of Chicamauga was fought for control of Chatanooga (Opposite Page, Above and Below Left). The Union lines were anchored on Lee & Gordon's Mill (Left), but the main struggle centered around Dyer House (Bottom), defended by Van Cleve's Division of General Thomas' corps, and in the surrounding woods. Lieutenant Van Pelt and the 1st Michigan Battery helped break the impetus of the Confederate attack (Below).

Opposite Page, Below Right: Troop movements before Chickamauga.

Chickamauga, Battle of, 1863

In 1863 the war in the west was reaching a crucial phase. In June, under pressure from President Lincoln to take Tennessee for the Union, Major General William S. Rosecrans' Army of Cumberland began to advance against the Confederate Army of Tennessee commanded by General Braxton Bragg. Bragg fell back to Chattanooga, then in August withdrew across the mountains south of Chattanooga to establish a position near Lafayette, Georgia. His army was augmented first by approximately 9,000 men from east Tennessee and Mississippi and the news that two divisions from Virginia commanded by Major General James Longstreet were also on their way meant that by September Bragg's army would total 60–65,000 men. His numerical superiority over Rosecrans' 55–60,000-strong army would enable him to take the initiative.

In early September Rosecrans, thinking the Confederates were still retreating, had spread out his three corps over a fifty-mile front as he advanced south of Chattanooga in pursuit of Bragg. Bragg, however, failed to capitalize on the chance to destroy Rosecrans' army piecemeal, and by September 13 Rosecrans, realizing the danger of his situation, began to concentrate his army west of Chickamauga Creek, twelve miles south of Chattanooga, where Union Major General Thomas L. Crittenden was established. Rosecrans' other two corps, under Major General George H. Thomas and Major General Alexander McCook, set off on a forced march of over fifty miles for the furthest troops and by the morning of September 19 Rosecrans was concentrating his

three corps along the two main routes to Chattanooga through the Chickamauga Creek Valley—the Lafayette Road and the Dry Valley Road. Meanwhile, Bragg was also moving north, planning to cross Chickamauga Creek and hold the vital routes to Chattanooga.

The two sides ran into each on the morning of September 19 when one of Thomas' brigades encountered Brigadier General Nathan B. Forrest's Confederate cavalry division and two infantry brigades near one of the crossings of the creek. As the fighting intensified both sides committed increasing numbers of reinforcements but although the Unionists were pressed hard by the end of the day they managed to hold their line along the Lafayette Road.

By nightfall the fighting had died down and the two sides prepared for battle the next day. That night Longstreet reached the Confederate camp and Bragg organized his army into two wings, the left under Longstreet and the right under Lieutenant General Leonidas Polk. Polk launched the first attack on the morning of September 20 against Thomas' corps. As the pressure grew, Thomas requested Rosecrans to send him reinforcements.

Rosecrans detached Brigadier General Thomas J. Wood's division from the center of his line to assist his left wing, and in doing so created a gap in his defenses. Longstreet saw his opportunity and sent his 20,000 men charging through, cutting the Union army in two by midday.

In disarray, McCook's and Crittenden's corps fled the battlefield, retreating to Chattanooga. Only Thomas' corps held firm, reinforcements helping him to hold his position on Snodgrass Hill

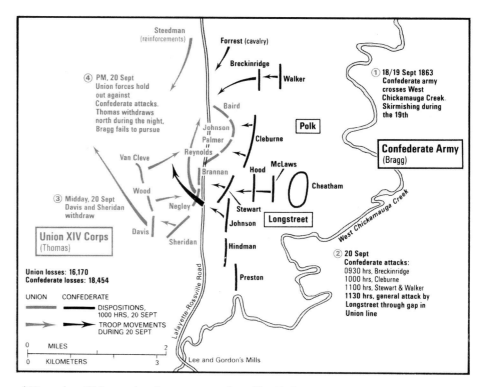

and Horseshoe Ridge against Longstreet and Polk until he was able to retreat at nightfall.

It had been a costly battle, the Confederates suffering 18,000 casualties and the Unionists 16,000. Although the Confederates had won the day, Thomas' heroic stand enabled the Union army to escape total destruction and reach Chattanooga.

Just two months later, on November 23–25, 1863, the revitalized Union army in the west, under the newly appointed command of Major General Ulysses S. Grant, defeated Bragg's forces at the Battle of Chattanooga, to regain the initiative in Tennessee.

City Point, Va

City Point lies on the James River between Richmond and Petersburg, and was the terminus of the railway line running from Petersburg. It was down this railway line that the Union troops under Meade and Baxter approached Petersburg in June 1864.

Above: The Battle of Chickamauga.

Below Left: The battles of Lookout Mountain and Missionary Ridge broke the Confederate siege of Chatanooga, and forced the Confederate army to withdraw south into Georgia.

Right: The Chickamauga battlefield.

Below Right: Another view of Lee & Gordon's Mills.

Bottom: In retrospect, the Battle of Chicamauga was a Pyrrhic victory for the Confederacy. The losses suffered by Bragg's men at Chicamauga weakened the Army of the Tennessee so much that it was unable to take advantage of its success.

Cold Harbor, Battle of, 1864

In the spring of 1864 Lieutenant General Ulysses S. Grant, newly promoted General-in-Chief of all Union land forces, embarked on a war of attrition to destroy General Robert E. Lee's Army of Northern Virginia. In a series of inconclusive but bloody battles, starting with the Battle of the Wilderness on May 5–6, Lee was forced back towards Richmond. By the end of May Lee had dug in northeast of Richmond, the seven-mile front extending from Totopotomy Creek in the north to the Chickahominy River in an attempt to halt Grant's probing drive towards the Confederate capital. Grant, fearing his advance would end in stalemate, decided after two days of inconclusive skirmishing to launch a frontal assault. Although Grant had 110,000 men at his disposal compared to Lee's force of 60,000, the Confederates were well entrenched. At dawn on June 3 Grant launched his attack, 60,000 troops charging from their trenches into concerted Confederate fire. Lee had arranged his forces so that he could defend his lines with interlocking fields of fire and the Union casualties were immense. In an hour the Unionists lost over 7,000 men, compared to Confederate casualties of 1,500, and Grant was forced to call off the attack. Grant realized that he was unable to smash through Lee's army and although fighting continued at Cold Harbor for several days, on June 12 Grant pulled the Army of the Potomac out of its lines and circled round Richmond, planning instead to attack from the south at Petersburg.

Colombia, South Carolina

Columbia, the capital of South Carolina, was one of the South's industrial centers and the site of the government powder mill supplying the wants of the Confederate navy.

On February 16 1865, Sherman reached Columbia following his March to the Sea and the sack of Atlanta and Savannah. The Mayor of Columbia surrendered the next day, and Columbia went up in flames.

Debate continues as to who was responsible for the razing of Columbia—while some accounts claim that Sherman's troops destroyed the city, others suggest that the Confederates deliberately burned everything of value.

The fall of Columbia cut Charleston off from the rest of the confederacy, and triggered its evacuation.

Colorado

Colorado was officially designated a territory on February 26, 1861, and although the region maintained its neutrality, geography dictated that its sympathies lay with the Union. It had no state militia organization, although several mounted militia companies were raised during the war to defend the territory against Indian attack. In February 1865, the 1st Volunteer Mounted Militia Regiment was formed to protect the stage route, not to fight in the Civil War. In addition, several volunteer regiments were raised in the Colorado Territory, and these fought in the western theater during the conflict.

Although General Grant's frontal attack at Cold Harbor was repulsed with appalling casualties, the Army of the Potomac was able to disengage, then renew the offensive to the south, over the James River. General Grant and his staff (head-quartered in the building pictured Below Left) maintained the strategic initiative over Lee's outnumbered troops.

Left: The battlefield photograph taken in 1865 shows the remains of the Confederate defensive breastworks.

Below: The battlefield of Lookout Mountain where Grant's troops finally broke the Confederate hold on Chatanooga in November 1863.

Command structure, Confederate

The land forces of the Confederacy were divided into (eventually) twenty-three armies, the majority of which were named after states (e.g. the Army of the Tennessee, the Army of Northern Virginia). In addition the Confederacy was divided into a number of districts, the majority of which followed state boundaries.

At the start of the war, these districts were allocated numbers, but by mid-1863 this system had been abandoned, and the districts were named after the state they encompassed. In the western theater, state boundaries were often transcended due to the nature of the theater, where rivers dominated the course of the war. For example, District 2 encompassed parts of Arkansas, Louisiana, Mississipi, and Tennessee adjacent to the Mississippi River. In July 1863 the district was renamed the Department of the Tennessee.

In most cases, armies operated within the district they were attached to. Commanders of armies and districts were answerable directly to the President Jefferson Davis, who played an even more active part in planning the strategy of the war than his Union counterpart, although his abrasive manner meant he went through six successive secretaries of war. Once the Mississippi River fell, General Kirby Smith was given independent control of all forces in the Trans-Mississippi region, as communication was impossible between the two parts of the Confederacy. In 1864, General Robert E. Lee was promoted to command of all Confederate Forces, although he also retained his post as head of the Army of Northern Virginia.

Command structure, Union

Field armies were the largest active commands established for much of the war, and eventually there were sixteen of them. In the majority of cases, these armies were named after the departments they served in, and both were usually named after rivers

Right: Grant—at left leaning over to examine a map—photographed conferring with his staff. In March 1864 Grant was appointed to command all Union forces.

COMMAND STRUCTURE, UNION

Right: General Robert E. Lee and his generals. When the Southern states seceded, he was offered command of the U.S. Army by Lincoln but preferred to serve in the Confederate forces. Lee was appointed commander of Confederate forces in February 1865 before being finally forced to surrender to Ulysses S. Grant on April 9, 1865, at Appomattox.

Below: The Union general staff at the beginning of the war.

Below Right: General Edward C. Ord and staff on the steps of Jefferson Davis' house, Richmond, Virginia.

Above: Captain James M. Robertson and Staff, 1st Brigade Horse Artillery at Brandy Station, Virginia

Opposite Page, Above: Communications were essential to the operations of the Civil War armies. This is the wagon train of the Union Military Telegraph Corps at Richmond, June 1865.

(e.g. the Army of the Cumberland, the District of the Potomac), although some were named after operating areas, such as the Army of the District of North Carolina. The departments in which the armies served varied greatly in size and importance, and were subdivided for administrative purposes into districts. The Department of the Potomac encompassed the campaigning area of Virginia as well as Maryland and Delaware. In addition, military districts grouped several divisions together, again as a largely administrative measure. Although General Winfield Scott was in charge of all Union forces until his retirement in November 1861, President Lincoln and his Secretary of War, Edwin M. Stanton, closely controlled the prosecution of the war. When Scott's successor George B. McClellan failed to live up to his promises of victory, the post of army chief was left vacant for two years. In March 1864 Congress created the grade of lieutenant general, and Grant was appointed to command all Union forces. He attached himself directly to the staff of

General Meade's Army of the Potomac, while he placed General Sherman in command of all active field armies in the western theater. In effect, he was a military district commander, but allocated an active rather than an administrative command.

Committee on the conduct of the war

In 1861, shortly after the beginning of the Civil War, the United States Congress established the Joint Committee on the Conduct of the War to monitor various matters related to the prosecution of the war. The chairman of the Committee was Senator Benjamin F. Wade, a Republican from Ohio. Other members of particular importance were Thaddeus Stevens and Zachariah Chandler.

Wade also sponsored the Wade-Davis Bill of 1864, which was an early attempt by Congress to have control of the Reconstruction process centered with it, rather than with the President. The bill stipulated Confederate disfranchisement, a loyalty oath of fifty percent of the

electorate, and abolition of slavery before a state could be readmitted to the Union. It was pocket-vetoed by President Lincoln. Later, during the Andrew Johnson Administration, Wade served as President Pro Tempore of the Senate, which under then-current law, placed him next in line to succeed to the Presidency (since Johnson had no Vice President). This was of benefit to Johnson during his impeachment, because Wade's opponents were afraid to remove Johnson and have Wade as President.

Communications

One of the reasons that the Civil War is referred to as "the first modern war" is the level of communications technology. It was the first major conflict in which virtually instantaneous, non-line-of-sight electrical communications was used to benefit tactical operations.

Prior to the Civil War, communication was by courier or by line of sight. Messages sent by courier often took hours, if not days, to be delivered. In order for messages to be sent and received in "real time," they had to be conveyed by "line of sight" through the use of flags, semaphores, signal fires, etc. The experiences of the Civil War demonstrated the utility and indispensable importance of the electric telegraph both as an administrative method

Left: President Abraham Lincoln maintained a tight control over his leading generals throughout the war.

and as a tactical weapon. Both sides in the Civil War made extensive use of existing commercial systems, and more than 15,000 miles of dedicated lines were also built and operated by military forces.

In 1861, because of the emergency situation of having Confederate forces nearby, the War Department seized the commercial systems around Washington, and Assistant Secretary of War Thomas A. Scott was made general manager of all such lines. In turn, he obtained the cooperation of E. S. Sanford of the American Telegraph Company, who imposed restrictions and censorship. In 1862, the scope of these operations was expanded by an act of Congress authorizing the seizure of any or all lines. The selection of operators for the War Department itself included D. H. Bates, A. B. Chandler, and C. A. Tinker, who are recalled as having been particularly skilful in the art of enciphering messages.

The need for an efficient field telegraph system was seen immediately by military commanders on both sides, and in the west, General Fremont ordered the formation of a telegraph battalion of three companies in August 1861. In the east, meanwhile, the commercial companies placed their personnel and equipment at the Government's disposal, but insisted on the use of civilian operators. Secretary of War Cameron acquiesced, and a purely civilian bureau was substituted. Even Fremont's battalion was to be disbanded.

Serving under the status of civilian employees of the U.S. Army Quartermaster Corps, the telegraph operators of the Military Telegraph Service performed work of vital importance, often in the heat of battle and under conditions of personal danger. Indeed, killing a telegraph operator was a more valuable action for an opposing sharpshooter than killing a dozen soldiers —or even officers. Few people, aside from the operators, understood Morse Code.

However, the operators suffered, not from only the natural impatience of military commanders, but from a sense of distrust of civilians.

Also of note is the work of Union codebreakers, which translated Confederate

cipher messages that fell into Union hands. A notable incident in the field was the translation of General Joseph E. Johnston's cipher message to General Pemberton, which was intercepted, relayed to General Grant before Vicksburg, and forwarded to Washington. More important were the two cipher dispatches from the Secretary of War at Richmond, in December 1863, which led to the arrest of Confederate conspirators in New York, and to the capture of contraband shipments of arms and ammunition. Other intercepted and translated ciphers revealed plans of Confederate agents for raiding Northern towns near the border. Most important of all were the cipher messages disclosing the plot for fire-bombing hotels in New York, which barely failed on November 25, 1864.

Both sides undertook wiretapping, although the Confederate forces were more successful because most of the fighting occurred within Confederate territory, with its sympathetic civilian population. The most successful wiretap was run by C. A. Gaston, General Lee's confidential operator, who tapped General Grant's direct line and remained undisturbed for six weeks during the siege of Richmond and Petersburg.

President Lincoln himself spent many long hours in the telegraph room at the War Department watching the progress of the war as it unfolded. This was not only because the White House had no telegraph office during the war, but because the quiet seclusion of the cipher room was a place where he could work undisturbed. Indeed, it was here that he wrote the original draft of the Emancipation Proclamation.

Companies, Organization of

The basic subunit of the infantry regiment in either army, the typical regiment contained ten companies. Companies were identified by a letter (A–K). In the prewar army, the company consisted of about a hundred men, commanded by a captain, who was assisted by two lieutenants, four sergeants, and eight corporals. During the war, Union companies tended to remain the same size (on paper), but included two musicians (usually drummers) and a standard bearer who carried a company guidon. There were also less NCOs in the typical company, and one less officer. While Confederate companies were larger on paper, in reality the companies on both sides were roughly similar in size for much of the war. The Confederates also tended to have more officers than Union companies. After a period of campaigning, company strength often shrank, and it was not unusual for companies on either side to have trouble finding one officer and three NCOs to command the unit. Even without taking part in a major battles, companies

brown red clouds red rays,
head red ring yellowish

Above Right: Drummers helped transmit the orders of regimental commanders on the battlefield.

Opposite Page, Above: William Waud's sketch of a crow's nest signal station.

Right: Company A, 6th Regiment Vermont Volunteers at Camp Griffin, Virginia. The company was the basic subunit of the infantry regiment in both Confederate and Union armies. The scene was captured by the photographer Matthew Brady.

could shrink to less than half their paper strength.

At the start of the war, companies were usually formed from a particular county, and often had their own company title. For example, in the 5th Virginia Regiment (part of the Stonewall Brigade), Company A was known as the Marion Rifles, Company B the Rockbridge Rifles, and Company E the Augusta Grays.

In battle, the companies of a regiment would form in line, three ranks deep, the officers located immediately behind their men.

Confederate States of America

The Confederate States of America was a national entity formed in 1861 from eleven Southern states that had previously been among the thirty-four states of the United States. In 1865, after the defeat of its armies in the Civil War, the Confederate States of America ceased to exist, and by 1870 all eleven states had been readmitted to the United States.

While the goal of the United States in the Civil War was to quell a rebellion, the Confederate States of America perceived the war as a war for independence. Indeed, the war was not described in the South as the "Civil War," but as the "War for Southern Independence."

The first Southern state to secede was South Carolina, which left the United States on December 20, 1860. Over the next six weeks, six additional states followed suit, Mississippi, Florida, Alabama, Georgia, Louisiana, and Texas. On February 4, 1861, delegates from these states (excluding Texas, whose delegation had not yet arrived) met in Montgomery, Alabama to organize a provisional Confederate government and to adopt a Constitution for the Confederate States of America. Montgomery was chosen as the provisional capital of the new nation.

The last four states of the Confederate did not officially join until April 15, 1861, after United States President Lincoln had ordered a call-up of Federal troops in the wake of the Fort Sumter crisis. These were Arkansas, North Carolina, Virginia, and Tennessee. Three "border states" where slavery was legal chose to remain with the United States. These were Maryland, Kentucky, and Missouri. The Confederacy did, however, set up parallel Confederate state governments in portions of Kentucky and Missouri that were occupied by

Above Right: Captain Otis and his company from the 22nd New York Infantry Regiment seen at Maryland Heights above Harper's Ferry.

Right: The great seal of the CSA.

Far Right: Confederate bank notes.

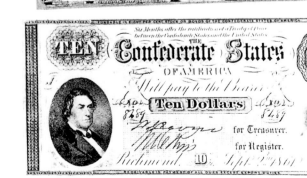

Confederate troops. Conversely, a section of Virginia seceded from that state to rejoin the Union. This area became the state of West Virginia, which still exists today.

With populations of 1.5 million and 1.1 million respectively, Virginia and Tennessee were the two largest Confederate states. When politically dominant Virginia joined the Confederacy, the national capital was officially transferred from Montgomery to Richmond, Virginia in May 1861.

At the February 4, 1861, meeting, the delegates held an election for a Provisional President. Of the three candidates, the radical R. B. Rhett and W. L. Yancey were passed over in favor of the more moderate Jefferson Davis of Mississippi. Alexander H. Stephens of Georgia was selected as Provisional Vice President.

In the first general elections for the Confederate Congress and for presidential electors, held in November 1861, the Davis and Stephens team ran unopposed. They were inaugurated as the Permanent President and Vice President of the Confederacy on February 22, 1862.

The Constitution of the Confederate States of America was patterned after that of the United States, with several important differences. Among these was the provision that the President and Vice President were to be elected for a single six-year term, with the President not allowed to run for reelection. This differed from the United States, where the term was four years, and where, until 1951 when a President was limited to two terms, the United States President would be allowed to run for reelection indefinitely.

The principal difference in the two Constitutions was in regard to the issue of slavery. The United States Constitution was moot on the issue, and would remain so until the adoption of the Thirteenth Amendment in December 1865. However, the Confederate Constitution explicitly recognized and legalized the holding of slaves, although the importation of slaves from any country other than the United States was prohibited.

The Confederacy was also seriously inferior in terms of material strength. The North retained a better than five to one ratio in total manufacturing capacity, and a thirty to one superiority in arms' production. Most of the prewar United States coal, copper iron, and steel production was centered on the North. Even the Southern textile industry was a mere seven percent of that of the North in terms of the value of its output. The North also retained virtually all of the prewar United States' financial and commercial resources. The total value of improved land in the North was two-and-a-half times that of the South, and its agricultural output was greater than that of the South. Of course, the South dominated the market for cotton, an important commodity on the world markets, but as the British brought the production of Egyptian cotton online, the importance of the Confederacy's key crop diminished.

Commercially, the North also dominated the South. Of the 31,000 miles of railroad in the prewar United States, only 9,000 miles were located in the South. Though it was never totally effective, the United States naval blockade of Confederate seaports reduced the ability operate a viable ocean-going commerce. Meanwhile, Northern seaports, which were already much larger and more commercially important than the Southern ports, operated virtually as normal throughout the Civil War. Before the war, only ten percent of United States foreign trade had been via Southern ports. During the war, traffic at these ports diminished while it expanded in the North.

While both sides suffered enormous casualties and enormous financial strain, the Confederate States of America suffered the worst. In the Union military services, just six percent of those in uniform were killed in action while estimates for the Confederate side range as high as twenty-five percent. By the time that the war ended, the Confederate States of America was bankrupt, with a worthless currency, while the United States economy remained intact. During the war, many South cities were the scenes of pitched battles, and some, such as Richmond and Atlanta were virtually destroyed. No major Northern city would suffer such a fate.

The Confederacy did extremely well militarily during most of the Civil War, but

Other differences in the two Constitutions were that Confederate cabinet members were give standing in the Confederate Congress to discuss legislation affecting their departments, and constitutional amendments could be adopted by votes of two thirds of the states without a vote in Congress.

By the census of 1860, the eleven states that would soon comprise the Confederacy had a combined population of 9,103,332. Of the total, an estimated 3.5 million were black slaves, compared to half a million black slaves held by Northern slave owners. While the Confederate population was 40 percent the size of the population of the 23 states that remained in the Union, the white population in the South was just a quarter of that of the North.

The Southern population had a higher proportion of men of conscription age than the United States, but the latter retained a better than two to one advantage over the Confederacy in manpower available for military service. Though both sides would utilize black soldiers to a varying extent, the Confederate armies were drawn almost entirely from the white population.

the economic superiority and larger population of the United States was clearly the dominant factor in the outcome. The Confederate States of America ceased to exist in 1865, and by 1870, after a period of military occupation, the secessionist states had been readmitted to the United States.

Congress

The acrimony between pro- and antislavery states during the decades preceding the Civil War meant that Congress became focal point for sectional rivalry. This reached a head over the issue of whether Kansas was to be considered a "slave" state or a "free" one. In May 1859 Senator Sumner of Massachusetts verbally attacked a Southern Senator, prompting South Carolina representative Preston Brooks to attack Sumner with a stick. Rivalry in Congress intensified following the election of President Buchanan (1857), and as Congressmen seemed unable to reach an amicable solution by debate, the slide towards armed conflict became unstoppable.

Conscription

When the Civil War began, the armies of both the Union and the Confederacy relied entirely on volunteers for their manpower needs. The way that the war was perceived on both sides is illustrated by President Lincoln's proclamation the day after the evacuation of Fort Sumter. On April 15, 1861, he called for 75,000 militia to serve for 90 days to put down "combinations too powerful to be suppressed by the ordinary mechanism of government."

The Civil War would not be over in 90 days, and Lincoln's anticipated requirement of 75,000 would grow to more than 2.1 million.

Initially, reliance on volunteers had been more than satisfactory. In fact, both sides were overwhelmed by the large numbers of young men who enlisted during the early months of the conflict. As the fighting progressed, however, and the dark reality of life in combat offset the initial euphoria, both governments reluctantly resorted to conscription.

The first general American military draft was enacted by the Confederate government on April 16, 1862. Even though Union forces were threatening the Confederacy from all sides, the draft was especially unpopular in the South because it was a law promulgated by the national government rather than the states. As such, it usurped the power of the states that had been one of the reasons for leaving the Union. Both Georgia and North Carolina sought to undermine the draft by the extensive granting of deferments. Such deferments were granted for men employed in

certain critical occupations, such as railroad and river workers, telegraph operators, miners, druggists, teachers and local government employees. The states were able to defer draftees simply by hiring them, thus making them local government employees.

Under the Confederate Conscription Act, all healthy white men between the ages of 18 and 35 were liable for a three-year term of service. It also extended all one-year the terms of enlistment to three years. A September 1862 amendment raised the age limit to 45, and in February 1864, the age range was expanded to 17 to 50. A controversial amendment to the Confederate law granted an exemption to anyone who owned 20 or more slaves and permitted a draftee to hire a substitute. Both of these provisions were seen as favoring the wealthy.

The first United States government draft, an act calling for "enrolling and calling out the National Forces," was signed into law on March 3, 1863 by President Lincoln. Like the Confederate law in effect at the time, the United States drafted men between the ages of 18 and 45, requiring them to join local militias and be available

for national service. Deferments were granted for some occupations, such as telegraph operators, railroad engineers and some government employees. Men with mental disabilities or with certain types of dependents were also exempted. Physical disabilities that would lead to a deferment included such things as lack of front teeth or missing more than one finger on the right hand or more than two fingers on the left hand.

The states were permitted to manage the United States draft, which usually used a lottery, such as would be used in World War II and late in the Vietnam War more than a century later. Each state was given a population-based quota, with draftees fill-

Above: 4th New Hampshire Regiment recruiting poster.

Opposite Page, Above: Black recruits are entrained for Meresfreeboro.

Opposite Page, Below: The original caption for this photo reads, "Arrival of recruits during the fight at Pebble Farm."

ing in for shortfalls in volunteer rates from the various states. Inducements of up to a year's salary were given to encourage volunteers because it was considered patriotic for a state to make its manpower quota without having to resort to the draft.

As was the case in the South, wealthy draftees were allowed to hire a substitute. This practice was as equally unpopular in the North, and the general disaffection with the procedure was the root cause of the bloody draft riots that occurred in New York City in July 1863. In four days of civil unrest, more than 1,200 persons were killed and a hundred buildings were burned.

Cooke, Jay (1821–1905)

A financier and investment banker, in 1861 Cooke founded his own banking house, Jay Cooke & Company, and loaned money to Pennsylvania. Cooke made his fortune during the war by selling war bonds, which raised more than $400 million for the Union.

Corinth, Mississippi

Control of Corinth was crucial to the control of the Mississippi and the rail line to Memphis. Originally a Confederate position, it was from Corinth that Beauregard and Albert Sidney Johnston planned their offensive to retake Tennessee—however, after two days' fighting at Shiloh they were beaten back to Corinth.

After Shiloh, Halleck set his sights on Corinth, and besieged Beauregard and Van Dorn. As illness overtook the Confederate troops, Beauregard was forced into a stealthy withdrawal. From May 1862 Corinth remained in Union hands—Van Dorn's attempt to retake the city in September 1863 proved abortive and was soon repulsed by Rosecrans' occupying forces.

Corinth Campaign

During the winter of 1861–62, Confederate forces were defeated in Kentucky at the Battles of Middle Creek and Mill Springs. After these setbacks came the losses of the Confederate garrisons at Fort Henry and Donelson on the Cumberland River, prompting Confederate General Albert Sidney Johnston to fall back from the unwieldy defensive line that he had established across southern Kentucky. In April 1862, after Shiloh, Confederate General Beauregard retreated to Corinth to regroup, a town which had already been singled out as a strategic objective by Union commanders for the reason that at Corinth, the Mobile & Ohio Railroad (M&O) and Memphis & Charleston Railroad crossed paths. Together, these two railroads connected the Confederate States of America

from the Mississippi River to the Atlantic Ocean and to the Gulf of Mexico. They were the backbone of the Confederacy, bringing troops from the deep South to Virginia and carrying war materiel—guns, ammunition, tents, clothing, shoes, and other equipment—from the factories in Richmond, Virginia, Knoxville, Tennessee, and Prattville, Alabama to the armies in the field. The Confederate war effort depended heavily upon them.

Furthrmore, Johnston's retreat from his defensive position in Kentucky forced the Confederacy to evacuate Nashville, as the Confederates had now lost control of the Cumberland River. With the loss of the Tennessee capital, the Southerners lost the city foundries that produced much of their artillery as well as small arms accoutrements. The loss of Nashville only served to heighten the strategic importance of Corinth to the Confederacy, because with it, the Army of the Mississippi lost one of its primary supply centers.

On April 11, Halleck assumed command of all the Union forces at Shiloh, and drawing reinforcements from all directions, increased his effectives to 110,000 men by the end of the month. General Ulysses S. Grant was his second-in-command. Meanwhile, Beauregard army was reinforced to 50,000 men. On April 30, Beauregard began his slow advance on Shiloh and early in May began to construct entrenchments; on May 9 he fought a brief engagement was fought and by May 28 he was within a mile of the Confederate main line. Two days later, however, it was learned that Beauregard had retreated from Corinth, which Halleck was able to occupy without opposition.

On October 1 of that year, Grant, who was in command of the Union forces in west Tennessee and northern Mississippi, had about 48,000 effective. Confederate General Earl Van Dorn believing that a successful attack on Corinth would drive Grant from west Tennessee, marched north with about 22,000 men. However, at the battle on October 3 that was fought some three miles northwest of Corinth, he failed in his attempt to recapture it for the Confederacy, and it remained in the hands of the Confederacy thenceforth.

THE BATTLE
After the Battle of Shiloh in April 1862 the Confederates withdrew from their defences at Corinth, leaving the town open to Union forces. In July 1862 Confederate General Braxton Bragg began an advance with the majority of the Army of the Mississippi towards Kentucky in an attempt to win back territory in the west for the Confederates. Bragg left behind Major General Sterling Price's Confederate Army of the West in Tennessee and Major General Earl Van Dorn's Army of West

Tennessee along the Mississippi to tie down Major General Ulysses S. Grant's Union forces west of the Tennessee River, widely dispersed at a number of garrisons, including Corinth. On August 11 Bragg ordered Van Dorn to move north and join Price, with the intention of taking advantage of the divided nature of Grant's forces to recapture Corinth then regain Tennessee. Although Grant dispatched Major General William S. Rosecrans' Army of the Mississippi to catch Price before the two Confederate armies could unite, the Unionists failed to destroy Price's army at the Battle of Iuka on September 19. Price managed to slip away with his men and at the end of the month reached Van Dorn, who took command of the combined Confederate force of 22,000 men.

On the morning of October 3 Van Dorn reached the Unionists' outer defences at Corinth, Rosecrans having retreated with his 23,000-strong army into Corinth the previous day, and launched an attack, exploiting a gap in the Union lines and pushing the Unionists back behind their inner defences. Confident of victory the next day, Van Dorn called off his advance in the evening, but by the time he renewed his attack on the next morning Rosecrans had regrouped his defenses and his artillery tore holes among the advancing Confederates. Although the Confederates managed to storm two batteries a Union counterattack forced Van Dorn's men into a general retreat. In all the Unionists lost 2,359 men in the battle, the Confederates 4,838, and Van Dorn's withdrawal enabled Rosecrans to move at the end of the year against Bragg in Tennessee.

Corps, Organization of

In 1861, no army corps had ever existed in the U.S. Army, and few senior officers had experience of command above the regimental level. The notion of the corps was relatively new, having been developed during the Napoleonic era in Europe. The basic premise was that each corps was virtually an army in miniature, containing all the elements it needed to fight independently, such as infantry, cavalry, artillery, engineers, and logistical units. During the Civil War, cavalry were kept in separate formations, separate from the army corps, and eventually both sides introduced whole cavalry corps to their armies.

Both sides were slow to introduce corps into their armies, and during the First Battle of Bull Run (July 21, 1861), the largest formation in either army was the infantry division. The Union army was the first to introduce the corps system before the start of the

Right: Major General Winfield Hancock of the Army of the Potomac, pictured with generals Barlow, Barney, and Gibbon.

Peninsular Campaign (1862), and the Confederates developed a "proto-corps" system during the campaign (having two "wing" commanders controlling three divisions each), and officially adopted the system by August. The first Confederate corps commanders were General Thomas "Stonewall" Jackson (Ist Army Corps) and General James Longstreet (IInd Army Corps). Following Jackson's death at the Battle of Chancellorsville (May 2–3, 1863), the Army of Northern Virginia was reorganised into three corps, commanded by Generals Longstreet, Richard Ewell, and Ambrose P. Hill. This corps organization was retained by the Army of Northern Virginia until the virtual disintegration of the Confederate army during the Petersburg campaign (1864–65). The Confederate Army of Tennessee adopted a smaller version of the Corps system in the last months of 1862, and during the Chickamauga campaign (1863) the small corps of the army were grouped into larger "wings", creating Corps similar in size to those used in Virginia.

In the Army of the Potomac, during the

Peninsular Campaign (1862), General George B. McClellan divided his army into six small corps. Although the corps commanders were appointed and fired on a regular basis, the same structure was retained throughout the rest of the war, although the numbers of corps increased steadily. Under experienced corps commanders such as generals John Reynolds, John Sedgewick, or Winfield Hancock, the cumbersome Army of the Potomac was divided into small, responsive subunits. Under commanders with less initiative, the system failed to work effectively.

Size was the key difference between the corps used by both sides during the war. At the Battle of Gettysburg, the average strength of a Confederate corps was around 20,000 men, and each of the three corps contained three divisions and a corps artillery reserve. In the Union Army of the Potomac, the typical corps was half the size of its Confederate counterpart, and contained two or three divisions which were also half the size of the Confederate formations. Each Union corps also contained a small artillery brigade. A similar size and

Above: The staff of III Corps, Army of the Potomac, pictured in September 1863. From left to right they are Brigadier General Mott, and colonels Farnum, Brewster, Ward and Austin.

Right: Heaps of canister sabots and piles of roundshot testify to the prodigious financial outlay made by the Union to defeat the secessionists.

type of corps was used by the Union armies in the Western theater, and Confederate Corps there followed the example of their opponents.

Cost of the war

The Civil War was more than three times as expensive in constant dollar terms than the combined cost of all of the previous wars that the United States had fought. Initially, it had been expected to last about 90 days. Few could have imagined the four bloody, costly years. It is clearly an understatement to assert that its cost in dollars (not to mention lives) was far greater than anyone could have predicted in 1861.

Both sides attempted for a time to finance

their war efforts through increased taxes and loans, but both ultimately turned to the printing press, creating an unprecedented level of inflation.

Prior to the Civil War, and during the conflict's early months, government intervention in the economy was generally hands-off, with few measures to control wages and prices. There were few exceptions. Railroads were under government regulation, and armament production was partially under state control, although more so in the South. Aside from these exceptions, the market economy dictated the material costs of war materiel and services.

The total cost to both sides is estimated to have been in the neighborhood of $5.2 billion in 1860 dollars. This translates to the equivalent of $104 billion at the turn of the twenty-first century. Of this, roughly 60 percent of the cost was borne by the North, although the per capita cost was greater in the South. On an equal basis, the Civil War cost every Northerner approximately $1,350 and every Southerner about $2,750.

By comparison, in turn of the century dollars, the American Revolution cost the United States about one billion dollars, World War I cost about $325 billion and Vietnam cost $500 billion. By this measure, America's most expensive war, World War II, cost the United States almost three *trillion* dollars.

Cotton

Cotton was the main cash crop of the slave-based plantation economy of the South and was seen by Confederate ministers and diplomats as the major weapon in securing southern foreign policy ambitions. An unsuccessful attempt was made to use control over the cotton exports Britain and France required for their crucial textile industries to prompt foreign intervention to break the Yankee naval blockade, or failing that at least to secure diplomatic recognition of the Confederate States. Despite the high price of cotton, which had boosted Southern confidence before the war, the Confederate war economy struggled to feed

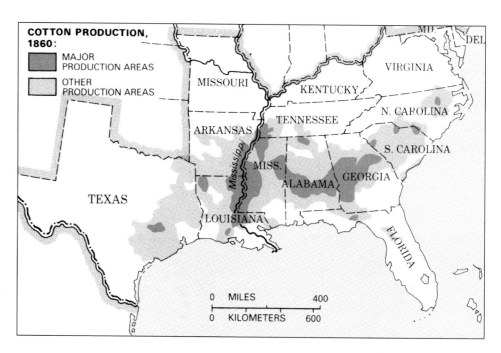

COTTON PRODUCTION, 1860:

◼ MAJOR PRODUCTION AREAS

▨ OTHER PRODUCTION AREAS

Top Right: Cotton production in 1860.

Above Right: Slavery was essential to the Southern economy.

Opposite Page, Above: Cotton pickers and overseer on a Southern plantation.

Opposite Page, Below: Slave coffle—the growth in cotton production created an internal slave trade.

its own people and support the war effort, with many planters resorting to smuggling cotton across Union lines.

Crittenden Compromise

The Crittenden Compromise was actually a series of measures advanced by Senator John J. Crittenden of Kentucky in which he hoped to head off the impending Civil War. Proposed to the United States Congress in December 1860, the measures included six constitutional amendments recalling the Missouri Compromise of 1820.

In order to induce the South not to secede from the Union, Crittenden proposed that the federal government would indemnify owners of fugitive slaves whose return was prevented by antislavery ele-

ments in the North. He also sought to sanction the right to decide whether slavery should exist in the territories and exempt slavery in the District of Columbia from Congressional action. In January 1861, he introduced a resolution calling for a national referendum on his Compromise, but the Senate tabled the measure. In a vote held on March 2, 1861, Crittenden's amendments were narrowly defeated. Two days later, Abraham Lincoln was inaugurated as President.

Cruisers, Confederate

Commerce raiding was one of the cornerstones of Confederate naval strategy. Several ocean-going cruisers were operated by the Confederate Navy, the first being the *Sumter*, commanded by Captain Ralph

Above: The blockade runner J. N. Maffitt.

Right: Rear Admiral David A. Porter commanded the Union naval forces which supported Grant's drive on Vicksburg. His fleet was spearheaded by casemate river ironclads of the "Cairo" class, including the USS *Carondelet*.

Semmes. Escaping through the Union blockade off the mouth of the Mississippi, Semmes captured 18 Union merchantmen in the Caribbean and the Atlantic before entering Gibraltar in January 1862. The ship was then sold and converted into a blockade runner. Semmes went on to command the *Alabama*, the most successful Confederate raider of the war. Although raiders such as the sidewheel steamer *Nashville*, the British-built steamer *Tallahassee*, and the ironclad

raider *Stonewall* had relatively unsuccessful careers, others proved spectacularly successful. The British-built raider *Florida* was fitted out in the Bahamas in the summer of 1862, but disease decimated her crew, so Captain John Maffitt sailed her into Mobile Bay. In January 1863 he again evaded the blockaders, and took the *Florida* on a successful Atlantic cruise before reaching Brest in August 1863. The *Florida* then cruised in the Caribbean before reaching Bahia in

Brazil in October 1864. Defying Brazil's neutrality, the USS *Wachusett* attacked and captured the raider. The last of the cruisers was the *Shenandoah*, a British-built steamer whose cruise began in October 1864, and took her into the South Atlantic, Indian Ocean, and Pacific, where she attacked the enemy whaling fleet. Her attacks continued until she returned to Britain in November 1865, where her crew discovered the war had ended seven months before.

Cumberland River

The Cumberland River divided the states of Kentucky and Tennessee. When Albert Sidney Johnston was placed in charge of these Western regions, he built Fort Donelson to defend the Cumberland. Johnston, however, erroneously esteemed the defense of the Mississippi a more important project than that of either the Cumberland or the Tennessee, with the result that his forts on both lesser rivers fell to Brigadier General Ulysses S. Grant in February 1862. The taking of Fort Donelson was effected by Grant moving in overland whilst Commodore Andrew H. Foote approached via the Cumberland itself.

Custer, George Armstrong (1839–76)

Custer, the 'boy general' of the Civil War, was appointed a brigadier general when only 23. Flamboyant, bold, and aggressive, he was an excellent Union cavalry general, and his long blond hair and gaudy uniform captured the public imagination.

Custer joined the Army of the Potomac fresh from West Point and commanded a cavalry brigade at Bull Run in 1861. He went on to fight with distinction throughout the Peninsular Campaign of 1861–62, earning his generalship before Gettysburg. He hounded Lee's army until the surrender at Appomattox, where he accepted the Confederate flag of truce.

Dana, Charles Anderson (1819–97)

An influential journalist, Dana worked for the *New York Tribune* 1847–62, the most strident anti-slavery journal of the time. In 1862 he became a member of the War Department and was an observer in the field for the Union army, 1863–64. A confidant of Lincoln, he became Assistant Secretary for War in 1864.

Davis, Jefferson (1808–89)

Jefferson Davis was President of the Confederate States and commander-in-chief of the rebel army during the Civil War. He was a man of contrasts, demonstrating courage, dignity, honesty, and energy—yet he was also proud, oversensitive to criticism, and a poor delegator.

Davis studied at West Point and entered Congress for Mississippi in 1845, before serving with distinction in the Mexican-American War. From 1853 to 1857 he was Secretary of War in Franklin Pierce's government. Rated as one of the most influential politicians in the country, he was elected President of the Provisional Government of the Confederate States of America in February 1861, with a six-year term of office, and a mandate to guarantee the right to own slaves. He was inaugurated on the steps of the new state capitol in Montgomery, Alabama; "Upon my head were showered smiles, plaudits, and flowers," he wrote, "but beyond them I saw troubles innumerable."

Tall, gaunt, aloof, obstinate, and formal, Davis was, according to Sam Houston, "cold as a lizard," but in private he was apparently a warm and loving individual. His wife summed up his character in a letter to her mother: "He impresses me as a remarkable kind of man, but of uncertain temper, and has a way of taking for granted that everybody agrees with him when he expresses an opinion, which offends me; yet he is most agreeable and has a peculiarly sweet voice and a winning manner of asserting himself."

Jefferson Davis may have charmed his wife, but one of his greatest failings was his inability to get along with his colleagues. One official noted in 1864 that Davis

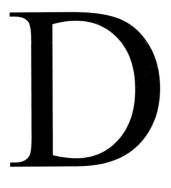

Left: President Jefferson Davis, the first and last President of the Confederate States of America, as a young senator.

Opposite Page, Above and Below: General Custer is, perhaps, better known for his fate at the Battle of the Little Big Horn in June 25, 1876, than for his exploits during the Civil War.

THE AMERICAN CIVIL WAR: A VISUAL ENCYCLOPEDIA

possessed "a most unenviable facility for converting friends into enemies." He wasted time in quarreling with congressmen, generals, governors, and the Press. He tended to promote his friends and remained fiercely loyal to them even in the face of evidence of their failings. When a group of generals questioned the competence of Braxton Bragg after Chickamauga, Davis sacked the ringleaders rather than Bragg.

Davis was not an extremist on the slave issue, but was completely devoted to the Confederate cause and wanted to defend the Southern way of life. He was all too aware of the realities of the situation: seven states (eventually eleven) were pitted against the industrial might and comparative wealth of twenty-three Northern states. Furthermore, the South lacked the diplomatic links and thus the foreign financial support available to the North. Davis struggled to fund the Confederate cause, but his unpopularity as time wore on did nothing to help the situation. He

Above Left and Above: President Jefferson Davis and his wife Varina, who shared and encouraged his secessionist views.

Above Right: Although a "slave state," the State of Delaware supported the Union in the conflict.

Right: The other Jefferson Davis—Union General Jefferson C. Davis (1828–79).

could not win approval for difficult measures, such as conscription or the impressment of supplies. He was in an almost impossible position: few of his supporters were far-sighted enough to recognize that some freedoms had to be sacrificed to the demands of the war.

In 1865 the Confederate government collapsed and Davis was captured by Union cavalry. He was imprisoned for two years and

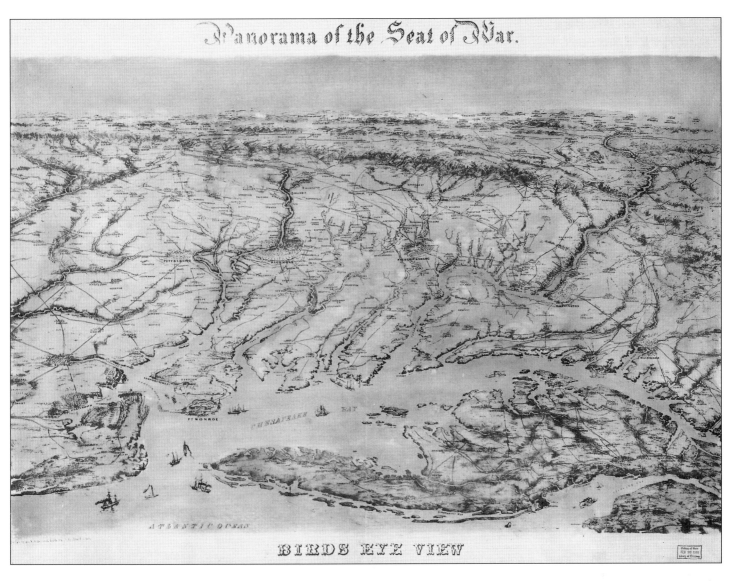

Panorama of the Seat of War.

BIRDS EYE VIEW

indicted for treason. Released in 1868 in the general amnesty, he spent the remainder of his life on an estate in Mississippi.

Davis, Varina Banks Howell (1826-1906)

Varina Banks met Jefferson Davis when she was only seventeen and he was some eighteen years older. They married in 1845. Well-educated and strong-willed, she supported her husband through the difficult years of the Civil War, fleeing Richmond in 1865 with her children and enduring her husband's vilification immediately after the war.

Delaware

One of the so called "Border States" at the beginning of the war, Delaware's allegiance was coveted by North and South alike. Delaware was a slaveholding state, and when on January 1, 1863, Lincoln abolished slavery, Delaware and the other border states were exempted from his ruling—a token of the strategic importance of the state's sympathies, as Lincoln was unwilling to alienate slave owners who were otherwise loyal Unionists. Despite this, in the election of November 8, 1864, Delaware was one of the states that did not go to the Republicans, voting instead for the Democrat party.

Democratic Party

Since 1850, the two major political parties in the United States have been the Democratic Party and the Republican Party. Ironically, the Democratic Party traces its roots to another

THE AMERICAN CIVIL WAR: A VISUAL ENCYCLOPEDIA

"Republican Party" which existed in 1792, long before the present Republican Party was formally created in 1854. The "Jeffersonian Republicans," as they called themselves, stressed the principle of popular government and opposed the Federalist Party's notion of a more imperial central government.

Officially known as the "Democratic Republicans" through the 1820s, and as the "Democrats" thereafter, the party held the presidency for four decades from 1801 to 1841. Thomas Jefferson, James Madison, James Monroe, and John Quincy Adams were all "Democratic Republicans," and Andrew Jackson was the first "Democrat" to hold the office. Between Jackson's term and 1860, four Democratic presidents—Martin Van Buren, James K. Polk, Franklin Pierce, and James Buchanan—would alternate with four presidents from the Whig Party.

By the 1850s, the Democrats had become divided over the issue of slavery in the new western territories that had not yet become states. The Southern Democrats, led by Jefferson Davis, wanted to see slavery legalized here, while the Northern Democrats, led by Stephen A. Douglas, wanted to allow the residents of the territories to ban slavery if they wished.

The internal conflict came to a head at the party's convention in 1860. A crisis was reached when the two wings of the Party split and each nominated a presidential candidate. The Northern Democrats nominated Douglas, and the pro-slavery Southern wing nominated Vice President John Cabell Breckinridge.

This split paved the way for the Democrats to lose the election to the Republicans, who had nominated Abraham Lincoln. In the election, Lincoln swept the North and Breckenridge took most of the South. Douglas was a strong second nearly everywhere, and won more popular votes than Breckenridge. Lincoln won with 1,865,908 votes to 1,380,202 cast for Douglas and 848,019 for Breckinridge. Together, the two Democrats outpolled Lincoln, but

Above: Women in Washington, D.C. helped the war effort by providing centers which fed soldiers on leave.

Right: A temporary supply depot used by Union forces in Virginia.

THE AMERICAN CIVIL WAR: A VISUAL ENCYCLOPEDIA

the Republican candidate emerged with a 180 electoral votes, a majority of those to be cast. Breckenridge would have seventy-two by virtue of taking most of the Southern states, while Douglas hare a mere twelve. The remaining thirty-nine went to John Bell of the Constitutional Union Party, which was itself a spin-off of the Democratic Party. From 1860 to the beginning of the Roosevelt era in 1933, the Democratic Party would hold the presidency for only sixteen years—during the two terms of Grover Cleveland (1885–89, 1893–97), and those of Woodrow Wilson (1913–21).

Depots

Because of the unprecedented number of troops in the field, the armies engaged in the Civil War were faced with an equally unprecedented logistical requirement. In order to support the Union and Confederate field armies, the respective quartermaster corps established field depots wherever possible. Supply depots were naturally located within reach of defensive positions, but because no advancing field commander wants to outrun his supply lines, forward supply depots had to also be established to support intended offensive actions.

The locations of both defensive and offensive supply depots were dependent to a large measure on the means of transportation that fed them. Obviously, large-volume transport was vital because huge piles of supplies had to be amassed as quickly as possible, especially for an army on the attack. For this reason, points that could be serviced by water or rail were preferable to locations that required delivery of supply overland by wagon. For this reason, the Mississippi River was a key supply line throughout the war and Mississippi River ports contained key depots.

District of Columbia

The District of Columbia was notorious as a slave-holding region, and as such was a bone of contention between North and South in the prewar years when it was hoped that Civil War might not be inevitable. Several years of negotiation and compromise preceded the outbreak of war, and it was part of the Compromise of 1850 that the District of Columbia's thriving slave trade should be discontinued.

In the end, no amount of compromise and negotiation could stave off war and the District of Columbia in general, and Washington in particular, had a significant part to play—both as the Federal Capitol and seat of government, but also as a location that could be threatened by the South (see page 426).

Divisions, Organization of

During the war a division was usually commanded by a major general or a senior brigadier general. Typically, these officers were experienced regulars, capable of independent action if required. The division consisted of two or more brigades (three brigades being the most common), and these were sometimes accompanied by their own integral artillery support. During the first years of the war, artillery was often attached to individual brigades within the division, but by 1863, artillery was more commonly formed into a unit of several batteries, under their own commander.

Above: Brigadier General John Buford (seated) seen with his staff. He commanded a division in the Cavalry Corps of the Army of the Potomac.

Above and Below Left: Two views of Pickett's Charge, one showing Major General George Pickett at the head of his men, hat on sword, the other the battle at bayonet point.

Below: Major General George E. Pickett.

A typical division was that of Major General George Pickett at Gettysburg (July 1–3, 1863). His 5,578 men were divided into three infantry brigades, each containing five regiments. Brigadier Garnett's Brigade contained 1,459 men, Brigadier Kemper's Brigade 1,634, while Brigadier Armistead's Brigade contained 2,055 men. In addition the division was supported by a divisional artillery unit of four batteries, each with four guns. The 419 gunners were commanded by Major James Dearing. Pickett's Division was one of the three divisions which formed part of Lieutenant General Longstreet's I Army Corps. The division was unusual in that it was composed exclusively of men from Virginia.

Pickett's Charge on the third day of the battle involved a frontal attack on the Union lines, in concert with troops from two other divisions. Pickett's men advanced across the 500 yards of open ground under constant artillery fire. By the time they reached the Union lines their formation was already decimated. After a bloody struggle, they were repulsed, with 3,000 losses in Picket's Division alone. When General Robert E. Lee asked Pickett to prepare his division to receive a Union attack, the divisional commander replied, "General Lee, I have no division now."

As a contrast, Pickett's men who reached the Union lines came into direct contact with the infantrymen of Brigadier General John Gibbon's division. Unlike the Confederates, Union divisions were numbered, and that of Gibbons was the 2nd Division of the Union II Army Corps, commanded by Major General Winfield Hancock. He commanded 3,608 men, divided into three brigades. His 1st Brigade (Brigadier Harrow) contained 1,366 men in four regiments, plus an attached company of sharpshooters. Each regiment came from a different state (Maine, Massachusetts, Minnesota, and New York). All four regiments of the 2nd Brigade (1,224 men commanded by Brigadier Webb) were from Pennsylvania. Gibbon's 3rd Brigade, commanded by Colonel Hall, contained 922 men in four regiments, from three states (Massachusetts, New York, and Michigan). The division contained no intrinsic artillery support.

In 1862, General Kearney's Division of the Army of the Potomac wore patches of red cloth sewn onto their hats as a unit insignia. In March 1863 this system was adopted by the rest of the Army of the Potomac, probably as a means of creating "ésprit de corps," and each division in a corps was identified by a particular color (1st: Red, 2nd: White, 3rd: Blue etc.). This simple divisional identification system was continued throughout the war.

Dix, Dorothea (1802–87)

An American social reformer, Dix was superintendent of Union army nurses. Tireless and forbidding, she recruited only respectable applicants over the age of thirty: "All nurses are required to be very plain-looking women." Her rigorous standards ensured that the standards of nursing care improved immeasurably. Furthermore, she stayed at her post throughout the war without pay.

Van Dorn, Earl (1820–63)

An enterprising and bold Confederate general, Van Dorn was given command of the Trans-Mississippi Department in 1862. Defeated by Union forces at Corinth, he redeemed his reputation by forcing Grant to retreat from his base at Holly Springs in December 1862 and harassing him at Vicksburg.

Douglas, Stephen Arnold (1813–61)

A U.S. senator for fourteen years and a Democratic presidential contender, Douglas is best remembered for his debates with Abraham Lincoln on the question of slavery in 1858. He believed that each territory should decide on the slavery issue after they achieved statehood, which alienated him from most Southern Democrats.

Douglass, Frederick (c. 1817–95)

A former slave and prominent black Abolitionist, Douglass struggled for the abolition of slavery by lecturing in the U.S. and Britain during the 1840s. An exceptional orator, Douglas was an advisor to President Lincoln, and fought for the enlistment of black men into the Union army, assisting in the recruitment of the 54th and 55th Massachusetts Colored Regiments.

Dupont, Samuel Francis (1803–65)

A naval officer, Dupont was instrumental in establishing the U.S. Naval Academy. In 1861 he organized the blockade of the Southern naval area by Federal forces, and captured the ports of South Carolina and Georgia. After the failure of an attack on Charleston in 1863, which ended in disaster, Dupont was relieved of his command.

Above Right: Frederick Douglass was one of the most prominent African-Americans of the age, and acted as a special advisor to President Lincoln.

Right: Major General Earl Van Dorn.

THE AMERICAN CIVIL WAR: A VISUAL ENCYCLOPEDIA

Early, Jubal Anderson (1816–94)

Lee's irascible "bad old man," Early cursed, "chawed terbaccy," and got results. A no-nonsense commander, he enjoyed Lee's complete confidence. Early graduated from West Point in 1837, but retired from the army to pursue a legal career in Virginia.

Although he opposed secession, Early was quick to volunteer for the Confederacy in 1861 and was appointed a colonel of volunteers. He fought well under Beauregard at Bull Run, impressing his superiors sufficiently to earn promotion to brigadier general. He served under Joseph Johnston in the Peninsular Campaign in 1862, defending Richmond from McClellan's forces. Wounded at Williamsburg, he recovered swiftly and went on to fight with "Stonewall" Jackson in the Shenandoah Valley. A flexible, quick-thinking commander, Early's strategic good sense preserved the lives of his brigade at Antietam, and at Fredericksburg he earned promotion to major general. Early's one failing was impatience with reconnaissance, and this proved to be his undoing at Chancellorsville.

Early attacked the outskirts of Washington itself in July 1864, terrifying the citizens. During the Wilderness Campaign of that year, "Old Jube" harassed Union forces so severely that Grant ordered "veterans, militiamen, and everything that can be got to follow" sent after him. Early laid waste to a number of Northern towns such as Chambersburg, Pennsylvania, exacting revenge for Sherman and

Sheridan's ravaging of the South. He liked cities, he said, because they burned easily. Finally, however, Sheridan drove him out of the Shenandoah in October 1864 in a victory widely celebrated in the North.

Early's Raid, 1864

By this action Lee, faced with a significant numerical disadvantage in men in the fourth year of the war, sought to divert some of Grant's strength from his front, in the hope that he could then destroy him by offensive action. Lieutenant General Early, who in May and June 1864 had defeated Sigel and Hunter in the Shenandoah Valley (see page 390) with four infantry divisions and a cavalry division, was ordered to undertake a renewed offensive in the Valley. This new Confederate "Army of the Valley" moved out on June 7, 1864, defeated Hunter's Federal forces at Lynchburg on June 18. In an attempt to relieve the pressure on Petersburg, Lee then ordered Early to threaten Washington.

In late June Early thrust at Staunton, before fording the Potomac into Maryland on July 5 and advancing toward Frederick. Reinforcements from the Army of the Potomac were ordered by Grant to Baltimore, but at Monocacy Wallace only succeeded in delaying Early before falling back to Baltimore. Using some of his cavalry to protect his line of communications, Early sent a cavalry brigade to threaten Baltimore, and with the remainder of his forces marched on Washington, D.C. On July 11 he arrived on the city outskirts but could find no weak spot in its hastily reinforced defenses.

The arrival of Federal reinforcements convinced Early that he lacked the necessary strength for a successful assault and

Below: Throughout the war, Washington was defended by a string of fortifications.

withdrew that night. In pursuit, the poorly coordinated Federal forces met with a reversal at Kernstown on July 23–24.

In its objective of diverting Federal forces, Early's raid was an unqualified success. It also highlighted the lack of an effective command system for the defense of the capital and convinced Grant that he would have to take more drastic action to eliminate Confederate use of the Shenandoah Valley for strategic diversions. He made plans to put Phil Sheridan in command of newly reorganized and consolidated Federal forces in the area. From a Confederate perspective the raid could be regarded as a useful delaying action.

Edged Weapons

Although firepower from gunpowder weapons dominated Civil War battlefields, a wide range of traditional edged weapons were used to equip the troops of both sides. Chief among these were swords, bayonets, and knifes. A few cavalry units were also temporarily equipped with lances, usually consisting of an eight-foot ash staff topped by a ten-inch metal spearpoint. However, these were quickly found to be of little practical use in combat and the overwhelming majority had been abandoned by the end of 1862.

KNIVES

In the opening state of the war, knives proved a highly popular item of equipment, with many being tucked into the waistband to give the owner a suitably aggressive posture. Both North and South paid little attention to combat knives and most were purchased by individuals. In reality, they were not greatly used in combat on the battlefield, although they had a number of other uses in camp or as an improvised entrenching tool.

A wide variety of knives were bought for personal use. Often of crude manufacture, they had blades of varying lengths, from six to eighteen inches, and wooden fittings. Blade widths also varied enormously, but the broad-bladed "Bowie" knife was popular, particularly among some Southern units. Generally, the carrying of such weapons continued for longer, and was more popular, among Southern units that in the North.

BAYONETS

In the mid-nineteenth century and beyond, the bayonet was considered one of the most important weapons available to the ordinary soldier. Artillery and musket fire might pave the way for an attack but cold

Left: In the U.S. Navy, sailors such as this yeoman were still trained to fight boarding actions using cutlasses, but improvements in gunnery meant such actions were rare.

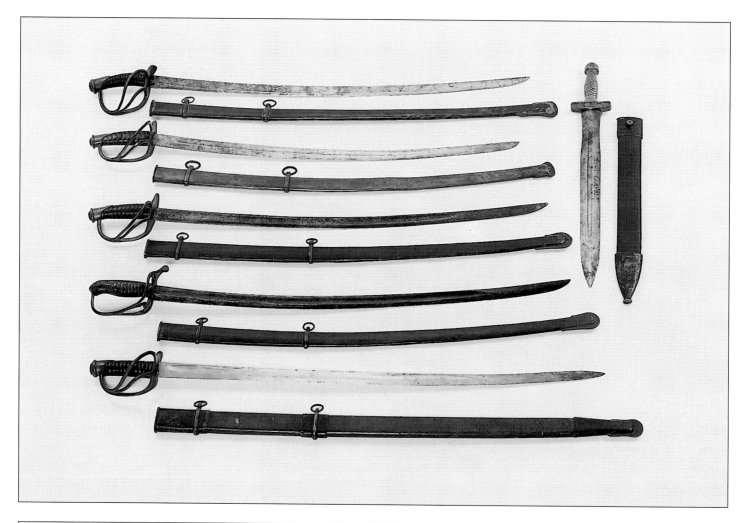

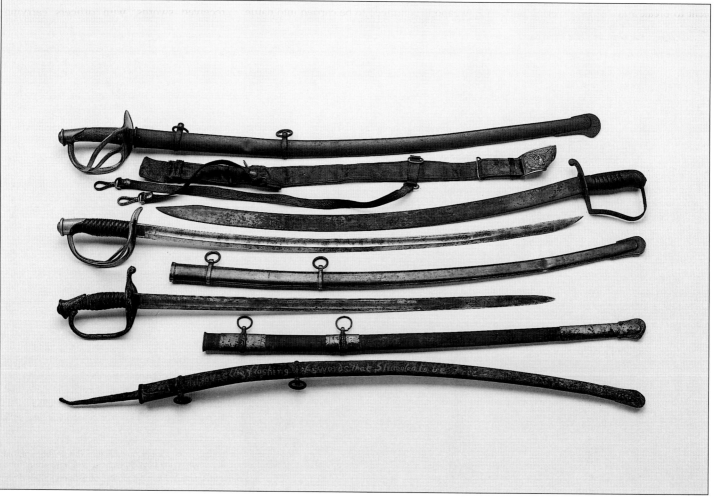

steel used at close quarters would deliver the *coup de grâce* on a wavering foe.

Reality on the battlefield of the Civil War proved to be entirely different. Hundreds of thousands of bayonets were manufactured and issued during the Civil War, yet few men on either side were wounded or killed by a bayonet thrust in the heat of battle. To put matters into perspective, during General Ulysses S. Grant's Wilderness Campaign in 1864, 7,302 Union troops were wounded in total, but only six are recorded as having received their injuries from either sword cuts or bayonet thrusts. As one Southern general remarked, "bayonets were fearful to look upon as they were leveled in front of a charging line, but they were rarely reddened with blood."

The chief reason for this was that firepower from artillery and smallarms so dominated the battlefield that the opportunity to launch a successful bayonet charge was rare. They did occur on occasion, but the likelihood of the attacker getting to close quarters was small, particularly if the defender was sheltering behind a natural barrier or purpose-built field defenses. Either the charge would be stopped in its tracks by enemy fire or the defenders, probably already softened up by heavy artillery bombardment, suffering casualties and with low morale, would simply melt away. Nevertheless, the sight of an approaching formation with leveled bayonets was sufficient to break an already wavering unit, so they did have a psychological impact. If a melee did take place, swords, knives, handguns, and rifles wielded as clubs were as likely to come into play as bayonets. Bayonets did find useful employment during the conflict, although not as their manufacturers had originally intended. They saw service as improvised entrenching tools, particularly as purpose-built equipment was often in short supply or not immediately available, or in camp as can openers or roasting spits.

Various types of bayonets were carried, although the overwhelming majority were of a similar design, fairly standardized, whether produced by Northern or Southern manufacturers, or sourced from overseas. The overwhelming majority were triangular in section, and were of the socket type. Northern designs tended to be of an all-steel construction, while their Southern counterparts were frequently just steel-tipped. Most bayonets were around eighteen inches long with a three-inch socket.

Union troops were issued with triangular, narrow-bladed steel socket types to fit their M1861 Springfield and P1853 Enfield rifled muskets. Both were eighteen inches long with a three-inch socket, although the Enfield's blade was very slightly wider, $^{13}/_{16}$th inch as opposed to $^{25}/_{32}$nd inch for the Springfield.

Scabbards for bayonets were made from either black or brown leather, and had brass, iron, or tin fittings. Southern-made bayonets for rifled muskets were similar, although made of iron with a steel tip. British Enfield bayonets were also widely used, and some rifles were also fitted with broad saber bayonets with twenty-two-inch blades and five-inch brass handles. These were often used with short rifles, thereby allowing the user a degree of reach more comparable to a man wielding a longer musket or rifled musket. They were also initially popular with some zouave units and used by naval personnel. However, they were more costly to produced than the triangle bayonets and proved of little value so production was halted in January 1864. Northern saber bayonets suffered a similar fate.

SWORDS

Despite their limited application during the Civil War, swords and other edged weapons continued to be carried into battle chiefly by officers of all services, cavalrymen, and members of the horse artillery. Clearly they were used in battle, particularly in cavalry charges, but they increasingly became seen as weapons conveying and symbolizing the authority of officership on the owner. Indeed, small nuances of design or embellishment were used to distinguish essentially similar swords used by different ranks. For example, the M1850 foot officer's light saber issued to captains and below was virtually identical to the M1850 staff and field officers' light saber worn by those above the rank of captain—except the later carried the letters U.S. on the hilt.

Despite the limited practical use of the weapon in the face of overwhelming firepower, the number of swords issued by North and South was huge. Apart from those cases already mentioned, they were also presented to non-commissioned officers, musicians, and field artillery units—although in many cases they would be abandoned or "lost". For all this, there was no doubting the general commitment to the sword, at least by the authorities. Between 1861 and 1866, for example, the U.S. Army issued 203,000 light cavalry sabers and 190,000 heavy cavalry sabers; smaller but nevertheless significant numbers were issued to other categories of troops. Some 86,000 non-commissioned officers' swords were distributed during the war.

Swords tended to be either slightly curved or straight, with varying lengths. The Union's light cavalry saber, the M1857, was some forty-one inches long and had a curved blade, which was one-inch wide at the hilt. The heavier cavalry sword, the M1840 saber, was similar, although marginally wider at the hilt. Sword carriers below full officer rank tended to received shorter swords, with straight rather than curved blades. In the case of Northern non-commissioned officers, they were entitled to wear the M1840 sword, which was a little under thirty-two inches long and had a straight blade.

The South made few original swords. With the exception of those distributed to musicians, the remainder were direct copies of U.S. types. For example, mounted troops were issued with, among others, copies of the M1840 cavalry and the M1860 light cavalry sabers. These copies were usually of inferior quality and finish to the Northern originals. As Southern manufacturers were unable to satisfy the demand for swords, the Confederacy turned to overseas suppliers. Chief among these was Britain, which shipped the P1853 cavalry saber in significant numbers. Others were produced in Germany, but many Confederates made use of better-quality Northern swords captured or abandoned on the battlefield.

Naval personnel of both sides also received swords, with officers carrying swords similar to those issued to their army counterparts. Ordinary seamen were issued with a range of cutlasses. The North supplied the M1841, which measured some twenty-one inches and had a straight blade, and the M1861, which was slightly longer (24⅞ inches) and had a slightly curved blade. Southern naval officers made use of copies of Northern types or imported British swords as well as a number of original designs.

Elections, Confederate

During the period of the Civil War, the Confederate States of America technically had two presidential elections, one to elect a Provisional President, and the second to elect a Permanent President—although the same man won both elections. The first election occurred on February 4, 1861, when delegates of six states of the Confederacy (South Carolina, Mississippi, Florida, Alabama, Georgia, and Louisiana) met in Montgomery, Alabama, then the capital of the Confederacy. At that time, there were seven states, but the Texas delegates were delayed and the vote was held in their absence.

In this election for a Provisional President, in which there were three candidates, the radical R. B. Rhett and W. L. Yancey were passed over in favor of the

Above Left: Various cavalry sabers and scabbards. The short sword was used by members of the Foot Artillery forces with the Confederacy.

Left: Union weapons used by the Confederacy. From the top: Model 1840 cavalry saber and scabbard; Union officer's sword belt; Model 1812 Starr saber; Model 1860 cavalry saber with scabbard below; Model 1850 infantry officer's sword with scabbard below; part of Model 1860 saber in scabbard with the inscription, "15th loved the flashing of swords that struggled to be free."

THE AMERICAN CIVIL WAR: A VISUAL ENCYCLOPEDIA

Right: Pauline Cushman photographed in a Union officer's uniform, holding a well-decorated infantry officer's sword.

more moderate Jefferson Davis of Mississippi. Alexander H. Stephens of Georgia was selected as Provisional Vice President.

In the first general elections for the Confederate Congress and for presidential electors, held in November 1861, the Davis and Stephens team ran unopposed. They were inaugurated as the Permanent President and Vice President of the Confederacy on February 22, 1862.

Under the Confederate Constitution, the President and Vice President were to be elected for a single six-year term, with the President not allowed to run for reelection. This differed from the United States, where the term was four years. Until 1951, when a President was limited to two terms, the United States President would be allowed to run for reelection indefinitely.

Thus, under the Confederate Constitution, Jefferson Davis's term officially ended on February 22, 1868—but, of course, the Confederate States of America had ceased to exist before there could be a second general election for presidential electors.

Elections, United States

The presidential election of 1860 took place against a backdrop of partisan and regional tension. This would culminate in a serious division in the Democratic Party and, in turn, to the election of the first Republican President of the United States.

The Democrats were divided along North-South lines, with the Southerners demanding a candidate who would be willing to protect the rights of slaveholders in the territories that were not yet admitted to the Union as states. The Northern and Border State wing of the party advocated "popular sovereignty"—the right of the people of the territories to decide whether they would be free or slave states. Most did not go so far as to advocate outright abolition in the Southern states. Indeed, a minority of the members of both the Democratic and Republican Parties favored abolition.

The front runner, and expected nominee of the party, was Stephen Arnold Douglas, a senator from Illinois who had emerged as the *de facto* leader of the party. At the Democratic National Convention in Charleston, South Carolina, Douglas's recommendations in a platform advocating nonintervention in slavery were adopted. In voting to select a nominee, Douglas himself led on fifty-seven consecutive ballots, but he failed to attain the necessary two-thirds of the votes of delegates to be nominated.

The convention adjourned and reconvened in Baltimore, where the Southern Democrats walked out. Acting alone, the latter bloc nominated John Cabell Breckinridge, who was then the sitting Vice President of the United States under Democratic President James Buchanan. Other Democrats left the party entirely to form the Constitutional Union Party, which nominated John Bell, a slaveowner who opposed the expansion of slavery in order to help preserve the Union. Douglas was easily nominated by what was left of the Democratic Party, now a primarily Northern institution.

The Republican Party, which had yet to win a presidential election, passed over nominal front runner William Seward to nominate an Illinois attorney and former congressman, Abraham Lincoln. Ironically, Lincoln had lost the 1856 Illinois senatorial race to Stephen Douglas.

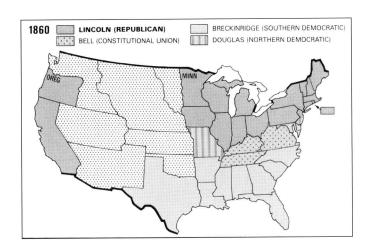

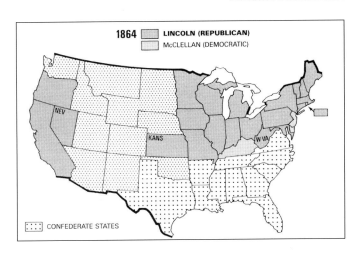

Above and Right: The three Presidential elections relevant to the Civil War period are shown graphically here. Above is Lincoln's 1860 triumph, showing how the Democrat vote was split. Above right is the U.S. wartime election won easily by Lincoln, with the Confederate States uninvolved. Finally, at right, is the third straight success for the Republicans, Grant's victory in 1868. The map shows the states that voted and those that were still unreconstructed.

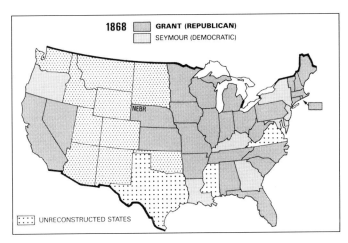

In November, Lincoln won the Northern states and Breckenridge won most of the South, although Douglas was a strong second nearly everywhere, and won more popular votes than Breckenridge. Lincoln won the election with 1,865,908 votes to 1,380,202 cast for Douglas, and 848,019 for Breckenridge. Together, the two Democrats outpolled Lincoln, but the Republican candidate emerged with 180 electoral votes, a majority of those to be cast. Breckenridge would have seventy-two, by virtue of taking most of the Southern states, while Douglas had a mere twelve. The remaining thirty-nine went to John Bell, who carried the key Southern states of Kentucky, Tennessee, and Virginia.

Though it was a mid-term election with the President secure in office, the elections of 1862 was essentially a referendum on the way President Lincoln was handing the Civil War effort. Polls at the time suggested that sixty percent of Northern voters, including members of both parties, favored defeating the Confederate States of America in battle and forcing the Southern states back into the Union. Meanwhile, thirty percent were Democrats who favored calling an end to the Civil War and letting the Confederate States of America remain independent. The remaining ten percent were Republicans who agreed with the majority, but also wanted full abolition of slavery in all areas of the prewar United States.

In November 1862, both parties could claim victory, although Lincoln did not receive the mandate that he craved. The Republicans lost the key governorships of New York and New Jersey and their legislative majorities in New Jersey, Illinois, and Indiana, as well as a total of thirty-four congressional seats. However, the Republicans retained seventeen of nineteen governorships that were up for a vote, and sixteen state legislatures. They also gained five seats in the Senate and retained a twenty-five-vote majority in the House of Representatives.

In 1864, Lincoln faced reelection with the United States still embroiled in the Civil War, and the most serious crisis the nation would face in the first two centuries of its existence. To run against Lincoln, the Democrats nominated the popular former general from New York, George "Little Mac" McClellan, whom Lincoln had fired as commander of the Army of the Potomac after the 1862 mid-term elections.

Polls indicated a tough campaign for Lincoln against McClellan, who was playing to the tide of support for ending the Civil War without a victory. The Republican Party spin doctors restyled it as the "Union" Party. Lincoln was retained as the party nominee for President, but Vice President Hannibal Hamlin of Maine was cast out in favor of a Southerner, Andrew Johnson, the former governor of Tennessee. Lincoln campaigned with a promise to see the Civil War through to victory, hence preserving the Union. He promised to give amnesty to Confederate soldiers, but to work toward passage of the Thirteenth Amendment to the United States Constitution, which would end slavery in the United States.

The Democrats, meanwhile, picked a Midwesterner, Ohio's George Pendleton, to run with McClellan. They promised an immediate ceasefire and negotiations aimed at restoring a the Union as it was in 1860, with slavery intact.

In November 1864, Lincoln won with 2,218,388 popular votes to 1,812,807 for McClellan. In the Electoral College, Lincoln's margin was 212 to 21.

Emancipation

At the outset of the war the emancipation of slaves was neither the personal goal of President Lincoln nor the policy of his administration. Lincoln was not an Abolitionist and, while he regarded slavery as a moral evil, he foresaw severe practical problems for race relations in ending it. In policy terms the focus of the Yankee cause was repeatedly stated to be restoring the Union rather than abolition of slavery. This was essential to avoid alienating important northern Democrats and the key pro-Union slave states of Maryland, Delaware, Missouri, Kentucky, and Western Virginia as well as to avoid strengthening hostility still further throughout the rebel states. By 1862 leading Republicans, who had previously adopted a gradualist approach towards the ending of slavery, had come to recognize that emancipation would seriously weaken the Confederacy and hence was vital to the future of the Union.

Abolitionists became increasingly influential. Congress began to debate measures to confiscate Confederate property, including slaves. On April 10, 1862, Congress passed a resolution from Lincoln offering aid to states that adopted measures for a gradual abolition, despite the opposition of Democrats and border state Unionists. When Lincoln's warning that failure to accept these measures would lead to the ending of slavery through "incident of war" was ignored, he abandoned efforts to reconcile conservatives and moved toward a more radical proabolition position. After holding off Democratic challenges in the fall elections, and bolstered by strategic success at the battle of Antietam, Lincoln gained Cabinet approval for an Emancipation Proclamation in September. Although limited in effect to rebel areas it was, as William Lloyd Garrison recognized, "an act of immense historical consequence."

From then on the Union was effectively fighting to abolish slavery, and calling on the African-American people to assist them in a struggle that culminated in 1865 in the passage of the Thirteenth Amendment.

Emancipation Proclamation

The Emancipation Proclamation issued by Abraham Lincoln, effective on January 1, 1863, was a major milestone in the ending of slavery throughout the United States. Although it explicitly freed only those slaves in areas at that time in rebellion against the Union, and thus in fact outside of Union authority, it was clear that victory would bring the total ending of slavery. The Proclamation stated:

"That on the first day of January, in the year of our Lord one thousand eight hundred and sixty-three, all persons held as slaves within any State, or designated part of a State, the people whereof shall than be in rebellion against the United States, shall be then, thenceforward and forever, free, and the Executive Government of the United States, including the military and naval authority thereof; will recognize and

maintain the freedom of such persons, and will do no act or acts to repress such persons, or any of them, in any effort they may make for their active freedom."

The Proclamation went on to formally authorize the recruitment of ex-slaves into the armed forces. Issued on September 22, 1862, it provided the key moral issue for the war from today's perspective.

Emerson, Ralph Waldo (1803–82)

A highly influential writer and poet, Emerson led the philosophical transcendentalist movement with its belief in the rights of the individual. He was a fervent Abolitionist, and applied his considerable eloquence and literary gifts to championing the cause in the late 1850s, publishing *The Conduct of Life* in 1860.

Right: A copy of *The New York Times* dated September 23, 1863, which carried the news of President Lincoln's Emancipation Proclamation.

Below: Scenes of jubilation following Grant's 1868 Presidential election.

The New-York Times.

VOL. XI—NO. 3432. NEW-YORK, TUESDAY, SEPTEMBER 23, 1862. PRICE TWO CENTS.

HIGHLY IMPORTANT.

A Proclamation by the President of the United States.

The War Still to be Prosecuted for the Restoration of the Union.

A DECREE OF EMANCIPATION

All Slaves in States in Rebellion on the First of January Next to be Free.

The Gradual Abolition and Colonization Schemes Adhered to.

Loyal Citizens to be Remunerated for Losses' Including Slaves.

WASHINGTON, Monday, Sept. 22.

By the President of the United States of America:

A PROCLAMATION.

I, ABRAHAM LINCOLN, President of the United States of America, and Commander-in-Chief of the Army and Navy thereof, do hereby proclaim and declare, that hereafter, as heretofore, the war will be prosecuted for the object of practically restoring the constitutional relation between the United States and the people thereof in which States that relation is, or may be suspended or disturbed; that it is my purpose, upon the next meeting of Congress, to again recommend the adoption of a practical measure tendering pecuniary aid to the free acceptance or rejection of all the Slave States so called, the people whereof may not then be in rebellion against the United States, and which States may then have voluntarily adopted, or thereafter may voluntarily adopt, the immediate or gradual abolishment of Slavery within their respective limits; and that the efforts to colonize persons of African descent with their consent, upon the Continent or elsewhere, with the previously obtained consent of the governments existing there, will be continued.

That on the first day of January, in the year of our Lord one thousand eight hundred and sixty-three, all perons held as slaves within any State, or any designated part of a State, the people whereof shall then be in rebellion against the United States shall be then, thenceforward, and forever, free; and the Executive Government of the United States, including the military and naval authority thereof, will recognize and maintain the freedom of such persons, and will do no act or acts to repress such persons, or any of them, in any efforts they may make for their actual freedom.

That the Executive will, on the first day of January aforesaid, by proclamation, designate the States and parts of States, if any, in which the people thereof, respectively, shall then be in rebellion against the United States; and the fact that any State, or the people thereof, shall on that day be in good faith represented in the Congress of the United States by members chosen thereto at elections wherein a majority of the qualified voters of such State shall have participated, shall, in the absence of strong countervailing testimony, be deemed conclusive evidence that such State and the people thereof have not been in rebellion against the United States.

That attention is hereby called to an act of Congress entitled "An act to make an additional article of war," approved March 13, 1862, and which act is in the words and figure following:

"Be it enacted by the Senate and House of Representatives of the United States of America in Congress assembled, That hereafter the following shall be promulgated as an additional article of war for the government of the army of the United States, and shall be obeyed and observed as such.

ARTICLE—All officers or persons in the military or naval service of the United States are prohibited from employing any of the forces under their respective commands for the purpose of returning fugitives from service or labor who may have escaped from any person to whom such service or labor is claimed to be due, and any officer who shall be found guilty by a Court-martial of violating this article shall be dismissed from the service.

SECTION 2. And be it further enacted, that this act shall take effect from and after its passage."

Also to the ninth and tenth sections of an act entitled "An act to suppress insurrection, to punish treason and rebellion, to seize and confiscate property of rebels, and for other purposes," approved July 17, 1862, and which sections are in the words and figures following:

SEC. 9. And be it further enacted, that all slaves of persons who shall hereafter be engaged in rebellion against the Government of the United States, or who shall, in any way, give aid or comfort thereto, escaping from such persons and taking refuge within the lines of the army; and all slaves captured from such persons or deserted by them and coming under the control of the Government of the United States, and all slaves of such persons found on (or being within) any place occupied by rebel forces and afterward occupied by the forces of the United States, shall be deemed captives of war and shall be forever free of their servitude and not again held as slaves.

SEC. 10. And be it further enacted, That no slave escaping into any State, Territory or the District of Columbia, from any of the States, shall be delivered up, or in any way impeded or hindered of his liberty, except for crime or some offence against the laws, unless the person claiming said fugitive shall first make oath that the person to whom the labor or service of such fugitive is alleged to be due, is his lawful owner, and has not been in arms against the United States in the present rebellion, nor in any way given aid and comfort thereto, and no person engaged in the military or naval service of the United States shall, under any pretence whatever, assume to decide on the validity of the claim of any person to the service or labor of any other person, or surrender up any such person to the claimant, on pain of being dismissed from the service.

And I do hereby enjoin upon and order all persons engaged in the military and naval service of the United States, to observe, obey and enforce, within their respective spheres of service, the act and sections above recited.

And the Executive will in due time recommend that all citizens of the United States who shall have remained loyal thereto throughout the rebellion, shall (upon the restoration of the constitutional relation between the United States and their respective States and people, if the relation shall have been suspended or disturbed,) be compensated for all losses by acts of the United States, *including the loss of slaves.*

In witness whereof, I have hereunto set my hand, and caused the seal of the United States to be affixed.

Done at the City of Washington, this Twenty-second day of September, in the year of our Lord one thousand eight hundred and sixty-two, and of the Independence of the United States the eighty-seventh.

ABRAHAM LINCOLN.

By the President.

WILLIAM H. SEWARD, Secretary of State.

GENERAL NEWS FROM WASHINGTON.

OUR SPECIAL WASHINGTON DISPATCHES.

WASHINGTON, Monday, Sept. 22.

THE PRESIDENT'S PROCLAMATION.

The great event of the day here is the proclamation of the President ordering the execution of the war measures of the last Congress, and promising freedom to the slaves in all States that persist in the rebellion against the Government. This act, so long expected, so long delayed, bids fair to simplify at once the issues of the war, and immediately to array against each other the unconditionally loyal and the rebellious of all shades and grades. If the cause of the Union and free institutions is strongest, this test will show it, and the only question of its triumph will then be the power in the Government to execute its policy with courage and vigor.

THE NEWS FROM KENTUCKY.

A special private dispatch, just received from Cincinnati, announces that BRAGG is marching on Louisville, Ky., and that Gen. NELSON has ordered the women and children to leave the city. BUELL is believed to have been outgeneraled, and to be several hours behind. The dispatch closes—"A General wanted for the West."

THE OLD ISSUE OF TREASURY NOTES.

I have the following statistics in regard to the old issue of United States Treasury Notes, receivable for duties, of the $60,000,0000 issue: $28,420,000 have been returned to the Department and burned; $43,000 have been returned, and are not yet burned; $4,000,000 have been redeemed, but not yet returned to the Department, leaving $27,537,000 yet outstanding. As only about half the whole issue has yet been redeemed, and as the Government will be able to get no gold in payment of duties, so long as any of these notes remain in possession of the public, it is plain that the specie required to pay the interest falling due on Oct. 1—$4,000,000—as well as that falling due Jan. 1—$5,000,000—must be procured by the Government by purchase or loan.

Thirty thousand dollars of small currency notes were to-day paid out at the Treasury Department, and were all taken within an hour.

CONDITION OF GEN. HOOKER.

Gen. HOOKER is now with his friend, Dr. NICHOLS, at the United States Insane Asylum Hospital, near Washington. His wound is a rifle ball through the left foot. Although the wound is painful, it is not considered dangerous; yet it is sufficient to disable him for active service.

THE CONVALESCENT CAMP.

The Convalescent Camp, under the regulations of Gen. BANKS, is becoming an institution of very great utility. All stragglers and convalescents are immediately sent there, as are officers who have been absent without leave, or have overstayed their leave under circumstances that entitle them to lenity. Soldiers are classified according to the corps to which they belong, and are placed in charge of officers belonging to the same corps, who subject them to the daily drill of camp instruction. When the accumulation becomes sufficient to justify their removal, they are sent to their regiments and commands.

PENSIONS.

The Commissioner of Pensions has commenced making appointments of surgeons to make examinations and give certificates in cases of applications for pensions. The fees will make the offices desirable. The following are the appointments already made: Cincinnati, James H. Oliver; Indianapolis, Geo. W. Mears; Leavenworth, Kansas, Selden W. Jones; New-Philadelphia, Ohio, Wm. G. Smith; Terre Haute, Ind., Geo. W. Clippinger; Lafayette, Ind., O. L. Clark; Boston, Geo. S. Jones; Bangor, Me. Ralph J. K. Jones; Rochester, N. Y., Harvey F. Montgomery; Oswego, N. Y., Chas. C. P. Clark; Lyons, N. Y., Nelson Peck; Norridgewack, Me., Uno Robbins, Jr.

ACTING REAR-ADMIRALS.

The following naval officers have been made Acting Rear-Admirals and assigned to the command of the following squadrons, respectively; C. H. BELL' Pacific Squadron; CHAS. WILKES, "Flying Squadron;" T. L. LARDNER, Eastern Gulf Squadron; C. H. DAVIS, Mississippi Flotilla.

From Salt Lake.

SALT LAKE, Monday, Sept. 22.

CHARLES MCBRIDE, from Virginia City, arrived here yesterday, one of a party of fifteen bound for the States. He says:

"The party were attacked by the Snake Indians at the City of Rocks, on the Humboldt route, 150 miles north. They fought the Indians for 20 miles, losing six killed and two wounded, and all of their outfit. JOHN CONNER, JOHN SHARPP, BENJAMIN WHITE, JAMES SHAW, WM. DAVIS and MR. GOODMAN were killed. JOHN FOSTER and SAM. KELLY had their arms broken."

Reports of Indian depredations northward are coming in daily, and much trouble is expected to emigration.

THE LATEST WAR NEWS.

A Raid of Stuart's Cavalry Across the Potomac at Williamsport.

NO DAMAGE DONE.

The Reoccupation of Maryland Heights by Our Forces.

THE REBELS CONTINUING THEIR RETREAT

No Further Collisions at Last Accounts.

LATEST REPORTS FROM HEADQUARTERS.

HEADQUARTERS OF THE ARMY OF THE POTOMAC, Saturday Evening, Sept. 20, 1862.

The firing heard last evening in the direction of Williamsport, turns out to have been a raid of STUART'S rebel cavalry. He crossed the Potomac on Friday night into Maryland, at that point, with his cavalry, one regiment of infantry, and seventeen pieces of artillery. The force sent up to drive him back, arrived near the town late in the afternoon. The firing heard was principally from the rebel guns. During the night they recrossed into Virginia and this morning they had disappeared from the opposite shore. No one was hurt.

The work of burying the dead is still continuing. They average about one thousand per day. To-morrow will probably finish it.

The Maryland Heights were yesterday occupied by a National force.

The indications are that the rebels are continuing their retreat into Virginia, leaving the line of the Potomac.

Divine worship was held at headquarters this evening, Bishop WHIPPLE, of Minnesota, officiating.

HEADQUARTERS, ARMY OF THE POTOMAC, Monday Evening, Sept. 22.

The following is the official report of loss in SUMNER'S corps at the battle of the Antietam:

GEN. RICHARDSON'S DIVISION.

Killed	212
Wounded	899
Missing	24

GEN. SEDGWICK'S DIVISION.

Killed	375
Wounded	1,577
Missing	321

GEN. FRENCH'S DIVISION.

Killed	293
Wounded	1,321
Missing	203
Total loss in Gen. SUMNER'S Corps	5,208

The loss in missing may be somewhat reduced by stragglers returning.

A train of cars crossed the Monocacy this morning. The road is now open to Harper's Ferry, where there is a sufficient Federal force for all purposes.

The rebels, in their hasty retreat from Maryland, left between 1,100 and 1,200 wounded between Sharpsburgh and the river. They are being paroled.

Twenty-six stands of colors were taken during the battle of the Antietam, and have been received at headquarters. Seven more are known to have been captured, and are in the hands of the different regiments which captured them.

OUR LATEST WASHINGTON DISPATCHES.

WASHINGTON, Monday, Sept. 22.

A special dispatch from Frederick states that some surgeons, just arrived from the army, report rebels still falling back from the Potomac. Not even their pickets are now to be seen.

Another dispatch states that our losses in the last fight are not nearly as great as at first reported, especially in SUMNER'S Corps. In the California Regiment only one commissioned officer was killed (Lieut. WILSE) and one hundred and fifty privates killed and wounded.

The last reports from headquarters represented "All quiet along the lines."

THE WAR IN MARYLAND.

Another Account of the Great Battle of Antietam.

LETTERS FROM THE BATTLE-FIELD.

The Strong Position Chosen by the Enemy—How the National Forces were Arranged—Desperate Character of the Fighting—The Results, &c.

ON THE FIELD NEAR SHARPSBURGH, MD., Wednesday Evening, Sept. 17, 1862.

This day will be memorable for one of the bloodiest fought battles on the American Continent. The combined forces of the enemy, under JACKSON, LEE, LONGSTREET, and the whole rebel set, have made a stand near Sharpsburgh, and all day long, from 5 o'clock in the morning until now, (9 o'clock P. M.,) have been contesting with the Union Army under MCCLELLAN, led by BURNSIDE, HOOKER, SUMNER, KEYES, and the other heroes of the war. Nothing, I am sure, since the battle of Pittsburgh Landing, can compare with this day's fight, either in its collossal proportions, or in the bloody character of the struggle. Our advance overtook the rebel forces, apparently in full retreat toward the Shepherdstown ford of the Potomac, yesterday morning, and a temporary halt was ordered near Kedysville, a little village three miles north from Sharpsburgh. The enemy had taken possession of the Antietam Hills, on the right of the creek by that name, with Sharpsburgh in their rear. They were attacked yesterday by our batteries across this creek, for the purpose of occupying them until our whole force should come up, but no general engagement ensued. The rebels were evidently preparing for a last desperate stand, before the final attempt to cross the Potomac. Their failure to check our advance here they knew would be fatal to their whole army, for they could not escape safely into Virginia with our artillery and infantry assailing their rear.

The day closed without any decisive results, except that in every encounter our artillery practice was found to be too accurate and terrible for them, and they doggedly yielded every position which they took up.

Meantime, LONGSTREET, who had succeeded in obtaining possession of Maryland Heights the day before, having *paroled the entire force found there,* (excepting the cavalry, which cut their way through and escaped,) abandoned the position, and was hurrying forward to reinforce the rebel troops at this point.

Thus the two armies, wearied by a harassing march over mountain ranges, and of four days' running fight from beyond Frederick, came together on this memorable field.

The enemy having chosen a strong position on the hills just beyond Kedysville, began a sharp cannonade at 5 o'clock in the morning. He found our boys wide awake, who replied firmly and steadily to the attack.

Gen. FITZ-JOHN PORTER had thoroughly examined the field on the previous day, and a council of the Generals had made a disposition of the various army corps for the grand contest. It will be sufficient, for the present purpose, to state that Gen. BURNSIDE took command of the extreme left, while the other Generals occupied the enemy's front and right. BURNSIDE, with Gens. RODMAN, WILCOX, COX and STURGIS Brigades, extended his lines as far as to the southeast of Sharpsburgh, with the stone bridge across the Antietam Creek in his front. Between their position and that of the enemy, who lay toward the village at the northwest, is a succession of hills running nearly north and south, the highest and most abrupt of which is that rising from the bed of the creek. Gens. HOOKER'S and SUMNER'S corps have been conspicuous throughout the bloody day, the early part of the fight being over their part of the field, while a fierce and protracted struggle was going on at the Stone Bridge, where Gen. BURNSIDE commanded in person. In the latter place we lost, in the forenoon, several brave officers and men. Gen. HOOKER is reported wounded; Lieut. Col. THOMAS BELL, of the Fifty-first Pennsylvania Volunteers, was mortally wounded while leading his men to the attack at this place, and died soon after. Lieut. BEAVER, of the same regiment; Capt. MALCOLM WILSON and Sergeant HARRY H. STEWART, of the Second Maryland Regiment, Co. A, were also killed. Col. KINGSBURY, of the Eleventh Connecticut, was mortally wounded; and Adjutant ANDREW FOWLER, of the Fifty-first New York, is dead. Sergeant DAVIS, acting Lieutenant in the Twenty-first Massachusetts, had a leg badly shattered; Capt. MARTIN, Co. E, Second Maryland, lost a leg; and Color Sergeants OSBORN and HOOVER, of the Second Maryland, are both severely wounded; also Capt. NEILL, Thirty-fifth Massachusetts. I saw all these lying at a barn near the Stone Bridge, while the battle was progressing, having visited the spot for the purpose of obtaining a list (which is only partial,) of the killed and wounded.

I also saw lying dead on the field the following privates: James Kirby, Co. A, Second Maryland; Peter Daily, Co. I; Wm. Kelly, Co. H; Sergt. Jas. Clark, Co. H; John Q. Adams, Co. C; Daniel Fisk, Co. F, Sixth N. H.; Corp. Chas. M. Noyes, Co. K, Ninth N. H.; S. H. Case, Co. B, Seventeenth Mich.; Sergt. Howard Rand, Co. K, Sixth N. H.; Michael Boland, Co. G, Second Md.; —— Connerty, Co. G, Fifty-first N. Y.; Corp. Keefe, Co. I, Fifty-first N. Y.; Thomas N. Stockwell, Co. I, Fifty-first N. Y.; Robert C. Dale, Co. G, Fifty-first N. Y.; Geo. Summerlock, Co. A, Fifty-first Penn., and Thos. Davis, Co. I, Fifty-first Penn. I saw some half-dozen others on the east side of the bridge, whose names I could not learn, lying on the field. It was not safe to cross the bridge, but I was told several others lay on that side. It is impossible, in the present state of affairs, to obtain anything like an estimate of the numbers killed and wounded, but our losses have been very heavy.

The Irish Brigade, Gen. MEAGHER, in SUMNER'S corps, occupied a very prominent position, and the brave General. I am told, had a horse shot under him. Some report him killed, but I cannot now learn that it is true. He rode in front of his brigade, and waving his flashing blade in the air, beckoned on his men to the attack. Wherever they made a charge the rebel lines were seen to waver and fall back.

The rebels kept as much as possible under cover of the ravines, and seldom advanced to the attack, but there has never been a battle, probably, where there was so little of woods for the rebels to conceal themselves in. The fighting has been mostly in the open field, with the exception of the sharp contest at the stone bridge, where woods (not dense) line both sides of the stream—and a considerable block of trees occupying nearly the centre of the right, where HOOKER was engaged.

The rebels have been driven back at least two miles since the fight began, so that Sharpsburgh has been, during the afternoon, about the centre of the rebel lines.

Three times the rebel caissons have been blown up by our shells. Five different conflagrations have occurred on the field of barns and houses which were set on fire by exploding shells, or purposely fired by the enemy. While I write the whole heavens are lighted up by burning barns and wheat stacks. It is an immense conflagration.

I made the following memoranda of events while overlooking the field:

Capt. COOK'S Parrot Battery, Eighth Massachusetts, occupies the east hill opposite Sharpsburgh and the bridge, and does excellent practice on the enemy's position. Lieut. BENJAMIN, in charge of CARLISLE'S Battery, also doing splendid execution. Twice the enemy's battery of six guns had been silenced or compelled to withdraw from the opposite hill.

The musketry firing down at the stone bridge, where WILCOX and STURGIS are engaged, is sharp and continuous. At 11 o'clock squads of rebels are seen "getting up" the hill. Our batteries are playing on them, which hurries their time. Shells burst, and solid shot plow up the ground all around them. Cheers from the ravine. The Seventeenth Michigan (new regiment and all brave boys) are charging down to the help of WILCOX. Our infantry are seen charging up the hill, and our batteries are ordered to cease firing to avoid hitting them. They are turned on the rebel batteries, which now open on the hill to the right of Sharpsburgh. Our infantry advance, and are shelled by the rebel batteries, and compelled to lie down and finally retire under cover of the next ravine. Our 20-pounder Parrots upset the rebel guns. Splendid shots by BENJAMIN. The Forty-fifth New-York come to the rescue, and are pressing by us toward the bridge. Gen. BURNSIDE has just sent orders for Gens. WILCOX and COX to cross the bridge with their brigades and occupy the hills south of the town. Our troops again advance, and as soon as they show themselves a new rebel battery of four guns, on the hill at the left opens upon us. At 12 o'clock a rebel caisson is blown up, the third one since morning.

Sharpsburgh is now the centre of the action in our front, while HOOKER is actively at work on the right. The firing in that part of the field is terrific and unceasing. The rebel lines are seen drawn up along the ravines at the northwest, and occasionally attempting to advance. In each instance they are met and driven back.

At 1 o'clock the fighting at the Stone Bridge has ceased, and WILCOX and COX have all passed over. We now have a large force on the hills confronting the rebel lines. They keep up a constant cannonade upon the Union troops. At 1½ P. M. a squad of seventeen rebels are brought to Gen. BURNSIDE as prisoners, who orders them sent to the rear. The spokesman of the party says: "I don't think there is a man of us who doesn't want to get out of the fight." Gen. COX is ordered to move up and occupy the hills south of Sharpsburgh. At 2½ P. M. there is a temporary lull of the firing, but it is very short. At 4½ P. M. our troops push up the hill (the rebels always continue to have us on the down-hill side of the fight) and a large force appears at their extreme left, advancing toward them over the hill. A perfect storm of shot and shell now greet the advance of our boys from a half dozen different batteries at once. On the right of our advance our troops push up toward the rebel lines and are met half way, at a ravine, where a fierce musketry fight continues for half an hour. The balls strike up the dust in the plowed fields in all directions. The fight thickens, and so many batteries are in play, from so many different quarters, it is difficult to distinguish friend from foe. Dust and smoke completely envelope the battle-field.

On the left of the town the Union forces have now gained the crest of the hill, the rebels giving back under their steady fire, and cheers and shouts ring along the line. The rebel flag waves sulkily in the heavy air, in close proximity to the cheerful Red, White and Blue, borne into the thickest of the fight by our brave boys. The Union troops hold their position at the Sharpsburgh road for half an hour, while a deadly contest is going on. Our artillery, which has crossed the bridge, now takes up a position at the left, to check the advance of the rebels, who are trying to flank us, and open a brisk fire. On come the rebel hosts in overpowering numbers, to flank the force on the hill, and WILCOX'S Brigade, which has stood their ground for over an hour, now retire part way down the hill. A tremendous onset was now made from the south, the enemy apparently having received reinforcements, and our left is pressed back. The sun has set, but the contest only thickens with the close of the day. The enemy's shell begin to burst over our hospital near the bridge, and the horses at BENJAMIN'S Battery are shot at the guns. He is ordered by Gen. BURNSIDE to withdraw them. Stragglers come in from the field, some wounded, some *tenderly* escorting comrades who are wounded—it generally takes two or three to perform this service for one man, and all hands wear a gloomy countenance and limp. Gen. BURNSIDE orders them back to their regiments, with a sharp reprimand. Among these delinquents is a Lieutenant of the Sixteenth Connecticut Regiment, whom the General reprimands, and orders his name to be taken. He goes limping, and says a ball hit him in the leg. "But you walked all the way from the field—why did you come here to exhibit your cowardice? You had better remained at home," said the General sharply. At the same instant a youth, not over fifteen, who had his arm torn by a shell or ball, came up, holding the bleeding member in his other hand. "Look at that boy, Lieutenant, he has some excuse for leaving the field," but you have none. Shells now began to hum and burst all over the ground where we stood, and your correspondent began to think there might be danger in remaining longer in *that* place, so he *quietly* mounted his horse and *slowly* moved to the rear.

The rebels received a check soon after dark, and the contest ended for the night. It has been a most sanguinary fight. Our dead lie mingled with the rebel corpses on every part of this wide field—over a space of three or four miles. Many a poor fellow will lie on the cold, damp earth to-night, and pray for death to relieve him of his sufferings.

I shall endeavor to send fuller particulars of the fight than I am now enabled to do, as soon as they can be procured.

Both armies encamped on the field. To-morrow the dead must be buried, and possibly a renewal of the contest be had.

We shall have reinforcements of COUCH'S Division this evening, from Harper's Ferry. E. S.

Events Succeeding the Great Battle—The Rebel Retreat Foreseen—Heavy Losses—Some of the Killed and Wounded—Incidents, &c.

ON THE FIELD, NEAR SHARPSBURGH, Md., Thursday, Sept. 18, 1862.

There has been no engagement to-day—only occasional firing between the pickets, who continue to confront each other on substantially the same field where the contest closed at sundown yesterday. The body of the enemy—if there be any body remaining—are at least three miles further toward the river than they were at the beginning of the battle yesterday morning. Competent judges, with whom I have conversed, among whom is Gen. GRIFFIN—a careful observer, and well versed in the ways of the rebels—believe that they are merely amusing us by these exhibitions of force, while the army proper is really on the retreat to the river, and should this hypothesis prove correct, we shall have a most mortifying result for all the labor, loss and bloodshed of this Maryland campaign. The rebel leaders have drawn after them from Washington an immense army, with its enormous train, which has marched, toiled, fought, and been dragged for fifty miles, over three mountain ranges, at an untold outlay of strength, expense and suffering; they will have supplied their starving army with all it needed; slaughtered and wounded thousands of our brave Union soldiers, and then have escaped back to Virginia to laugh in their sleeve at our laggard way of following up our successes. The old-fashioned way of waiting for the rebel army to make the first move to attack; to choose their own field of operations to fight us; lie still or retreat as *suits their convenience,* seems to be the humor of the hour.

What motives of "strategy" or mysterious plans requiring *time* for development, explains this failure to attack the rebels to-day, a mere novice in warfare has no right to draw in question. But one thing seems apparent to me, the Union army are eager to be "up and at them," and make an end of this rebel *canaille,* and of the rebellion, while we have them and it in our power. The humblest Union soldier will feel the mortification of permitting this ragged and wolfish lazaroni to escape our clutches, by crossing again into Virginia.

In order to ascertain the number of the killed and wounded, as near as might be, so soon after the battle, and to obtain such names of prominent persons who have suffered, I passed over the field to-day, and went to nearly all the hospitals where the wounded are being gathered in.

While the wounded are still on the field, and no official returns are made, it is, of course, impossible to obtain anything like a correct list of the killed and wounded. Lists will soon be prepared, however, and full accounts be sent forward. Every house and large barn contiguous to the field, is occupied by the wounded, where, I am happy to say, provision has very promptly been made for dressing wounds and rendering them comfortable.

The troops in HOOKER'S, SUMNER'S and RICHARDSON'S corps have suffered greatly. Some officers of the General Staff estimate the number of wounded at 13,000, and say there are 5,000 on the field. My own judgment, after going pretty well over the ground is, that this estimate is greatly exaggerated, and that they do not amount to half that number, while the killed is very small in proportion to the wounded. I think six to eight hundred will cover the *killed,* and twenty-five hundred to three thousand the wounded, making a total of not to exceed *four thousand of killed and wounded.*

Gen. Rodman was shot through the body, the ball passing through the lung. Gen. Mansfield was instantly killed. Gen. Hooker was wounded in the foot. Gen. Hartsuff, of Rickett's Division, wounded in the right iliac region; a serious wound. Col. Beal, 10th Maine, in the thigh. Col. Richard Oakford, of Scranton, Penn., (132d Penn. Vol.,) was killed. Robert A. Abbott was seriously wounded in the lower jaw. Lieut. Jno. C. Dolan, injured in the hip by a shell. First Lieut. Sawyer, 7th Maine, killed, and about 100 privates of the same regiment wounded. Lieut.-Col. Fillebrown was thrown from his horse and injured, but not seriously. Gen. Max Weber was wounded seriously in the arm, and amputation may be rendered necessary. The Lieutenant-Colonel of the 49th New-York Volunteers, was dangerously wounded. Col. Kingsbury, of the Eleventh Connecticut, who was shot through the body twice and wounded in both feet, died this morning. Col. Childs, of the 4th Pennsylvania Cavalry, was killed while leading a charge on the right of the field. Gen. Richardson was wounded, and Gen. Hancock takes his command. Capt. Kelley, of the 6th Illinois Cavalry, was badly wounded on Monday in the mountain fight. Gen. Pleasanton's command, (his cavalry division and four batteries of horse artillery lost several other officers and men, whose names I cannot now obtain.

In Gen. King's Division the loss has been heavy; Col. H. A. V. Post, of the Second United States Sharpshooters, was wounded; also, Lieut. Chas. E. Cushing, Co. E, 22d New-York; Lieut. Whitman, Co. D, had his leg shot off—dead; Capt. Myers, Co. I, 14th Brooklyn—dead; Capt. O'Brien, Co. I, 24th Brooklyn—dead; Adgt. Parmele, 2d U. S. Sharpshooters—dead; Lieut. Seabury, 2d U. S. Sharpshooters—wounded; Lieut. Guest, 2d U. S. Sharpshooters—wounded; Capt. Chase, Co. A, 2d U. S. Sharpshooters—wounded; Sergeant-Major Shoot, 2d U. S. Sharpshooters—wounded.

In Caldwell's Brigade the loss was severe. The Fifth New-Hampshire Regiment have 119 killed and wounded, among which are fourteen officers. Some of these wounded are the following: Col. Cross, wounded in the head, slightly; Capt. Long, Co. G, wounded in the arm; Capt. Ranlet, Co. E, wounded in the thigh; Lieut. Graves, Co. H, forearm, slight; Lieut. Bean, Co. H, severely; Lieut. Gay, Co. H, mortally; Lieut. Parks.

KILLED IN MICHIGAN SEVENTEENTH REGIMENT.

Phelix Randall, Co. B.	Israel Colf, Co. C.
Andrew Saller, Co. C.	John A. Troy, Co. C.
Samuel Huut, Co. D.	S. H. Hooley, Co. D.
Martin V. Moore, Co. D.	Daniel McMartin, Co. D.
Benjamin Ward, Co. D.	Almeron Palmeter, Co. D.
H. A. Smith, Co. D.	Henry Tomlinson, Co. D.
Wm. Woodward, Co. E.	Alex. McKinnon, Co. D.
Robert C. Irvin, Co. E.	Corp. Miron Hawley, Co. D.
Ephriam Micks, Co. F.	[illegible] Gardner, Co. D.
Delos Vandeberg, Co. H.	Mason Kearney, Co. I.
Frank Belknap, Co. I.	Wm. Clay, Co. K.
Oliver Cheeney, Co. K.	Leonard Ives, Co. K.
David D. Tompkins, Co. K.	Total, 25.

Mr. IVES, of Providence, an Aid of Gen. RODMAN, received a severe flesh wound in the thigh by a piece of shell. Probably not mortal. Mr. IVES is a brother of Capt. J. POYNTON IVES, who commanded the *Picket* in North Carolina, under Gen. BURNSIDE.

The Seventh Maine regiment (Third Brigade, SMITH'S Division,) commanded by Major HYDE, went into the fight with 175 men and 14 officers, and came out with only 65 men and four officers unhurt.

Lieut. Butler, Co. A, was wounded and is missing; Capt. Jones, Co. B, wounded slightly; Adjt. Haskell was shot through both legs and his horse was killed; Lieut. Beason, Co. C, wounded in leg; Lieut. Goodman, Co. D, killed; Lieut. Emery, Co. E, wounded slightly; Lieut. Shorey, Co. F, wounded in the leg; Lieut. Warren, Co. H, wounded and missing; Capt. Cook, Co. I, wounded in leg; Lieut. Brown, Co. I, supposed killed; Capt. Cochran wounded in foot; Major Hyde wounded in hand and horse shot under him; not serious.

This regiment is now the body-guard of Gens. FRANKLIN and SMITH. The loss in this regiment is said to have been heavier than any regiment engaged, in proportion to numbers, since the beginning of the war. Their colors with "Williamsburgh" inscribed on them, were riddled with bullets. Capt. J. W. CHANNING has three bullet-holes through his clothes, and both he and Major HYDE came off the field with their clothing all bespattered with the blood of their comrades.

THE TURNER RIFLES.

Officers Killed.

Capt. Gustav A. Loreng, Co. C.

First Lieut. Jacob Pabol, Co. D.

Second Lieut. —— Krano, Co. G.

Some of the Wounded.

Capt. Robert Meikle, Pauls (?) Frick, —— Lohman, Capt. Weber, Lieut. Voelker.

Of enlisted men, there were twenty-six killed and eighty wounded.

THE FIRST DELAWARE—*Complete.*

Killed.

Capt. Watson, Co. A.	Corp. John Brierly, Co. A.
Capt. Leonard, Co. B.	Benjamin Lee, Co. A.
Capt. Richards, Co. C.	Minus J. Nelson, Co. E.
Ed. Moseley, Co. A.	Thomas Oskins, Co. A.

Wm. McCoy, Co. D—shot in both hands.
Emanuel Delasse, Co. F—left elbow.
Thos. G. Chance, Co. F—right knee.
Sergt. Chas. F. Holland, Co. E—right side.
Sergt. J. Spensley, Co. H—left foot.
James E. Clark, Co. K—right thigh.
John Marshall, Co. A—left leg.
H. L. Savage, Co. G—little finger and right hand.
Geo. R. Ellis, Co. E—left leg.
Thos. Y. McCullen, Co. B—right shoulder.
Clarkson Cloud, Co. K—right shoulder.
Jos. Windser, Co. A—left leg.
Robt. Brierly, Co. A—abdomen.
James P. Dickerson, Co. F—abdomen.
Perry Wright, Co. D—right hand.
Wesley Freeman, Co. G—ball through right shoulder.
Wm. Porter, Co. H—bayonet thrust in hip.
Jesse Hurd, Co. K—struck by shell in the breast.
James Forgsum, Co. I—ball through right leg.
James Hilleyard, Co. F—right hand.
James Ross, Co. F—hand.
Ed. Ingham, Co. A—spent ball in breast.
Albert Nelson, Co. A—ball in back.
Corp. Geo. Camperson, Co. D—left knee.
Thos. Thornton, Co. I—flesh wound in left arm.
Corp. Patrick McClusky, Co. C—arm.
Jesse D. Furls, Co. A—wrist.
Sergt. J. Martin, Co. A—hand.
J. J. Kerbaugh, Co. A—right hand and one thumb amputated.
David M. Johnson, Co. E—left shoulder.
Henry Morris, Co. F—leg.
Patrick McGarraty, Co. C—right eye.
Corp. Henry Vinning—spent ball.
Jos. Fitzsimmons, Co. F—hip and back.
John Barton, Co. F—flesh wound in leg.
Thomas Workman, Co. F—neck.
Wm. Veach, Co. A—flesh wound in hand.
H. S. Chaffer, Co. I—flesh wound in left ear.
Sergt. M. Hill, Co. C—right foot.
Lieut. C. Tanner, Co. H—breast.
Jno. Walker, Co. H—left leg.
Jno. Curry, Co. H—left hand and right thigh.
Corp. Jos. Booth, Co. H—groin and leg.
Anthony Cheevers, Co. H—shoulder and leg.
Color Corp. Lewis Corell, Co. H—flesh wd. finger.
Daniel Reed, Co. H—flesh, left shoulder.
Jno. Shepherd, Co. A—left shoulder.
Wm. Wahl, Co. G—flesh wound in finger.
Patrick O'Brien, Co. E—flesh wound in left breast.
C. Platt, Co. A—hit by butt of a musket in breast.
Corp. Duley, Co. H—head and breast.
John Sweeney, Co. A—left side.
Jasper Calhoun, Co. A—left wrist.

In Gen. BURNSIDE'S Corps there has been severe losses in officers and men. The great conflict culminated on the left, where he commanded, and a desperate effort was made to outflank WILCOX and COX'S Divisions, which had gained the summit of the hills, and were fast turning the tide of battle. The contest here was desperate and bloody. To-day I can see our dead scattered over the hill side up which our gallant boys fearlessly charged the enemy. Nothing in modern warfare could exceed the steadiness and courage of the troops, who fought on this part of the field. To-day they occupy the hill, only a quarter of a mile in rear of the position which they took yesterday. The enemy's batteries of seven guns on the left of Sharpsburgh and about the same number on the right of the town continue to threaten our front lines. No material change has occurred since last evening in the position of the forces, but *we occupy the field of battle.*

Gen. BURNSIDE and Staff have remained constantly on or near the field, watching intently every movement of the rebels, who keep themselves habitually out of sight. We ought to learn a lesson from them in this respect. This afternoon the General and his Staff and his Aids might all have been seen lying on the ground, under the shelter of a large wheat stack during a heavy rain. Let those who covet the glory and labors of the battle-field follow the march, and share the toils of our *working Generals,* and they will soon have enough of war.

On the right, in the extreme front, I found General COCHRANE, this morning, with his entire brigade engaged in picket service. Two hundred yards in advance of where he and Adjutant ROOME were, our lines of sharpshooters were lying along the ground, within short rifle range of the enemy's pickets. Every two or three minutes the sharp crack of rifles, and the "bim-m-m" of the bullet was heard, in some cases passing directly overhead or on either side. Behind them, in a large plowed field, the rebel dead lay very thickly scattered about, in every conceivable position; while muskets, bayonets and the *debris* of the previous day's battle covered the ground. Beside the fence of a small square burying-ground I counted

[*Continued on Eighth Page.*]

10

Engineering

As they had in the Mexican War of 1846–48, military engineers played a significant role in the Civil War, providing both mapping and construction services. Union and Confederate engineers constructed forts and batteries, demolished enemy supply lines, and conducted siege warfare. They are possibly best remembered for building pontoon and railroad bridges quickly and, often, under fire. In support of the Union attack on Fredericksburg, Virginia in December 1862, Union engineers laid six pontoon bridges across the Rappahannock River under devastating fire from Confederate sharpshooters. The 2,170-foot pontoon bridge, which Union engineer troops laid across the James River in June 1864 as the Army of the Potomac approached Petersburg, Virginia, was the longest floating bridge erected before World War II.

Also during the Civil War, many officers with an engineering background served as combat leaders. Drawn largely from the top of their graduating classes at the U.S. Military Academy at West Point, the men of the prewar U.S. Army Corps of Engineers included many excellent military strategists who rose to leadership roles during the war. Among them were Union generals George McClellan, Henry Halleck, and George Meade, as well as Confederate generals Robert E. Lee, Joseph Johnston and P. G. T. Beauregard.

Engineers/Pioneers

Before the war, the U.S. Army Corps of Engineers consisted of less than 600 men, who were responsible for all engineering work undertaken by the regular army. In addition a small unit of Topographical Engineers was charged with mapmaking and surveying. The formation served in the Army of the Potomac, and often functioned as a combat unit as well as serving in their technical capacity. Additional volunteer engineering units were also raised; two regiments from New York and the 1st Michigan Engineers and Mechanics Regiment. Other independent engineering companies were also formed, and specialist pontoon and bridging units were attached to most Union armies. On both sides, the importance of the engineering arm was understood, and engineering officers were frequently attached to the staff of senior commanders.

In the Confederacy, a Corps of Engineers was formed in Virginia and merged with other State engineering units to form the Confederate Corps of Engineers in early 1861. By 1863, the corps contained two regiments. When required, infantrymen were drafted into *ad hoc* Pioneer Corps by both sides in order to assist in the construction of field fortifications.

Right: Artist's impression of Lincoln's Emancipation Proclamation being read by a Union soldier to a slave family in their cabin.

Below: The original caption for this photograph was "a full sap." the earthworks are being prepared by men of the 1st New York Engineers as men of the 54th Massachusetts look on.

ENGINEERS/PIONEERS

In the Confederacy, slaves or civilians could also be employed in this manner. As the war progressed, the Confederacy placed an increasing emphasis on the use of field fortifications in order to help offset the Union's numerical superiority. During the Siege of Petersburg, Virginia (1864), engineers were assisted by thousands of temporary "pioneers" in order to build the most extensive field fortifications of the war.

Right: In both armies, engineers such as these became increasingly important as the Confederates came to rely on field fortifications to offset the Union army's numerical superiority. These men are part of the U.S. Engineer Battalion in front of Petersburg, August 1864.

Below: Lieutenant Colonel Quincy Gillmore was an engineer who achieved success as a field officer when he used heavy guns to destroy the walls of Fort Pulaski at the mouth of the Savannah River and effect its capture, spring 1862.

Right and Below Right: Bridge-building was crucial to the logistical elements of the Civil War. Men, ordnance, provisions—all had to be moved by train (wagon or railroad) and had to cross the many wide rivers of the United States.

Europe during the war, Role of

For the Confederacy, the prospect of overt support from the major European powers, particularly Britain and France, was the major goal of foreign policy. At the very least they hoped for diplomatic recognition of secession, while the Europeans could also have intervened to break the Union naval blockade, or even to impose a peace settlement. In pursuit of these goals, diplomatic missions were backed up by attempts to use cotton as an economic weapon. The diplomacy of the Union was directed in turn to frustrating these possibilities. Despite British and French government sympathy for the Southern cause, neither recognition nor intervention followed.

Both sides turned to Europe for shipbuilding capacity and imports vital to the war effort, although the significance of these was far greater for the South with its much weaker domestic economic base.

Ewell, Richard Stoddart (1817-72)

A career soldier, Ewell resigned his commission in the Union army in 1861 and became a brigadier general with the Confederacy. He fought under "Stonewall" Jackson and succeeded him as commander of the Confederate II Corps in 1862 after fighting through the Shenanadoah Valley. Ewell's column led Lee's army across the Potomac in June 1862 after an impressive victory at Winchester, where his troops scattered the Union garrison and took 4,000 Union prisoners. Ewell appeared to be a worthy successor to Jackson, but his style of leadership was very different.

"Old Baldy" lost his leg at Second Bull Run, and although the wound had healed by the time of Gettysburg, Ewell was uncharacteristically hesitant. At the end of the first day he missed an opportunity to seize the hills south of the town that could have led to a decisive Confederate victory. He was shot on the first day of Gettysburg while talking to General Gordon. "Are you hurt, sir?" enquired Gordon. "No," Ewell replied. "It don't hurt a bit to be shot in a wooden leg."

Ewell led II Corps throughout the hard-fought Wilderness Campaign of 1864, but at Spotsylvania one of his divisions was virtually destroyed and Ewell relinquished command shortly after. Ill-health had provoked his departure, but Lee made it permanent. Ewell took over the defense of Richmond in 1865, but finally surrendered after being captured at Sayler's Creek in April 1865.

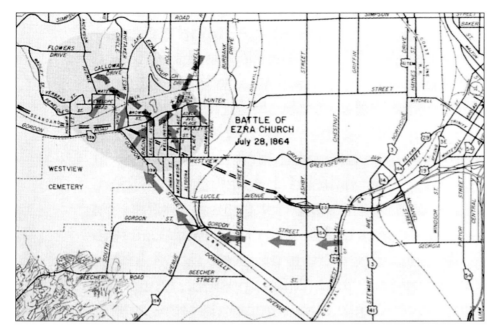

He was a capable officer, but as a commander, he demanded precise instructions, and lacked the brilliance and initiative of some of his peers.

Ezra Church, Battle of, 1864

In May 1864 Union Major General William T. Sherman embarked from Chattanooga on his campaign to take Atlanta. By July 21 the Confederate commander facing him, General John B. Hood, and his Army of Tennessee had been forced within Atlanta's defenses. After the Battle of Atlanta on July 22, Sherman decided to send Major General Oliver O. Howard in command of the 30,000-strong Army of the Tennessee round the city to attack it from the west. Hood sent out Major General Stephen D. Lee's corps, followed by Major General Alexander P. Stewart's corps, and the two sides met at Ezra Church crossroads on July 28.

The Confederates were beaten back and the 3–5,000 losses they sustained (compared to approximately 500 Union casualties) would further weaken Hood's hold on Atlanta.

Above Left: The Battle of Ezra Church was one of a number of engagements which resulted from General Hood's policy of aggressive defense around Atlanta.

Left: Pontoon bridges built by the Army of the Potomac's Corps of Engineers at Brunswick (formerly Berlin), Maryland, October 1, 1862, during the pursuit of Lee's army after Antietam.

Below: General Richard Ewell was one of Lee's most able lieutenants, and served in the Army of Northern Virginia until his capture during the Appomattox campaign.

THE AMERICAN CIVIL WAR: A VISUAL ENCYCLOPEDIA

175

Fair Oaks/Seven Pines, Battle of, 1862

Since the Unionists' disaster at Bull Run in 1861, Union Major General George B. McClellan had built up the powerful Army of the Potomac. In March 1862 McClellan moved his army of over 100,000 men by water onto the Virginia peninsula, to march on Richmond inland. Facing him on the peninsula was General Joseph E. Johnston with 60–70,000 troops, but by May Johnston had retreated to ten miles west of Richmond, behind the Chickahominy River. As McClellan advanced he split his army in two, with the two corps of Major General Samuel P. Heinzelman and Major General Erasmus D. Keyes (40,000 men) south of the Chickahominy. Spring rains had rendered the river impassable along much of its course, and Johnston knew that this was his chance to strike a damaging blow against McClellan's divided forces. Johnston planned a two-pronged attack on Keyes' isolated corps in the van, but confusion, however, dogged the Confederates' attack on the morning of May 31. Although Major General D. H. Hill's Confederate division on the right wing reached Brigadier General Silas Casey's Unionist division, Hill waited in vain for the left wing led by Major General James

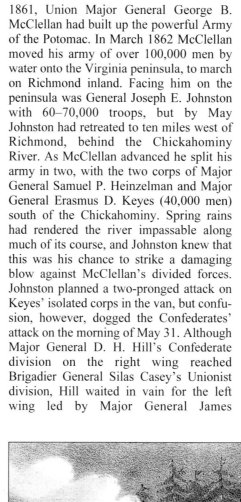

THE AMERICAN CIVIL WAR: A VISUAL ENCYCLOPEDIA

Longstreet. By 1:00pm Hill could wait no longer and launched his attack on Casey. The attack pushed the Unionists back to their second line at Seven Pines, held by the majority of Keyes' corps, but there the Confederates' attack stalled. The delayed Confederates' left wing had also been also halted north of Seven Pines at Fair Oaks Station by the unexpected arrival of Union Brigadier General Edwin V. Sumner's corps which had crossed the river on a precarious bridge. Johnston was seriously wounded in the fighting at Fair Oaks and the Confederates withdrew towards Richmond the next day. The Confederates

lost 6,000 men in the inconclusive battle compared to Unionist losses of 5,000.

Farnsworth, Elon John (1837–63)

A Union cavalry general, Farnsworth enjoyed a brief, but spectacular, career. With little military experience, he was appointed lieutenant in September 1861, and was promoted to brigadier after heroic work at Chancellorsville. He was killed at Gettysburg while charging Confederate infantry dug in behind stone walls—a dangerous maneuver whose wisdom Farnsworth questioned.

The Battle of Seven Pines (Left) halted the advance of General McClellan's Army of the Potomac across the Chickahominy Creek (Above), part of his drive on Richmond.

177

Farragut, David Glasgow (1801–70)

At the outbreak of the Civil War, Farragut was an experienced but undistinguished naval officer, having joined the navy as a midshipman at the age of nine.

In 1862 he was tasked with capturing New Orleans, a major Northern objective that would open up the Mississippi and split the Confederacy. He ran the gauntlet of the guns on Forts Jackson and St. Philip, sank four ships in a small Confederate squadron, and captured New Orleans in a daring night raid. The Union now had a base from which to attack the deep South.

Farragut's approach to battles combined a fixed purpose with flexible tactics, and these methods ensured his success. At Mobile Bay in 1864 Farragut faced similarly strong defenses. Although he was by now fifty-three years old, frail and suffering from vertigo, he lashed himself to the riggers of his flagship *Hartford*, and navigated his ship into mine-strewn waters, famously urging the fleet on with the command, "Damn the torpedos! [the contemporary name for mines] Full speed ahead!" He described the battle as "one of the fiercest naval contests on record," and his victory, which closed the Confederacy's last Gulf port, played an important part in Lincoln's reelection.

Farragut was a native of Virginia and his loyalty to the Union was questioned at the start of the war. By the end, he was a Northern hero and the first to hold the U.S. ranks of rear admiral, vice admiral, and admiral.

Inset: Portrait of David Farragut in 1866 just before he became Admiral of the Navy.

Right: Shelling Forts Jackson (Right) and St. Peter (Left) as the fleet passed on April 24, 1862. The vessels illustrated are the USSs *Varuna*, *Brooklyn*, *Pawnee* (although she wasn't present at the action), *Hartford*, *Pensacola*, *Mississippi*, *Louisiana*, and *Manassas*.

Field Defenses

Experience soon taught the senior officers and ordinary troops that traditional cavalry and infantry charges across open ground to engage in hand-to-hand combat with the enemy were an increasingly risky tactic. They were as likely to result in the attackers suffering severe casualties well before they could reach the enemy line. An example of the risks involved can be illustrated by the Union's 81st Pennsylvania Regiment at the Battle of Fredericksburg in December 1862. The unit consisted of 261 officers and enlisted men, and suffered close to sixty-eight percent casualties during an attack. Firepower was becoming so devastating that it could smash any attack or pulverize any unit left in the open to protect a vital position. Consequently, cover became increasingly important to both the attack and defense. Attackers used field defenses to secure captured ground, while defenders, often outnumbered, used them to keep what they had.

Aside from making increasing use of natural or man-made preexisting cover on the battlefield—such as woods, sunken roads, and railroad embankments, for example—troops quickly learned to shift for themselves. If an important but exposed position was to be held at all costs, an area's natural defensive features enhanced, or an attack imminent, they constructed field defenses. It was rare for officers to need to tell their men to carry out such duties. Their scale, sophistication, and the degree of protection they offered very much depended on the time available and the materials to hand. At their most basic, they might consist of simple scrapes in the ground, dug out using knives, bayonets, tin cups, and plates—or bare hands. The evacuated soil was simply piled up in front of the shallow hole, which would accommodate anything from a single individual to a handful of men.

As a rule, entrenching tools were not issued to ordinary soldiers, and pioneers with the necessary tools were in short supply. Suitable entrenching equipment might be borrowed from nearby artillery units, which tended to be better equipped with the necessary tools. Despite their apparent crudeness, such scrapes were often sufficient to stop a bullet. If more time was available, these simple defenses might become more elaborate. They might be reinforced by materials close at hand, including logs, picket fencing, rocks, and boulders, and be camouflaged. They might also become deeper, thereby allowing the occupants a better chance of reloading their weapons without exposing them to enemy fire.

Not all field defenses involved digging rifle pits, however. Some were built above ground, but these tended to be more time-consuming to construct. Revetted earth embankments of chest height were built on occasion and proved sufficient strong to protect the defenders from both smallarms and artillery fire. Other barriers that found a place on the battlefield included walls of felled trees and branches.

However, field defenses were not considered permanent features, ones to be manned for weeks, if not months as in sieges. In the end the ordinary soldier had to leave his field defenses behind and defeat his opponent in open battle or by maneuver.

Finance

Though the Civil War was expected to be short and relatively low in cost, it would end up as the most expensive activity yet undertaken in the history of the United States government. Initially, it had been expected to last about ninety days. Few could have imagined the four bloody, costly years. The Civil War was more than three times as expensive in constant dollar terms than the combined cost of all of the previous wars that the United States had fought. The total cost to both sides is estimated to have been approximately $5.2 billion in 1860 dollars. This translates to the equivalent of $104 billion at the turn of the twenty-first century.

Prior to the Civil War, and during the conflict's early months, government intervention in the economy was generally hands-off, with few measures to control wages and prices. There were a few exceptions. Railroads were under government regulation, and armament production was partially under state control, although more so in the South. Aside from these exceptions, the market economy dictated the material costs of war materiel and services.

Treasury Secretary Salmon Chase initially financed the war effort by borrowing, but within a year, this was seen as no longer viable. The Lincoln Administration turned to taxes, seen as necessary not only to provide partial funding, but to maintain the confidence of the banks to continue to lend money to finance the war. The Revenue Act of July 1862 increased taxes dramatically and introduced the first Federal income tax, which was collected by the dreaded Office of Internal Revenue, a precursor to the Internal Revenue Service. Intended to be temporary, the income tax was not repealed until 1872. (Though the concept of income tax was declared unconstitutional in 1894, it was to be institutionalized in 1913 by the 16th Amendment.)

The income tax rates under the Revenue Act were slim compared with today, being three percent on incomes between $600 and $10,000 and five percent above that. At the same time, there were taxes on stocks, deposits, profits, and inheritance. Tax stamps were introduced for use on medicine, cosmetics, and playing cards. The income tax rates were raised in 1864 to five percent on incomes from $600 to $5,000, ten percent on incomes over $10,000, and 7.5 percent in between.

Increasingly, battles in the war became dominated by the use of field defenses. Confederate generals were forced to exchange maneuverability for protection in an effort to offset Union superiority in numbers. The field defenses around Atlanta (Right) were typical of these entrenched lines.

Five Forks, Battle of, 1865

By March 1865 Lieutenant General Ulysses S. Grant's stranglehold on General Robert E. Lee's Confederate Army of Northern Virginia besieged at Petersburg was nearing its conclusion. Lee's last chance to continue the conflict was to break away and join General Joseph E. Johnston's Army of Tennessee in North Carolina. Although Major General John B. Gordon managed to take Fort Stedman for Lee on March 25, Grant counterattacked with Major General Philip E. Sheridan's cavalry, supported by an infantry corps. Lee reinforced the line with five brigades led by Major General George E. Pickett, but on April 1 Pickett's forces on the Confederate right wing collapsed at the Battle of Five Forks, with the loss of up to 5,000 men, compared to Unionist casualties of 2,500.

Lee was forced to evacuate Petersburg and Richmond, and a week later surrendered his army to Grant.

Flags

Flags were used for a variety of reasons during the war—as signs of allegiance, as symbols of a military unit's origins and its battles, and as a means of communication. The most obvious flags were those chosen to represent the Union and the Confederacy. The Union, not willing to acknowledge the breakaway of the South, continued to fly the flag of the United States, while the South adopted a number of designs to reflect its independence. These generally appeared in a combination of the colors red, white, and blue, with a number of white stars, reflecting the first group of states to secede or the final number.

Unit flags included those used by corps (more common in the North) and those carried into by individual regiments. In the latter case, Northern units flew two flags—the national color, which had the unit's details placed on the central strip, and a regimental color, usually comprising an eagle on blue background. Beneath the eagle was a scroll, again detailing the unit.

Southern units tended to carry two types of flag. First, there was the battle flag of the Confederacy; second, a state flag—examples might include the Texan "Lone Star." Battle honors were common on flags of most types. Infantry flags tended to be roughly square.

Flags were also used as a means of signaling. Semaphore, the waving of colored flags in a set pattern to convey messages, was used by both sides, but had obvious limitations—it only worked in daylight and needed a clear line of sight. The use of flags was only one of several methods of transmitting information, which included couriers, flares, lights, and telegraphy.

Left: The Battle of Five Forks was fought almost four years after General McClellan's unsuccessful drive on Richmond.

Below left: Pickett's Charge, complete with "Old Glory."

Below: Various configurations of the Union flag were encountered during the war, bearing thirty-two stars in several patterns. Although today the Confederate "battle flag" is that which is most readily identifiable, it was not the national flag of the Confederacy. After 1863, the battle flag design was incorporated into the upper canton of the national flag.

Above Left: The battle flag of Battery "K," 1st U.S. Artillery, lists the engagements in which the unit took part. These included battles in the Mexican-American War as well as the Civil War.

Left: The regimental color guard of the 7th Regiment, New York State Militia, displays the national color, the regimental flag, and company guidons.

Above: Confederate troops garrisoning northern Florida were at a disadvantage, given the unchallenged Union control of the state's coasts. These are seen in the Warrington Naval Yard, Pensacola, in 1861.

Florida

Florida was one of America's eleven slave-holding states at the outbreak of the Civil War, and seceded on February 1, 1861. On May 9, 1862, Major General David Hunter, the Union commander responsible for Florida, Georgia, and South Carolina, took it upon himself to abolish slavery there without Lincoln's knowledge or permission—this proved a politically unsound move, providing fodder for the Confederate, anti-Union Press and driving many of the people of Florida to ally themselves to the Confederates.

In 1863–64, when the Confederates were most hard pressed for want of food and supplies, they found themselves unable to transport Florida's abundant resources to where they needed them. The Southern forces in Florida surrendered in early May 1865.

On January 1861, as Florida seceded from the Union, U.S. Army officers stationed at Pensacola and Key West moved to secure Fort Pickens near Pensacola, Fort Taylor in Key West, and Fort Jefferson in the Dry Tortugas for the Union, ensuring they had access to strategic outposts in the South. Subsequently, the Union army occupied most of Florida's coastal forts and

towns. After this Florida saw minimal large-scale fighting, however, and with the exception of the Olustee campaign and several small raids into the interior, the Union army usually remained near its forts and occupied cities.

Immediately following the southern bombardment of Fort Sumter, on April 12, 1861, Union forces landed at Pensacola, Florida to reinforce Fort Pickens. The ensuing standoff at Pensacola continued for several months, during which time the Union forces carried out a raid in which they burned a southern ship, and in early October the Confederates launched a large, nighttime raid on Santa Rosa Island. On October 9, approximately a thousand Confederate troops assaulted the island and overran the Union army regiment that was camped there. They were forced to withdraw, however, after Union reinforcements from Fort Pickens arrived.

Following defeats in Tennessee in early 1862, most Southern troops were transferred out of the state, Confederate national officials having determined that Florida's long coastline was too large an area to defend. By May 1862, Confederate forces had withdrawn from Pensacola, thus ending the year-long standoff.

After the withdrawal from Pensacola in early 1862, Union troops quickly occupied the area of extreme northwest Florida. On the northeast Florida coast, at Fernandina, Jacksonville, and St. Augustine, a large Union naval force pressured the southern forces to evacuate.

Although military action on its soil was limited, Florida made a major contribution to the Confederate war effort, namely through supplying much-needed foodstuffs the southern armies. These resources were a target for regular, small scale Union military operations, including cavalry raids in south Florida to seize cattle, navy raids against saltworks along the coast, and the Union naval blockade to prevent the import and export of goods.

Foote, Andrew H. (1806–63)

A highly experienced naval officer, Commodore Foote was placed in command of Union naval operations on the upper Mississippi. He led the fleet of Union gunboats that assisted Grant's capture of the vital Fort Henry and Fort Donelson in Tennessee in 1862.

A teetotaller, he helped abolish the liquor ration in 1862.

Forrest, Nathan Bedford (1821–77)

A brilliant Confederate cavalry tactician, Forrest was a wealthy planter in Tennessee before the Civil War. In 1861 he enlisted as a private, then raised a cavalry battalion at his own expense. Known as "the wizard of the saddle," he ended the war a lieutenant general, the only man on either side to rise so far from the ranks.

As part of the Army of Tennessee, he escaped capture at Fort Donelson in 1862 by leading his force through a gap in Union lines. He excelled at lightning raids and at winning battles when the odds were stacked against him. At Murfreesboro in 1862 he led a raid behind Union lines to capture 1,000 prisoners and valuable supplies. He led from the front and, as a consequence, was wounded four times and had thirty horses shot from under him during the war.

Forrest had an uncanny ability to predict his opponent's next move. At Brice's Cross Roads, in 1864, he realized that given the muddy roads and extreme heat, Union cavalry would arrive well before the infantry, giving him time to fight the cavalry alone, on his own terms. Sherman acknowledged Forrest as "the most remarkable man our Civil War produced on either side," but in 1864 he was so rattled by Forrest's highly effective raids that Sherman vowed to capture Forrest "if it costs ten thousand lives and bankrupts the Federal treasury."

Forrest was charged with the slaughter of surrendering black soldiers in April 1864, although he denied responsibility.

Fortifications

Forts are military works constructed to protect installations, localities, and troops. Two basic classes of fortification can be identified:

Right: Nathan Forrest was a gifted Confederate cavalry commander, but his reputation was tarnished by his ideological belief in white supremacy.

Far Right: During the siege of Petersburg, Union field fortifications were protected by powerful siege guns, such as this Confederate ten-inch Rodman smoothbore.

Below: Fort Sumter.

permanent, usually of great strength and built in times of peace as protection against surprise attack; and field, usually built during campaigns to meet the needs of the moment. Permanent fortifications are initially more elaborate than field fortifications, but in protracted campaigns the latter often develop into the form of permanent fortifications.

The development of fortifications is directly related to the advance in weapons, for, as weapons grew more powerful and achieved greater range, the defender was forced to strengthen and extend his fortifications. The earth and wood barriers of early forts gave way to masonry, yet by the sixteenth century artillery had gained the ascendancy and even heavily fortified structures became vulnerable. Military engineers were forced to return to earthworks, and developed a style whose principal features persisted in practically all fortifications constructed before the outbreak of World War I. The works were based on a wide ditch, retained on the near side by the scarp wall and on the far side by the counterscarp. Earth excavated from the ditch formed a sloping parapet, which gave elevation above the foreground; the upper step of the reverse side of the parapet formed a platform for infantry and the lower one for artillery. On the opposite bank of the ditch, which was the key to the fortress defense, the glacis slope protected the rampart from direct fire and gave protection to troops assembling for a sortie. To ensure that all parts of the ditch could be covered by flanking fire, projections known as bastions were built into the outer wall. Later the simpler and cheaper polygonal fort was introduced. A fine surviving example of a polygonal fort can be seen at Fort Monroe, Virginia, and another at Governor's Island, New York.

In the nineteenth century, the ever-increasing range of artillery caused major changes in the art of fortification. The outerworks, developed to keep the artillery at a safe distance from the area to be protected, proved inadequate. Redoubts (short entrenchments open to the rear) were constructed around the defended area and several hundred yards to the front.

Right: A Union gun crew serve their piece on the Water Battery of Fort Brady, a fortification built to contain the Confederate naval forces operating on the James River.

Page 190–91: Fort Mahone was the lynchpin of the Confederate defenses around Petersburg in Virginia. This photograph was taken after its capture by the Union IX Corps.

THE AMERICAN CIVIL WAR: A VISUAL ENCYCLOPEDIA

Forts were developed early in North America to protect the civilan population against hostile attack, and on the frontier developed into centers of commerce and trade.The U.S. Army had built a large number of these forts by the mid-nineteenth century, some of which remain in use as military outposts even to this day. Strategically situated at important road and river junctions, or on prominent high ground, during the Civil War they were hotly contested. The inland forts east of the Mississippi River were generally fortifications surrounded by a wall or stockade; in the west they were usually buildings for housing troops, arranged around a rectangular parade ground.

Examples of permanent fortifications that played a prominent role in the Civil War are found at Fort Pickens and Fort Pulaski, Florida, Fort Monroe, Virginia, Fort Jackson and Fort St. Philip on the Mississippi, and Forts Henry and Donelson on the Tennessee and Cumberland Rivers respectively. With the exception of Henry and Donelson, these were all built prior to the war in accordance with current doctrine, typically featuring masonry outer walls.

Fortifications came in many forms, ranging from the permanent yet vulnerable brick-built structures such as Fort Morgan, Alabama (Inset) pictured after its capture by the Union in 1864, to field fortifications (Left).

THE AMERICAN CIVIL WAR: A VISUAL ENCYCLOPEDIA

193

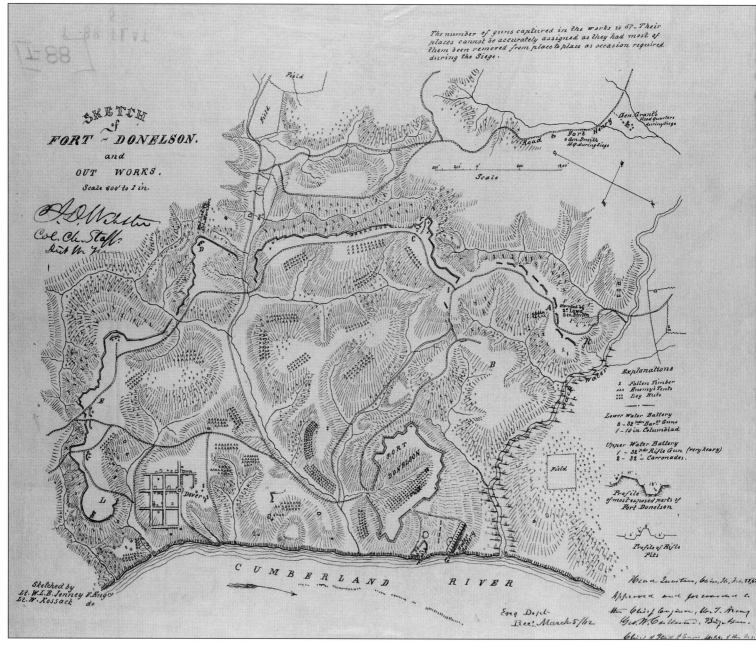

FORT DONELSON

Success in the Battle of Fort Donelson made Brigadier General Ulysses S. Grant's name as a leading Union commander. In February 1862, under the command of Major General Henry W. Halleck, Grant led a force against the strategically crucial Fort Henry on the Tennessee River and Fort Donelson on the Cumberland River, which commanded the water routes into Confederate Tennessee. Grant's 15,000 men were carried on river transports and escorted by a fleet of shallow-draft ironclad gunboats commanded by Flag Officer Andrew Foote. Fort Henry was only lightly defended and fell on February 6 following a bombardment from Foote's gunboats, without Grant's troops having to fire a shot.

Grant's next objective was Fort Donelson, twelve miles east of Fort Henry, but this was in a stronger defensive position high above a bend of the Cumberland River, with two creeks to the landward side, and its batteries included twelve heavy

guns and eight additional field guns. The garrison initially numbered 6,000, under the command of Brigadier General Bushrod R. Johnson, but General Albert S. Johnston, who had command of all Confederate forces from the Appalachian mountains to the Mississippi, sent a detachment of 10–12,000 troops under Brigadier General John B. Floyd and Brigadier General Simon B. Buckner from his main army at Bowling Green, and a further detachment under Brigadier General Gideon Pillow, to reinforce Fort Donelson.

The winter weather slowed Grant's progress along the roads from Fort Henry to Fort Donelson, but by February 12 his infantry and cavalry were in position to besiege the fort. Grant's first attack on the 13th, on the Confederate left, was beaten back. On the 14th, Grant's force was reinforced by a division under Brigadier General Lew Wallace sent from Major General Don C. Buell's army to the west which was facing Johnston's Confederate

army at Bowling Green and the same day Grant launched a serious assault on the fort.

At 3:00pm, Foote took six gunships, which had arrived the night before, to attack the fort from the river, but the Confederates' water batteries inflicted heavy damage to the fleet, including seriously wounding Foote, and by the end of the day it became clear that the fort's defenses were too strong for a water-borne assault.

Fort Donelson's commanders, however, decided they could not survive a siege, and planned to break out through Grant's lines and escape to the south. On the morning of the 15th the Confederates attacked and succeeded in breaking Grant's right wing, leaving the way open to for the garrison's forces to escape towards Nashville. However, confusion and hesitation between the Confederate commanders led to the Confederate advance being halted, and by the end of the day the Unionists, despite losing 2–3,000 men compared to

Confederate losses of about 500, had pushed the Confederates back to their original defenses. That night the Confederate generals decided that they were unable to break out and had no option but to surrender the garrison. Floyd and Pillow escaped upriver with a small number of troops, and on the morning of February 16 Buckner requested a cease-fire to discuss surrender terms. Grant famously replied, "No terms except an unconditional and immediate surrender can be accepted." Buckner ordered the garrison to lay down its arms and although 7,000 Confederates escaped, 13,000 were captured. The loss of Fort Donelson was a serious blow to the Confederates as it broke open Johnston's defensive line, forcing him to fall back through Tennessee.

FORT FISHER
Wilmington lay on the Cape Fear River, whose entrance was guarded by Fort Fisher. Built on a sand spit, the fortification used sand earthworks to form the strongest defensive position in the Confederacy; forty-four heavy guns, guarded by minefields and trenches. A Union fleet of sixty vessels was assembled; the largest naval force of the war. An initial assault on Christmas Day 1864 was

a failure, but on January 13, 1865, the fleet began a non-stop bombardment of Fort Fisher which lasted for sixty hours. The 40,000 shells fired into the position demoralized the garrison, and caused 300 casualties. On the afternoon of January 15 a force of 8,000 Union troops assaulted the fort, coming under heavy canister and rifle fire. Despite heavy casualties, the attackers entered the fort, and after a bitter hand-to-hand struggle lasting into the night, the defenders were forced to surrender.

FORT HENRY
Built by Albert Sidney Johnston to defend the Tennessee, Fort Henry fell to Grant (then under Halleck) on February 6, 1862, and was part of the campaign in which Grant first established a name for himself in the Union camp.

The attack on Fort Henry was Grant's idea, as he had correctly identified it as a weak point in Johnston's line—the fort was built on a low bank overlooked by hills and vulnerable to flooding. On February 5, Grant launched his attack on land and water simultaneously, and as most of Johnston's 2,500 men had been sent to defend Fort Donelson, Henry fell easily. The capture of Fort Henry put Grant between Johnston's two main forces.

Above: Armstrong gun defending Fort Fisher, North Carolina. The photograph was taken in January 1865.

Above Left: A sketch map of Fort Donelson and the defensive works surrounding it.

FORT HINDMAN
Standing on the White River, Arkansas, Fort Hindman boasted mounted eleven guns. On January 4, 1863, Major General John A. McClernand joined forces with Sherman and Rear Admiral D. D. Porter with the intention of capturing it. Troop transports towed eleven gunboats up the Arkansas River towards the fort in a bid to save fuel, and after more than a day of bombardment the Confederate commander, Brigadier General Thomas J. Churchill, surrendered with thirty-six officers and men. The taking of Fort Hindman yielded 6,500 prisoners and an important post for the Union.

FORT JOHNSTON
Together with Fort Moultrie in the north and Fort Sumter in the center, Fort Johnston defended Charleston Harbor. This was the southernmost of the three forts, and was taken at once by the Confederates upon

Above and Below: Fort Mahone was one of the string of forts defending Petersburg.

Right: The coal and wood yards of the Quartmaster Department, Fort Monroe.

Below Right: Fort Sumter, in Charleston Harbor, against which the opening shots of the war were fired.

the secession of South Carolina in January 1861. Confederate defenses remained in place at Fort Johnston until February 17, 1865, when, following the fall of Columbia, they were forced to abandon their posts and marched to join Lee and the Army of Northern Virginia.

FORT MACON
The Confederate Fort Macon was located near Beaufort, North Carolina. It took over a month of siege before the Southerners were forced to surrender their position—from March 23, 1862, the rebels put up a dogged resistance. However, on April 25 the Union forces under John G. Parke bombarded the fort from the water side, dismounting half the Confederate guns—surrender followed that same afternoon.

FORT MAHONE
This fort defended the Confederate city of Petersburg, whose fate was bound up inextricably with that of the Confederate capital of Richmond. Following the Union victory at Five Forks on April 1, 1865, Grant ordered a general assault on Petersburg the very next day. Fort Mahone held out against the onslaught of Parke's IX Corps on April 2, but further west VI Corps under

Above and Below: Two similar views of the bombardment of Fort Sumter in April 1861 which led to its capture by the Confederacy.

Above Right: The Federal position inside Fort Sumter.

Below Right: Union soldiers celebrate the fall of Fort Fisher.

FORTIFICATIONS

Wright made a decisive breakthrough and Vicksburg was taken

FORT MONROE
Located on the James River, Virginia, Fort Moultrie was the base from which General McClellan mounted his siege of Yorktown, moving his troops there by steamboat on April 1, 1862, prior to the Yorktown campaign. Following his success at Yorktown, President Lincoln himself traveled to Fort Monroe to personally command the gunboat operations against Sewell's Point on the James.

Fort Monroe was a traditional point for "flag-of-truce" boats to move between Confederate and Union lines, and as the Southern surrender approached in 1865 Lincoln issued passes for three Confederate Commissioners to enter Union lines there.

Right: Fort Sumter.

Below Right: the storming of Fort Fisher.

Below: Grant's first major victory in the west—the capture of Fort Donelson on February 15, 1862.

FORT MOULTRIE
Together with Fort Johnston to the south and Fort Sumter in the center, Fort Moultrie was one of the forts defending Charleston Harbor. Located on Sullivan's Island to the south of the harbor mouth, it was from here that Major Robert Anderson moved his Federal garrison to the more defensible and commanding Fort Sumter on December 26, 1860, when hostilities between North and South became a looming inevitability, spiking the guns and cutting down the flagpole to ensure a Confederate flag would not fly from it.

FORT SUMTER
Positioned on a man-made island in the center of Charleston Harbor, this fort commanded Forts Moultrie to the south and Johnston to the north, and it was to Sumter that Major Robert Anderson moved his Federal garrison in December 1860 when war became inevitable.

The opening shot of the Civil War was fired on Fort Sumter, which fell to the Confederates on April 13, 1861, without casualties and following two days of bom-

bardment. After twenty-two months under siege and bombardment, it was finally retaken for the Union by Sherman after the evacuation of Charleston following his "total war" campaign. On April 14, 1865, now a major general, Robert Anderson raised the Stars and Stripes over Sumter again.

FORT WAGNER
Fort Wagner was a Confederate earthwork defending Charleston Harbor. The doomed Union attack on the fort on July 18, 1863, was a minor battle in the Charleston campaign, but one which would change northern perceptions of black American soldiers, earning them respect at a time when anti-Abolitionism and racial distrust were growing amongst the Northern population. Of the two units that launched a bold frontal attack on Fort Wagner, one was the 54th Massachusetts Infantry—a crack corps of black soldiers under Abolitionist Robert Gould Shaw. The 54th penetrated and held the fort for an hour before falling back, and their repulse cost them half of their regiment, including Shaw.

Forts Henry and Donelson Campaign

Confederate reverses in coastal areas were accompanied early in 1862 by serious setbacks in Kentucky and Tennessee. Federal forces under Major General Henry Halleck, commander of the Department of the Missouri, and Brigadier General Don Carlos Buell, commander of the Department of the Ohio, faced Confederates under Albert S. Johnston. These forces clashed in January at Mill Springs, driving southern troops from eastern Kentucky. Of more significance was a move into western Kentucky and Tennessee initiated in January by land troops from Halleck's department led by Brigadier General Ulysses S. Grant, which held the prospect of breaking the thinly held Confederate line extending from Columbus, Kentucky in the west to Cumberland Gap in the east, as well as cutting a number of important railroads including the vital route running from Memphis to Chattanooga. This connected at Chattanooga with roads that extended to Richmond, Virginia, and Charleston, South Carolina. By following the Tennessee, Cumberland, and Mississippi rivers, Union commanders recognized that they could penetrate to the heart of the Confederacy.

From the outset their Southern adversary recognized that the Cumberland and Tennessee rivers, which coursed deep into Confederate territory, would be high on the list of strategic targets for the Union. However, although the Tennessee plunged right into the heart of the Confederacy, Johnston's immediate concern was the Cumberland, which coursed past Clarksville, Tennessee, the site of the South's second largest ironworks, and Nashville, his base of supply. If Union gunboats were allowed free passage on this waterway, they could destroy the bridgeheads and render his fragile rail supply situation untenable.

To countermand this threat, the Confederacy ordered the construction of Fort Henry and Fort Donelson at sites along the Tennessee and Cumberland, respectively, at a point where the rivers were only twelve miles apart. However, Fort Henry was badly sited on low ground subject to flooding and dominated by high ground across the river. Johnston's engineer, who arrived in late November 1861, noticed the

Above Right: Confederate Major General Patrick R. Cleburne who was killed at Franklin on November 30, 1864.

Right: General John Hood led the Confederate Army of Tennessee against the isolated defenses of General Schofield's XXIII Corps at Franklin, and although the attack led to the retreat of the defenders, over 7,000 Confederate soldiers were lost in the assault. In late 1864 the Confederacy could ill afford such heavy losses.

problem immediately but despite his labors, by mid-January had still not found a solution.

Fort Henry fell to Flag Officer Foote's Federal ironclad fleet and the rising flood waters on February 6, 1862. Fort Donelson was sited much better, and Foote's fleet came out on the worse end of a heavy artillery duel with the fort. It was left to Ulysses S. Grant's infantry to take Fort Donelson, which fell on February 16, 1862. This, in turn, gave the Union access to the Cumberland River and opened the way to Nashville, one of the Confederacy's most important supply centers, and forced Johnson to concede territory as he moved from his defensive positions across Kentucky.

France during the war, Role of

The French ruler, Louis Napoleon, although ultimately unwilling to break ranks and recognize the Confederacy without British backing, was able to play on Southern expectations both in the hope of securing cotton imports and to boost his own imperial ambitions in Mexico. Although British and French diplomats often expected a Union defeat and did discuss joint intervention to break the blockade, in the event no such action was taken. French troops captured Mexico City in June 1863 and installed the Hapsburg

Archduke Maximilian as Emperor, but by early the following year French interests within Europe had shifted and Southern efforts to use Mexico to secure recognition failed.

Franklin, Tennessee, Battle of, 1864

After the fall of Atlanta to Major General William T. Sherman on September 1, 1864, General John B. Hood took the remaining 35,000 Confederate troops of the Army of Tennessee southward. He then moved north of Atlanta, planning to cut off Sherman's vital rail supply link with Chattanooga and to lure the Unionists away from Atlanta. Sherman left Atlanta in late September to pursue Hood, but when Hood in October decided to continue north through Tennessee towards Nashville, ultimately to join General Robert E. Lee's army in Virginia, Sherman returned to Atlanta and dispatched two corps under Major General D. S. Stanley and Major General John M. Schofield to join Major General George H. Thomas' divisions already in Tennessee to deal with Hood.

In mid-November Hood linked up with Major General Nathan B. Forrest's cavalry corps and headed for Nashville, now with 40–50,000 troops. Thomas had not yet fully concentrated his Army of Cumberland and ordered Schofield's approximately 30,000-strong corps to

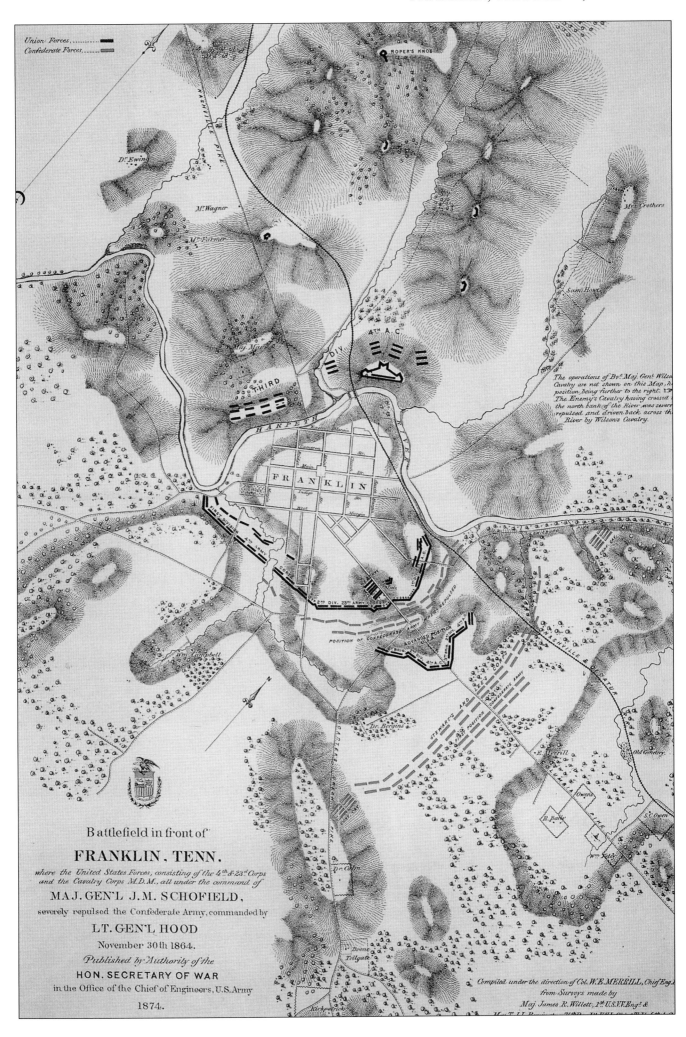

Union Forces.
Confederate Forces.

The operations of Bvt. Maj. Genl. Wilson's Cavalry are not shown on this Map, his position being further to the right. The Enemy's Cavalry having crossed to the north bank of the River, was severely repulsed and driven back across the River by Wilson's Cavalry.

Battlefield in front of

FRANKLIN. TENN.

where the United States Forces, consisting of the 4th & 23d Corps and the Cavalry Corps M.D.M., all under the command of

MAJ. GEN'L J.M. SCHOFIELD,

severely repulsed the Confederate Army, commanded by

LT. GEN'L HOOD

November 30th 1864.

Published by Authority of the

HON. SECRETARY OF WAR

in the Office of the Chief of Engineers, U.S. Army

1874.

Compiled under the direction of Col. W.E. Merrill, Chief Eng.l from Surveys made by Maj. James R. Willett, 1st U.S.V.V. Eng.s &

delay Hood until he could join him with a greater force. Schofield managed to block Hood's advance on Columbia, Tennessee on November 26 and then evaded the pursuing Hood, fighting a delaying action at Spring Hill on November 29 to take up position to the north around the town of Franklin. On the afternoon of November 30 Hood finally caught up with Schofield and launched a massive frontal attack, sending two corps of infantry (20,000 men) across open ground toward the Union defenses. Hand-to-hand fighting continued for over five hours during which the Confederates suffered heavily, losing 6,500 men, including five generals killed, compared to the Unionists' 2,300 casualties, and Schofield managed to withdraw his forces that night towards Nashville.

Fredericksburg Campaign

After Pope's defeat at the Second Bull Run, Lee made a customarily bold and audacious move against Federal forces in Maryland. He split his force, sending a third to attack Harper's Ferry, while advancing against a army nearly twice as strong as his own. The 12,500-man garrison at Harper's Ferry surrendered to Jackson on September 15, but Lee's invasion of Maryland was disrupted when the plan of operations fell into McClellan's hands and only by hasty replanning was McClellan's resulting attack repulsed at South Mountain and Crampton's Gap. At Antietam Creek on September 17, 1862, the two armies met again and the Confederates were comprehensively beaten. Following this action, McClellan failed to press home the initiative against a much-reduced Confederate force. Lee retreated from Antietam the following night, but despite continuing urging from Lincoln, McClellan could not be induced to pursue. During the period of October 10–12, Stuart's cavalry again rode completely around the Federal army and did over $250,000 in damages, causing the government much embarrassment. On November 7, Lincoln fired McClellan and replaced him with Ambrose E. Burnside.

General Burnside inherited the 120,000-strong Army of the Potomac on November 7, 1862. Within two days, he proposed abandoning McClellan's ponderous southwesterly advance in favor of a forty-mile dash across country to Fredericksburg. Such a maneuver would position the Federal army on the direct road to Richmond, the Confederate capital, as well as ensure a secure supply line to Washington.

President Lincoln approved Burnside's initiative but advised him to march quickly. Burnside took the President at his word and launched his army toward Fredericksburg on November 15. Two days later the lead units arrived opposite Fredericksburg on Stafford Heights.

Burnside's swift march placed General Robert E. Lee and his Army of Northern Virginia at a perilous disadvantage. After the Maryland Campaign, Lee had boldly divided his 78,000 men, leaving Lieutenant General Thomas J. "Stonewall" Jackson in the Shenandoah Valley, while sending Lieutenant General James Longstreet to face the Federals at Culpeper. Lee had not anticipated Burnside's shift to Fredericksburg and now neither of his wings was in position to defend the old city. The Confederate army thus guarded a long stretch of the Rappahannock, unsure of where the Federals might attempt a crossing.

Burnside's offensive began well enough, stealing a march on Lee and moving rapidly down the Rappahannock River, planning to cross over to Fredericksburg on December 19, 1862. The Rappahannock was the largest of several river barriers that flowed across his path to Richmond. Once across the river, the Federals would strike Longstreet's overmatched defenders, outflank Jackson, and send the whole Confederate army reeling toward Richmond.

Because the civilian bridges had been destroyed earlier in the war, Burnside directed that pontoon equipment meet him at Stafford Heights. A combination of miscommunication, inefficient army bureaucracy, and poor weather delayed the arrival of the floating bridges. This gave Lee the opportunity to shift his forces to cover the crossing. Excellent defensive terrain overlooked Fredericksburg on the south bank and Lee proceeded to construct prepared positions for his troops. When the pontoons finally appeared on November 25, so had the Army of Northern Virginia.

Failing to recognize the perils of an attempt on Lee's strengthened lines, Burnside assaulted across the river at the Confederate positions, but his troops were

Above Right: Union troops attack Fredericksburg across the Rappahanock. Note the pontoon bridge-building at right.

Below: The southern outskirts of Fredericksburg, Virginia, photographed shortly after the battle. Marye's Heights are marked by the trees in the distance, beyond the last houses on Hanover Street.

FREDERICKSBURG CAMPAIGN

cut down before they even came near the enemy lines. So were the repeated, costly attacks that followed. However, Lee had insufficient troops to launch his own counterattack and on the evening of December 15–16, Burnside skillfully withdrew his army to Stafford Heights, dismantling his bridges behind him, thus bringing an end to the Fredericksburg Campaign and Burnside's career—Lincoln dismissed him in January of the next year.

Although undoubtedly a tactical triumph, the Battle of Fredericksburg proved to be a hollow victory for the Confederates. The limitless resources of the North soon made good the losses in manpower and materiel. By contrast, Lee struggled to replenish both. The Battle of Fredericksburg, although profoundly discouraging to Union soldiers and the Northern populace, made no decisive impact on the war. Instead, it merely postponed the next "On to Richmond" campaign until the spring.

THE BATTLE
The delay in the arrival of Burnside's bridging equipment was crucial for Lee. It enabled him to rush Lieutenant General James Longstreet's corps to Fredericksburg. It dug in on the ridge above the town on November 21, followed by Lieutenant General Thomas J. Jackson's corps. Even after his bridging equipment arrived, Burnside was slow to act but in early December he made up his mind to attack Fredericksburg across two sets of pontoons built directly across the river from the town, with another set a mile or two to the south. Lee had advised the citizens of Fredericksburg to evacuate the town, and although the Unionists starting building the bridges on the night of December 10/11, Confederate sharpshooters in the buildings on the waterfront held up the Unionists' progress across the river the next day. From his positions on the high ground above Fredericksburg Lee could see exactly where the battle would be fought and concentrated his 78,000-strong Army of Northern Virginia at the two crossings, with Jackson's corps forming a line to the south of the town and Longstreet's corps and artillery along rising ground behind the town.

Burnside eventually managed to get his troops across the river on December 11/12 and was ready to attack at dawn on December 13. He had arranged his army in three wings: Major General Edwin V. Sumner's and Major General Joseph

THE AMERICAN CIVIL WAR: A VISUAL ENCYCLOPEDIA

207

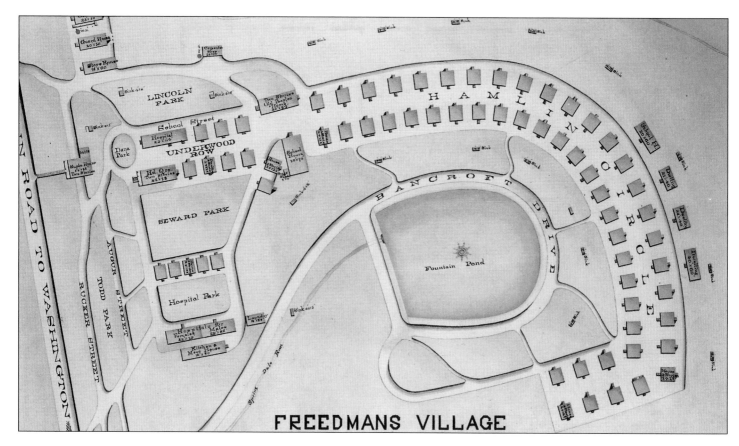

FREEDMANS VILLAGE

Hooker's divisions on the Unionists' right were to advance on Longstreet's corps on Marye's Heights behind Fredericksburg while Major General William B. Franklin's divisions on the left wing were to take on Jackson. Franklin sent forward a division in the south under Major General George C. Meade, but although it broke through Jackson's lines, it was poorly supported and was driven back by a Confederate counterattack. By the afternoon the fighting died down in the stalemate.

At midmorning the Unionist attack on the Confederate left wing started, Sumner's and Hooker's divisions attacking Marye's Heights in waves. The Confederates held their line behind a wall protecting the Sunken Road and their concerted rifle fire, supported by artillery, inflicted huge casualties amongst the Unionists attacking across the open ground. The Unionists attacked in vain until nightfall, when Burnside was persuaded by his generals to halt the assault. They had suffered 12,600 casualties compared to Confederate losses of 5,300. On December 15 the Unionists recrossed the Rappahannock, abandoning the campaign.

Freedman's Village

When President Lincoln emancipated the slaves of Washington, D.C. on April 16, 1862, liberated slaves seeking refuge from their previous owners were originally housed at the Old Capitol. However, this accommodation soon proved unsanitary and unsafe, as former slave owners would often raid the camp to steal back what they saw as their "property." In May 1863 Arlington House was finally chosen as the new home for freed slaves, and was dedicated to them on December 4 of the same year. Originally designed as a temporary refuge, it was inhabited by these "Freedmen" for over thirty years, and soon developed into a real community with schools, farms, hospitals and churches—this settlement was known as "Freedman's Village."

Frémont, Major General John Charles (1813–90)

A celebrated explorer known as "the Pathfinder," Frémont was an ambitious and talented man, but his talents did not lie in the field of military leadership. His exploration of the American West made

him a national hero and he was a presidential candidate in 1856. He was a keen Abolitionist and the South threatened to secede if he was elected. In 1861 Lincoln gave him command of the Western Department, but was removed after he emancipated Missouri's slaves on his own authority. As commander of the Mountain Division in 1862, he was humiliated by "Stonewall" Jackson and resigned when Pope replaced him.

Front Royal, Battle of, 1862

Major General Thomas J. Jackson's brilliant Shenandoah Valley Campaign of spring 1862 successfully tied down a large number of Unionist soldiers in the defense of Washington. His three divisions of 17,000 men bettered three Unionist armies in the campaign, notably at the Battle of Front Royal. Threatened from the north by Major General Nathaniel Banks with 9,000 men and Major General John C. Frémont's 15,000 men from the south, Jackson was able to use the speed of his "foot cavalry" to defeat Frémont on May 8, and then on May 23 he forced Banks' army into retreat when 3,000 of his troops overran the 1,000-strong Union garrison at the Battle of Front Royal, capturing most of the defenders for the loss of fifty-two Confederate troops. Following his victories, Jackson eluded the Unionists in a rapid march to join General Robert E. Lee's Seven Days' Campaign.

Fugitive Slave Acts

The Fugitive Slave Acts of 1873 and 1850 were a major source of friction between North and South. Northern Abolitionists mobilized to thwart attempts to return escapees under the acts, while Southern slaveholders became increasingly outraged by the failure of Northern courts to enforce their property rights.

The 1793 Act proved hard to enforce in the face of anti-slavery magistrates and free state personal liberty laws. In 1850 as part of the Clay compromise, Congress passed a much more effective act imposing penalties on those aiding escapees and enjoining federal marshals to recapture fugitives. Bitter disputes followed, notably the case of Anthony Burns in Boston in 1854, which aroused further hostility on both sides of the sectional divide.

Left: Major General John C. Frémont was a noted explorer and national hero, but his reputation was tarnished by his lackluster military performance.

Far Left: Freedman's Village was located across the Potomac River from Washington, in Arlington, Virginia.

GEORGIA

Georgia

Seceding on January 19, 1861, Georgia was the fifth state to do so. Initially non-committal in its politics, the consistent ill treatment of Georgia by the Union drove more and more Georgians towards Confederate sympathies. In May 1862 Major General David Hunter announced the abolition of slavery in Georgia, without Lincoln's sanction, and began confiscating the property of slaveholders. In 1864, Georgia suffered Sherman's "total war" campaign, as he marched through the state leaving a swathe of destruction fifty miles wide between Atlanta and Savannah—although the fall of Atlanta prompted the Georgian mayor to exempt his militia from the need to serve in the Confederate army, it also drove anti-Union sentiment to its peak.

Above: In 1864, General Sherman invaded Georgia along this road, leading south from Ringgold toward Dalton, Georgia. In the distance to the south is Mill Creek Gap, the site of the first line of Confederate defences.

Left: The temporary prison camp in Andersonville, Georgia, expanded into the largest and most notorious prisoner of war facility in the South. This photograph, by A. J. Riddle, was taken on August 17, 1864, at a time when some 33,000 prisoners were housed in the camp.

THE AMERICAN CIVIL WAR: A VISUAL ENCYCLOPEDIA

Gettysburg Address

One of the most memorable and important speeches in American history, the Gettysburg Address is all that more amazing for its having been penned on the back of an envelope as President Abraham Lincoln was traveling by train to Gettysburg, Pennsylvania, to dedicate the military cemetery there in November 1863. The Battle of Gettysburg, which occurred between July 1 and 3, 1863, had been the turning point of the Civil War, and the bloodiest battle fought in the Western Hemisphere. For the latter reason, the dedication of the National Cemetery was expected to be an especially emotional moment.

The main event of the dedication ceremony, which occurred on November 19, 1863, was a two-hour speech by Edward Everett, the most celebrated public speaker of the age. After he spoke, Lincoln "added a few words" with his own address. The brilliance of his "few words" stunned the audience, and within days the address had been quoted in newspapers throughout the United States. The next day, Everett wrote to Lincoln, "I wish that I could flatter myself that I had come as near to the central idea of the occasion in two hours as you did in two minutes."

In the coming years, the Lincoln address would become a cornerstone of American oratory. Over the next century, nearly every child attending school in America would memorize the speech. However, after the 1960s, when American history as taught in schools was deeply purged of much of its important substance, this practice was largely abandoned.

There were several versions of the speech written in Lincoln's hand. The accepted version is that which he rewrote after the fact to include some ad-libbing he'd done while he was speaking. It is as follows:

"Four score and seven years ago our fathers brought forth on this continent a new nation, conceived in Liberty, and dedicated to the proposition that all men are created equal.

"Now we are engaged in a great civil war, testing whether that nation or any nation so conceived and so dedicated, can long endure. We are met on a great battlefield of that war. We have come to dedicate a portion of that field, as a final resting place for those who here gave their lives that that nation might live. It is altogether fitting and proper that we should do this.

"But, in a larger sense, we can not dedicate—we can not consecrate—we can not hallow—this ground. The brave men, living and dead, who struggled here, have consecrated it, far above our poor power to add or detract. The world will little note, nor long remember what we say here, but it can never forget what they did here. It is for us the living, rather, to be dedicated here to the unfinished work which they who fought here have thus far so nobly advanced. It is rather for us to be here dedicated to the great task remaining before us—that from these honored dead we take increased devotion to that cause for which they gave the last full measure of devotion—that we here highly resolve that these dead shall not have died in vain—that this nation, under God, shall

Right: The bloody battle of Gettysburg that prompted Lincoln's Gettysburg Address.

have a new birth of freedom— and that government of the people, by the people, for the people, shall not perish from the earth."

Gettysburg Campaign

The Battle of Gettysburg was the culmination of a two-month campaign in the summer of 1863. It has been said that no more important battle was fought between Waterloo and the Marne than the one at Gettysburg. It was the turning point in the war, not only in time but in military fact, for after it the Confederate fortunes began to wane.

Although the Gettysburg battle itself looks on paper to have been an almost circumstantial encounter, the Confederacy laid the path to the Pennsylvania battleground well in advance. In the aftermath of the successful Chancellorsville campaign, Lee was faced with a dilemma, this stemming from the knowledge that his recent defeat of the Federal Army of the Potomac at the Battle of Chancellorsville—daring example of superior generalship though it had been—had really only bought him time. True, the battle had succeeded in repelling the Federal armies from much of Virginia and eased the threat to the vitally important capital of the Confederacy at Richmond, but Lee knew it would only be

a matter of time before the powerful Federal host moved south again.

Lee's dilemma was defense or attack— whether to dig in and prepare to fight another defensive battle for Richmond, or to assume the initiative and attack. Some Southern politicians thought he should stand on the defensive and that Johnston or Bragg should be reinforced for a major offensive in the west, but Lee advocated following up the advantage won at Chancellorsville. The attacking option was obviously the more dangerous, since the Confederates were significantly outnumbered, but it did present certain advantages, and Lee was making a name by his ability to overcome against long odds. Besides the

advantage of retaining the initiative, the Confederate army was short of supplies, including food, clothing, and—no less important to a marching army—shoes. A thrust into Pennsylvania presented an opportunity to correct those deficiencies, and as an additional potential benefit, foreign recognition for the Confederacy. Also, it would strengthen the position of the Northern Democrats, who were pressing for peace with the South. Perhaps the greatest influence on Lee's decision, however, was his natural aggression; relinquishing the military initiative to the enemy and siege warfare were alien to him. The matter was debated by the Confederate Cabinet and despite some objections and misgivings about such a bold venture on the part of the Confederate President, Jefferson Davis, Lee was eventually granted permission to undertake an invasion of the North.

At Chancellorsville, Lee had lost his best commander, his "right arm," General "Stonewall" Jackson. Jackson was but one of many good commanders that Lee could call on—Longstreet, the "Old Warhorse," Ewell, and Hill all had proven ability in battle—but however capable, none of these men had the gift of military genius that Jackson had demonstrated. For the campaign, the Army of Northern Virginia was reorganized into three corps; Longstreet retained command of I Corps, and Ewell and Hill were promoted to the command of II and III Corps, respectively. Lee's cavalry commander, J. E. B. Stuart, was another who had proved himself, although in the upcoming campaign his relentless

Above Left: John Reynolds of the Union I Corps was one of the Army of the Potomac's best corps commanders. He was killed on the first day of the battle.

Above: Much of the fighting on the second day centered around Little Round Top.

Left: The battlefield, viewed from the Union lines looking towards Seminary Ridge.

self-agrandisement began to color his decision-making.

While the leadership of this Army of Northern Virginia was little afflicted by personal differences, the opposite is true of its Federal counterpart. Powerful, large, well-clothed, and well-armed, but much misused, the Army of the Potomac was a "long-suffering" organization. In two years past its veterans had fought six battles, incurring five defeats and a draw that could only be called a bitter failure. During this period, they had served under as many commanders, each of whom had demonstrated command inferiority to his Southern counterpart.

Despite the setbacks, the men in the ranks displayed no air of being a defeated army, which is a credit to their tenacity. Among them was the pride and cohesion that had been a trademark of the Southern forces from the outset. Some of the credit for this can be attributed to the army's corps and division commanders—men like Sedgwick, Sickles, Hancock, Reynolds, and Slocum. All of them would prove critical in the upcoming campaign. The Army of the Potomac's latest commander, appointed only on June 28, was Major General George Gordon Meade. While having little time to cope with his new responsibilities, a decisive struggle was about to be thrust upon him without warning.

The invasion of the North began on June 15, when the leading divisions of Ewell's corps crossed the Potomac river near Sheperdstown into Maryland. Officially still loyal to the Union, the state had provided several excellent combat units to Lee's army. On June 19, Confederate troops marched over the Maryland-Pennsylvania border, creating a threat to the cities of Baltimore and Washington that was intended to provoke a response from Meade. At no stage, it would seem, did Lee have a clear idea of where exactly he wished to fight the decisive battle. His orders to Ewell were unspecific, only to advance on a broad front, allowing progress and directions to be determined by the "development of circumstances."

During the preliminary fighting, Ewell used his freedom well. Early in the campaign, during the advance north, he orchestrated the capture of three Federal garrisons near Winchester, Virginia. As a new corps commander, this was an impressive start. The ebullient Stuart, by contrast, was deflated at the Battle of Brandy Station on June 9, the largest cavalry fight of the war. Although his forces eventually repulsed the Northern horsemen, whose attack had caught him by surprise, Stuart's reputation was tarnished. His chastisement led him to perform another "glory ride" to redeem his reputation, and while off on this enterprise, he left Lee's army virtually blind to Federal positions and movements.

Gettysburg was a small, prosperous farming town. When a Southern brigade first passed through it, its commander noted that it contained a shoe factory. On June 30, a Confederate brigade was sent to appropriate some of these shoes, but withdrew because of a large Federal force seen heading towards the town. On July 1 it was the scene of the final decisive battle of the war, and when it ended, it ended in defeat for the Confederacy, or at least for its hopes of bringing a crushing defeat upon the North. But in the aftermath of the desperate three-day struggle, which culminated in the famous Pickett's Charge, Meade failed to launch the counter-punch that would have surely brought crushing defeat.

After the battle, Lee ordered his army into a defensive posture, and as July 4 came and went, he decided to retreat back into Virginia. Meade, to Lincoln's chagrin, was slow to pursue and by July 14, despite some clashes with the Federal cavalry in rearguard actions, Lee was back across the rain-swollen Potomac River. Meade crossed in pursuit, but Lee managed to cross both the Rappahannock and the Rapidan rivers, and by August 4, the two armies were more or less back where they

had started at the beginning of the campaign. It seems certain that had Meade followed up his resounding victory with a hot pursuit of the defeated and extremely vulnerable Confederate forces, the Civil War would probably have ended in autumn of that year, rather than dragging on for two more long and bloody years. After Gettysburg, no other major land actions occurred in the east until spring of 1864.

THE BATTLE

In June 1863 General Robert E. Lee invaded Unionist territory for the second time in the war. On June 23 Lee's Confederate Army of Northern Virginia crossed the Potomac River and entered Pennsylvania. When news of the invasion reached Washington, the Unionist Army of the Potomac, under the command of Major General Joseph Hooker, set off north in pursuit. Although neither army knew the exact whereabouts of the other they were converging on the small crossroads town of Gettysburg, which was to become the site of the most famous battle of the war. Although Hooker was replaced in command by Major General George C. Meade on June 28, the Unionist pursuit continued, forcing Lee to

turn before he could cross the Susquehanna River to establish his invasion of the North. On June 30 Major General John Buford led two advance cavalry brigades into Gettysburg and set up a defensive position on McPherson's Ridge. That afternoon a Confederate patrol ran into Buford's troops and as news of the close proximity of the two armies reached Meade and Lee, the commanders ordered their forces—94,000 Unionists and 77,000 Confederates—to close in on Gettysburg.

At 8:00am the next morning, July 1, Confederate Major General Henry Heth's division reached Buford's defensive positions. Although initially outnumbered, the Unionists managed to hold their line until Major General John F. Reynolds' Unionist infantry corps arrived later in the morning. The battle expanded as the Confederates' attack was joined by Lieutenant General Ambrose P. Hill's corps on the west flank and Lieutenant General Richard S. Ewell's corps to the north. The Unionists were hard pressed by the superior Confederate forces, Reynolds being killed, and as Lee arrived on the battlefield midafternoon, Ewell broke through the Unionists' line, despite it being reinforced by Major General Oliver

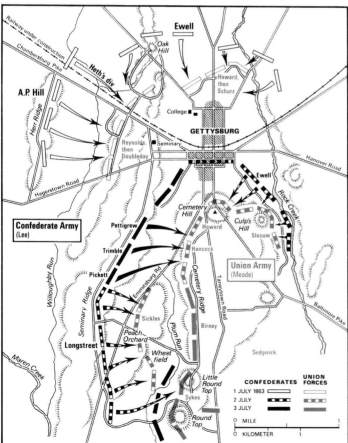

O. Howard's corps. Ewell did not follow up this breakthrough and the Unionists were able to fall back to join Major General Winfield S. Hancock, who had assumed command of Reynold's troops, on Cemetery Hill. As the fighting died down on the first night of the battle, both sides received further reinforcements. Meade arranged his forces in a defensive line along the high ground centered on Cemetery Ridge, with Major General George Sykes' corps at the south, then (from south to north) Major General Daniel Sickles' corps forming a salient, Hancock's corps, Howard's corps and Slocum's corps holding the north, to the right. Lee's attack did not occur until 4:00pm when Lieutenant General James Longstreet's corps assaulted the Unionists' left at the south. The Confederates reached the high ground several times, almost breaking through the Unionists' line on both their left, and later right where Ewell launched his attack late in the day, but again the Unionist line held, and at nightfall the Confederates fell back.

Having tried Meade's flanks Lee resolved on a frontal assault the next day, July 3. Meade still held the ridge, his line strengthened with the arrival of Major General John Sedgwick's corps on the far left wing of the Unionists' line, but Lee also had fresh troops— Major General George E. Pickett's division and Major General

Above: The battlefield around the Devil's Den, looking west from Little Round Top.

Left: Map of the battle.

Far Left: On the third day of the battle, the Union defense of Cemetery Ridge proved too tough for the Confederates to break.

J. E. B. Stuart's cavalry. At 1:00pm Longstreet started an artillery bombardment of Cemetery Ridge, answered by Unionist artillery, then as the guns fell silent Longstreet launched his attack on Meade's center.

At 3:00pm 13,000 Confederate infantry led by Pickett marched in formation across the open ground towards Cemetery Ridge, into a wall of fire from the well-placed Unionist infantrymen and artillery. Thousands of Confederates fell in the attack, although a handful reached the Unionists lines before the attackers were forced to fall back. Lee was forced to admit defeat and the next day withdrew his army towards Virginia. The bloodiest battle of the war had claimed 28,000 Confederate casualties and 23,000 Unionist casualties, and although Meade's army was too exhausted to pursue Lee, it marked the end of Confederate ambitions to bring the war home to the North.

Gilmore, Quincy Adams (1825–88)

Gilmore was a skilled Union engineering officer. An instructor at West Point before the war, he devised the plan to capture Fort Pulaski, Georgia in 1862 and recaptured Fort Sumter in 1863, a propaganda coup, if not a critical military objective. He earned steady promotion from captain in 1861, to major general in 1864.

Gorgas, Josiah (1818–83)

General Gorgas was chief of the Confederate Ordnance Bureau. He supervised the construction of arsenals and foundaries, despatched agents to smuggle arms from the North, and sent blockade-running ships to the Caribbean to collect munitions delivered from Europe. More than any other individual, he kept the Confederate war machine supplied.

Grand Gulf, Mississippi

Grand Gulf, thirty miles north of Vicksburg, was the site of Confederate defenses designed to obstruct the passage of vessels down the Mississippi. The defenses there were not equal to the Union bombardment that was leveled at them, however, and were soon destroyed in the first heavy attack they suffered.

Grant, Ulysses S. (1822–85)

Ulysses S. Grant was one of the outstanding commanders of the Civil War, a man of courage, conviction and strategic genius.

He grew up in Ohio, the son of a tanner and farmer; as a child he acquired considerable skill in handling horses and in 1839 he won a place at West Point, despite having absolutely no interest in things military. Having fought in the Mexican-American

THE AMERICAN CIVIL WAR: A VISUAL ENCYCLOPEDIA

Above Right: Panorama of Gettysburg and its surroundings viewed from the southeast, showing how the small Pennsylvania town formed the hub of a network of roads.

Right: Ulysses S. Grant, one of the outstanding commanders of the Civil War.

Far Right: Union dead litter the battlefield around Peach Orchard. Over 50,000 American soldiers lost their lives in the battle which proved the turning point of the war.

War, he married Julia Dent, the sister of his roommate, in 1848. When the Civil War broke out, he was a civilian, working in his father's tanning business. In September 1861 he was appointed brigadier general, and he swiftly proved his competence.

Grant's capture of the Tennessee Forts Henry and Donelson in February 1862 opened up the west to the Union, and the victory at Shiloh, although costly, was critical. Dissenting voices called for his dismissal, but Lincoln refused, saying, "I can't spare this man. He fights." Halleck assumed field command and Grant considered resigning, but Sherman persuaded him to carry on. "You could not be quiet at home for week," he said, "when armies are moving."

Grant moved on to Vicksburg, the last major Confederate stronghold on the Mississippi, and with characteristic aggression and independent determination, forced the city's surrender on July 4, 1863. It was the decisive victory of the war: he eliminated a Confederate army and cut the Confederacy in half. He earned the personal gratitude of Lincoln and became a hero. In 1864 Grant became commander of all U.S. armies and planned to destroy the Confederate forces one by one. Displaying immense strategic vision, he pinned down Lee at Petersburg, while Sherman's army cut a swathe through Georgia on his "March to the Sea," and Sheridan destroyed communications and supply lines in Virginia.

After a series of running battles in the spring of 1865, Lee was forced to surrender at Appomattox on generous terms. Grant curbed the jubilation of his men, saying "The war is over. The Rebels are our countrymen again."

Grant undoubtedly had superior resources at his disposal, but this should not detract from his achievements. He faced several calls for his dismissal with great moral courage, and did not allow high casualties to sway him from his ultimate goal; he was certainly not careless of human life, but equally he recognized that success on

Above and Left: Ulysses S. Grant rose to prominence in the western theater, and was rewarded with the supreme command of all Union Army forces in 1864–65. He is seen here (Above) on the cottage porch at Mount McGregor four days before his death from throat cancer.

the battlefield was not without cost. He was self-reliant and decisive, always courteous to his officers and personally courageous. He remained clear-headed under fire and utterly focused on the ultimate goal.

Contemporaries regarded him with mixed feelings. He was an unassuming, quietly spoken man, who had a reputation for drinking when times were hard. "Grant is certainly a very extraordinary man, [but] he does not look it and might well pass . . . for a dumpy and slouchy little subaltern, very fond of smoking," wrote the diplomat Charles Francis Adams. Crucially, Grant had Lincoln's confidence and was highly respected by his troops.

Guerrilla warfare

Guerrillas are irregulars who operate without typical military discipline and with or without the support of regular armies, but with similar aims. The term "guerilla," meaning "small warrior" in Spanish, was coined during the Peninsular War of 1808–14, to describe the Spanish partisans who were never subdued by Napoleon's regular troops. Guerrillas operate in small groups, utilizing deception and ambush, rather than massed battles. They usually depend on rugged terrain and sympathetic local civilians. Though large-scale guerilla warfare has been an important part of he geopolitical landscape in the developing world throughout the latter part of the twentieth century, it played an important part in American history in the eighteenth and nineteenth centuries. During the American Revolution, partisan leaders such as Francis Marion were a key to American successes.

During the Civil War, it was mainly the Confederates that practiced guerilla tactics, although the exact extent is not known because many of the records of partisan units were destroyed in 1865. Also, several of the units designated as "partisan rangers" operated as regular units and only used the designation to attract volunteers.

Governor John Letcher of Virginia was the first to organize irregulars. In 1861, the state general assembly authorized him to organize ten companies of partisan rangers. D. M. K. Campbell of Alabama, who

offered to Secretary of War Leroy Pope Walker to "organize companies to fight without restraint, under no orders," was rebuffed with the reply that, "The Confederate government preferred that these companies be armed and tendered for the war in the usual way. They would have to conform to the rules of war of civilized nations. The government must commission the officers and the companies be paid for by the state. If the Alabamians proceeded according to their own ideas they would have to be regarded as outlaws and pirates."

General Thomas C. Hindman of the Confederate District of Arkansas, however, was an eager supporter of partisan operations to "cut off federal pickets, scouts, foraging parties, and trains, and to kill pilots and others on gunboats and transports, attacking them day and night, and using the greatest vigor in their movements."

Some of the more colorful Confederate guerilla leaders became legendary. Two of the most feared were William Clarke Quantrill, who operated in Missouri and Kansas, and John Singleton Mosby of Virginia. Quantrill is regarded today as mainly a bandit and opportunist, because of his having targeted civilians. His massacre of 150 people in Lawrence, Kansas in August 1863 was especially brutal, and did nothing to help the Confederate war effort. (See photograph on page 110.)

Mosby had served as a cavalry under J. E. B. Stuart until January 1863, when he began his partisan operations in Northern Virginia. Though they were ruthless fighters, his "Gray Ghosts" directed their attacks against Union troops, destroying communication lines and hijacking supplies. At one point, Mosby captured a Union general in his bed. Among Mosby's "Ghosts" were

Baron Robert von Massow, the son of one of the chamberlains of the King of Prussia and a veteran of the Prussian army (who later commanded a corps during the Franco-Prussian War, and all of German Cavalry before World War I) and Captain Bradford Smith-Hoskins, who had served with Her Majesty's 44th Royal Infantry in the Crimea, and with Giuseppe Garibaldi in Sicily.

Though heavily outnumbered by Union forces sent to bring them to heel, Mosby's rangers were never defeated in combat.

Other important guerilla leaders included Captain R. C. W. Radford, who offered to raise and mount a company of a thousand active men for irregular service if the Confederate government was willing to arm them with long-range guns and pistols.

Among those who served as Confederate guerrillas during the Civil War were many of

the legendary outlaws of the postwar Wild West, including Jesse James and Cole Younger.

Gunboats

The majority of warships which participated in the war were not ironclads or ocean-going steam frigates but small gunboats. Although an increasing number were purpose-built as the war progressed, many were converted from merchant ships or river paddleboats. Although unable to take on ironclads, they were more than able to fight vessels of their own kind, to maintain the blockade of the Confederate coastline, or to contest control of the rivers and inland waterways of the Confederacy. For the Confederates, when the war started the navy had no vessels, so numerous gunboats were converted from existing vessels. Armament of these vessels ranged from one

Above: Bands led by irregular commanders such as Mosby or Quantrill proved highly successful in disrupting Union lines of communication. This is Colonel William T. Anderson, "Bloody Bill," who perpetrated the massacre of September 27, 1864, at Centralia, Missouri. He was killed by militia units within a month.

Left: Although both sides used guerrillas to some extent, it was the Confederates who were the most successful.

THE AMERICAN CIVIL WAR: A VISUAL ENCYCLOPEDIA

to twelve guns, depending on size, and by July 1861 around twelve were in service in various state navies. The Confederate Navy subsequently commandeered these gunboats. A gunboat building program produced a range of vessels, the most successful being those designed by Commander Matthew M. Maury for use along the Atlantic seaboard.

For the Union, while civilian vessels were pressed into service in the Atlantic states as well as on the Mississippi, the Union's emer-gency shipbuilding program led to the "ninety-day gunboats," the "Unandilla" class of twenty-three vessels, designed specifically to enforce the blockade of Southern ports. These were augmented by small screw sloops, double-ended paddle-wheel gunboats designed for use on Southern rivers, and an entire fleet of Mississippi rams designed by Commander Ellet and others. In all naval areas of operations, these small wooden gunboats played a vital part in the prosecution of the naval war.

Right: The "Cairo" class ironclad gunboat USS *Essex* participated in the destruction of the Confederate ironclad CSS *Arkansas*.

Below Right: Gunboat flotilla on the Mississippi River.

Below: The Union Mississippi fleet consisted of converted and specially built ironclads and wooden gunboats. This force played a major role in the splitting of the Confederacy in two.

Halleck, Henry Wager (1815–72)

A capable administrator, but a poor field commander, Halleck was a remote West Point tactician whose scholarship earned him the nickname "Old Brains." When his subordinate, Grant, won the day at Shiloh, Halleck was promoted to general-in-chief of the Union armies, despite his evident failings as a field commander. He failed to make his intentions clear to his subordinates, and tended to blame others for his failures. Gideon Welles, Secretary of the Navy, said, he "originates nothing, anticipates nothing . . . takes no responsibility, plans nothing, suggests nothing, is good for nothing," a harsh assessment, but a view that was widely held.

Hampton Roads, Battle of, 1862

Following the capture of Norfolk in 1861, Confederate engineers raised the remains of the frigate USS *Merrimac* and converted her into the ironclad CSS *Virginia*. Reports of this activity caused consternation in Washington, so the U.S. Navy produced an ironclad of their own, the USS *Monitor*. The *Virginia* was completed in early March 1862, and on March 8 she steamed down the Elizabeth River into Hampton Roads, watched by thousands of onlookers. Commanded by Admiral Franklin Buchanan, the *Virginia* would attempt to single-handedly break the Union blockade.

Six wooden warships lay at anchor in Hampton Roads, including the USS *Congress* (fifty-gun frigate) and the USS *Cumberland* (twenty-four-gun sloop). The *Virginia* headed for the *Cumberland*, whose shot bounced off the Confederate ironclad. She rammed the *Cumberland*, the impact tearing off the *Virginia*'s ram. The *Cumberland* sank rapidly, allowing the *Virginia* to concentrate on the *Congress*, which had run aground. She was soon left burning on the shore. As night fell, Buchanan decided to retire, and continue the action the next morning.

At dawn on March 9 the *Virginia* got underway and set course for the wooden

H

frigate USS *Minnesota*. Another low-lying vessel lay beside the *Minnesota*, which turned toward the ironclad.

It was the USS *Monitor*, which had arrived during the night. What followed was the first ever clash between two ironclads. The *Monitor* opened fire, but her shot failed to damage the *Virginia*. For the next hour the two warships circled, firing continually and trying to gain an advantage over their adversary. Both vessels tried and failed to ram their opponent, and it appeared both ironclads were impervious to enemy fire. At one point the *Virginia* ran aground, but pulled herself off. The *Monitor* then retired to shallow water to replenish her ammunition, and after a pause the battle was resumed. The stand-off continued for another half-hour, but a falling tide eventually forced the *Virginia* to return to Norfolk.

The contest was never resumed. Although a stalemate, the arrival of the *Monitor* effectively ended the *Virginia*'s attempt to break the Union blockade.

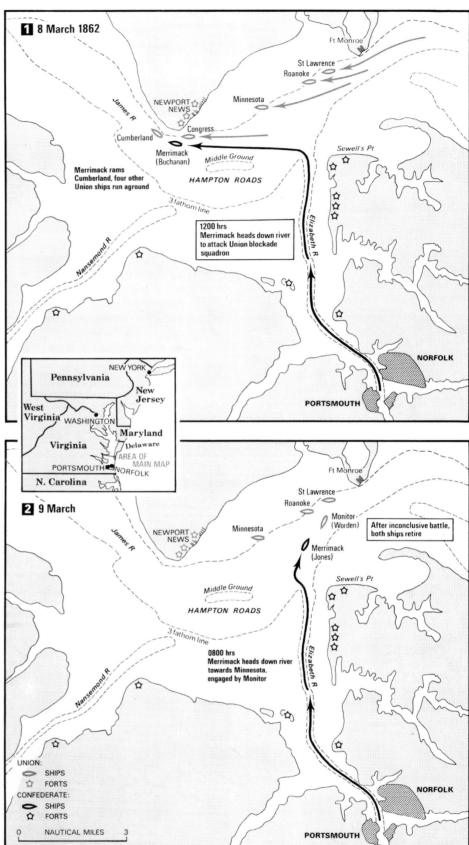

Above: Map of the battle of Hampton Roads.

Left: The Confederate ironclad CSS *Virginia* (formerly the USS *Merrimac*) attacking the USS *Cumberland* on March 8, 1862. The following day the Confederate warship fought in the first duel between two ironclads.

Hancock, Winfield Scott (1824–86)

A professional soldier who always wore a clean white shirt, Hancock was possessed of a calm and inspiring manner. His resolution on Cemetery Hill at Gettysburg stopped the Confederate advance and earned him the nickname "Hancock the Superb." From 1863 he led Union II Corps, contributing to the final drive on Richmond in 1865.

Handguns

Due to the need to equip troops quickly, a bewildering range of both pistols and revolvers found their way into service during the Civil War. These included virtually obsolete flintlocks to the most modern revolvers. Many were conventional single-barreled types, although some had multiple barrels, including the Sharps four-barreled .32-caliber rimfire and various six-barreled "pepperbox" revolver. Many of those to see wider service were home-produced, although the South always lagged behind the North in the output of handguns, and its troops often had to acquire weapons abandoned on the battlefield or taken from Northern supply dumps. Both sides also made great use of imports from Europe to offset any shortages. Handguns enjoyed enormous popularity among troops of all types at the outbreak of the war and many soldiers provided their own, either brought from home or purchased privately, but the officially sanctioned handguns were chiefly used by officers, cavalrymen, and naval personnel.

The U.S. government produced no handguns in its own armories, and so turned to private manufacturers, among which was Colt. This company provided the Union forces on both land and sea with the greatest number of handguns. Of the 374,000 revolvers purchased during the war, something in the region of forty percent were produced by Colt, chiefly the "Army" and "Navy" types. These were single-action six-shot types made in steel that used percussion caps and self-consuming cartridges.

However, Colt was by no means the only supplier—others included Starr and Savage. Although the U.S. government bought around 1,402 of Starr's M1860 "Navy" revolvers, the company's greatest success were with two "Army" types—selling 31,000 M1862s and 23,000 M1858s.

Savage delivered 11,284 "Navy" revolvers, which had two triggers; one to rotate the cylinder and the other to actually fire the weapon. In the event, the Savage revolvers, which were bought between late 1861 and mid-1862, did not prove a success and were little used in the latter states of the conflict. Whitney produced a "Navy" revolver in considerable quantities—

around 32,000 in total—but less than half of them, some 14,000, were acquired by the U.S. government. Remington and Sons, based in New York, supplied 12,500 of its "Army" and 1,901 "Navy" revolvers. Among the smaller companies involved with handguns were Allen and Wheelock, Joslyn, Pettengill, and Rogers & Spencer. These supplied revolvers in much smaller quantities. For example, Rogers and Spencer delivered some 5,000 and Joslyn just over 1,000.

The U.S. authorities also looked overseas to fill their requirements for handguns, chiefly to Britain and France. Among the manufacturers from Britain were Adams, Deane, Kerr, and Tranter, while the French company of Lefaucheaux produced 12,400 weapons for the U.S. Army.

Southern handguns were also available in a variety of designs, with many being

Above: General Winfield S. Hancock's resolute defense of Cemetery Ridge during the Battle of Gettysburg led to Lee's first defeat, and turned the tide of the war.

Right: Although most people's image of a cavalry charge involves swords, in fact the handgun and carbine were the cavalryman's main weapons. This is a group of reenactors depicting a typical charge.

somewhat crude copies of designs such as the Colt revolvers. However, the South did have its own producers, including the Columbus Fire Arms Manufacturing Company, but its output was comparatively small compared with its rivals in the North. Consequently, the South looked overseas to satisfy its needs. As in the North, most of the suppliers were based in Europe.

COLT

Samuel Colt was the most successful handgun manufacturer of the Civil War as the company's weapons quickly won a reputation for their robustness and reliability. So popular did the company's range of handguns prove, that they were used extensively by both the North and South, equipping both land and naval forces. The U.S. government, which had no facilities to produce handguns itself, turned to Colt, and others, to satisfied its requirements and purchased close to 150,000 examples of the former's designs during the war period, while many ordinary soldiers of both sides bought them out of their own pockets. The South also made copies of Colt designs and a range of companies was involved, including Leech and Rigdon.

There were two basic types of Colt to see service between 1861 and 1865, although the company produced a number of models in a range of calibers. First, there was the M1851 "Navy" revolver, which had a .36 caliber, and second, the M1860 "Army" revolver, which had a slightly larger .44 caliber. A third revolver was available, the M1861 "Navy" revolver. This was essentially a smaller version of the "Army" revolver, but it did not prove a great success and was only produced in comparatively small numbers. The U.S. authorities took delivery of 129, 730 "Army" revolvers and a total of 17,110 of both types of the "Navy" design. It should be noted that the various types of Colt available were not exclusively used by army or naval personnel; in fact, the "Navy" revolver proved popular with members of the Northern land forces, who often purchased their own weapons.

The Colt revolver was single-action and six-shot, and used self-consuming cartridges with separate percussion caps, or the powder and round could be loaded separately. The cylinder, frame, and barrel were made from hardened steel, the trigger guard was of brass, and it had walnut grips. Some revolvers also had notched frames to which longer wooden shoulder stocks could be fitted to improve accuracy—the M1851 "Navy" even had a shoulder stock that included a small canteen—but these were rarely used. Cartridges were of several types, chiefly foil, paper, or hide. Bullets were either cone-shaped or round. The Colts had chambers that were somewhat smaller than the ball diameter; in the case

Left: Colt revolvers were loaded one chamber at a time, inserting a prepared charge containing powder and shot, then ramming it home as shown. Percussion caps were then placed on the appropriate nipples, and the gun was ready for use.

Right: American and imported pistols used by the Confederacy.
At left from top to bottom: Wesson and Leavitt Army revolver; British Kerr .44 caliber with its belt and holster; British Webley, .44 caliber; Colt Model 1848 3rd Model Army revolver; French pin-fire revolver.

At right from top to bottom: British Beaumont-Adams revolver; tin of British Eley percussion caps; belt and holster for Beaumont-Adams revolver; British Tranter single-trigger revolver; British Tranter double-trigger Navy revolver; pistol bullet mold; British Tranter double-trigger Army revolver.

Left: More Confederate pistols and revolvers. At left from top to bottom: Virginia Manufactory 1st Model pistol; Virginia Manufactory 2nd Model flintlock pistol and ramrod; holster; Palmetto Model 1842 with integral ramrod unstowed; J. and F. Ggarret pistol with integral ramrod stowed; J. H. Dance & Brothers Navy revolver; J. H. Dance & Brothers Army revolver.

At right from top to bottom: Le Mat 1st Model revolver; Le Mat 2nd Model revolver; Columbus Fire Arms C revolver; T. W. Cofer revolver; Tucker, Sherrard & Co. revolver; Griswold & Gunnison early model revolver; Clark, Sherrard & Co. revolver; Le Mat holster.

of the .36-caliber "Navy" model, the ball was .38 caliber. This minor difference made sure that their was a good fit over the powder charge. The weapon's loading lever was hinged and placed under the barrel. As all Colts were single-action, cocking was done by hand.

As mentioned, the South copied Colt designs on a significant scale. These were usually of .36 caliber and the leading manufacturers were the Columbus Fire Arms Manufacturing Company (7,500), Griswold & Gunnison (3,600), Leech & Rigdon (350), Rigdon & Ansley (2,330), and Schneider & Glassick (14). However, many of these manufacturers had to compromise on the original Colt design due to a shortages of steel. Brass was often used for the revolvers' frames instead.

LE MAT

This imaginative, if rather impractical and rarely used revolver was the brainchild of one Dr. LeMat, who was of French origin but had settled in New Orleans before the Civil War. As his adopted home suggests, his weapon only saw service with the forces of the Confederacy. In fact, LeMat fled New Orleans when it fell to Union troops and his revolver was actually manufactured in Belgium and France, and then shipped back to the South. There appears to have been little standardization in the design, with the revolver appearing in two calibers, .35 and .40.

The LeMat's claim to fame was that it was unique in that it could fire both standard revolver rounds and buckshot, the latter giving it the capability of a hand-held close-range shotgun. The revolver had two barrels, one above the other, with the lower smoothbore barrel designed for the buckshot round. The device had a nine-round cylinder, and a nose on the hammer was reset depending on whether conventional rounds or the buckshot was to be fired.

While there were potentially considerable benefits in having a weapon that could spray buckshot around in a close-quarters melee, the LeMat saw little service, not least because of its poor quality and unreliability, although it was issued in small numbers to Southern cavalrymen and some members of the navy. Perhaps it greatest claim to fame is that the most renowned Confederate cavalrymen of the Civil War, J. E. B. Stuart, is known to have been armed with a LeMat at some point.

Right: A reenactor fires a .44-caliber Colt "Army."

SOUTHERN HANDGUNS

As the South lacked the facilities for designing and manufacturing handguns on the scale of the North, it had to fulfill its needs in two main ways. First, it simply copied designs that had been developed by Northern arms firms, and second, it placed orders with a variety of companies based overseas. A third source was somewhat more haphazard—the appropriation of weapons abandoned on the battlefield by Northern forces.

In terms of Northern copies, the most commonly manufactured designs were those of Samuel Colt, although the Southern versions were generally of an inferior quality due to a lack of high-grade steel, which necessitated the use of brass. Generally, the Southern Colts were based on the M1851 "Navy" revolver, which the Confederacy's Ordnance Department had designated as its standard weapon in its Field Manual from 1862. However, the scale of the Southern output of Colt-style weapons was comparatively small during the war, due to its limited facilities and lack of key supplies. The leading manufacturer, the Columbus Fire Arms Manufacturing Company, produced a relatively modest 7,500 revolvers. The smallest output was recorded by Schneider and Gassick, which delivered a mere fourteen of the Southern Colt copies. Other Northern revolvers that were produced in the South included the .36-caliber Whitney. These were manufactured with brass frames due to the ongoing supply difficulties by two enterprises, the Macon arsenal and the private firm of Spiller & Burr. However, their output was again small, with just 1,400 being delivered throughout the conflict.

Again due to supply shortages, these Southern Whitneys were produced with brass frames. It also seems likely that copies of the Whitney manufactured by a company in St. Louis, Missouri, Shawk & McLanahan, immediately before the Civil War found their way into Southern hands, but in very small numbers.

Supplies from overseas came from a number of sources, although handguns produced in Britain and France overwhelmingly predominated. Among the British manufacturers selling revolvers to the Confederacy were Beaumont-Adams, Deane-Adams, Kerr, and William Tranter. The Deane-Adams design was of .44 caliber and had a five-shot double action; interestingly it was also imported by the North and manufactured under licence in Massachusetts.

French arms firms involved in the weapons trade with the Confederacy included Devisem, Houllier and Blanchard, Lefaucheaux, Perrin, and Raphael. In fact, several of these designs were produced in both France and Belgium, and some were used by both sides. The .45-caliber Lefaucheaux revolver, itself manufactured in both France and Belgium, was certainly used by both Union and Confederate forces. Unlike most revolvers to see action, the Lefaucheaux operated with a pin-fire rather than the more common percussion caps. One of the rarest revolvers produced overseas to see action in the South was the unusual LeMat. Designed by a Frenchman living in New Orleans, it was actually produced in France and Belgium. It could fire both regular rounds and buckshot, but proved costly to produce and unreliable in action, and actually saw very little service. Some were used by cavalrymen and naval forces, however.

Hardee, William Joseph (1815–73)

A distinguished Confederate general, Hardee, "Old Reliable," was an outstanding commander throughout the war. Wounded at Shiloh, he led the Army of Mississippi into Kentucky under Bragg and took over Polk's corps during the Atlanta campaign in 1864. Unable to stop Sherman, he withdrew into North Carolina with Johnston and surrendered in April 1865.

Harper's Ferry

Harper's Ferry is a strategically located West Virginia town in the Blue Ridge Mountains. It is situated at the confluence of the Shenandoah and Potomac rivers, where today, the states of West Virginia, Virginia, and Maryland converge. (Prior to the Civil War, West Virginia was still part of Virginia.) The town takes its name from Robert Harper, who operated a ferry across the Potomac in 1734 and a grist mill on the Shenandoah. the ferry operator who was active here before the construction of the several bridges here.

Prior to the Civil War, Harper's Ferry (then in Virginia) was the site of an important United States military arsenal. Indeed, George Washington himself picked the site

Above: Harper's Ferry on the Potomac and Shenandoah rivers was the site of a major arsenal, and provided a gateway to the strategically important Shenandoah Valley.

Left: Federal troops enter the arsenal at Harper's Ferry defended by John Brown's sons.

Far Left: William J. Hardee's book on infantry tactics was essential reading for all field commanders on both sides. He practiced what he preached, and was regarded as one of the finest divisional commanders of the war.

to manufacture rifles because of its abundant water power. As a former Virginia surveyor, President Washington was very familiar with Harper's Ferry.

On October 16, 1859, a group of Abolitionists, headed by the fiery and outspoken John Brown, raided the arsenal as part of a complex plan to establish an autonomous colony of liberated slaves in the Blue Ridge wilderness. State and federal authorities responded with force, but Brown held out for two days. Though seventeen of twenty-three in his group were killed, Brown and his sixty local hostages were surrounded by Marines under Lee and J. E. B. Stuart. Brown himself survived, to be captured on October 18 and, later, hanged for treason.

During the Civil War, Harper's Ferry was an important strategic position in the campaigns fought in Northern Virginia. In July 1861 Robert Patterson tried unsuccessfully to decoy Johnston to Harper's Ferry in order to keep him from joining the fighting at Manassas, and in September 1862 Lee narrowly escaped entrapment there when Union troops gained access to his operational orders. General Hooker resigned control of the Army of the Potomac following disputes over Harper's Ferry.

In September 1862, General Thomas J. "Stonewall" Jackson captured the town,

Above: This view shows *Hartford*'s afterguard in August 1864.

Right: The USS *Hartford* was the flagship of Admiral David G. Farragut, and participated in the naval battles of New Orleans and Mobile Bay. Her crew served her broadside armament without the benefit of protective armor, but she emerged from both battles battered but victorious.

taking over 12,500 Union prisoners, the largest number to surrender at any point during the war. After the war, the town's strategic importance faded, and the arsenal was eventually closed. However, the town became a strategic railroad intersection, operated by the Baltimore & Ohio Railroad (now part of CSX Corporation).

Today designated as the Harper's Ferry National Historic Park, the town itself has been administered by the National Park Service since 1944.

USS *Hartford*

The 2,900-ton steam sloop USS *Hartford* served as the flagship of Admiral David G. Farragut for most of the war. One of five powerful wooden steam warships, together with her half-sister, the USS *Brooklyn*, she formed the backbone of Farragut's Gulf Blockading Squadron. In that capacity she fought in the Battle of New Orleans (1862), then she led the Gulf Squadron upriver. She ran past the batteries of Vicksburg, Mississippi, in June 1862 to join forces with the Union river fleet. After her brush with the ironclad CSS *Arkansas* she returned down the Mississippi in mid-1864. In August 1864 she served as Farragut's flagship during the Battle of Mobile Bay (1864), when she exchanged broadsides with the ironclad CSS *Tennessee*.

Heavily damaged in the battle, the warship underwent repairs for the remainder of the war.

Dimensions: 225 feet x 44 feet x 17 feet
Armor: Unarmored
Armament: 20 smoothbore guns
Commissioned: May 27, 1859

Hill, Ambrose P. (1825–65)

"A. P. Hill you will, I think, find a good officer, with whom you can consult," wrote Lee to Jackson. Reliable and hard-hitting, Hill was one of Lee's most trusted, if somewhat unimaginative, lieutenants. He fought all over the eastern theater of the war, leading by example in tenacious attacks against the Union. A courteous man, he was popular with his troops, but he was also exceptionally sensitive and had a longstanding feud with "Stonewall" Jackson.

Hill became a Confederate infantry commander on the outbreak of the war, first demonstrating his skills on the Virginia Peninsula in 1862. He was promoted to major general and led his "Light Division" in the Seven Days' Battles in June 1862, repulsing Federal attacks at Second Bull Run. At Antietam he arrived just in time to reinforce Lee's right wing, and heroically prevented disaster at Sharpsburg.

Hill was wounded at Chancellorsville in 1863, and had not entirely recovered by the time of Gettysburg. He fought anyway, but was not at his best, and suffered from poor health throughout the latter half of the war. He fought hard to defend the Confederacy against the relentless Union forces in the Wilderness Campaign. Characterized by the bright red shirt he always wore in battle, he said that he had no wish to see the end of the Confederacy, so his death at the hands of Union infantrymen outside Petersburg on April 2, 1865, although a blow to the Confederacy, was somehow fitting.

Hill, Daniel Harvey (1821–89)

Like his brother-in-law, "Stonewall" Jackson, Daniel Harvey Hill was a deeply religious, rather puritanical figure. He was a graduate of West Point and served in the Mexican-American War, where he was decorated for bravery. He resigned his commission to teach mathematics at Washington College from 1849–54. An excellent teacher, he inspired his students and was the author of several textbooks and religious tracts.

In 1861, Hill organized North Carolina's first military instruction camp. He was commissioned colonel and took charge of the defences of Yorktown. In September 1861 he was promoted to brigadier general and served under J. E. Johnston. At Seven Pines, Hill demonstrated his bravery and tactical expertise; Longstreet noted, "The conduct of the attack was left entirely to Major General Hill. The success of the affair is sufficient evidence of his ability, courage and skill."

Hill went on to hold back Federal attacks during the second Manassas campaign, and at Sharpsburg he withstood the onslaught of McClellan's troops at Crampton's Gap. Three horses were killed under him, but he continued to lead his men unperturbed. At Chickamauga in 1863 he captured 5,000 prisoners and, together with Longstreet and Forrest, attempted to exploit the Confederate success, but was prevented by the cumbersome leadership of Bragg. They petitioned to have Bragg removed, but instead, Jefferson Davis relieved Hill of command.

Hill served on the staffs of Beauregard and Hoke, and finally, at the request of Johnston, commanded the remnants of the Army of Tennessee.

Right: John B. Hood led his Texan contingent for most of the war before gaining command of the Army of the Tennessee in 1864.

Holly Springs, Mississippi

Grant's first attempt to take Vicksburg was launched from here. He planned to coordinate his overland advance from Holly Springs with the advance of 32,000 men under Sherman, who were simultaneously moving up the Mississippi. Grant's 40,000 troops established their base there in December 1862, but on December 20 Van Dorn surprised them with a raid that caught Colonel R. C. Murphy's troops asleep in their tents and destroyed $1.5 million of supplies. So ended Grant's first assault on Vicksburg, as his men consequently failed to join Sherman's forces at the appointed time.

Homer, Winslow (1836–1910)

Popular magazines could not reproduce photographs and so employed "special artists" to sketch the scenes of battle. *Harper's Weekly* commissioned Homer as a pictorial reporter and he concentrated mainly on scenes of camp life, rather than battles. *Prisoners from the Front* (1866) admirably captured the public mood of reconciliation after the war.

Hood, John Bell (1831–79)

A belligerent and competent divisional commander, John Bell Hood was a cavalry officer who spent the earlier part of his career on frontier duty in Texas and California. On the outbreak of the Civil War, he joined the Confederate army and by March 1862 was a brigadier in command of the Texas Brigade, a body of men who quickly acquired a reputation as fierce fighters.

They fought hard throughout the Peninsular Campaign, and in October Hood was promoted to major general. Under James Longstreet, he commanded the reserve division at Antietam, unleashing a withering attack on Union forces that broke their assault. It was a costly action, however, with only forty percent of the Texas Brigade surviving. When asked where his division was, Hood replied, "Dead on the field."

He replaced Joseph Johnston as commander of the Army of the Tennessee outside Atlanta in July 1864—Davis wanted a more aggressive leader to face Sherman's onslaught. Hood attacked Union forces three times, trying in vain to save Atlanta.

Hood was an hard-hitting commander who was widely admired for his bravery and well respected by his men. He was a fighting general who led from the front and suffered several grievous injuries as a result. He mangled his arm at Gettysburg and lost a leg at Chickamauga. By the end of the war he had to be strapped in his saddle each morning but his fighting spirit was untouched. "We will fight you to the death," he warned the Yankees.

Hooker, Joseph (1814–79)

Hooker graduated from the U.S. Military Academy in 1837. He served along the Canadian border and during the Mexican War before resigning his commission in 1853 to become farmer in California. After the secession in 1861 he became a Union brigadier general of volunteers. Nicknamed "Fighting Joe" Hooker (which he hated), he commanded Union I Corps at Antietam on September 17, 1862, a corps which led the dawn attack from Hagerstown Pike. He then conspired against Burnside, who demanded that Lincoln replace him, but Lincoln instead promoted Hooker. This proved to be a popular choice amongst the men and Union morale improved quickly as a result.

However, Hooker was to be defeated by Robert E. Lee at Battle of Chancellorsville on May 2, 1863. Prior to the battle, the Union forces had invaded Northern Virginia but were easily outflanked in the dense forest of the region. The defeat, in which Hooker was slightly injured, allowed Lee to cross the Potomac and

Below: Texans of Longstreet's corps retaking the outer line of entrenchments on the south side of the James River.

Right: "Fighting Joe" Hooker was a more cautious commander, and his defeat at the hands of Lee at Chancellorsville cost him his position as the commander of the Army of the Potomac. A Mathew Brady photograph.

ultimately forced Lincoln to seek a replacement commander. Reactivated by Lincoln, Hooker was given command of the expeditionary force that gathered at Chattanooga in October 1863; 20,000 men with artillery and equipment gathered in eleven days—the fastest logistical gathering in military history until the twentieth century. Grant eventually took over command of the gathered army with Hooker serving under him as corps commander at Lookout Mountain on November 24, 1863. Later he served with Sherman during the latter's campaign against Atlanta. Subsequently, he resigned his command when overlooked for promotion, and served thereafter as Commander of the East and the Lakes until retirement in October 1868 after suffering a stroke. He died in October 1879 in Garden City, New York.

CSS *Hunley*

The submarine *Hunley* was built in Mobile, Alabama, early in 1863, and was named after her designer. She was built using a large boiler, and fitted with ballast tanks, an iron keel, a hand-cranked propulsion system and two small hatches. She was armed with a spar torpedo. After testing, she was taken to Charleston in August 1863. She foundered at her dock on August 28, but was raised and recommissioned. She foundered again in October, this time taking all of her nine crew with her. She was raised again, and fresh volunteers were found. On February 17, 1864, she attacked the USS *Housatonic* off Charleston Harbor and sank her, but the *Hunley* was also lost following the attack. All her crewmen were killed. The *Hunley* was recently discovered and raised, and the submarine will eventually become a museum exhibit.

Dimensions: 40 feet x 3 feet 6 inches x 4 feet
Armor: Unarmored
Armament: Spar torpedo
Commissioned: Spring 1863

Hunter, Robert Mercer Taliaferro (1809–87)

Senator for Virginia who was strongly pro-slavery, he was quoted as saying that, "there is not a respectable system of civilization known to history whose foundations were not laid in the institution of domestic slavery." He was chairman of the Senate's Financial Committee in the early 1850s and was one of the southern senators involved in the disputed creation of the states of Kansas and Nebraska in 1853–54. Hunter strongly supported Jefferson Davis as President of the Confederacy and became temporary President of the Confederate senate at the end of the war. Hunter was one of the three-man commission appointed to negotiate peace with the Union at Hampton Road in February 1865. The negotiations, however, failed as a result of the Union's demands for unconditional surrender.

Right: The Confederate submarine *Hunley* was designed to challenge the Union blockade of Charleston. After two crews were drowned in her when she sank twice in the harbor, she was raised, refitted, and given a new crew of volunteers. She attacked and sank the steam sloop USS *Housatonic*, but the submarine was sunk during the attack. This drawing is taken from Conrad Wise Chapman's painting.

Idaho

Idaho saw very little action during the Civil War. The only engagement of note took place in late January 1863 when, in response to Shoshoni raids during the winter of 1862–63, Union troops decided to retaliate. Troops under Colonel Patrick E. Connor caught up with the Shoshoni Chief Bear Hunter at his camp in the Battle Creek ravine west of Bear River, north of Preston, Idaho. On January 29 the Union forces crossed the river and attacked frontally, losing many casualties in the process. After this setback they moved on to the edges of the ravine, blocking the Shoshoni escape routes and began to fire into the camp killing the warriors and many of the women and children present.

Illinois

The state of Illinois was uncertain in its allegiance and politics—no slaves were held there, but as in Wisconsin, no free Negroes were permitted in the state either. A Union state, Illinois had a large contingent of "Peace Democrats" (also known as "Copperheads")—Northerners who advocated peaceable negotiations with the South, and who were responsible for an attack on Union soldiers in the state in March 1864.

Immigration

The Civil War occurred midway through what has been termed the century of immigration, with almost thirty-six million migrants arriving in the United States in the hundred years after 1820. Three million arrived from 1845 to 1855 alone, part of a process of rapid Northern industrialization and of the opening up of new states in the West that contributed to the growing economic backwardness and social distinctiveness of the old South. Not surprisingly immigrant numbers fell sharply at the outset of the war, but by 1863 higher wages due to labor shortages in the North had prompted a new influx. Immigrants constituted about a quarter of servicemen in the U.S. Army, a slight under-representation of the proportion in the population as a whole.

Indiana

Brigadier General Morgan's 1863 campaign in Indiana, Kentucky, and Ohio enjoyed a moment of glory at Corydon, Indiana on July 2, 1863. Morgan, together with 2,450 hand-picked cavalry men, was on a mission to disrupt the communications of the Army of the Cumberland in Kentucky. Following his capture of the confederate garrison at Lebanon, Kentucky, Morgan disobeyed orders and crossed into Indiana where the surprised Union officials struggled to put up a defense. On July 9, near Corydon, Indiana, Morgan's force encountered about 400 Home Guards and captured most of them, before moving off towards Ohio leaving destruction in his wake.

Right: Scouting party of the 9th Indiana Volunteers.

Below: Indiana did not play a great part in the war although some units were formed such as those pictured in this photograph.

Industry and technology

In terms of industrial capacity, the Union had an overwhelming advantage over the Confederacy. The industrial factories of New York City alone produced more goods than all the factories in the South combined. Similar · production centers in Pennsylvania and Illinois each provided a similar level of industrial capacity, meaning that in industrial terms, the Confederacy began the war with an overwhelming disadvantage. Prewar arms production centers were also concentrated in the North, as were most Federal arsenals. By mid-1861, the Federal arsenal in Springfield, Massachusetts, began the mass-production of modern rifled muskets, while the Confederate army had to be content with a haphazard supply of weapons and munitions.

The largest factories in the South were located in Richmond and New Orleans. Richmond's Tredegar Ironworks produced most of the armor plate required for the Navy's ironclads, as well as artillery. Smaller armament centers were located in Selma, Nashville, Atlanta, and Augusta.

Despite the best efforts of the Confederates, the combined industrial output of military related products was only a fraction of that produced in the North. The Union also attracted innovators such as John Ericsson, the designer of the USS *Monitor*, and Samuel Colt, the firearms' manufacturer. This ensured a succession of technological military innovations, such as the widespread introduction of repeating rifles. Faced with this industrial and technological imbalance, the only hope the Confederacy had was to ensure that the war ended quickly, before this industrial might could be brought to bear.

Right: The ruins of a factory in Atlanta, destroyed when Hood's ammunition train was blown up as the Confederates withdrew from Atlanta. Industry was hard hit in the battle areas.

Infantry, Confederate

Unlike the Union army, the Confederates had no body of regular troops to build their army around, although over 300 regular officers offered their services to the Confederacy. Consequently, the army was formed from volunteers, backed by a scattering of existing state militia units.

Prewar volunteer militia units were swelled by fresh volunteers, and a wave of popular enthusiasm for the war led to the creation of hundreds of new regiments. Individuals raised or sponsored these volunteer formations, often inspired by the same motives as their Northern counterparts. The organization of volunteer units in both armies was similar. Each individual state raised regiments, and these were usually brigaded together. Some of these were prewar militia formations, such as the Clinch Rifles (Georgia), who already had distinctive uniforms, and a modicum of training. While several volunteer formations were also issued with particular uniforms, as the war progressed these distinctions disappeared. By 1862, all Confederate infantry were effectively dressed and equipped in a similar fashion, at least when supplies permitted. In many units, volunteers had to provide their own clothes, and Confederate infantrymen commonly wore civilian dress. Each state was responsible for the equipping of its own troops, and some state administrations were more efficient at supplying their troops that others.

Initially, volunteers signed up for a ninety-day or a 180-day period of service, but as the war continued, this was changed. By 1862, volunteers signed on for three years, or for the duration of the conflict, if the war lasted longer. In effect, all recruits served from the moment they enlisted until the end of the war, unless discharged through wounds, or they were killed in service.

While many Southerners genuinely believed in the cause for which they fought, in the poorest parts of the country others saw it as a way to ensure regular food, clothing and a pair of shoes. Where in the North, political zeal was the main reason for volunteering, the typical Confederate infantryman volunteered to defend the rights of his home state, and to ensure the

survival of his society. In 1862 conscription laws were introduced in an attempt to maintain the level of 50,000 fighting men in the Confederate army (of all arms of the service). Replacements were added to infantry units after they were created, and although regimental strengths dwindled as the war progressed, this meant that each

Left: Although many came from a privileged background, infantry officers shared the same privations as their men. The Confederate officer pictured is Colonel Hugh A. Garland, of the 1st Missouri Infantry, photographed in November 1864.

Below: Confederate volunteers drilling in their camp in Virginia.

infantry regiment had its own "*ésprit de corps*," and retained a sizeable body of combat veterans.

Unlike the Union army, all Confederate infantry units shared similar levels of pay, conditions, and social standing. Organization, pay, conditions of service, and discipline were all established by the Confederate Congress in March 1861. Although pay was regular, a lack of provisions and rampant inflation meant that, in most cases, the Confederate infantryman fought for no financial gain. By 1865, the handful of Confederate infantrymen who remained in the field were ragged, half-starved veterans who longed for an end to their suffering through capture, wounding, or even desertion.

Infantry, Union

The prewar U.S. Army was in poor condition when the war began. Over a third of its 1,000 officers "went South," although only twenty-six of the 15,000 regular soldiers followed suit. Poor pay and conditions made military service unpopular, and of all the arms, the infantry had the worst conditions of service. When the war began the majority of regular units were scattered in outpost on the western frontiers, guarding against Indian attacks, or serving as garrison troops in static fortifications. This regular army was kept intact, as it was considered the regulars would provide a dependable body of reliable troops. The infantry arm of the regular army was also expanded to a force of approximately 60,000 men by the end of the war.

It soon became evident that an expansion of the regular army was insufficient to fulfil the requirements of the wartime army. While new regular soldiers were recruited, the majority of infantry recruits joined newly raised state regiments. Existing or potential regional politicians realized that participation in the war might further their postwar careers, so there was widespread regional support for the creation of Volunteer regiments. In addition, each state also controlled state militia regiments, and further militia formations were raised as the

Above: A rifleman from the Iron Brigade posing for a formal photograph.

Above Left: Soldiers from the Union garrison on parade in Fort Pulaski, Georgia, near Savannah.

Left: A group of veteran Union infantry pose beside their field defenses.

war continued. A series of acts of Congress provided a framework for the administration of this amalgam of units, and Congress introduced a draft system when the initial influx of volunteers dried up in 1863. Although by 1863 there was little effective difference between regular, volunteer, or state militia infantry formations, different levels of pay, discipline, and social standing continued to influence the relationship between the various types of units. Enlistment bounties were higher for state-run regiments than for regular units, and local publicity ensured the state units received the majority of the military glory.

Over 2,750,000 soldiers served in the army at various times, the majority serving as infantrymen. A total of 1,666 infantry regiments of all types were raised during the war, of which ninety percent were volunteer units. To the regulars, the volunteer infantry were little more than an untidy mob, while the volunteers considered themselves a cut above the soldiers of the existing army. For the officers, service in a state regiment offered greater political and

financial rewards, although for the 500 original infantry officers of the regular army, the war offered greatly enhanced promotion prospects. Officers who were lieutenants or captains before the war could find themselves in command of infantry regiments by the summer of 1861.

If a typical Union infantry regiment existed, the foot soldiers in the unit were almost all willing volunteers, recruited from the same part of a state. Before they joined the army on campaign, they would have spent a minimum of three to six months learning their new trade, and were proficient in drill and weapons-handling. As the war continued, war-weariness set in, and reluctant draftees replaced the volunteers, although the corresponding lack of enthusiasm was countered by an increasing professionalism in the service.

Inflation

Neither the United States nor the Confederate States of America anticipated the overall economic impact of the Civil

THE AMERICAN CIVIL WAR: A VISUAL ENCYCLOPEDIA

War. Both nations began the war expecting it to be of relatively short duration and relatively nominal cost. When it dragged on into its second and third years, and as costs spiraled beyond what anyone had imagined, extreme measures were necessary. Both sides increased taxation and their level of borrowing. When these measures fell short, both sides turned to the printing press.

The United States government printed an estimated $432 million ($4.8 billion in terms of twenty-first century dollars) worth of non-redeemable, non-interest-bearing paper called "greenbacks." The Confederate States of America, meanwhile, printed more than $1.6 *billion* ($18 billion in turn of twenty-first century dollars) worth of similar currency. The theory was that, when the Confederacy won the Civil War, such paper would become a stable entity on world currency markets. However, the Confederacy printed so many bank notes that 150 years later, even their value as collectibles is worth barely more than their original face value!

Runaway inflation—of a kind never experienced by the people alive at the time —did severe damage to both economies,

although it was much worse in the South. By 1864, inflation within the Confederate States of America had reached 2,600 percent. It cost a thousand Confederate dollars to buy a barrel of flour in the South, and United States dollars became the preferred medium of exchange for merchants in the region. Even if the Confederacy had won the Civil War militarily after 1864, it is probable that its economy would have collapsed, forcing it into a currency union with the United States.

Iowa

The Union state of Iowa's contribution to the Northern war effort stretched to the provision of 75,797 white soldiers, five sailors and marines, and 440 black soldiers. Iowans made up nine cavalry regiments, four light artillery batteries, forty-five infantry regiments, and two infantry battalions of the Union Army. Out of these over 119 officers and 1,946 enlisted men were killed in battle, 82 officers and 1,393 enlisted men died of wounds, 107 officers and 8,906 enlisted men died of disease. Together with those deaths attributed to other causes that meant that the state of Iowa lost over 300

Above and Left: Two views of the "den," the headquarters of the Irish Brigade of the Army of the Potomac in their encampment in Virginia during the winter of 1862.

officers and 13,000 enlisted men killed during the course of the war.

Irish Regiments

Many Irish immigrants who arrived in Boston or New York were recruited into Union regiments. Irish units such as Meager's Zouaves (69th New York), the Irish Volunteers and the St. Patrick's Brigade all joined the Army of the Potomac, along with dozens of other all-Irish formations.

Irish regiments usually adopted Irish emblems such as the harp on their unit insignias and standards. Historians have suggested that many Irish soldiers were active in anti-British Fenian organizations, giving their units a uniquely political aspect. The majority of these Irish units earned a well-deserved reputation for bravery and tenacity in action.

Ironclads

During the Crimean War (1854–56), the French used armored floating batteries during the siege of Sevastopol. After the war, French designers took this concept a stage further, and in 1859 they produced the world's first steam-powered ironclad warship, the *Gloire*. Overnight, she rendered wooden warships obsolete. Within a year the British responded by launching HMS *Warrior*, an even more powerful ironclad. During the 1860s, both nations produced further ironclads, with the British maintaining a significant lead in numbers and quality.

In America, naval analysts watched this arms race with interest, but no ironclad warships were commissioned before the start of the Civil War, although several designs had been considered. Robert L. Stevens of New Jersey proposed a steam-powered ironclad as early as 1841, and an experimental vessel was commissioned, work was delayed until 1854. A casemate design, the "Stevens Floating Battery," was never completed.

Following the outbreak of the war, the Confederates produced an ironclad floating battery during the bombardment of Fort Sumter in April 1861, and an entrepeneur from Louisiana converted an ice-breaker into the first ironclad warship produced in America, the *Manassas*. During the first months of the war, the Confederates adopted an ironclad production program which favored the use of casemated warships, while for its part, the U.S. Navy commissioned three ironclads, the USS *New Ironsides*, *Galena*, and *Monitor*. Of these the first two were casemate ironclads, but the third, the *Monitor*, proved so successful that most subsequent Union ironclads followed its design.

CONFEDERATE

Following the outbreak of the war, Confederate Secretary of the Navy Steven Mallory decided to counter the numerical superiority of the Union with technological superiority. He envisaged a fleet of ironclad warships which were capable of defeating the wooden warships of the Union blockade, and work began on his prototype, the CSS *Virginia*, in late 1861. Converted from the hull of the frigate USS *Merrimac*, the *Virginia* was a "casemate" ironclad, where her upper hull was protected by a four-inch thick sloping iron shield, giving the vessel the appearance of an upturned bathtub. The casemate protected the vessel's main

Above Right: The Confederate Navy adopted pre-war designs for casemate ironclads. One exception to the rule was the CSS *Manassas*, built as an ironclad privateer, but drafted into naval service.

Below Right: The Federal *Mississippi* attempts to ram *Manassas*.

Below: The deck of a Union "Passaic" class monitor, with its pilothouse mounted on top of its twin-gunned turret.

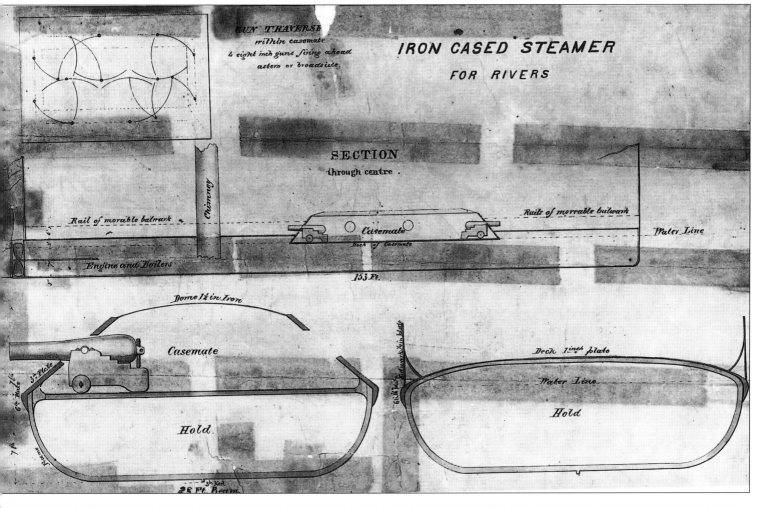

IRON CASED STEAMER
FOR RIVERS

GUN TRAVERSE
within casemate
4 eight inch guns firing ahead
astern or broadside

SECTION
through centre.

Rail of moveable bulwark

Chimney

Rails of moveable bulwark

Water Line

Casemate

Deck of Casemate

Engine and Boilers

153 Ft.

Dome 1½ in Iron

Casemate

Deck 1 inch plate

Water Line

Hold.

Hold

28 Ft. Beam.

A. LOCKHARDT. SC

Main Picture: U.S. monitor *Lehigh* operating on the River James in spring 1863.

Inset Left: USS *Cincinnati.*

Inset Right: USSs *Baron de Kalb*, *Cincinnati*, and *Mound City* off Cairo, Illinois, in 1863.

battery, a combination of broadside guns and bow and stern guns mounted on pivoting carriages, capable of firing ahead or to the sides.

Although a handful of ironclads were converted from existing vessels during the first years of the war (such as the CSS *Manassas*, *Mobile*, and *Atlanta*), the majority of Confederate ironclads were produced from the keel up as warships. All of these followed the principles employed in the production of the *Virginia*, although improvements to the casemate design, to the propulsion systems and the armament continued throughout the war.

Two massive unfinished ironclads (*Louisiana* and *Mississippi*) as well as the CSS *Manassas* were lost when New Orleans fell in April 1862, and the *Virginia* was destroyed when Norfolk was abandoned in May 1862. On the upper Mississippi, only the CSS *Arkansas* was brought into operation, but her career ended when she was lost in August 1862.

During 1862–63, ironclads designed by John Porter were produced in most Confederate ports, and his "Richmond" class of six ironclads was followed by other, even more advanced designs. Following experiences in action, later designs favored shorter casemates, smaller but more powerful rifled guns, and thicker armor. Throughout the war, twenty-two Confederate ironclads were commissioned, although numerous others were abandoned before completion due to a shortage of materials or Union advances. Given the limited industrial capacity of the Confederacy, it is a testimony to the ingenuity and perseverance of Mallory and his naval design team that these vessels were built at all.

UNION

Union strategists determined that control of the Mississippi River was vital if the Confederacy was to be defeated. When the war began, the Union had no warships on the river, and while wooden gunboats were rapidly converted from civilian riverboats, plans were laid to create a flotilla of ironclads. Given the limited shipbuilding capacities of the Union's river yards, monitor designs were abandoned in favor of a simpler casemate design. Designs were produced for a series of lightly-armored casemate ironclads (known as "tinclads"). The "Cairo class" of seven vessels was built in Mound City and St. Louis during late 1861, and commissioned in January 1862. These vessels featured a rectangular casemate enclosing a stern paddlewheel. Most of these vessels participated in the attacks on Fort Henry, Fort Donelson, Island No. 10, Fort Pillow, and Vicksburg. Two additional ironclads, the USS *Essex* and USS *Benton* were converted from civilian river steamers.

During 1862 a second generation of river ironclads was produced using a combination of captured or converted paddlewheel steamers while three others were designed specifically for naval use. None were particularly successful. In 1863, three types of river monitors were produced, the most powerful and numerous being the "Milwaukee" class, which were capable of operating in coastal waters. The Confederates were unable to match the number and quality of Union warships on the Mississippi and its tributaries. These river ironclads proved decisive in wresting control of the river from the enemy, and splitting the Confederacy in two.

Island No. 10, Battle of, 1862

Any advance down the Mississippi was blocked by extensive Confederate fortifications at Island No. 10 on the Kentucky-Tennessee border, and at Fort Pillow, upstream from Memphis, Tennessee. The island lay in a bend in the river near New Madrid, which was captured by the Union in March 1862 when engineers cut a channel to bypass the Confederate defenses. The Union flotilla bombarded the island from a distance, then on April 4 the USS *Carondolet* ran past its defenses at night. The island was duly attacked from the rear and captured on April 7. Some 7,000 Confederates surrendered, opening the river as far as Fort Pillow. The defenses were bombarded by continual mortar fire, and a Confederate naval attack on the mortar flotilla on May 10 was fought off by the Union ironclads. Unable to counter the mortar fire, Fort Pillow was abandoned four weeks later.

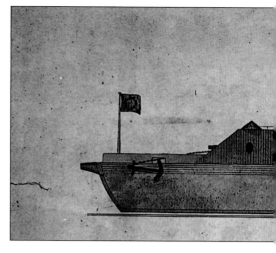

Above Right: The CSS *Virginia* was the first Confederate ironclad to see action.

Right: On the Mississippi, Union casemate ironclads were used to subdue the defenses of Forts Henry, Donelson, Pillow, and Island No. 10.

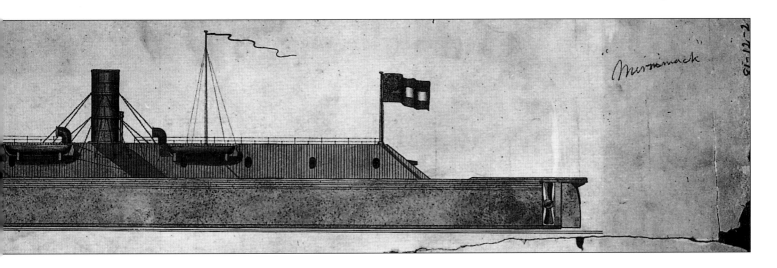

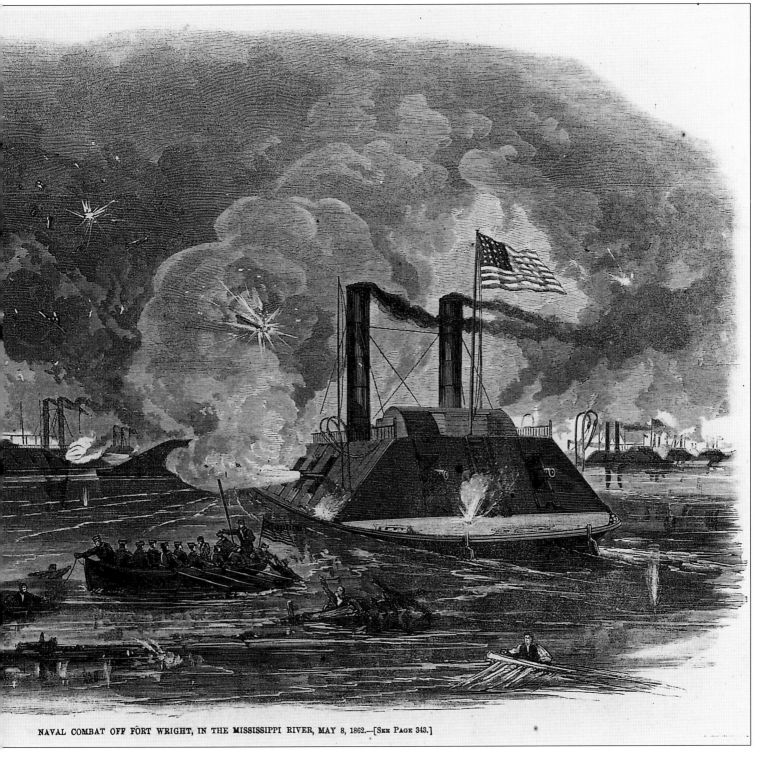

NAVAL COMBAT OFF FORT WRIGHT, IN THE MISSISSIPPI RIVER, MAY 8, 1862.—[SEE PAGE 343.]

J

Jackson, Thomas Jonathan "Stonewall" (1824–63)

One of the most famous Civil War generals, Jackson was a professional soldier. He graduated from West Point in 1846 and served in the Mexican War before resigning from the army to teach at the Virginia Military Institute. Austere, godly, and faintly eccentric—he remained standing while eating in order to improve digestion—he was held in great esteem by contemporaries, particularly his own troops.

Jackson had no great reputation before the Civil War, indeed he was known as "Fool Tom Jackson" at the Virginia Military Institute. He joined the Confederate army in 1861, convinced that the Southern cause was sacred, and commanded a brigade of Virginian troops. He earned his famous nickname at the battle of First Bull Run in 1861, where he arrived with his army by train, the first time in combat history that troops were transported by rail. As Federal forces drove back the Confederates, Jackson and his men remained firmly in position, "like a stone wall," according to General Bernard Bee, and were instrumental in the Southern victory.

In the spring of 1862, Jackson went on to command a Confederate army in the Shenandoah Valley, demonstrating outstanding tactical and operational skills. His campaign was characterized by lightning-quick marches and belligerent offensives, and he eluded, and then defeated, superior Union forces. Possibly exhausted by rigorous campaigning during the spring, Jackson arrived at Richmond a day late in June during the Seven Days' battles, hampering, although not ruining Lee's efforts against General George B. McClellan. In August 1862 Jackson marched right around the Union army of General John Pope, then stood off, luring them into an attack and waiting until the rest of the Confederate army could crush Pope's troops at Second Bull Run. The following month, Lee sent Jackson to capture the strategically important town of Harper's Ferry at the confluence of the Shenandoah and Potomac rivers, which he did before commanding one of Lee's wings at Antietam.

Left: "Stonewall" Jackson was one of the most celebrated commanders of the war, capable of inspiring his "foot cavalry" to perform amazing deeds.

Below: "Stonewall" Jackson speaks to his men.

Promoted to lieutenant general, he commanded the right wing at Fredericksburg in December 1862, crushing Ambrose Burnside's ill-advised attack on the well-entrenched Confederate positions. The following spring, at Chancellorsville, Lee divided his army, an innovative move that sent Jackson marching around the rear of a larger Federal force. Jackson launched a surprise attack on the exposed Union flank, but at the moment of victory, disaster struck. Jackson was accidentally shot by one of his own men when returning from reconnaissance at dusk, depriving the Confederacy of its most talented general. "I know not how to replace him," wrote a mournful Lee.

Jackson combined a fierce religious fervor with unyielding combative skill; it was said that, "he lives by the New Testament and fights by the Old." His most effective quality was his decisiveness; time and again he proved himself capable of seizing opportunities and exploiting them to the Confederate advantage. He marched towards his objectives with a speed unmatched by his colleagues and

was undoubtedly the most able of Lee's generals.

James River Squadron

Following the loss of Norfolk in May 1862, the partially completed CSS *Richmond* was towed up the James River to the safety of Richmond. A Union advance up the river in late May was halted at Drewry's Bluff, several miles short of the capital. No further attempts were made, enabling the Confederates to build up a squadron of ironclads and wooden gunboats to protect the city. Known as the "James River Squadron," the force centered around the ironclads CSS *Richmond* (commissioned in November 1862), the CSS *Fredericksburg* (completed in May 1863), and the CSS *Virginia II*, commissioned in May 1864. Their primary role was to cooperate with the army in the defense of Richmond, and the squadron only fought one inconclusive engagement with Union warships at Trent's Reach on January 24, 1865. The entire squadron was scuttled off Drewry's Bluff just before Richmond was abandoned in April 1865.

James River

The James River runs through the center of Virginia, emptying into Chesapeake Bay at Norfolk—home to the largest Navy yard in the South.

McClellan's bold Peninsular Campaign of April and May 1862, designed to win back some of the favor that he had lost through hesitation at Manassas, involved a strike up the peninsula between the James and York rivers with the Confederate capital of Richmond (itself built on the James River) as its goal. The campaign was starved of the manpower that McClellan felt that he needed, however, and again he hesitated. In June 1862, Lee engaged McClellan in the seven days of fighting that would see the Union commander beaten back to Harrison's landing, a point on the James River. McClellan emerged the tactical victor, but remained entrenched on the James until mid-August, his campaign effectively over.

Johnson, Andrew (1808–75)

Johnson became president of the United States after Lincoln's assassination in April 1865. Despite his own pro-slavery beliefs, he followed Lincoln's Reconstruction Plan to restore the Union, abolishing slavery and pardoning Southerners, but he was the center of bitter struggles over Reconstruction during the late 1860s, leading to his impeachment in 1868.

Johnston, Albert Sidney (1803–62)

Regarded by many as the most able soldier in the Confederacy, Johnston had studied at West Point with Jefferson Davis. In 1834 he left the U.S. Army to go to Texas where he served as commander of the Texan army (1837–39). During the Mexican War his quick thinking saved both his life and that of his friend Jefferson Davis. Davis remained devoted to him for the rest of his life, convinced of Johnston's talent.

On the outbreak of the Civil War, Johnston was serving in California, but he returned when Davis appointed him to one of the most senior positions in the Confederate army. He assumed command of the Western Department in September 1861, the area between the Appalachian Mountains and the Mississippi River. Facing terrific problems, not least being insufficient troops to hold a large, vulnerable area, Johnston succeeded in organizing an army to defend the line from the Mississippi to the Allegheny Mountains.

The Union regarded the Mississippi as a vital corridor of invasion; control would split the Confederacy, and the key to domination was the neutral state of Kentucky. In a preemptive move in the autumn of 1861, Confederate troops under Leonidas Polk marched into Kentucky, closely followed by the Union forces of Ulysses S. Grant. With the borders of the Confederacy now exposed, Davis sent Johnston to recapture the area.

Johnston advanced to Bowling Green, Kentucky, stretching his army thinly along the Tennessee border. He realized that his troops could not withstand a concerted Union attack and sent his political masters in Virginia a dispatch in January 1862: "All the resources of the confederacy are now needed for the defense of Tennessee." Unfortunately, two weeks later in February, Grant captured Fort Henry and Fort Donelson, the key defensive points in western Tennessee, forcing Johnston to abandon Kentucky and most of northern Tennessee and withdraw into northern Mississippi. There were calls for Johnston's resignation, but Davis remained loyal to him.

Massing his troops at Corinth, Johnston succeeded in launching a surprise attack on Grant's forces at Shiloh on April 6, 1862. "We are sweeping the field," he told Beauregard, "and I think we shall press them to the river." Johnston led the final charge to clear Union troops from a peach orchard, but was wounded in the leg and bled to death on the field. Command passed to Beauregard, who was forced to retreat on the second day of the battle.

Davis wept when he heard of his death at Shiloh ("our loss is irreparable—there

exists no purer spirit, no more heroic soul") and with hindsight believed that Johnston's demise was a turning point for Confederate forces in the war.

Johnston was a professional soldier, with a commanding, magnetic personality, but like most Civil War generals had no experience of commanding large numbers of men in battle. Shiloh was the bloodiest battlefield of the Civil War up to that point, with 3,477 dead, among them Johnston, the great hope of the Confederacy.

Photographs of the James River—a Union supply depot (Left); the conflict-ravaged river, strewn with semisubmerged vessels and lined by earthworks (Above); and the Confederate battery on Drewry's Bluff (Right) that guarded the river approaches to Richmond.

Johnston, Joseph Eggleston (1807–91)

Joseph Johnston was one of the most formidable Confederate generals and survived the war without suffering a direct defeat in battle. A graduate of West Point and a native of Virginia, he was U.S. Quartermaster General at the start of the war, but resigned his commission in 1861 in order to serve with the Confederacy. His decision was a difficult one that typified the dilemma of many; one in three regular army officers joined the forces of the South. "I owe all that I am to the government of the United States," he wrote. "It has educated and clothed me with honor. To leave the service is a hard necessity, but I must go. Though I am resigning my position, I trust I may never draw my sword against the old flag."

Appointed brigadier general, Johnston, together with Beauregard, took the credit for the great success of First Bull Run in 1861. He was promoted to general, but almost instantly quarreled with President Davis over his seniority, a disagreement that became a long-running feud between the two men and hampered Johnston's career.

During the Peninsular Campaign in April 1862, Johnston withdrew to defend the Confederate capital of Richmond. He was seriously wounded the next month at the Battle of Seven Pines and command of the Army of Northern Virginia passed to Robert E. Lee. Pragmatic and generous, Johnston wrote, "the shot that struck me down was the best ever fired for the Confederacy, for I possessed in no degree the confidence of the government, and now a man who does enjoy it will succeed me and be able to accomplish what I never could."

Johnston returned to command Confederate forces in Tennessee and Mississippi in December 1862. When Federal forces threatened Vicksburg in May 1863 he warned General Pemberton to evacuate the city, but Jefferson Davis ordered Pemberton to hold it all costs. Johnston lacked the troops to relieve Pemberton and he cautiously held back a relief effort. Pemberton was forced to surrender before Johnston could launch an offensive.

Despite being heavily criticized, Johnston took command of the Army of Tennessee as Union forces under Sherman drove steadily south towards Atlanta. Outgunned and outnumbered, Johnston pursued a policy of tactical withdrawal in order to avoid costly battlefield defeats, yet he also failed to inflict a defeat upon the Northerners. Anxious for more positive results, and under pressure from his cabinet, President Davis finally removed Johnston in July 1864 and replaced him with John Bell Hood. In February 1865, Johnston was recalled to face Sherman in the Carolinas, but he led exhausted troops in a short-lived and desperate defense of a dying nation.

Johnston was an extremely competent, if slightly cautious commander. Davis blamed him for failing to lift the siege of Vicksburg, but he was immensely popular with the troops under his command. When he was removed in July 1864, one Confederate veteran remarked that, "This act threw a damper over this army from which it never recovered."

Jonesboro', Battle of, 1864

The Battle of Jonesboro' was the last attempt by the Confederates to hold Atlanta. By mid-July 1864 Unionist Major General William T. Sherman's 100,000-strong force, comprising Major General John Schofield's Army of the Ohio, Major General George Thomas' Army of the Cumberland, and Major General James McPherson's Army of the Tennessee, was closing in on Confederate General John B. Hood's 50,000-strong Army of Tennessee defending Atlanta. Hood launched a series of desperate attacks, the last of which occurred fifteen miles south of Atlanta. Sherman had decided to outflank the Confederates to the south of the city, sending six corps to cut off two vital railroads. Hood sent out two corps under Lieutenant General William J. Hardee to attack the Unionist right at Jonesboro on August 31 but Hardee was repulsed in the ensuing battle, losing approximately 2,000 men to 1,149 Union casualties. Hood had failed to prevent the encirclement and evacuated Atlanta the next day.

Left: Joseph E. Johnston was one of the most successful defensive commanders of the war, but his career was hampered by a long-running feud with Confederate President Jefferson Davis. His performance during the Atlanta campaign was exemplary, but it failed to prevent the President removing him from command of the Army of the Tennessee in July 1864.

Below: The battlefield was a dangerous place, even for officers of general rank. Both "Stonewall" Jackson and Joseph Johnston were shot, Jackson dying of his wound.

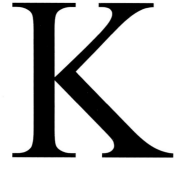

Kansas

When Kansas applied to join the United states in 1850, the decision as to whether it would join as a free or slave state was put to the vote under the new Kansas-Nebraska Act. Kansas was flooded by campaigning pro-slavery Missourians and anti-slavery Iowans, each hoping to tip the balance of the vote. Missouri won, but many Iowans stayed in Kansas, establishing anti-slavery settlements and giving "border ruffians" from Missouri the political excuse that they needed to pillage and raid the borderlands. Radical John Brown—of Harper's Ferry fame—led his first assault against the settlers on the Pottawatomie River, branding it retribution for the border ruffians' sack of Lawrence; this set the tone for the guerrilla warfare that plagued Kansas until the war's end.

Kansas-Nebraska Act

The Kansas-Nebraska Act of May 1854 provided that the organization of the territories of Kansas and Nebraska under the doctrine of "popular sovereignty." This meant that the residents of the states who opposed slavery could choose to ban the practice if they wished. The act was sponsored by Democratic Senator (and later 1860 presidential candidate) Stephen A. Douglas of Illinois as an effort to stem the advance of slavery into territories outside the South. The Southern states opposed the act, seeing it as a blow to their cause, but it was also opposed by "free-soil" and anti-slavery groups as a sellout because it did not ban slavery outright. The dissatisfaction with the Kansas-Nebraska Act led to the establishment of the Republican Party as a political organization opposed to the expansion of slavery into the territories.

In the wake of the Kansas-Nebraska Act, both pro-slavery and anti-slavery immigrants poured into the territories, especially Kansas, in an effort to weight the vote on slavery in their favor. The result was the violent era that is known as the "Bloody Kansas" period. In retrospect, it was this Act that started the United States down the slippery slope toward outright Civil War.

Right: Franklin Pierce sits on the shoulders of the Speaker of the House, Lynn Boyd. At left Stephen Douglas holds the Nebraska Bill; Thomas Benton is at right.

Below: The 1863 Quantrill Raid on Lawrence, Kansas (see also picture on page 110).

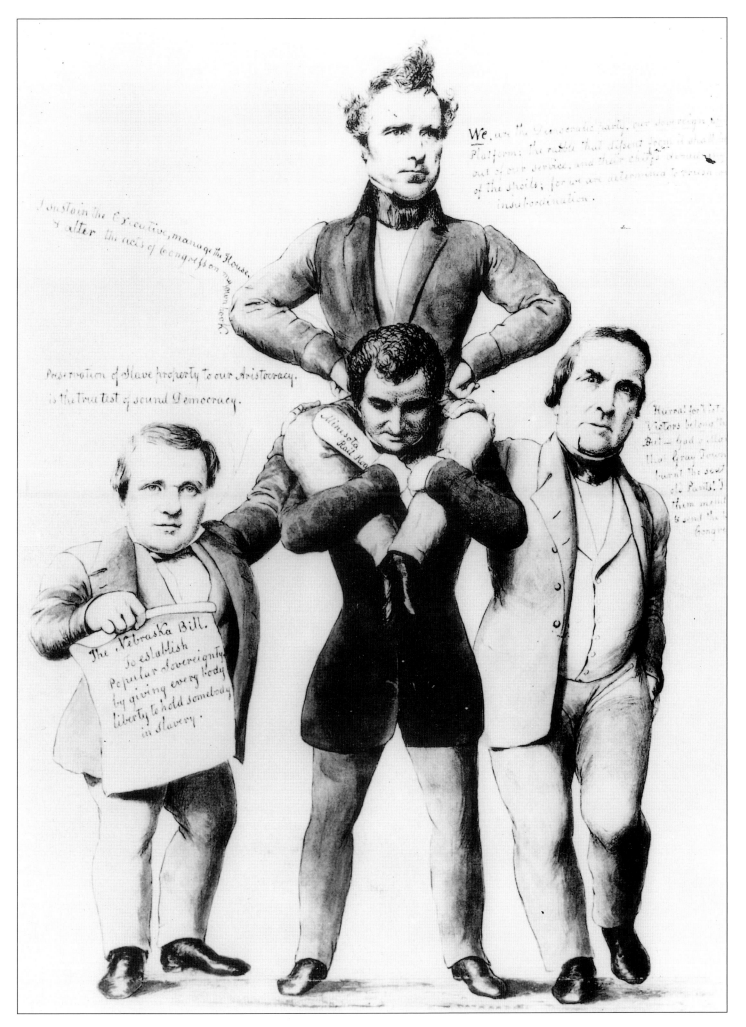

USS *Kearsarge*

The USS *Kearsarge* was a 1,550-ton steam sloop of the "Mohican" class, built at the Portsmouth Navy Yard in Maine. Constructed during the Union's emergency shipbuilding program, she was typical of the cruisers employed by the Union Navy to hunt Confederate raiders. Under Captain John Winslow she spent three years on patrol without encountering the enemy. Then, in mid-June 1864, the *Kearsarge* arrived off Cherbourg, France, where the cruiser CSS *Alabama* was undergoing repairs. On June 19, the *Alabama* sallied out, and the ships fought a duel just outside the port. Both ships were roughly comparable in armament, but in an hour-long fight, the *Kearsarge*'s superior gunnery proved decisive, and the Confederate raider was sunk. The *Kearsage* later participated in the hunt for the raiders CSS *Florida* and CSS *Stonewall*, but she never saw action again

Left: Captain John Winslow and his officers on board the USS *Kearsage*, photographed after their battle with the Confederate raider CSS *Alabama* in 1864.

Above: Kennesaw Mountain formed part of the Confederate defenses which blocked General Sherman's route to Atlanta. His attack on the position in May 1864 was repulsed with heavy losses.

Dimensions: 198 feet x 34 feet x 16 feet
Armor: Unarmored
Armament: Seven smoothbore guns
Commissioned: January 24, 1862

Kennesaw, Battle of, 1864

On May 4, 1864, Unionist Major General William T. Sherman began his advance on Atlanta. Opposing him was General Joseph E. Johnston's Confederate Army of Tennessee. Although Sherman had the numerical advantage (100,000 men opposed to eventually 60,000), Johnston fought a careful defensive campaign in the mountainous terrain. In a series of flanking maneuvers, Sherman forced Johnston back through Georgia until deciding on a frontal attack at Kennesaw Mountain on June 27. Johnston was in a strong defensive position and despite a heavy Unionist artillery bombardment his entrenched troops repulsed the attack launched by Sherman at 9:30am. After two hours Sherman called off the attack, having lost 3,000 men to 500 Confederates.

Kentucky

When war broke out Kentucky declared itself neutral, turning down calls to arms from both forces. Just one year later, it was in Kentucky, more than any other state, that brother was pitched against brother, with

50,000 fighting for the Union and 35,000 for the Confederacy.

Kentucky's neutrality ended on September 18, 1861. In the early months of the war, North and South alike coveted the high bluff at Columbus, Kentucky, esteeming it crucial to control of the Mississippi. The Confederates attempted to seize it first, and so drove the see-sawing state toward the Union, but an unofficial ordinance of secession followed on November 18 and Davis readily admitted Kentucky as the thirteenth Confederate state.

Kernstown, Virginia, Battle of, 1862

Having been driven out of the Shenandoah Valley at the end of March 1862 by superior Union forces, Major General Thomas J. "Stonewall" Jackson, with around 3,400 men, was led into believing that the Union forces garrisoning the strategically vital town of Winchester were only about 3,000 strong. He reentered the valley intent on driving them out. On March 23, 1862, Jackson's forces encountered around 8,500 Union troops under the temporary command of Colonel Nathan Kimball entrenched just outside the town of Kernstown. Jackson's attacks were unable to take the strong Union positions and Kimball's counterattacks turned his left flank forcing him into a retreat that came perilously close to a total rout.

Above: Troops from Kentucky played an important part in the Civil War—this is the Kentucky State Guard at Camp Boone.

Right: Colonel D. W. Lindsey of the 22nd Kentucky Volunteers.

Far Right: Although technically a defeat, "Stonewall" Jackson's attack on a superior enemy unnerved his opponents, and forced them to overestimate the troops at Jackson's disposal. Nevertheless, Kernstown forced Lincoln to divert troops to counter the threat of an attack on Washington. This map is by Jedediah Hotchkiss, who often drew in the saddle and whose maps were used by Generals Jackson, Ewell, and Early while he was attached to the Army of North Virginia.

THE AMERICAN CIVIL WAR: A VISUAL ENCYCLOPEDIA

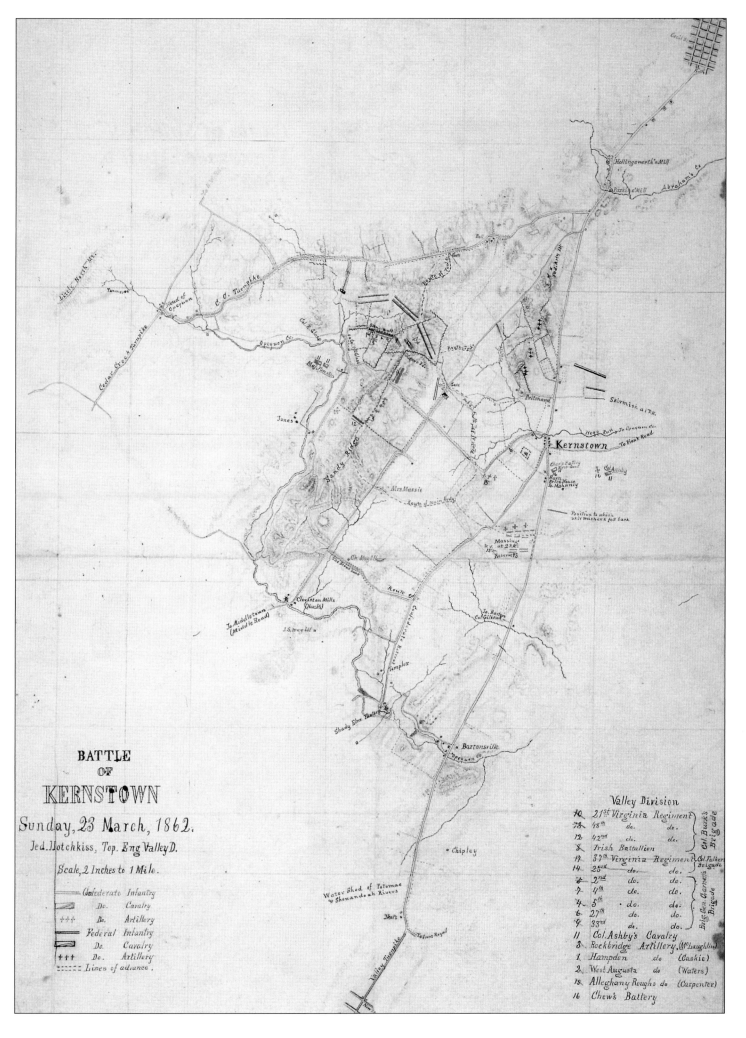

BATTLE
OF
KERNSTOWN

Sunday, 23 March, 1862.

Jed. Hotchkiss, Top. Eng. Valley D.

Scale, 2 Inches to 1 Mile.

Confederate Infantry
Do. Cavalry
+++ Do. Artillery
Federal Infantry
Do. Cavalry
+++ Do. Artillery
Lines of advance.

Valley Division

10	21st Virginia Regiment	
18	48th do. do.	Col. Burks Brigade
12	42nd do. do.	
8	Irish Battalion	
17	37th Virginia Regiment	Col. Fulkers Brigade
14	23rd do. do.	
5	2nd do. do.	
7	4th do. do.	
4	5th do. do.	Brig. Gen. Garnett's Brigade
6	27th do. do.	
9	33rd do. do.	
11	Col. Ashby's Cavalry	
3	Rockbridge Artillery (McLaughlin)	
1	Hampden do. (Caskie)	
2	West Augusta do. (Waters)	
15	Alleghany Roughs do. (Carpenter)	
16	Chew's Battery	

L

Robert E. Lee was probably the most famous commander of the war. His spirited leadership of the Confederate Army of Northern Virginia resulted in a string of victories, but at Gettysburg his luck changed. From that point on, his battles were defensive, as the Union Army of the Potomac forced his army south toward Richmond and Petersburg. His surrender at Appomatox Court House effectively marked the end of the war. Right and Opposite Page, Above: Here he is seen in characteristic pose, the far photograph taken in 1865, shortly before he left his home to become president of Washington University.

Opposite Page, Below: Alfred Waud's sketch of Lee as he leaves the McLean House on his final return to his headquarters having surrendered.

Lee, Fitzhugh H. (1835–1905)

A nephew of Robert E. Lee, Fitzhugh Lee was a Confederate cavalry officer. He commanded the southern cavalry when the Union forces attempted to capture a crossroads called Cold Harbor on May 31, 1864. The Union success in this engagement was a precursor to a longer battle at Cold Harbor in early June 1864.

Lee, Robert Edward (1807–70)

Lee was a native of Virginia and the son of Harry Lee, who had been a general during the War of Independence. Having passed through the U.S. Military Academy in 1829, Lee began his military career as an officer of the Union. He was commissioned into the engineers—where he helped compile many early maps of the United States—before serving as an engineer in Mexico. However, by the outbreak of the Civil War he had become a cavalry officer.

When the Southern states seceded, he was offered command of the U.S. Army by Lincoln but preferred to serve as a commander of Confederate forces, being commissioned in May 1861. His first campaign, in West Virginia, was not successful, being defeated by Rosecrans at Philippi (June 3, 1861) and Reynolds at Cheat Mountain (September 1–15, 1861) and he was then sent to inspect coastal defenses. In March 1862 he was back in Richmond, acting as an adviser to Jefferson Davis, before being appointed commander of the Army of Northern Virginia, following Johnston's wounding at Seven Pines on May 31, 1862, holding this position until his final defeat (despite a heart attack in 1863). The year 1862 saw his army achieve several victories—Cold Harbor (June 27–28), White Oak Swamp (June 30), Groveton (August 28–29), Second Bull Run (August 30), Chantilly (September 1), Blackford's Ford (September 19), and Fredericksburg (December 13)—which inflicted heavy losses on Northern army, particularly at Fredericksburg. He was, however, also to suffer several reverses during this period, such as Oak Grove (June 25) and Antietam (September 17).

The pattern was followed in the spring of 1863—with victory at Chancellorsville (May 1–5) being contemporary with defeat at Salem Church (May 3–4)—before he marched northward. However, his invasion of the North was thwarted by General Meade, and Lee suffered a critical defeat at Gettysburg (July 1–3, 1863) before being forced to retreat. Back in Virginia—one of the criticisms of Lee's activity during the war was that he tended to concentrate on the local war rather than the whole of the conflict, ignoring, in particular, critical events in the western theater—Lee again achieved both victories, such as Richmond

(February 28–March 1), Cold Harbor (May 31–June 12) and New Market Heights (September 28–30)—and defeats, such as Haw's Shop (May 28) and Poplar Springs Church (September 30–October 2). Lee was appointed commander of Confederate forces in February 1865, before being finally forced to surrender to Ulysses S. Grant on April 9, 1865, at Appomattox. The surrender effectively marked the end of the war and thereafter, Lee strongly supported reconciliation and reconstruction of the South. He later became president of Washington College—now Washington and Lee University—in Virginia. Robert E. Lee died in 1870.

Lee was a great tactician, but a less successful long-term strategist and, during the war, his contemporaries were not always firm believers in him. In particular, there were many who believed that he did little to create good morale within his army.

Letters of Marque, Confederate

Privateering—the commissioning of private armed vessels to attack enemy shipping in time of war—was outlawed by the Treaty of Paris in 1856. Following the outbreak of war, President Jefferson Davis was bombarded by pleas from Confederate shipowners to sanction privateering. The dubious justification for this was that the Confederacy was not a signatory to the treaty, although the Federal government was. On April 17, 1861, Davis invited shipowners to apply for "Letters of Marque," the traditional form of contract between privateers and the state. In retaliation, Lincoln stated he regarded any such "privateer" a pirate, liable to be hanged if captured. Despite this threat, 3,000 Letters of Marque were issued, although only a handful of privateers put to sea. As the Union blockade grew stronger, privateering became proportionately less popular, and many Southern shipowners turned to blockade-running as a more reliable source of profit.

Lexington, Virginia

Following the victory at Wilson's Creek, Confederate forces under Major General Sterling Price marched on Colonel James A. Mulligan's Union garrison entrenched at Lexington. On September 18, 1862, Price launched his assault, and soon pushed the Northerners back into the inner works of their stronghold. Consolidating their positions the following day, Price's men made a final rush forward on September 20, and by noon Mulligan had requested surrender terms. Lexington was evacuated of Union forces by 2:00pm the same day, and the victory at Lexington consolidated Confederate control in the Missouri Valley west of Arrow Rock.

Libby prison camp, Virginia

With an undeservedly infamous reputation second only to that of Andersonville, the Confederate's three-story prison in Richmond, Virginia, was formerly Libby &

Right: Libby Prison in Richmond was a prison reserved for Union officers. Although conditions were primitive, these prisoners were treated humanely. Over 125,000 Union prisoners-of-war passed through its gates during the conflict.

Sketched by W. C. Schwartzburgl? A. 24th Wis. Vol?

PRISON, RICHMOND, VA

Son Ship Chandlers & Grocers. No enlisted men were held at Libby—it was reserved for Union officers, of whom 125,000 passed through its doors by May 1864. Despite Northern reports of inhumane conditions, unusually for a prison camp of the era Libby boasted running water and even primitive flush toilets. Outside observers, invited to visit the camp by Confederate authorities keen to preserve a humane reputation, reported excellent standards of welfare and hygiene. Following the war, Libby was dismantled and reerected in Chicago as a tourist attraction.

Lincoln, Abraham (1809–65)

Born in 1809, the son of a poor and illiterate farming family in a Kentucky township, Abraham Lincoln spent much of early life in Indiana (where his family moved in 1816 and where he received his limited education) and Illinois (where his family moved in 1831). In New Salem, Illinois, Lincoln—who was a tall man at six feet four inches—ran a store, served as postmaster, and studied law. He was admitted to the bar in 1836, before moving to Springfield, Illinois. Active, at this time, as a Democrat politician, he served four terms in the state legislature and also spent a short period in Congress (1847–49), before changing to the Republican party in 1856 as a result of his belief that slavery was irreconcilable with freedom and equality. He stood for the Senate in 1858 against Stephen Douglas (a supporter of slavery) but lost. His reputation, however, saw him selected as the Republican candidate for President in 1860, and he became the sixteenth President of the United States in 1861, being reelected in 1864. At his inauguration on March 4, 1861, his speech rejected compromise over slavery and his

record resulted in seven slave-owning states seceding from the Union in 1861. It was his decision in April 1861 to send provisions to Fort Sumter—a policy opposed by his own cabinet—that led to the Civil War. Confederate forces started shelling Fort Sumter on April 12—two days later the fort surrendered. The following day, April 15, Lincoln proposed that insurrection in the South had occurred, and on April 27 declared Martial Law. From the outset of the Civil War he insisted that the Union

Right and Below: Two portraits of Lincoln, the latter with General McClellan, one of a famous series of photographs of the two on the battlefield of Antitietam.

must be preserved and that his aims did not necessarily include the complete abolition of slavery (even as late as August 1862 he said, "My paramount object is to save the Union and not to save or destroy slavery."). Following the outbreak of war, he called up a citizens' militia, strengthened the army and suspended *Habeas Corpus* in the South.

After the Northern victory at Antietam, Maryland, in September 1862 he made abolition of slavery in those states still in rebellion on January 1, 1863, a priority. Although ultimately to prove victorious in the war, Lincoln was often ill-served by his generals and there were often complaints about the confusing command structure that weakened the Union's strategy. He was also, however, fortunate that he was ably assisted by figures such as Gideon Welles who were able immeasurably to improve the Union's fighting capacity at the outset of the war. Lincoln was fatally shot on April 14, 1865 (Good Friday), by John Wilkes Booth at Ford's Theater Washington (the play was *Our American Cousin*, a popular comedy), dying at 7:22am on the following day. Slavery was abolished by the thirteenth Amendment to Constitution on December 18 1865. Lincoln's vision of "government of the people, by the people, for the people" was given most strikingly in his Gettysburg Address of November 19, 1863.

Longstreet, James
(1821–1904)

Longstreet, who was perhaps Lee's favorite among his subordinate generals

(Lee referred to him as "My Old Warhorse"), graduated from U.S. Military Academy in 1842 and served during the Mexican War and later as Paymaster. He wished to serve as Paymaster of Confederate forces but was given a field command in June 1861. Nicknamed "Ole Pete," his success at the First Bull Run and during the Peninsular Campaign led to promotions to major general in October 1861 and to lieutenant general in October 1862. He served with Jackson to the north of Richmond, Virginia, during the Seven Days' Campaign (June 25 to July 1, 1862) and was also one of the Confederate commanders at the Battle of Second Bull Run, on August 30, 1862, when Lee defeated the Union army under Pope. He was commander of Lee's I Corps in the invasion of the North in 1863—although he suffered a reverse at Suffolk, Virginia, in April/May 1863 when he was defeated by the Union forces under Peck—and dislodged the Federal forces from Gettysburg town during the Battle of Gettysburg on July 1–3, 1863, but forced them into a better

Above Left: James Longstreet, photographed after the war.

Above: Longstreet's assault on Fort Sanders, Tennessee.

defensive position with the result that the Confederate army was defeated and forced to retreat. On July 3, 1863, part of Longstreet's force, under George Pickett, was ordered to attack the Union's center under Hancock; known as Pickett's Charge, this action was to prove costly for the attacking Confederate forces.

Gettysburg was not the only occasion when Longstreet's alleged tardiness resulted in a weakening of the Confederate position; he was also believed to have reacted with hesitation when ordered to make a move at both Bull Run and during the Peninsular Campaign. There may, however, be an element of scapegoatism in deflecting criticism for this crucial defeat away from Lee himself.

After Gettysburg, Longstreet linked up with Bragg—although this relationship was not successful personally—in September 1863 for the Confederate victory at Chickamauga in Tennessee (September 19–20, 1863) before acting independently at Knoxville (Battle of Fort Sanders, November 29, 1863), where he was defeated by the Union forces under Benjamin. The weather conditions made an assault difficult and, before a second attack could be mustered, Longstreet had received a telegram from Bragg announcing the retreat. Longstreet remained at Knoxville until early December 1863, believing that his presence there would assist Bragg to

effect a safe retreat by splitting the Union forces. He reached Bragg at Russellville and remained with Bragg until his transfer back to the eastern theater. Following this reverse, Longstreet rejoined the army of Northern Virginia in March 1864. He was wounded at the Wilderness (May 5–7, 1864)—accidentally by his own men—where the Confederate forces under Lee were successful.

Ultimately, Longstreet was one of a number of Confederate commanders who surrendered at Appomattox on April 9, 1865. After the war he became a Republican, serving on behalf of the U.S. government in Turkey and later as commissioner of Pacific Railroads. He was the last of the Confederate commanders to pass away, when he died in Georgia in January 1904.

Lookout Mountain, Battle of, 1863

Following the Confederate victory at the battle of Chickamauga on September 19–20, 1863, the Union Army of the Cumberland was bottled up in Chattanooga by the Confederate Army of Tennessee.

Right: A war artist at work on top of Lookout Mountain.

Below: Union troops under the command of General Hooker stormed up the near vertical face of Lookout Mountain, sweeping the defenders off the crest.

Realizing that extreme measures must be taken to assist the beleaguered Army of the Cumberland, the Union authorities dispatched General Joseph "Fighting' Joe" Hooker with 20,000 men from Virginia and General Sherman with 16,000 men from Mississippi to effect a relief. General U. S. Grant was put in overall charge of the operation. The plan of attack was for Sherman to attack on the right flank, securing the northern heights of Missionary Ridge, while Hooker's divisions would attack on the far right, crossing Lookout Mountain and the Chattanooga Valley before approaching Missionary Ridge from the Southern end.

On November 24, 1863, the two flanks began their attacks. Hooker's 12,000 men, one division from each of the three armies involved, was vastly superior in numbers to the 1,200-man brigade that defended the base of the mountain. Therefore, when he forced a crossing, the Confederates fell back, withdrawing up the mountain. As they did this, they were reinforced by a further Confederate brigade that had been stationed on the mountain's crest. After a period of hard fighting, confused by a thick layer of cloud or mist that hung over Lookout Mountain, the Confederates fell back once more, and Hooker decided to rest his men in preparation for a further assault the following day. However, that night the Confederate forces were ordered to withdraw leaving Hooker, unbeknown to him, in sole possession of the battlefield.

Louisiana

Bought from France in 1803 for $15 million, Louisiana was crucial to the navigation of the Mississippi. Ever a disputed area, President Thomas Jefferson bought it to keep rival European nations from warring over it. He intended to relocate the Indian population from east of the Mississippi to Louisiana—Southerners, meanwhile, saw the territory as a vast cotton field.

In an attempt to reconcile Northern and Southern ambitions for Louisiana, the Missouri Compromise of 1820 drew a notional line through the region, north of which there could be no slavery save in Missouri. The compromise was designed to preserve peace, but it effectively cut Louisiana in half and made a violent future inevitable.

Above: Following the fall of New Orleans, Louisiana proved a fertile recruiting ground for former slaves, who served in colored regiments in the U.S. Army with distinction.

Machine guns

The American Civil War saw the advent of the use of rapid-fire and automatic weapons. Both the Union and the Confederacy issued them widely to their infantry units throughout the war, although after late 1861, Confederate machine-gun deployment fell off due to an acute shortage of brass for cartridges.

An interesting footnote to U.S. cavalry weapons' efforts was the production of the Spencer auto-carbine, a submachine gun with a spring-driven loading mechanism and fifty-round drum magazine. Theoretically capable of firing 400 rounds per minute, barrel warping due to excessive heat and the buildup of black powder residue kept it from acting as a fully automatic weapon. The feed action was subsequently modified to allow for the firing of three-round bursts. Even so modified, the carbine was dangerously prone to jamming and virtually impossible to maintain in the field, due to the number and complexity of its component parts. U.S. mounted troopers routinely discarded the weapon after it was issued, preferring the pump-action carbines. U.S. forces stationed in major Northern cities (primarily New York after the 1862 draft riots), liked the auto-carbine because its rapid rate of fire and large magazine gave them an edge over hostile crowds armed with pistols and conventional repeaters.

The first truly successful machine gun was invented by Dr. Richard Jordan Gatling, and although it saw only limited use in the Civil War by Union forces, it gave notice of the terrifying destructive power that was fully unmasked during World War I, particularly when used in a defensive role.

The Gatling gun was a hand-crank-operated weapon with six barrels revolving around a central shaft. The cartridges were fed to the gun by gravity through a hopper mounted on the top of the gun. Six cam-operated bolts alternately wedged, fired, and dropped the bullets, which were contained in steel chambers. Gatling used the six barrels to partially cool the gun during firing. Since the gun was capable of firing 600 rounds a minute, each barrel fired 100 rounds per minute.

The gun had a number of problems, however. The bores were tapered, and often the barrels and chambers did not exactly align, affecting accuracy and velocity. The chamber system itself, in which a paper cartridge was contained inside a capped steel chamber, was both expensive and fragile. While the gun showed much promise and fired the standard .58-caliber ammunition, it had so many drawbacks and was so radical in both design and purpose that Gatling was unable to interest the U.S. government.

The army purchased none of his guns, but Major General Benjamin F. Butler, after a field test, purchased twelve for $1,000 each and two were used on the Petersburg front in 1864 and apparently were considered successful. Admiral Porter acquired one to test its usefulness as a naval weapon and Hancock ordered twelve for his I (Veteran) Corps.

In January 1865, Gatling's improved Model 1865 gun was tested by the Ordnance Department. Among other things, this weapon used rimfire copper-cased cartridges instead of the steel-chambered paper variety. Though this model did not see service, it was adopted officially in 1866. Having at last received government approval, Gatling began to sell

Although a novelty, machine guns designed by firearms manufacturers such as Agar and Gatling were effective weapons.

Left: General John B. Magruder.

Right: James B. McPherson.

his guns throughout the world; they achieved lasting fame in the postwar years.

McPherson, James B. (1828-64)

McPherson, one of Sherman's favorite combat officers, was victorious at Raymond, Mississippi, on May 12, 1863, against the Confederate forces led by Gregg, and under Grant, was one of the commanders who proved victorious at Jackson, Mississippi, on May 14, 1863, before being involved in the march on Vicksburg that resulted in Grant's victory there on July 4, 1863. The appointed commander of the Army of the Tennessee in March 1864, he was killed in action, along with 1,988 dead or wounded, at the Battle of Atlanta on July 22, 1864, against Confederate forces led by Hood, although Union forces were to prove ultimately victorious.

Magruder, John B. (1807–71)

A Confederate general, Magruder defeated the Union army led Benjamin Franklin Butler at Big Bethal, Virginia, on June 10, 1861. He was the defender of the Virginia peninsula when it was invaded by McLellan in 1862. His wily strategies convinced McClellan that the peninsula was better defended than it was in reality—he encouraged his artillery to fire salvos and his officers to shout orders to non-existent troops, for example—thereby causing Union officers to believe that his forces were greater than they were and thus allowed for Confederate reinforcements to aid the defense of Richmond. However, he was to be defeated by McLellan at Yorktown, Virginia (April 5–May 4 1862), and at Williamsburg, Virginia (May 4–5, 1862).

Maine

The population of Maine were particularly fervent supporters of the Union cause, and members of the Volunteer Militia of Maine (VMM) were augmented by thousands of volunteers. These were subsequently formed into volunteer units; a total of thirty-four Maine infantry regiments, two cavalry regiments and eight artillery units were raised throughout the war, in addition to independent garrison units. These formations served with distinction, but the most celebrated unit was the 20th Maine Volunteer Infantry Regiment, which was commanded by Colonel Joshua Chamberlain during the fight for Little Round Top.

Mallory, Steven Russell (1813–73)

Hailing from Florida, Mallory had chaired the Senate's naval affairs committee before 1861. Following the secession he became Confederate Secretary of the Navy and devised the strategy to try and keep Southern ports open. Notorious for his penchant for women of easy virtue, he was successful in creating a Confederate navy from a variety of ill-suited vessels. It was Mallory who adopted the policy of mining ports and river estuaries—activities which sank forty-three Union warships during the war—and developed the first military submarine (the CSS *Hunley*). It was also Mallory who authorized the conversion of the damaged USS *Merrimac* into the CSS *Virginia*, the first ironclad to be deployed by the Confederacy.

Malvern Hill, Battle of, 1862

The final battle of the Peninsular Campaign fought east of Richmond, Virginia, the Army of the Potomac under General McClellan was drawn up on Malvern Hill, with its rear close to the James River. The 100-foot-high hill was stormed by General Lee's Confederate army in a series of frontal attacks, by five divisions. These futile assaults were repeated until 9:00pm, when Lee gave up the attempt. The Confederates lost 15,000 men, the Union 5,000. This defensive victory brought McLellan time to withdraw his army, evacuate the peninsula, and abandon his drive on Richmond.

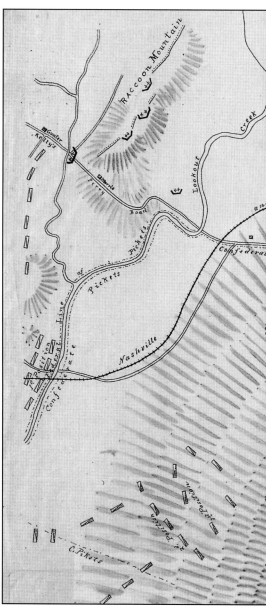

Right and Below: Civil War period maps range from the detailed U.S. Coastal Survey maps such as this of the defenses of Charleston Harbor Right) to this Confederate hand-drawn map of positions on Lookout Mountain.

Maps

Accurate topographical information was vital to the successful prosecution of the war, and in 1861, many of the areas where the war's campaigns were fought were inadequately mapped. A uniform system of large-scale topographic maps did not exist before the war, although various state legislatures sometimes produced their own series of maps. In the eastern theater, both sides initially relied on a series of nine maps of Virginia published there in 1859. These works were produced by Herman Böye, based on original state maps first published in 1826. Together with similar maps of Maryland and Pennsylvania, these maps were drawn to a scale of five miles to the inch. The most detailed maps were ones

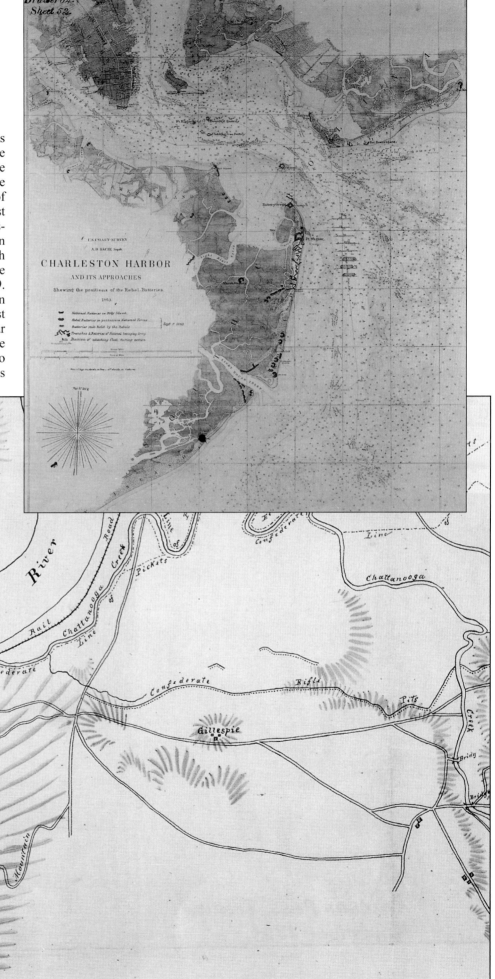

of individual counties, produced at a scale of one mile to the inch. These contained the level of detail required by military commanders, and showed every road, stream, river, and hill, as well as naming every town and hamlet, and even appending the names of the owners of individual farms or buildings. Not every county was mapped in this way, and gaps had to be filled by military cartographers after the war began.

The Union placed great emphasis on mapping, and the Corps of Topographical Engineers produced a series of detailed studies, as well as recording the topography and military movements of battles. The Confederates had problems supplying their officers with suitable maps throughout the war due to a lack of trained cartographic personnel in the South, and a shortage of mapping equipment.

Marines

In the U.S. Navy, although the Marine Corps had existed since 1775, only around 1,500 marines were in service at the start of the war, although numbers doubled during the conflict. Marine detachments served on all major Union warships, and ad-hoc marine battalions operated in several land and amphibious operations. During 1863–65, brigade-sized operations were conducted in the Carolinas, including an expedition to sever the Savannah–Charleston railway (1864) and an attack on Fort Fisher (1865).

The Confederate Marine Corps also grew in size as the war progressed, reaching a peak of over 500 men in October 1864. A Marine detachment served on every major warship, and provided gun crews. The largest contingent to see action were the fifty-five marines attached to the CSS *Virginia*, who later served at Drewry's Bluff, Virginia. A marine contingent even campaigned with Robert E. Lee in April 1865, when the Confederate capital was abandoned.

Right: Union sailors and marines.

Below: The other source of maps of the Civil War are the Press of the time and commercial ventures—such as this "Pocket Map showing the probable theater of war"—published by M. H. Traubel of Philadelphia in 1861.

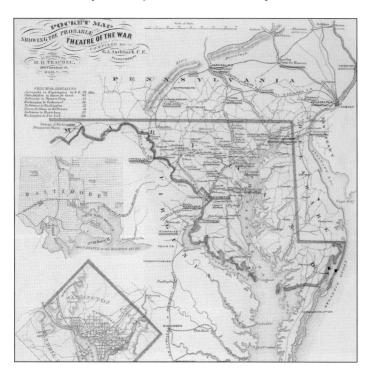

Maryland

Maryland's split political allegiances led it to declare itself neutral, but bordered as it was by Washington on three sides and Virginia on the fourth, it was economically bound to the North and eventually allied itself with the Union. Although two-thirds of the fighting population sided with the Union, secessionists held on throughout the state, and following the Confederate victory at Manassas on July 21, 1861, Lincoln felt so threatened by them that he ordered the ringleaders imprisoned.

On September 5, 1862, Lee attempted to bring the war to the North, marching into Maryland with 60,000 men and publishing a secession invitation—however, he had chosen a Union segment of Maryland and met a with cold reception.

Mason, James Murray (1798–1871)

Mason was one of two ministers—the second being John Slidell—sent by the Southern states to London and Paris. They slipped through the Northern blockade but the Union naval commander in the region, Captain Charles Wilkes, became aware of their presence on Cuba where they had boarded the British mail-steamer *Trent*. Wilkes seized the *Trent* and forced the vessel into Boston harbor, where Mason and Slidell were incarcerated in Fort Warren. Known as the *Trent* Incident, Britain reacted with hostility, threatening war and reinforcing her forces in Canada. Ultimately, to prevent war—which neither Britain nor the Union wanted—the two were released and allowed to complete their journey. In the end, however, the journey was to prove fruitless as neither Britain nor France intervened on behalf of the Confederate states.

Massachusetts

The Union state of Massachusetts was the first state to respond to Lincoln's call to arms, when, on January 18, 1861, it offered men and money to support the emergency situation and to maintain the nation. The 6th Massachusetts Regiment, the first to march to Lincoln's aid in Washington, became caught up in the riots in Baltimore and it was on account of the ensuing altercations that Baltimore severed all transport and communication links to Washington.

Right: The original caption to this illustration identifies, "The Rebel invasion of Maryland and Pennsylvania—the Rebel cavalry crossing the Potomac."

288

Maury, Matthew F. (1806-73)

When the Confederate Navy established its Naval Submarine Battery Service in October 1862, the new operation was placed under the command of Captain Matthew Fontaine Maury, a well-known hydrographer. With torpedo (mining) stations established at Richmond, Wilmington, Charleston, Savannah, and Mobile, the service was able to claim more than forty Union warships. After the Confederate defeat, Maury was one of a number of ex-Confederate officers who went into exile, joining the service of the Emperor Maximilian in Mexico, where he served as Imperial Minister for Colonization.

Maury, William L. (18??-??)

A Confederate naval officer, Lieutenant William L. Maury was the commander of the CSS *Georgia*. This was a 690-ton brig that entered service on April 9, 1863, and patrolled the Atlantic for six months, during which time she captured nine prizes. Following these actions, the ship entered Cherbourg harbor in France on October 28, 1863, where she was decommissioned and sold.

McClellan, George Brinton (1826–85)

Born in 1826, McClellan graduated from the U.S. Military Academy in 1846. Serving in Mexican War in the 1840s, McClellan was then in Europe as an observer during the Crimean War in the early 1850s. Nicknamed "Little Mac," he was summoned by Lincoln after successfully clearing the mountains of West Virginia of Confederate forces—with victories at Philippi (June 3, 1861), Rich Mountain (July 11), and Carrick's Ford (July 13, 1861)—to train the new Army of the Potomac. While he was undoubtedly popular with his troops, bringing improved discipline to the army, he was perceived by Lincoln and Northern public opinion as overly cautious and his timidity allowed the South to regroup. In April 1862, having been relieved of his position as Commander-in-Chief of the Union Army as a result of his unwillingness to advance in North Carolina, he was forced to act; taking advantage of Union control of the sea, McClellan moved his army by sea to land on the peninsula of Virginia where he besieged Yorktown and aimed for the capture of Richmond. Having secured his base at Fort Monroe, he moved toward his target

Right and Below: Massachsetts provided many men for the Union cause. These (Right) are the 8th Infantry at Camp Essex early in the war.

but speed was not his strength and this allowed the South to improve weak defenses. McClellan's natural hesitancy was compounded by cunning defense of the peninsula by Magruder, who convinced his Union counterpart by subterfuge that the defending force was much greater than it was in reality. Despite the delays, McClellan gradually advanced on Richmond, where he was faced by a Confederate counterattack—the Seven Days' Battle (June 25–July 1, 1862). The Confederate general, Joe Johnston, was wounded and replaced by Lee, who attacked McClellan's flank and inflicted a heavy defeat. Faced by this defeat, Lincoln replaced McClellan by Pope; however, Pope was to be defeated in a number of engagements, including Second Bull Run and Groveton. It was widely believed that McClellan had stood by and allowed Pope to be defeated in order to regain his command. Despite this belief, McClellan was recalled to Washington in order to reorganize the Army of the Potomac. He pursued Lee, aided by fortunate capture of a copy of Lee's orders, to the Battle of Antietam in Maryland (September 17, 1862—the single bloodiest day of the war). Despite severe losses on both sides, the Confederate forces won but were so severely mauled that Lee's strategy was thwarted and Lee was forced to retreat to Virginia; however, McClellan failed to take advantage of Lee's retreat and was sacked for the final time on November 7, 1862. He ran for president as a Democrat in 1864, but was defeated by Lincoln, and later served as governor of New Jersey prior to his death in 1885.

McDowell, Irvin (1818–85)

Born in 1818, McDowell graduated from the U.S. Military Academy in 1838 and acted as an instructor there between 1841 and 1845. Having served in Mexican War, he was appointed Brigadier General of Volunteers in May 1861. Initially he became field commander of Union forces in succession to Scott (who was suspect as a Virginian, as well as being old and fat) and led the Union forces against the Confederate forces led by Beauregard at Manassas Junction on July 21, 1861—the Battle of First Bull Run. McDowell's position was not helped by the desertion of the Pennsylvania Militia halfway through the battle when the ninety days of service, for which they had signed up, had expired! With the Confederate forces gaining the upper hand, the Union forces panicked and fled. If the Confederate forces had been better prepared, Washington could have been captured, but instead they were satisfied merely to have cleared Virginia of Union forces.

This was the end of McDowell's short and inglorious command. After being involved in the defense of Washington, he joined Pope as a corps commander, but after Second Bull Run he was relieved of all command until July 1864, when he was given command of the Department of the Pacific. He remained in the army after the war, becoming a major general in 1872 and retiring in 1882.

Meade, George Gordon (1815–72)

Born in Spain, where his father was U.S. naval agent, Meade was educated at West Point, graduating in 1835. He resigned from the army in 1836 but rejoined in 1842 to serve in Mexico. After secession, he was commissioned as Brigadier General of Volunteers in August 1861 in the Union army. He served in the Peninsular Campaign, being twice wounded, before returning to lead his

George McClellan (Right and Above Right) was replaced as commander of the Army of the Potomac by two other commanders before George Meade (Opposite Page, Below) was given the command in 1863.

Opposite Page, Above: Appomattox—Meade would hold his command through to final surrender of the South.

division in the Second Bull Run on August 30, 1862. He subsequently saw service in command of a division at South Mountain and Antietam, and then had control of V Corps at Fredericksburg on December 13, 1862—where his troops penetrated the Confederate defenses along Prospect Hill but where the potential breakthrough was not exploited by Franklin—and Chancellorsville. In June 1863 his appointment as commander of the Army of the Potomac, in place of Hooker, to defend Washington was so unexpected he thought the messenger relaying the appointment, who woke him, had in fact come to arrest him.

Despite this inauspicious start to this command, he defeated Robert E. Lee's invasion of the North at Gettysburg on July 1–3, 1863. After Gettysburg, Meade eventually pursued the Confederate army southward. (Lincoln commented on Meade's tardiness in exploiting the victory that, "They will be ready to fight a magnificent battle when there is no enemy there to fight." Meade discovered Lincoln's complaint and resigned his command; however, Lincoln was in no position to accept the resignation of the officer who had saved Washington and routed Lee, and refused to accept the resignation, writing Meade a letter of praise referring to the "magnificent

success" at Gettysburg.) Crossing the Rappahannock River on November 7, Meade had victories on that day against Lee at Rappahannock Bridge and Kelly's Ford, although was not able to force Lee into a decisive action. Meade's slow advance had given Lee time to strengthen his position at Mine Run and, rather than risk an assault at this stage, Meade withdrew to the north bank of Rapidan and prepared for the winter.

He retained his command, under Grant's overall command of the Union army, through to the Confederate surrender at Appomattox on April 9, 1865, with victories at Saylor's Creek, Virginia (April 6, 1865), and Farmville/High Bridge, Virginia (April 7, 1865). In May 1864, the Army of the Potomac again crossed the Rapidan, but the inconclusive Battle of the Wilderness, fought on May 5–7, 1864, saw the Union forces suffer greater casualties than those suffered by Lee's army. Meade was, however, to be defeated at Falling Waters, Virginia, on July 14, 1864.

He remained in the army after 1865, becoming a major general in the regulars, but was irked by the fact that this promotion occurred after that of his one-time subordinate, Sheridan. Meade died in 1872 in Philadelphia.

Mechanicsville, Battle of, 1862

Following the preliminary battle of Oak Grove, Mechanicsville was the first major encounter of the Seven Days' Battles. General Robert E. Lee began his attack against the Union right flank north of the Chickahominy River using A. P. Hill's division, reinforced by one of D. H. Hill's brigades. A series of frontal attacks against Brigadier General Fitz John Porter's V Corps were repulsed with serious losses to the Confederate attackers—they suffered 1,500 casualties compared to the 400 suffered by the Union troops. Nonetheless, McClellan was convinced that he faced overwhelming odds and began his withdrawal to Gaine's Mill.

The battle of Mechanicsville was part of McClellan's Peninsular Campaign against Richmond, and took place on the second of seven days of heavy fighting. Mechanicsville was one of the first major battles where Lee commanded the Confederate troops, as he replaced Joseph E. Johnston who had been injured the previous day at Fair Oaks. On June 27, 1862, Lee planned to use his 65,000 men to overwhelm 25,000 Union troops—however, his plan fell apart when his General A. P. Hill took it upon himself to launch an attack without Lee's permission, and the day ended as a bloody repulse for the Confederates.

Medicine

At the start of the war, both sides were unprepared for the effect the conflict would have on hospitals and medical services. Diseases such as malaria, dysentery, and typhoid took a greater toll on the rival armies than the enemy did. Of the 360,000 Union soldiers who died during the war, about 200,000 of these deaths were caused by disease, while thousands of others died due to insufficient medical attention. When a soldier was wounded a medical officer administered first aid, then regimental bandsmen carried him to a field hospital. Later in the war, both sides employed specially trained medical corpsmen. A surgeon would determine the seriousness of the wounds, and treat his patient accordingly. Amputation was a frequent recourse, and especially in the Confederacy, anaesthetics such as chloroform were rarely available. By modern standards medical practices were primitive, and a lack of understanding of sterilization, germs, or medical hygiene caused numerous deaths. Wounded soldiers frequently died from blood poisoning or sepsis caused by poor medical practice. Records indicate that in approximately twenty percent of all operations, gangrene or erysipelas resulted from insanitary operating procedures. After treatment in a field hospital, the wounded who survived were evacuated by ambulance to a general or army hospital. There the facilities were generally better than those in the field, and many contained highly trained medical staff. Patients remained there until they died, or were fit enough to be returned to duty, or were discharged as being medically unfit for service.

The severity of the conflict took both sides by surprise, and medical facilities were stretched to the limit. Field ambulance units and field hospitals provided front-line care for the wounded, who were then evacuated to permanent hospitals to recover.

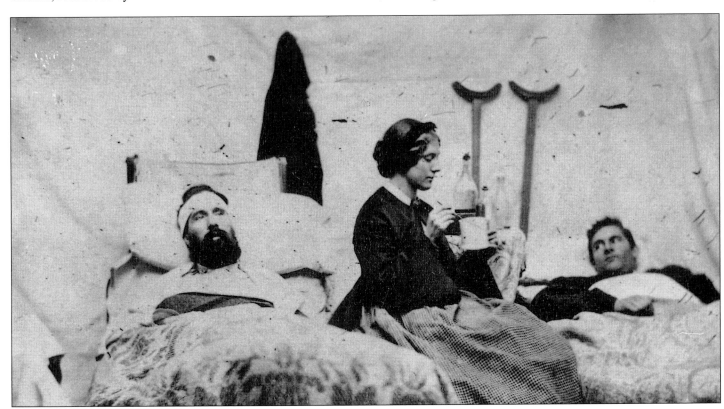

Memminger, Christopher Gustavus (1803–88)

Memminger, an expert in banking and commercial law, was the Confederacy's Treasury Secretary. It was under Memminger that the Southern states raised the bonds and taxes that funded their war effort. The costs of the war were, however, so great that the Confederacy was forced to print vast amounts of money that were to depreciate rapidly in value. Memminger, effectively a proto-monetarist, warned that printing money was a recipe for disaster. However, the scale of the war effort was such that $1.5 billion were printed during the war.

Memphis, Tennessee

Situated on the Mississippi, Memphis became a trading center between North and South. While blockades largely prevented Southerners from obtaining supplies from overseas, there was no ruling to keep them from trading with the North, and in Memphis bribery and corruption were rife as Southerners obtained trading permits to sell cotton and salt into the North.

Following his evacuation of Corinth, it was in Memphis that Beauregard made his stand against the naval might of the Union Ellet family—within two hours, however, he was defeated, and on June 6, 1862, Memphis was taken. Despite Grant's and Sherman's best efforts, however, the Union occupation of Memphis did nothing to stop illegal trading.

Memphis, Battle of, 1862

Following the loss of Fort Pillow, Tennessee, and New Orleans in April 1862, only Mempis and Vicksburg remained as Confederate bastions on the Mississippi. The remaining Confederate naval forces were gathered at Memphis, their strength reduced to eight wooden rams, commanded by Captain James Montgomery. At dawn on June 6, 1862, five Union ironclads descended on Memphis, followed by a flotilla of five wooden rams, converted and commanded by Colonel Charles Ellet. Both sides exchanged long-range fire. At that point, Ellet's ram fleet passed through the ironclads, and the two fleets of wooden rams charged each other. Ellet's flagship *Queen of the West* steered for Montgomery's *General Lovell*, which backed water just before impact. The *Lovell* was struck amidships and sank. The *Queen of the West* was rammed in turn by the *General Beauregard*, forcing Ellet's ship to beach herself on the Arkansas shore where Ellet was mortally wounded by Confederate sharpshooters. The *Beauregard* then turned on the *Monarch*, who was simultaneously charged by the *Sterling Price* from the opposite side. She escaped, and the Confederate vessels collided. The *Monarch* circled round and rammed the stationary *Beauregard*. At this point the Union ironclads arrived, sinking the *Beauregard* and blowing up the *Jeff Thomson*. The remaining Confederate rams retreated downriver, pursued by the Union fleet. One by one they were destroyed, leaving only the *Van Dorn* to escape to the safety of Vicksburg. Around noon infantry landed and took control of the city to complete the Union victory.

Left: Facilities were generally better in hospitals than in the field, and many contained highly trained medical staff. Patients remained there until they died, or were fit enough to be returned to duty, or were discharged as being medically unfit for service.

Mexican War

The Mexican War of April 1846–February 1848 resulted in the annexation by the United States of a half-million square-mile swath of territory from Texas to California. The conflict was significant militarily because it was where many of the important leaders on both sides during the Civil War got their original combat experience. In the Mexican War, of course, they were all fighting on the same side.

The background issues of the Mexican War were a combination of disagreements over the southern border of Texas and an American interest in the acquisition of the territory between Texas and the Pacific Ocean (including California). Mexico had inherited this area when it was abandoned by Spain, but it was inhabited primarily by American settlers. After ten years as an independent country, Texas had joined the United States as a state in 1845. Mexico claimed sovereignty as far north as the Nueces River in central Texas, while the United States claimed that Texas extended to the Rio Grande.

In September 1845, President James Knox Polk sent John Slidell to Mexico City to negotiate the Texas border dispute and to offer Mexico $30 million ($600 million in terms of twenty-first century dollars) for the additional territory west and north of Texas. The Mexicans refused to see Slidell, so Polk ordered the U.S. Army into the disputed area of south Texas. In April 1846, Mexican forces entered the region and attacked the Americans. Interpreting this as an invasion of the United States, Congress declared war on May 13. A force under General (later President) Zachary Taylor marched south into Mexico, while a second force under Stephen Kearney occupied the area between the present states of New Mexico and California. In March 1847, General Winfield Scott captured the port city of Vera Cruz and marched inland to Mexico City, which was occupied in September.

On February 2, 1848, Mexico and the United States signed the Treaty of Guadalupe Hidalgo. Having won a resounding military victory, the Americans were generous to a fault. Even though Mexico had been defeated, the United States withdrew from Mexico proper, assumed all claims by Americans against the Mexican government and paid Mexico $15 million for the former Spanish territory that was settled by Americans.

Above Right: The Battle of Churubsco from a painting by Chappel.

Right: The storming of Monterey—an attack on the Bishop's Palace under the command of General Zachary Taylor.

THE AMERICAN CIVIL WAR: A VISUAL ENCYCLOPEDIA

After the war, however, the new territory became a pawn in the slavery issue. The South naturally wanted to have slavery legalized in this area, and Abolitionists wanted it banned. In 1846, Congressman David Wilmot of Pennsylvania attempted to add an amendment to an appropriations bill banning slavery from any territory acquired from Mexico. The "Wilmot Proviso" was not passed, but the debate that it caused helped to drive the wedge between North and South that would ultimately lead to the Civil War.

Mines and mining

Both land and submarine mines were used during the Civil War, and during its course mining took of two distinct forms—first, as a means of controlling access to waterways and impeding the movements of enemy ships; second, as an offensive measure against fortified land positions.

Submarine mine warfare has a history dating back to the American Revolution, although before 1870 mines were generally known as torpedoes, and all reference to torpedoes in early accounts should be so understood. Early submarine mines were fired by clockwork, by levers or by triggers pulled by hand. A significant advance was made when electric triggering was introduced, making it possible to plant mines which were connected by wire to the shore. The next step was the introduction of percussion type mines, which could be exploded by contact with a ship. The current technology was crude and the mines unreliable, but after the Crimean War (1853–56) they exerted a powerful influence on naval tactics and strategy. During the Civil War a number of vessels were lost to mines, and at Mobile Bay in August 1864 they might have reversed the result. Approaching the entrance to Mobile bay in two columns, the lead ship of the Union fleet under Farragut struck a mine and sank almost immediately. Ignoring warnings of the presence of more mines, Farragut steamed ahead. Had his ship, the *Hartford*, struck a mine, there is

every chance that the Union fleet would have withdrawn.

Land mines were used with some success, particularly against strongly held entrenchments. Mining was a specialty of the engineers, but most officers were schooled in the techniques, which had been practiced since the Middle Ages. Usually, an offensive mining operation involved excavating a downward-sloping shaft of calculated length from behind the front line toward the enemy position, and then constructing lateral shafts under them. Explosive would then be packed into the lateral shafts and fuzes laid.

The most famous use of this technique was during the Siege of Petersburg. In the latter part of June 1864 Lieutenant Colonel Pleasants, an officer of the 48th Pennsylvania, submitted a plan to his superior officer for the mining of a Confederate redan in front of his position, and agreed to conduct the operation. General Burnside authorized it to be done, though he was not confident of success. The redan was held by part of B. R Johnson's division, and was opposite the center of IX Corps, where the opposing lines were only some 120 yards apart. Pleasants began work in late June, his men tunneling with considerable difficulty through difficult soil toward and under the redan. The main gallery was some 511 feet in length, with two lateral galleries of thirty-seven and thirty-eight feet, in which were eight magazines. The works were completed ready for charging on July 23, and 1,000 pounds of powder was placed in each of the magazines. It was intended that, upon the explosion of the mine, the artillery on the right and left would lay down a furious barrage, and the two brigades of infantry should lead the assault on the wrecked position. The whole army was then to advance and take advantage of the general confusion anticipated in the Confederate lines. Burnside was to trigger the mine at 3:30am; his guns were to begin at once a bombardment of the whole line, and of Cemetery Hill, 400 yards to the rear of the mined works; his assaulting columns

were to rush forward; seize a crest of ground 150 yards beyond the breach in the line caused by the explosion, reform and push on, closely followed by supporting infantry.

However, the fuzes failed, and once they had been relighted half an hour had been lost. Finally, at 4:40am, the 8,000lb mine exploded, throwing men, guns, carriages, dirt and timbers into the air and leaving a crater 170 feet long, sixty feet wide and

Above Left: The Confederates helped offset the Union's naval supremacy by using torpedoes (mines) to protect their harbors.

Above: A sergeant from the 54th Missouri Volunteers.

Below: The Union fleet on the Mississippi included hospital ships and floating offices as well as warships.

thirty feet deep. The mine did its job, as did the artillery bombardment, but the accompanying infantry assault was poorly coordinated, and the dazed Confederate troops had time to regroup and repulse the attack. The Union soldiers who had rushed into the breach were mown down with artillery fire; few of them ever made it back to friendly lines.

Another interesting attempt at offensive mining, if it can be called that, was at Fort Fisher on Christmas Eve, 1864. Union forces under Porter sailed from the Hampton Roads to the vicinity of the formidable Confederate fort at the entrance to the port of Wilmington with the old steamer *Louisiana*, which had been packed with 240 tons of explosive and was to be exploded under the walls of the fortress. At 1.40am, when the ship was still some 400 yards from the fort, the powder was exploded but caused scarcely any damage, and plans for an assault had to be abandoned.

Minnesota

At the outbreak of war the Union state of Minnesota was distanced from the main action, its only involvement being its obligation to send its quota of soldiers to fight.

Minnesota, however, was home to large numbers of Native Americans, and their mistreatment by the corrupt Federal Indian agency left them poor and hungry and soon led to all-out war between the Sioux nation and their Union settlers. Union rumor had it that a Confederate plot had sparked the Santee Sioux uprising—in fact, it was provoked entirely by the Northerners themselves, but served the Confederate cause in that it occupied Union soldiers who would otherwise have traveled south to the war.

Mississippi

Having joined the Union in the January of 1817, Mississippi withdrew its representatives from the United States House of Representatives on January 12 ,1862. The struggle for control of the important Mississippi River took place across the state of Mississippi, with fighting at Corinth, Grand Gulf, Holly Springs, and, notably, Vicksburg.

Mississippi River

Control of the Mississippi River was recognized by both forces as a key to success in

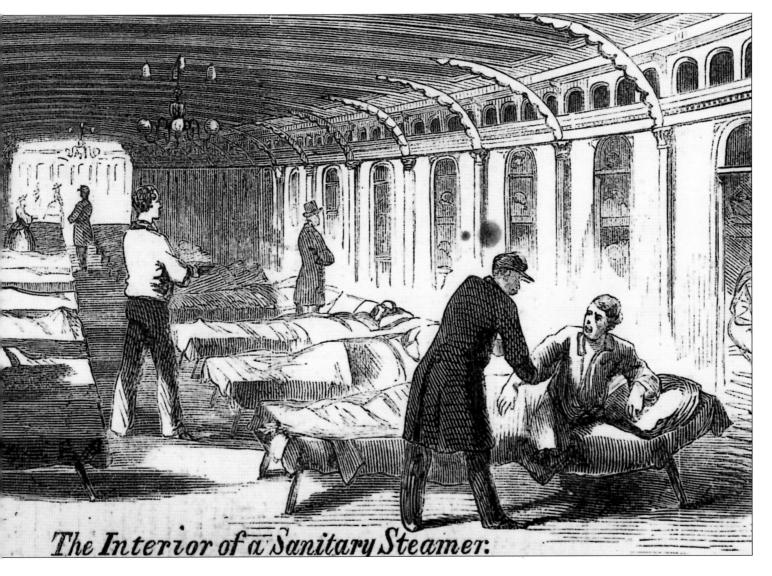

The Interior of a Sanitary Steamer.

the American Civil War, and in January 1812 Confederates raided Federal arsenals and seized their artillery with the sole purpose of sending their spoils to Vicksburg to help stop traffic on the Mississippi.

In October 1862, rebel forts all along the Mississippi were taken by Grant, in the campaign which would culminate with the taking of Vicksburg in July 1863—the river itself was used extensively in the launching of Union attacks.

Mississippi River Defense Fleet, Confederate

Following the loss of Forts Henry and Donelson in early 1862, a Confederate flotilla was hastily built or purchased to protect both New Orleans and the northern reaches of the Mississippi River. At various stages the fleet incorporated Louisiana State vessels, naval warships, and army gunboats. By April, twenty-two small river gunboats were available, having been built or converted in New Orleans and Memphis. Six gunboats helped defend Island No. 10 near the Tennessee state line, and on May 10, the Confederate "fleet" fought its first battle in defense of Fort Pillow. Following the fall of Fort Pillow and the destruction of the New Orleans squadron (eight vessels), the remaining River Defense Fleet was concentrated at Memphis, Tennessee. All but one of these gunboats were destroyed in the Battle of Memphis (June 6, 1862), and the remaining vessel was subsequently lost at Vicksburg a year later.

Missouri

The Missouri Compromise of 1820 enabled Missouri to join Congress as a slaveholding state, and when in 1850 Kansas applied for statehood, Missourian pro-slavery lobbyists ensured that their neighbor state also became a slaveholding region. Missouri itself remained politically divided at the outbreak of war, with a Confederate government and Union legislature. When the Unionist Frémont proclaimed the emancipation of slaves there and began confiscating Confederate property, an illegitimate minority vote led to Missouri's secession, but although it was a Confederate state, from November 28, 1861, most of the population fought for the Union. The state soon fell into Union hands, and for the duration of the war guerrilla fighting raged in Missouri.

Right: A band of Confederate irregular cavalry make camp in the backwoods of Missouri. The state was subjected to frequent guerrilla raids throughout the war.

THE AMERICAN CIVIL WAR: A VISUAL ENCYCLOPEDIA

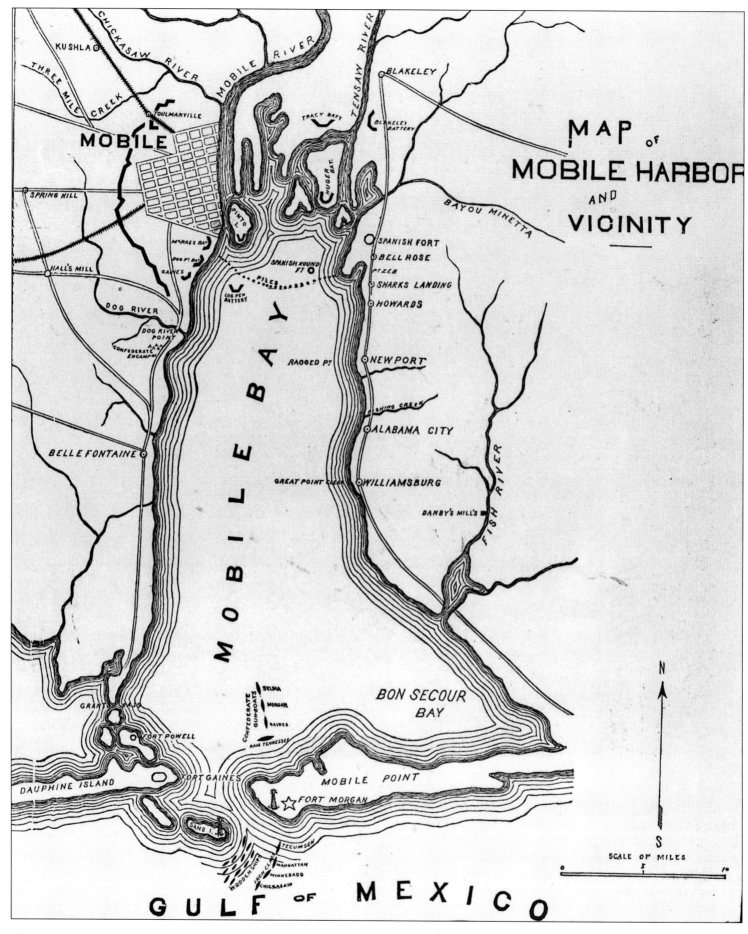

MAP of MOBILE HARBOR and VICINITY

Above: By 1864, Mobile was the only major port on the Gulf of Mexico which was still in Confederate hands. On August 5, 1864, Admiral Farregut forced his way past the forts guarding the entrance to the bay, and battered the defending ironclad CSS *Tennessee* into submission.

Above Right: Commodore Josiah Tattnall (nicknamed "Old Tat") was a compatriot of Admiral Buchanan, and commanded Confederate naval forces in Virginia and the Carolinas during the war.

Right: Ericsson's innovation—the *Monitor*. (See page 308.)

Mobile, Alabama

Mobile became the Confederates' primary Gulf port following the loss of New Orleans in April 1864, and its bay was the last blockade-running port to fall to the Union. The town of Mobile remained in Confederate hands after the Union seizure of Mobile Bay.

Mobile Bay

Mobile Bay was thirty miles long, and protected by three forts (including Forts Morgan and Gaines which were seized for the Confederacy on January 5, 1861), three gunboats and the famous Confederate ram *Tennessee*. It was the last blockade-running port in the Gulf east of Texas, and Rear Admiral David Glasgow Farragut was charged with the task of taking Mobile Bay, while his former colleague Franklin Buchanan defended it. Farragut launched his attack on August 5 at 6:00am, leading fourteen conventional gunboats and four ironclad monitors into the bay. The Confederate fleet was soon disabled, and all three forts had fallen to the Union by August 23, 1864.

Mobile Bay, Battle of, 1864

By early 1864, the only significant port on the Gulf of Mexico still in Confederate

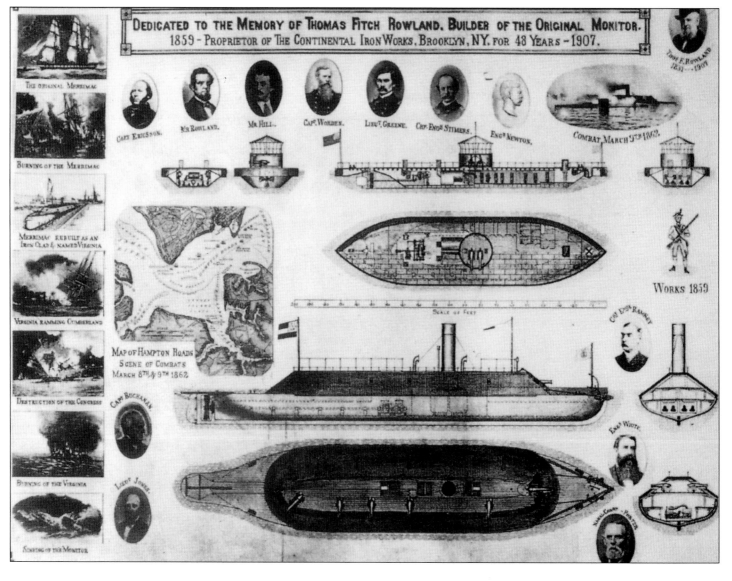

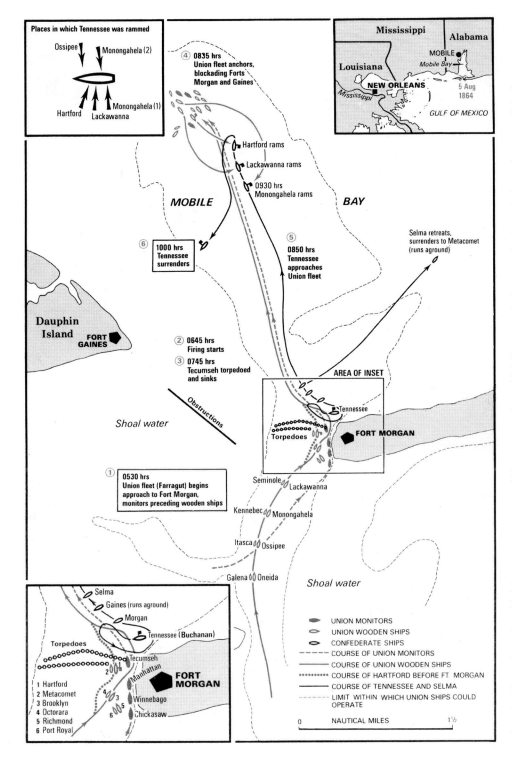

At dawn on August 5, 1864, his fleet advanced toward the channel, a column of fourteen wooden warships lashed together into pairs. The weaker warships were stationed on the port side of their consorts, protected from Fort Morgan, which would be passed at close range to starboard. The USS *Brooklyn* led the column, while Farragut followed behind in his flagship, the USS *Hartford*. In addition, four "Manhattan" class monitors provided additional firepower. By 6:45am the first shots were fired, and the fleet drew close to the fort, which was pounding the leading Union warships. The monitor *Tecumseh* then struck a mine and sank in thirty seconds, taking most of her crew with her. The advance halted while Confederate fire continued to pummel the Union fleet. Farragut then ordered the *Hartford* to take the lead, and his exclamation; "*Damn the Torpedoes!*" became the most famous naval quotation of the war. The gamble paid off, as no further mines detonated, and the fleet passed into the bay. The smaller ships were cut loose and while most of these engaged and destroyed the Confederate gunboats, the rest of the Union fleet concentrated on the *Tennessee*. The Confederate ironclad was rammed twice to no effect, then exchanged point-blank broadsides with the *Hartford*. The monitors also fired on the *Tennessee*, crippling her steering gear. Immobile, and surrounded by enemy vessels, Buchanan continued fighting for another thirty minutes before bowing to the inevitable. The *Tennessee* surrendered, yielding the bay to the Union fleet. Both forts surrendered before the end of the month, and although Mobile remained in Confederate hands until April 1865, she was effectively closed as a port.

USS *Monitor*

Designed by Swedish-born engineer John Ericsson, the USS *Monitor* was the Union's first ironclad. Built in New York, construction began in October 1861, and she was finished in four months. Unlike other ironclad designs, the *Monitor* mounted its armament of two smoothbore guns inside a revolving turret. The iron hull was partly submerged, presenting a minimal target to the enemy. Once commissioned, she was immediately sent to Hampton Roads, Virginia; arriving on March 8, when she immediately went into action with the Confederate ironclad *Virginia*. The resulting Battle of Hampton Roads was a stalemate, but the monitor design had demonstrated its effectiveness. The ironclad remained in Hampton Roads and the James River before being ordered to Charleston. She foundered off Cape Hatteras on December 31, 1862. The wrecksite is now a marine sanctuary.

Above Left: The battle between the *Monitor* and the *Merrimac*.

Above: The Battle of Mobile Bay.

Left: The USS *Monitor* was a revolutionary design for a warship, employing a tunnel on a low armored deck. By contrast the Confederate ironclad CSS *Virginia* mounted its guns in a more conventional broadside battery.

hands was Mobile, Alabama. The port lay at the head of a large bay, whose only navigable entrance was protected by the powerful fortifications of Fort Morgan and Fort Gaines. The entrance channel was also sown with mines (torpedoes), and covered by secondary gun batteries. A small Confederate flotilla consisting of the powerful ironclad CSS *Tennessee*, and three wooden gunboats (*Selma*, *Morgan*, and *Gaines*) protected the bay itself. In command was Admiral Franklin Buchanan, the man who led the *Virginia* into action against the *Monitor* in 1862. Union forces gathered off the entrance of the bay during the early summer, and by August Farragut was ready.

Dimensions: 172 feet x 41 feet x 11 feet 4 inches
Armor: Eight inches of iron (turret)
Armament: Two eleven-inch smoothbore guns
Commissioned: February 1862

Monitors, Union

The USS *Monitor* proved the effectiveness of the turreted ironclad, and her name became the generic term given to all subsequent Union ironclads of that type. Of the thirty seagoing ironclads in Union service during the war, twenty-eight were monitors. Of these the most numerous types were the "Passiac" class of ten ships, and the "Canonicus" class of five monitors. Experiences gained during the war led to the introduction of better-armed monitors with two turrets, and improved armored protection. By 1864 the "Milwaukee" class (four ships) were armed with two fifteen-inch smoothbore guns, making them the most powerful monitors afloat until the introduction of the twin-turreted *Onondanga* and *Monadnock*, the latter carrying four fifteen-inch guns. The least successful monitors in the fleet were those of the "Casco" class, whose turrets were replaced with a mounting for a spar torpedo. A drawback of the monitor design was the low freeboard of the hull, making these ships susceptible to swamping. The USS *Weehawken* and the USS *Keokuk* both foundered off Charleston, as had the USS *Monitor* before them. Although they had their faults, the Union monitors were a success, and played a crucial part in the defeat of the Confederacy.

Right: Capture of Confederate flagship CSS *Tennessee* on August 5 in Mobile Bay by Admiral D. G. Farragut in *Hartford*. From a painting by Xanthus Smith.

Monocacy, Battle of, 1864

In June 1864, General Jubal Early invaded Maryland to divert Union attention from Lee's army in Virginia. On July 9, his 8,000 veterans encountered the improvised Union force of General Lew Wallace at Monocracy Junction, Maryland.

Outnumbered, Wallace ordered his 6,000 troops to entrench behind the Monocracy River. Early's Confederates assaulted these entrenched positions, and after heavy casualties they forced Wallace to withdraw at nightfall, leaving 1,300 casualties behind him. The Union stand gained time for other Union troops to gather to defend Baltimore and Washington, forcing Early to abandon his advance on Washington a week later.

Morrill Tariff Act (The Tariff Act of 1861)

A Republican Representative from Vermont, Justin Smith Morrill was a chief sponsor of the Tariff Act of 1861, which introduced a series of tariffs that are often referred to as the "Morrill tariffs." On the surface, the idea was the familiar one of protecting American industry from overseas competition by making foreign products artificially more expensive that American ones through the use of import duties. However, the Tariff Act of 1861 became one of the causes of the Civil War by forcing the Southern states, with their minimal industrial base, to become dependent on Northern industry.

During the war, Congressman Morrill acted a strict financial conservative, strongly opposing the printing of paper money to finance the war, and fighting efforts to take the United States off the gold standard.

He is best remembered for the Morrill Act of 1862, which provided grants of land to state colleges for teaching subjects "related to agriculture and the mechanic arts" against a backdrop of science and liberal arts. The "land grant" colleges ultimately became the backbone of higher education throughout much of the United States.

Morton, Oliver Perry (1823–77)

Oliver P. Morton was the Republican Governor of Indiana; an enthusiastic supporter of the Union, he raised more troops in the state than Lincoln had initially called for in 1861. He was to vent his frustration in the amateurish organization of the Union forces at the start of the war when he commented, "Why has there been such delay in sending arms? . . . No officer here yet to muster troops into service. not a pound of powder or a single ball sent us, or any sort of equipment. Allow me to ask what is the cause of all this?" When the Democrats gained a majority of the state's legislature in 1863 (thereby threatening to demand an armistice), Morton persuaded the Republican members to refrain from attending, thus preventing the legislature from acting as a result of a lack of a quorum. For the next two years Morton acted without the legislature, raising money through methods that were probably verging on the illegal. The belief was, however, that the constitution needed to be stretched in order, ultimately, to preserve it.

Right: The Battle of Monocracy was fought in Maryland during Jubal Early's raid on Washington, D.C. in 1864.

Below: A Union monitor of the "Passaic" class, USS *Saugus*. These warships were an improved version of the original monitor design.

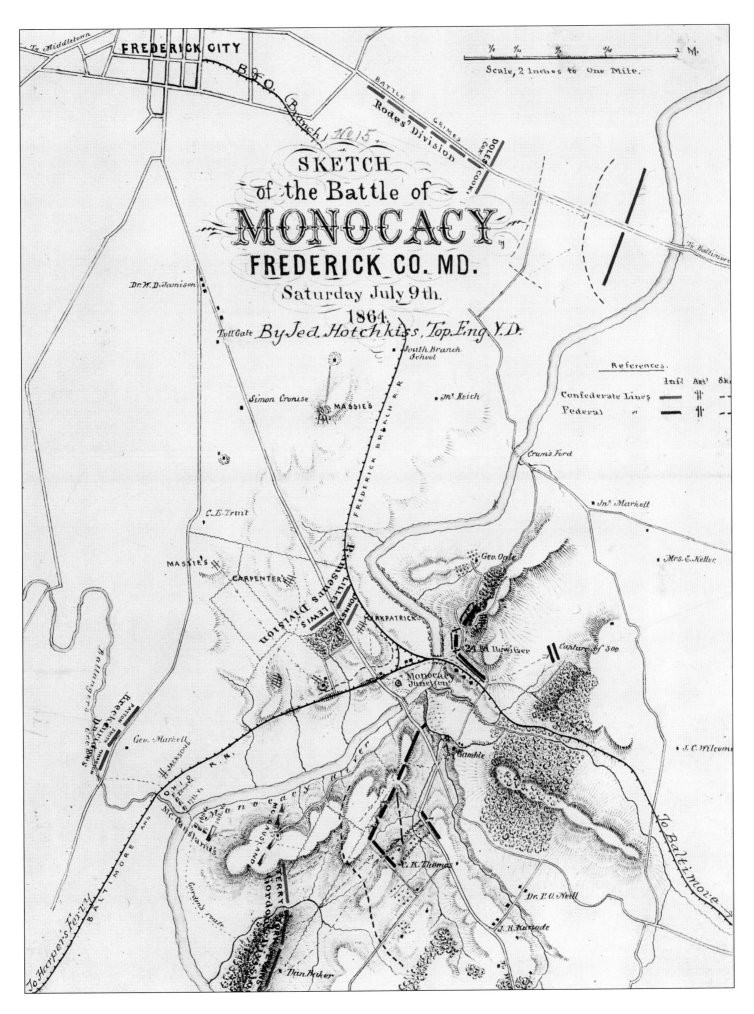

Murfreesboro, Battle of, 1862–63

Following the battle of Perryville on October 8, 1862, General Bragg moved his Army of the Mississippi through the Cumberland Gap into Tennessee. Here he concentrated at Murfreesboro from where, on November 20, his Army of Mississippi was combined with the Army of Kentucky to become the Army of Tennessee. Following Buell's failure to pursue Bragg after the battle of Perryville, Lincoln had replaced him with Major General William S. Rosecrans, and he now led the Union Army of the Cumberland from Kentucky to Nashville in pursuit of Bragg. The two armies encountered each other along the edge of the Stones River (the Confederate name for the battle) on December 30 just to the west of Murfreesboro. Unbeknown to either one of them, they had decided upon identical battle plans, each planning on enveloping the other's right flank.

At dawn on the 31st, Bragg's men attacked first, Rosecrans deciding to wait until his men had had their breakfast. The initial Confederate charge was particularly successful, Hardee's corps swept round to the left, supported by Polk's corps and managed to push the Union troops back to the Nashville Turnpike, though not before Sheridan's division had withstood several Confederate charges and held up the advance till midday. By this point Rosecrans had realized the perilous situation that he was in and had taken steps to reinforce his beleaguered right flank. The Union advance on the Confederate right flank was canceled and two divisions were sent to the right lank. By the end of the day the Union position had held and the Confederate advance had petered out. Bragg had lost around 9,000 men yet considered himself to be in a strong position and believed that the Union forces would withdraw to their Nashville entrenchments. However, Rosecrans, even though he had suffered over 12,000 casualties throughout the day, had consulted his corps commanders and decided to stay and fight.

Very little of note occurred on New Year's Day—both sides remained more or less in the positions they had occupied the previous evening and awaited developments. Bragg remained convinced that Rosecrans would withdraw, but the following morning he still remained in position. On January 2 Bragg planned a further offensive for the 3rd, he intended to resume the attack with Polk's division, but first he

Right: The Battle of Stones River—Murfreesboro to the Union—was fought over the three days of the New Year of 1862–63, and although technically a stalemate, it resulted in the strategic withdrawal of Confederate troops from northern Tennessee.

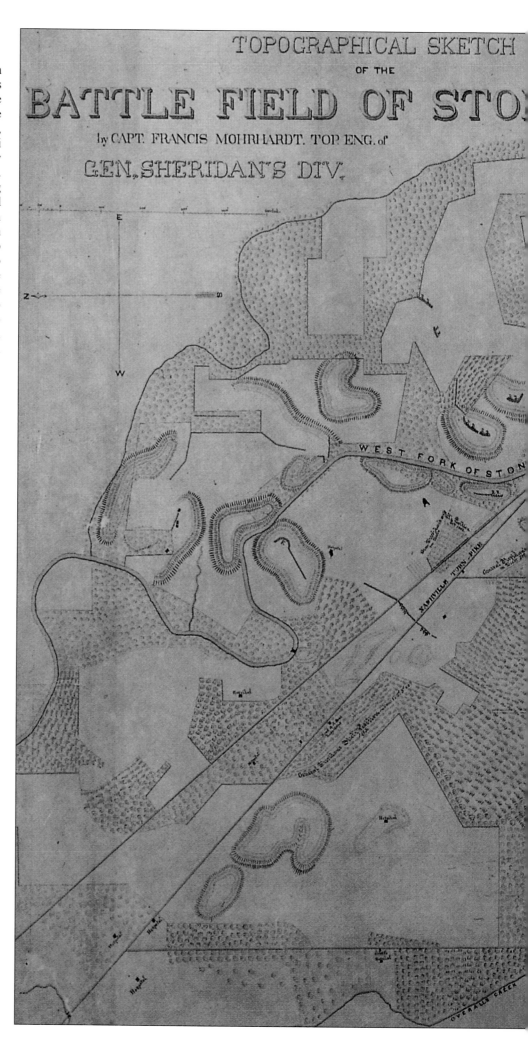

TOPOGRAPHICAL SKETCH
OF THE
BATTLE FIELD OF STO[NES]
by CAPT. FRANCIS MOHRHARDT. TOP. ENG. of
GEN. SHERIDAN'S DIV.

E RIVER

MURFREESBORO

SHELBYVILLE T

CHATTANOOGA R.R.

SALEM TURN PIKE

NASHVILLE N.

WILKINSON TURN PIKE

FRANKLIN DIRT ROAD

WEST FORK OF STONE RIVER

had to drive back a Union division that had crossed Stones River the previous day. To this end he ordered Breckinridge's corps to attack it in the late afternoon of the 2nd, thus preventing any Union counterattack before nightfall.

Under protest Breckinridge complied and his forces were decimated by well-sited Union artillery, before being pushed back to their original start line. After a further day of inaction on the 3rd, the Confederate Army of Tennessee began to withdraw in the evening. Although he had made no effort to harass Bragg's withdrawal, nor, in fact, had he made many offensive moves since the 31st, Rosecrans claimed the victory as he was left in possession of the field. Over the course of the three days the Union forces had lost over 12,900 while the Confederates had lost 11,700, and Bragg's Army of the Tennessee was now incapable of offensive action.

Muskets and Rifles

Once the Civil War had begun, both North and South had to equip their rapidly growing forces with basic firearms. Initially, there were too few of the most modern weapons to go around, and a variety of old and even obsolete firearms were issued. However, gradually, a measure of standardization was achieved, with certain guns being issued in their hundreds of thousands. However, due to the shortages a wide variety of rifled muskets and other types were employed, many of which came from overseas.

Union forces were equipped with weapons from a variety of sources, although as the war progressed a high degree of standardization was achieved. Among the older weapons available was the M1842 smoothbore musket, a number of which—some 14,000—were modernized with rifling and longer-range sights being added in the late 1850s. Next, came the M1855 rifled musket, which took the conical, pure lead Minié ball. These were produced by government arsenals and also under contract by Eli Whitney. In an attempt to reduce the high costs associated with this weapon, a more basic version was introduced. This, the M1861 Springfield, became the standard rifled musket of the Union forces during the war. Some 671,000 were produced in total during the conflict, of which around 265,000 were actually

Left: Confederate muskets and rifles. From right to left: Morse smoothbore muzzle-loading musket with bayonet; State of Georgia smoothbore muzzle-loading musket with bayonet; J. P. Murray muzzle-loading rifle; Boyle, Gamble & Macfee bowie bayonet and scabbard; cartridge box embossed with Georgia State seal plate; C. Chapman muzzle-loading rifle and ramrod; Pulaski muzzle-loading rifle; W. J. McElroy knife and scabbard; H. C. Lamb muzzle-loading rifle; late design Read and Watson muzzle-loading rifle.

manufactured by Springfield. Foreign designs were headed by the British P1853 Enfield rifled musket of which 428,292 were issued. The Enfield was in some ways a slightly better design that the more common Springfield. Other foreign imports included Austrian, Belgian, French, and German designs, of which 226,294, 57,467, 44,250, and 141,570 came from each country respectively

The North also equipped some units with breech-loading rifles, although they were considerably more expensive that the much more common rifled muzzle-loaders. Some 9,141 M1859 Sharps rifles were bought by the U.S. Army, along with 12,471 Spencers, and a very modest number of Henry repeating rifles, just 1,731. The Sharps used a linen cartridge, while both the Sharps rifle and the Henry repeater made use of brass cartridges, and thus heralded a new generation of breech-loaders.

The South was at a decided disadvantage in equipping its forces with firearms as it lacked a large armaments industry. Indeed, it was not until the latter part of 1862 that its troops were ale to surrender the outmoded flintlock muskets, with percussion muskets. Many of these were smoothbore rather that the more advanced rifle musket.

The South's troops received firearms from three sources: Southern manufacturers, overseas suppliers, and captured Union weapons. The importance of the latter source cannot be overestimated—in the twelve months after September 30, 1863, the South took around 45,000 Union smallarms. Northern types chiefly consisted of two rifled muskets—the M1861 Springfield and the British P1853 Enfield. Overseas suppliers were wholly European. Britain accounted for seventy-five percent of the total, mostly Enfields, while the Austrians provided twenty percent, of which the most common was the M1854 rifled musket. The remaining five percent came from a number of Belgian, French, and German manufacturers. Local manufacturers copied Northern and European designs, mainly the Springfield, Enfield, and the U.S. M1855 rifle.

ENFIELD

The British-manufacturer Enfield was one of the best standard muzzle-loading rifled muskets of the era and was one of the most widely used smallarms of the Civil War. It was introduced partly because it was a fine

Right: Confederate muskets and rifles. From right to left: Palmetto Armory Model 1842 smoothbore musket with bayonet; D guard side knife with scabbard; Dickson, Nelson & Co. muzzle-loading rifle; Davis and Bozeman muzzle-loading rifle; D guard side knife with scabbard; tin drum canteen; later Fayetteville muzzle-loading rifle; unidentified muzzle-loading rifle; waist belt with oval CS plate; Mendenhall, Jones & Gardner muzzle-loading rifle with shoulder strap and British Lancaster saber bayonet and scabbard.

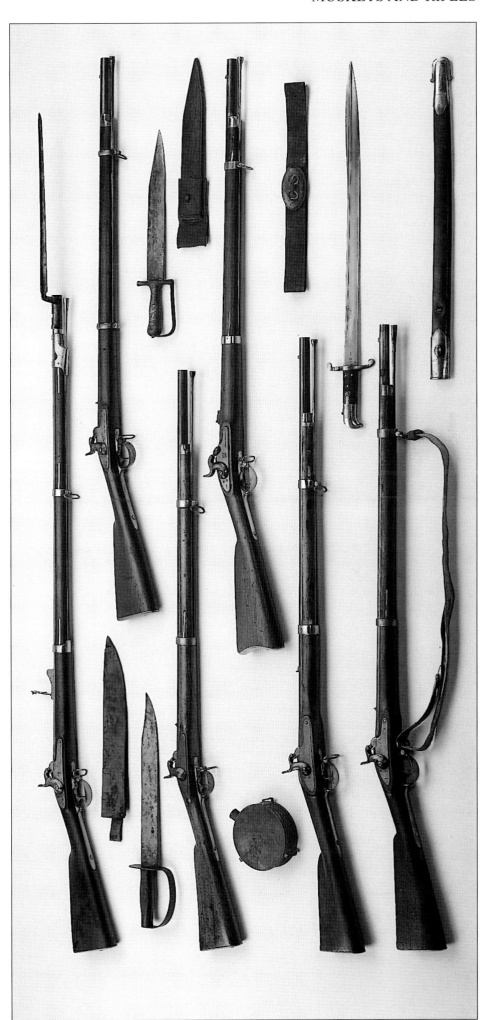

weapon and partly because U.S. manufacturers could not keep pace with demand for such equipment. The Enfield was so widely imported that it became virtually the standard weapon of Confederate infantry and stood only second to the M1861 Springfield in its use by Union forces. The U.S. Army alone took delivery of some 428,000 Enfields during the conflict and the South very slightly less. The South also contrived to produce its own copies of the Enfield, but these were rather cruder versions of the British original. Cook & Brother manufactured modified versions of the design with some success, but others made by other private concerns proved less successful. In fact, many of the Enfields that saw service in the Civil War were generally not produced in the company's armory, but elsewhere in Britain.

The Enfield rifled musket, which was officially designated the P1853, was in many ways similar to the famed M1855 Springfield. Its chief differences lay in its .577-inch caliber, its fifty-five-inch overall length, and the use of brass for its nose cap, butt plate, and trigger guard. The Enfield also had special long-range sights graduated to a distance of 1,000 yards that were not found on the Springfield. The Enfiled had a similar maximum range to the Springfield and its battle range was also similar, being between 200 and 300 yards.

EUROPEAN IMPORTS
Neither North nor the South was prepared for a war on a grand scale in 1861, one involving forces numbering in the hundreds of thousands. Equally, neither side had the weapons available in the numbers required to equip such vast armies. The North was in general better prepared in the medium to long term to provide weapons for its troops due to its larger industrial base, but like the Confederacy for the entire war, it had to purchase weapons from overseas to cover the shortfall in the short term. Europe became the key supplier of firearms to both sides.

The main supplier to both sides was Britain, whose greatest contribution was the P1853 Enfield rifled musket. This became the most common firearm carried by Southern troops and the second commonest in Northern use. The North also purchased a number, some 8,000, of another Enfield weapon, the P1856 rifle, which had a barrel measuring thirty-three inches. However, Britain was by no means alone in supplying the rival war efforts. Among other European nations to become involved where Austria, Belgium, France, Germany, and Italy. Together, the supplied something like 364,000 firearms, in some cases taking the opportunity to unload obsolete weapons from their own arsenals, to the U.S. government between 1861 and 1866. Austria was the main provider with 226,294 items, while Italy shipped a more modest 5,995

firearms. Southern imports were on an equally grand scale. Some seventy-five percent of the imports were from Britain, chiefly Enfields, with most of the remainder (twenty percent, some 100,000, which were mostly M1854 rifled muskets) came from Austria.

REPEATING
Although repeating rifles were destined to play a profound part in the history of the United States in the final decades of the nineteenth century, they had only a limited impact on the course of the Civil War. There were several reasons for this. Repeating rifles were a new, revolutionary weapon and signaled a great leap forward in arms technology. Consequently, they were still expensive and time-consuming to produce, and were considerably more expensive to buy than more established weapons that were being mass produced at comparatively small cost. Finally, there was a degree of in-built conservatism within military circles that was wary of innovation. Indeed, it was believed by some senior figures that quick-firing firearms would allow troops to simply waste ammunition.

Despite these issues and problems, two repeating rifles did see service, albeit in a very limited capacity, during the war years. These were the Spencer and the Henry. Unlike standard breech-loaders, which had to be reloaded after each shot, these had magazines that could hold a number of brass cartridges—seven in the case of the Spencer and fifteen in the Henry. Official interest in both weapons was somewhat limited, particularly in the case of the more advanced Henry. A mere 12,471 Spencers were purchased by the U.S. Army and an even smaller number of Henrys—just 1,731. However, in the latter case considerably more were probably purchased by individuals as the total production during the war totaled around 10,000. Anecdotal evidence suggested that whatever their superiors thought of the repeaters, the frontline soldier was eager to acquire a weapon that greatly magnified his personal firepower. The direct descendant of the Henry was the famed and widely admired Winchester, suggesting that the man at the front was correct.

RIFLED
The rifled musket gave the Civil War infantryman unparaleled firepower, and such weapons were essentially standard issue during the conflict, being available in their hundreds of thousands. The two most widely used by both Union and Confederate forces were the M1861 Springfield and the British-made P1853 Enfield, although others, often European designs, were available in smaller numbers.

Rifled muskets had been around for twenty years or so before the Civil War, but

had not been seen on the battlefield in such great quantities. The rifled muskets were far more accurate that their smoothbore predecessors and had a greater range, chiefly due to the spin imparted to the round, usually a spherical ball or a conical Minie, by the rifling. Such rounds had a muzzle velocity of around 950 feet per second and the large soft bullets caused terrible wounds to the body. Other rounds included a mixture of buckshot and a single ball, or just buckshot, although these were comparatively rare. Rifled muskets had a maximum range of around 1,000 yards but a top marksman was likely to score a hit on a particular target at ranges of up to 500 yards. On the battlefield, fire was considered to be most effective at ranges of 200 to 300 yards.

Such firepower forced a sea change in tactics. Troops could not advance in densely packed lines or columns against an enemy as they were likely to be shot to pieces. Therefore, troop formations became more fluid and greater advantage was taken of cover and concealment.

SMOOTHBORE
The Civil War confirmed that the age of the smoothbore musket was over as rifled muskets, such as the M1861 Springfield and the British P1853 Enfield, proved to be more accurate over greater distances. However, traditional muskets did not immediately disappear from the battlefield. There were several reasons for this. Chief among them was the problem of equipping armies of a size that had never been seen in North America before. Neither the North nor the South had sufficient quantities of the up-to-date rifled muskets to equip all of their rapidly expanding forces. In the case of the South, matters were made worse by its lack of arms manufacturers that could turn out the newer firearms; even those that could were in no way comparable in size or experience to their Northern counterparts.

Before late 1862 the Confederacy still very much relied on old smoothbore muskets, often flintlock types, and these were often replaced by percussion muskets, again smoothbore rather than rifled. Among some of the former weapons brought out of retirement were some dating back to the early part of the nineteenth century and even earlier, such as copies of the British Short Land Model of 1775 and the U.S.-manufactured M1795 and M1808 muskets. An official Southern manual from 1862 detailed the plethora of similar weapons available, including .69-caliber M1822 and M1840 smoothbore flintlocks. Similar weapons were also to be found in armories in the North, although the need to press them into frontline service was somewhat less urgent due to the Union's larger base of arms manufacturers.

SNIPERS

While many ordinary soldiers considered themselves to be above-average marksmen, the reality was somewhat different. This was particularly true of Union troops, many who had never handled a weapon before being issued with one. The level of marksmanship among Southerners was considered generally higher as many, especially men from agricultural communities, had long experience of handling weapons. In both cases individuals with the requisite skill were earmarked as snipers or sharpshooters. Men who enlisted in the Union's Berdan's Sharpshooters had to be able to put ten shots within an average of five inches from a bull's eye at a distance of 600 yards.

In general, rifles used by snipers were individual owned, often fitted with basic telescopic sights, and could weigh anything up to thirty pounds. The very best snipers had some chance of hitting a target at up to 1,200 yards. The South did import a small number of sharpshooter rifles, mainly from Britain. Among these was a model produced by Enfield, which resembled that company's P1858 rifle, as well as examples from Whitworth and the Kerr. All were .45 caliber and, in the case of the Kerr, resembled the Enfield P1858. The Whitworth, which had an hexagonal bore and fired special fitted ball rounds, seems to have been the better weapon. Tests indicate that when fired from a fixed rest, a skilled marksman could consistent put his bullets into a twelve-inch circle at a distance of 500 yards. Accuracy declined at longer distances, but the weapon was nevertheless sufficient for the needs of a Civil War sniper.

SPRINGFIELD '61

The .58-caliber M1861 Springfield was the most widely used rifled musket of the Civil War, not least for its ruggedness and reliability. Although a Northern design it so saw considerable service with Southern troops. Something like 670,617 Springfields were manufactured in the North between early 1861 and mid-1866, not only by Springfield by also by twenty-two subcontractors, while Southern armories managed to make 23,381 copies. Its greatest advantage in production terms that it was a fairly straightforward standardized weapon, which could be produced rapidly. Bulk production also brought the cost of an individual weapon down to around thirteen dollars, which compared very favorably with its rivals.

Right: Imported British longarms. From right to left: Pattern 1853 Enfield rifle-musket; Belgian Pattern 1842 short rifle; Pattern 1853 short rifle with saber bayonet and scabbard; Kerr's Patent rifle; Brunswick rifle with bayonet; pattern canteen; cartridge box for Pattern 1853 rifle-musket and short rifle; Whitworth Patent rifle with telescopic sight.

Above: Union longarms and accouterments. From top to bottom: U.S. Model 1816 smoothbore musket with bayonet in place and scabbard below; cap box and waist belt; U.S. Model 1842 smoothbore musket with socket bayonet below; cap box, waist belt and bayonet scabbard; rifle-musket cartridge box with shoulder strap; U.S. Model 1861 muzzle-loading rifle-musket with cap box, socket bayonet and scabbard; British Pattern 1853 muzzle-loading Enfield rifle-musket with Tompion plug for top of barrel and socket bayonet, scabbard and frog; gun tools; Justice muzzle-loading rifle-musket and ramrod; NCO's waist belt with plate; .58 caliber paper cartridges.

Above: Confederate rifle-muskets, rifles and accouterments. From top to bottom: early Richmond muzzle-loading rifle-musket with ramrod and shoulder strap; Raleigh Bayonet Factory socket bayonet and scabbard; early Fayetteville muzzle-loading rifle with saber bayonet below; Confederate embossed cap box, cartridge pouch and carrying strap and cartridge box, cap box and waist belt; early Read and Watson muzzle-loading rifle; Cook and Brother muzzle-loading rifle; Confederate enmbossed cap box; Georgia Armory saber bayonet in its scabbard; embossed cartridge box and tin drum canteen with shoulder strap; late type Richmond muzzle-loading rifle-musket; three waist belts.

The origins of the weapon lay with the need to overcome two shortcomings of its immediate predecessor the M1855 Springfield, which was considered difficult to manufacture and costly. The M1861 dispensed with the M1855's most expensive items—its adjustable ladder sight and the Maynard primer, which were replaced by a basic leaf sight with three settings (100, 300, and 500 yards) and copper percussion caps. The M1861 had an overall length of 55¾ inches, and a weight of 8.88 pounds. The basic design underwent minor modifications in 1863 and 1864 but remained basically unaltered. The M1861 could hit targets at up to 1,000 yards, but its true effective range, where a decent marksman might expect to hit precisely what he was aiming at, was near 500 to 600 yards. The chances of a hit on a specific target by an average shot were highest at battle ranges

of between 200 and 300 yards. The rate of fire was three rounds per minute.

Below: Confederate rifle-muskets, rifles and accouterments. From top to bottom: early Richmond muzzle-loading rifle-musket with ramrod and shoulder strap; Raleigh Bayonet Factory socket bayonet and scabbard; early Fayetteville muzzle-loading rifle with saber bayonet below; Confederate embossed cap box, cartridge pouch and carrying strap and cartridge box, cap box and waist belt; early Read and Watson muzzle-loading rifle; Cook and Brother muzzle-loading rifle; Confederate enmbossed cap box; Georgia Armory saber bayonet in its scabbard; embossed cartridge box and tin drum canteen with shoulder strap; late type Richmond muzzle-loading rifle-musket; three waist belts.

NASHVILLE, TENNESSEE

Nashville, Tennessee

The evacuation of Nashville on February 23, 1862, made it the first Confederate capital and industrial center to fall. Major General John Hood's attempt to retake Nashville in the December of 1864 was easily repulsed by the combined forces of Thomas and General John M. Schofield, who between them outnumbered Hood's surrounding forces by two to one. The Confederate army was driven off, and in the ensuing two-week chase, only Forrest's excellent rearguard action saved them from utter destruction.

Nashville Campaign

On November 15, 1864, Sherman turned back from his pursuit of General Hood to begin his march through Georgia to the sea, leaving General George Thomas to act for the defense of Tennessee or else take renewed offensive actions in neighboring Alabama. The Confederate Army under General John Bell Hood, strengthened by General Nathan Forrest's cavalry, was then threatening Nashville from positions at Decatur and Tuscumbia on the Tennessee River, with an army of 44,000 men. Another force under Stephen Dile Lee was encamped across the river and in advance of Florence. Hood was making active preparations for a move on Nashville, with Ohio a possible objective. Thomas had been sent to Nashville early in October to organize a force to resist Hood, but his command was much smaller in number, and those men that he had were thinly strung from Chattanooga to Nashville.

At the end of October, General John Schofield's XXIII Corps and D. S. Stanley's IV Corps were ordered to Thomas, who sent them to Pulaski, Tennessee, some eighty miles to the south of Nashville, with orders to delay Hood, should he advance, until the army could be concentrated and Nashville reinforced.

On November 21, while Thomas was still making energetic efforts to organize a force to meet Hood, Hood made a move against Schofield's right flank. Schofield's stubborn rearguard action baffled Hood for a time, and he was frustrated in his attempt to intercept Schofield at Pulaski, which he quit on the 22nd. The Federals retreated as far as Columbia, and held the Confederates there for three days before withdrawing to the north bank of the river. By skillful work Schofield arrived at Franklin in advance of Hood, and took position around the town. Hood threw the full weight of his army at the Federal troops. The desperate assault, launched at 4:00pm, cost the lives of five general officers. On the night of the 30th Schofield withdrew to Nashville, to be reunited with Thomas' army on December 1st. He was followed by Hood, who

established lines in front of the city on December 2. Only at this point, with Hood's entire army and 10,000 cavalrymen threatening, did the Federal authorities recognize the fact that Thomas had been left with in adequate means to resist the advance. A mild panic set in at Washington; many feared that Hood would simply avoid Thomas and advance on into Ohio. Grant was prompted to send an order to Thomas urging him to man the defenses with "quartermaster's employees, citizens etc." Thomas responded calmly to other frantic orders from Washington compelling him to attack at once, and in the two days' battle that was fought at Nashville between December 15–17, he demonstrated great leadership.

After the action, Hood was driven back over the Mississippi, having suffered a loss during his campaign of over 13,500 men and seventy-two guns. More than 2,000 of his deserters came into the Union lines. After Nashville, Hood's once splendid force of Confederate fighting men did not again appear as an army on the battlefield. His complete defeat at Nashville removed the threat of an advance on Ohio, yet this did not fully allay the panic in Washington lest Sherman's March to the Sea had left the west without sufficient protection. Desiring the utter destruction of this threat, Grant and Halleck badgered Thomas to maintain his pursuit of Hood's army, until he felt obliged to point out in a plainly worded despatch that he was doing all in his power to achieve this end, but was in no small way hindered by the fact that Sherman had taken with him most of the equipment of the Military Division of the Mississippi.

THE BATTLE
Having advanced northward in an attempt to force Sherman to fall back from Atlanta General John Bell Hood led the Army of Tennessee toward Nashville in November 1864. He encountered Schofield's Union Corps at the battle of Franklin on November 30 and was beaten, suffering over 6,000 casualties, and Schofield was allowed to fall back on Nashville and join up with Major General George H. Thomas in secure entrenchments around the city. Hood reached the outskirts of Nashville on December 2, occupied positions on a line of hills parallel to those of the Union and began erecting fieldworks. From December 1–14, Hood could do nothing but wait for Thomas's next move, when it came it would be a devastating one. On December 10, having been delayed by five days by an ice storm, Thomas launched his attack. His plan was to launch a coordinated attack on both flanks of Hood's army, committing his main strength against the left flank while pinning the right flank with a diversionary action. By the end of the first day the

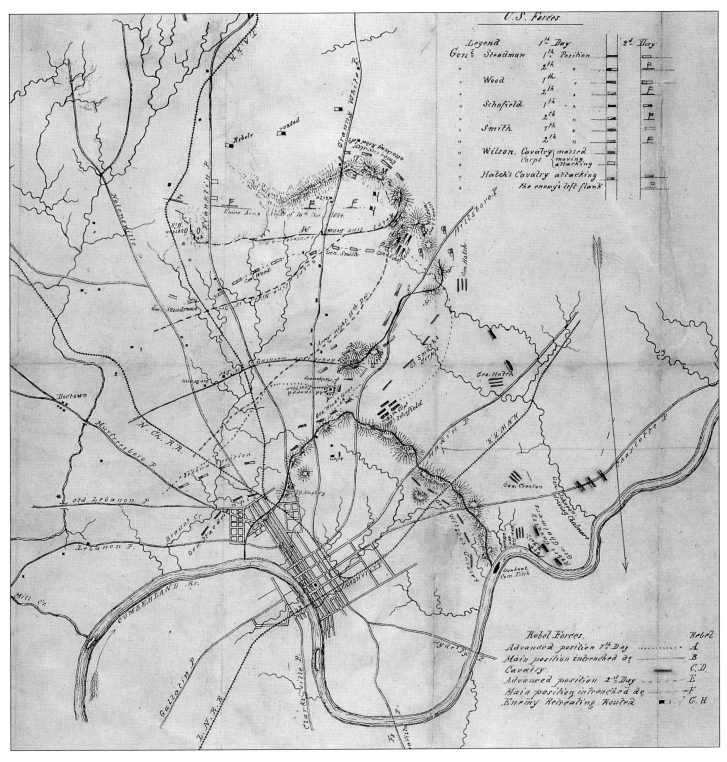

Confederates had been considerably pushed back, but were still holding firm and erecting breastworks to protect their reduced positions. On the 16th Thomas repeated his tactics of the previous day and Hood's army broke and fled, with its total destruction only being prevented by desperate rearguard cavalry actions. As a fighting force the Army of the Tennessee was no more and Hood resigned his command. The only army now left to the Confederacy was Lee's Army of Northern Virginia.

National Banking Act

Although the United States had a de facto national currency prior to the Civil War, most state banks issued their own currency. Because they were theoretically backed by gold, all of the currencies were, again theoretically, interchangeable. However, there was a wide gulf between theory and reality. The so-called "wildcat" banks issued unsound bank notes secured by questionable paper, such as mortgages and other instruments. During the Civil War, this system was seen as antiquated and in need of reform. Passed in 1863, the National Bank Act provided for the Federal charter and supervision of a system of banks known as national banks. The idea was the circulation of a stable, uniform national currency secured by Federal bonds deposited by each bank with the comptroller of the currency

Above: The Battle of Nashville saw the virtual destruction of the Confederate Army of Tennessee. General Hood's impetuosity had left the South at the mercy of Sherman's Union army.

or the national banking administrator. The Act regulated the minimum capital requirements of national banks, the kinds of loans they could make, and the reserves that were to be held against notes and deposits. The new law did not actually prohibit state banks from issuing currency, but Congress imposed a ten percent tax on state banknotes, thus ending their viability. The National Bank system was further refined by the formation of the current Federal Reserve Bank and banking system in 1913.

Native Americans

The situation of Native Americans in the Civil War was a complex one. The consolidation and expansion of government and settler control over vast areas of the west continued despite the war, involving numerous Native American peoples in an ongoing tragedy of conflict, massacre, and retreat. Among the most notorious incidents of the Civil War years was the Sand Creek massacre in Colorado, in which militia volunteers wiped out an entire village of Arapaho and Cheyenne, killing some 500—mostly women and children.

Elsewhere, however, a number of Native Americans became directly involved in the war, either on an individual basis or as a nation. The most notable instance was that of the Cherokee people, who had split into two factions after a minority of leaders had signed a treaty agreeing to their removal from Georgia to Oklahoma territory some twenty years earlier. Chief Stand Watie, one of the treaty signers, gave allegiance to the Confederacy, organizing a regiment that became the First Cherokee Mounted Rifles and saw action at Wilson's Creek, Elkhorn, and many small conflicts along the border of Indian Territory. Several

other regiments of Cherokee, Creek, Choctaw, and Seminole were enlisted and Brigadier General Chief Stand Watie became the best known Native American figure among Confederate forces. On the Union side Colonel Ely Parker, who was present at the surrender of Robert E. Lee at Appomattox was the best known of more than 3,500 Native American soldiers.

Naval Crew

At the outbreak of the war there were only 7,600 enlisted men in the U. S. Navy, and most of these were Northerners. Unlike the

officer corps, very few Southern enlisted men were given the opportunity to "go south." As a consequence, the Confederacy began the war with no ships and no crewmen. By war's end the U.S. Navy had over 51,000 sailors in service, compared to the 4,000 enlisted men in Confederate service. A lack of trained sailors on both sides led to the mass recruitment of "landsmen," and even the drafting of soldiers to naval vessels. The introduction of ironclads meant that traditional maritime tasks were augmented by technical ones, creating a growing demand for engineers and machinists. Conditions were primitive, particularly on ironclads, and it is a testimony to the endurance of the sailors of both sides that they performed their duties with such fortitude.

Naval Officers, Confederate

The officers of the Confederate Navy were all former U.S. Navy officers who resigned

Opposite Page and Below: The struggle between North and South offered little respite for the Native Americans, who continued to suffer at the hands of American soldiers from both sides in the far west.

Left: The expansion of the U.S. Navy and the creation of its Confederate counterpart meant that experienced seamen were at a premium during the war.

their commissions and "went south." In 1862 the navy established posts for four admirals, ten captains, thirty-one commanders, 125 lieutenants (first and second), plus corresponding non-line posts. Promotion was by merit, and a midshipman training program introduced fresh volunteers into the service. Promotion prospects were poor due to a lack of posts, and the former commanders of large Federal warships were often found commanding small gunboats in the Confederate Navy. Senior commanders controlled a naval station such as Charlestown or Mobile, and their remit often included the control of shore defenses within the area. Otherwise, the officer structure reflected the organization and traditions of the old Federal navy. In most cases, the officers of the Confederate Navy distinguished themselves, demonstrating a resourcefulness that allowed them to continue the unequal contest for so long.

Naval Officers, Union

Of around 1,000 commissioned naval officers, about a third resigned and "went south." Southerners who remained continued to be viewed with suspicion until able to demonstrate their loyalty through action. Other aged officers were also weeded out, while Congress authorized a volunteer officer corps to augment numbers. Over 4,000 volunteer officers served during the war, 1,800 of who were engineers, giving the Union Navy a technical edge over their adversaries, although professional line officers continued to regard themselves as superior to all other types.

In July 1865 the ranking structure was reorganized, introducing the ranks of lieutenant commander and ensign. In all, nine admirals, eighteen commodores and thirty-six captains were authorized. As the war progressed, appointments to these top positions were made on merit rather than rank. While early volunteers were recruited from the merchant service, most other officers were trained at the Naval Academy at Annapolis.

Right: Rear Admiral David Dixon Porter, U.S. Navy, with his staff aboard USS *Malvern* in Hampton Roads, Virginia, December 1864.

Navy, Confederate

On 21st February 1861, the Confederate Congress founded the Confederate Navy, appointing Stephen Mallory as its head. He had no warships at his disposal, or crews to man them, only Southern naval officers who returned to serve Confederacy. While Mallory sent commissioners to Europe to buy or build warships, he also planned to build a navy at home. As the Confederacy lacked shipyards and industrial facilities, the capture of Norfolk Navy Yard in April 1862 was a major boon. At the start of the war several states formed their own navies,

Above: The CSS *Arkansas* depicted fighting the Union ironclad USS *Carondelet* on the Mississippi River. The Confederate ironclad had a brief but distinguished career, and at one stage she single-handedly engaged the entire Union fleet anchored above Vicksburg.

Right: The Confederate Navy struggled to come to terms with the more powerful Union forces. This is the CSS *Albermarle* (see page 8) seen at the Union Norfolk Navy Yard after being salvaged, circa 1865.

each consisting of small gunboats. These were amalgamated into the Confederate Navy, and sailors were recruited to man these vessels. Although Confederate gunboats continued to be produced, Mallory placed his faith in technological innovation to overcome Union superiority in numbers.

Despite a lack of industrial facilities, rail transportation and experience, the Confederate Navy succeeded in building a powerful ironclad fleet, which played a major part in the defense of the ports and rivers of the Confederacy. The prototype was the CSS *Virginia*, built using the burned-out hull of the wooden steam frigate *Merrimac*. Although the performance of the ironclad and its immediate successors proved to Mallory that these vessels had little offensive capability, they were well-suited to the defensive role forced upon the Confederacy by numbers and geography.

While a number of Confederate cruisers harried Union shipping abroad, the defense of Southern ports and rivers was considered the primary role of the Confederate Navy. The South lacked the ships, men, guns or shipbuilding facilities to effectively contest control of either the Mississippi or the blockaded ports. Mallory's ironclad policy was his only option, but lacking strategic maneuverability, these ironclads could only defend their home port or region. On the other hand, the Union could concentrate and strike wherever it chose. Despite the courage of its men, the Confederate Navy was an unequal opponent for the Union Navy. The Union Navy possessed overwhelming numbers and the port facilities to build and repair warships. Unable to produce the ships needed to break the Union blockade, the Confederacy was doomed.

Navy, Union

When war was declared in April 1862, on paper, the U.S. Navy consisted of over ninety warships. In reality, twenty-one were unfit for service, twenty-seven were undergoing repairs, and twenty-eight were spread around the globe on overseas

Right: Sketch by Theodore R. Davis—for *Harper's Weekly*—of the Union mortar fleet on the Mississippi at Vicksburg in 1862.

Opposite Page, Top: The backbone of the Union blockading fleet were wooden steam frigates, this USS *Housatonic* drawn by R. G. Skerrett.

Below: A Union gun crew manning an eleven-inch Dahlgren smoothbore.

Opposite Page, Bottom: USS *General Bragg* seen at Cairo in 1862–63; USS *Maria Denning* is in stream. The CSS *General Bragg* was captured near Memphis in June 1862, and was commissioned into the Union river fleet.

deployments. The remaining fourteen ships were unable to put into effect the blockade of the Confederacy demanded by Lincoln, so Secretary of the Navy Gideon Welles instituted a massive naval expansion program. This included the conversion of merchant ships for blockading duties, of specially-built warships for ocean-going and riverine service, and the creation of a fleet of ironclad warships, most of which were of the monitor type. In addition, the navy often pressed captured Confederate vessels into service. By 1865, over 690 vessels had been commissioned, of which only 160 were specially built naval vessels. The remainder were converted, or captured warships.

The Union's strategic goals were twofold; to maintain a blockade of the Southern coast to constrict its commerce (a strategy known as the "Anaconda Plan"), and to launch a major thrust down the Mississippi River to split the Confederacy in two, opening the river to Northern commerce. In addition the employment of high-seas raiders by the Confederacy forced the Union to deploy high-seas cruisers to hunt these commerce raiders down. Most of the existing steam warships on overseas deployment when war broke out were eventually employed in this vital role. The navy's ships were eventually well suited to achieve the goals it was set.

On the Mississippi River, a convoluted command system involving army and navy cooperation caused initial problems, but by mid-1862 a Union river fleet was produced which was able to counter and destroy any Confederate naval initiatives on the river. This fleet also supported the Union advances along tributary rivers such as the Cumberland, Tennessee, Yazoo, and the Red River. By 1864, over 140 riverine vessels had been employed on these rivers. Along the Confederate seaboard, an increasing number of monitors augmented the wooden warships blockading the Confederate ports, and these fleets also assisted numerous amphibious attacks, which

Left and Above: The Union fleet contained vessels of all types, purpose built as warships or converted for the purpose. Several converted New York ferry-boats such as the *Commodore Perry* (Left) were used by the navy to patrol the sounds and rivers of the Confederate Atlantic seaboard. The Union navy used purpose built cruisers such as the USS *Pensacola* (Above, seen off Alexandria, Virginia) to hunt down Confederate raiders on the high seas.

THE AMERICAN CIVIL WAR: A VISUAL ENCYCLOPEDIA

seized vital sections of the Confederate coastline.

New Hampshire

The Union state of New Hampshire joined the fighting as soon as the first shot had been fired at Fort Sumter, and by the end of the war New Hampshire had contributed over 30,000 men to the Union war effort. Infantry, cavalry, and light and heavy artillery regiments were all raised in New Hampshire, while other men from the state joined state organizations or fought under the broad umbrella of the United States Military.

New Market, Virginia, Battle of, 1864

As part of Grant's spring offensive of 1864 the 23,000 men of Major General Sigel's Army of West Virginia were to march down the Shenandoah Valley and threaten the Virginia Central Railroad. Major General John C. Breckinridge, instructed by Lee to attempt hold him, scraped together just over 4,000 men including the cadets from the Virginia Military Institute. On May 15, the two forces met at New Market. After a Confederate cavalry advance on the right and left flanks, Breckinridge managed to take a battery that proved to be the key to the whole Union position, after which he

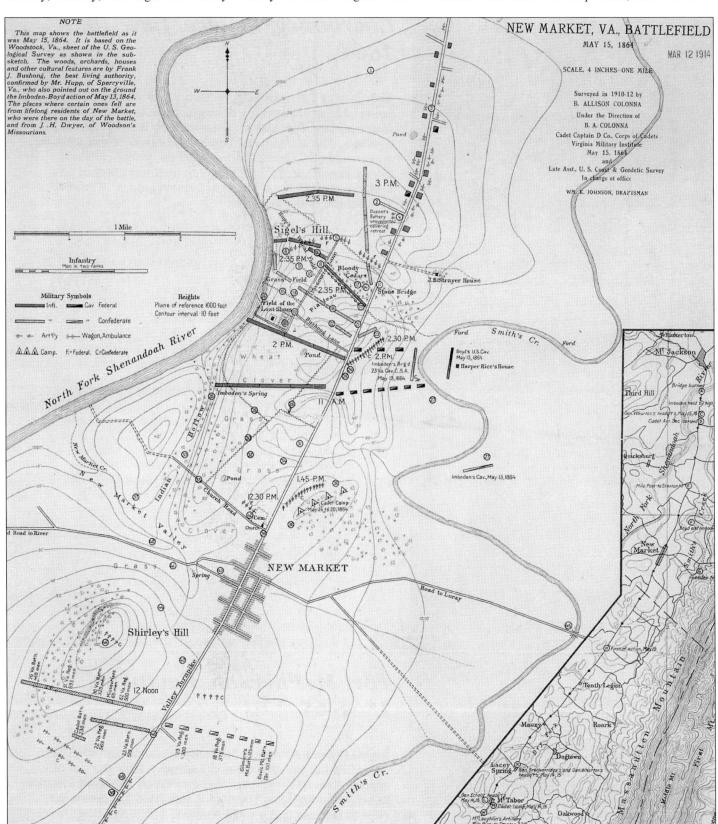

Above: Confederate defense lines outside Atlanta.

Left: The Battle of New Market is best known as the battle where the cadets of the Virginia Military Institute charged and defeated a superior Union force.

ordered a general advance. Sigel's defense collapsed and he withdrew, being relieved of command two days later.

New Mexico

New Mexico was a pawn in the struggle to offset war. It originally applied for statehood at the same time as California, but both its slaveholding status and Texas' claim to own part of it, made its application problematical.

Union politicians later used the issue of the region's admission as a lever to keep control of the upper South, as disputes divided the South in terms of opinion. Positioned as it was in the middle of the

Southern territories, the allegiance of New Mexico would have been of next to no use to the Northern cause anyway, but the wrangling over its fate helped Northerners to win over the upper South.

New Orleans, Louisiana

Commanding the mouth of the Mississippi, New Orleans was the South's largest city and most important port—the Union capture of New Orleans effectively cut the Confederacy in half.

David Glasgow Farragut's attack on the city began on April 24, 1864, with the commencement of his assault on Forts Jackson and St. Philip. After a week of bombardment he stormed past the forts up the Mississippi, effectively cutting them off and leaving New Orleans to the Union. General Benjamin Butler subsequently controlled New Orleans, and while his actions (including the infamous "woman order") earned him the nickname "Beast", his harsh martial law effectively cleansed the city of disease and crime.

New Orleans, Battle of, 1862

In April 1862 the Union was ready to launch an attack on the New Orleans. The city was an important prize, being the largest city in the Confederacy, a major port, and the gateway to the lower Mississippi River. Admiral David G. Farragut was chosen to execute the attack, and he quickly secured control of the entrance to the river some 30 miles below the city. By April 18, his fleet was less than two miles from the Confederate defenses. The Confederate position was strong, centerd on the two fortifications of Fort St. Philip and Fort Jackson. A boom spanned the river, augmented by a line of underwater obstructions. Immediately upstream lay the Confederate river fleet, including the immobile floating battery *Louisiana*. The battle commenced with a day-long bombardment of the forts by twenty-one mortar-schooners. Farregut then sent work parties to cut the boom and clear a path through the obstructions, allowing the Union fleet to run past the forts.

Farragut divided his fleet into three sections and on April 24 he ordered them to proceed upstream in line astern. The vanguard consisted of five large wooden warships and three gunboats. Although badly battered, it passed the forts without mishap, as did the second section commanded by Farragut himself, consisting of the flagship USS *Hartford* and two large wooden cruisers. The Union ships then engaged the outnumbered Confederate naval squadron, commanded by Commander John Mitchell. As the third Union squadron of a steam sloop and five gunboats ran past the forts, the two fleets became embroiled in a close-range engagement. In a brutal melee, the ironclad CSS *Manassas* and the wooden gunboat CSS *Governor Moore* sank the USS *Varuna* and seriously damaged one other vessel before being destroyed themselves. While the other Confederate gunboats were overpowered, the Union fleet steamed on to New Orleans. On May 1, 1862, the city was occupied by Union troops, and within a week the bypassed forts and batteries below the city were surrendered or abandoned. The loss of New Orleans was a blow from which the Confederacy never recovered.

New Orleans, Defense of

One of the two largest shipbuilding ports in the Confederacy, New Orleans was vital to the Confederate war effort. Soon after Louisiana seceded, a State Navy was established, consisting of the wooden gunboats *Governor Moore and General Quitman*. While other small gunboats were built or converted in shipyards in the city or in Memphis, Tennesee, contracts were issued for the construction of an ironclad squadron to defend the city's approaches. During early 1862 work began on the massive casemate ironclads *Mississippi* and *Louisiana* in New Orleans shipyards, but the ambitious scale of the project and a lack of available men and resources delayed production. By the time the Union attacked the city's river defenses in April 1862, neither ironclad was completed, although the *Louisiana* was towed into position to be used as a floating battery. One additional ironclad, the CSS *Manassas* was built as a privateer by private owners, then commandeered into Confederate service. In April, the local naval squadron consisted of the ironclad *Manassas*, plus eight wooden gunboats of various sizes. The most effective defenses on the river were the forts of Fort Jackson and Fort St. Philip, one on each side of the Mississippi below the city, containing a total of 126 guns. Additional smaller batteries, mobile batteries and sharpshooters augmented these well-guarded fortifications. Underwater obstructions and a boom also blocked the river, stretching across the Mississippi just below Fort Jackson. As an added precaution, fire-rafts were readied for use against any Union attack.

New York

New York's loyalties remained divided throughout the war, and as a state it was far from unquestioning acceptance of Union rulings. At a time when healthcare and

Below Left: This dramatic—but inaccurate—depiction of the Battle of New Orleans shows the battle as a free-for-all engagement. In reality, the Confederate forts and river gunboats were unable to prevent the ordered progress of Admiral Farragut's Union fleet up the Mississippi River below the city.

Right: Map of the Battle of New Orleans.

Below: Soldiers of the 22nd New York Volunteer Regiment in their encampment in Virginia. Over 40,000 New Yorkers served in the eastern theater during the war.

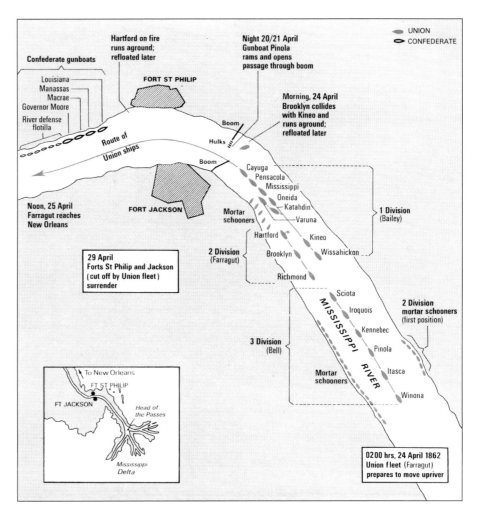

Confederate gunboats

Louisiana
Manassas
Macrae
Governor Moore

River defense flotilla

FORT ST PHILIP

Hartford on fire runs aground; refloated later

Route of Union ships

Night 20/21 April Gunboat Pinola rams and opens passage through boom

Morning, 24 April Brooklyn collides with Kineo and runs aground; refloated later

Boom

Hulks

Boom

Noon, 25 April Farragut reaches New Orleans

FORT JACKSON

Mortar schooners

Cayuga
Pensacola
Mississippi
Oneida
Katahdin
Varuna

Hartford

Kineo

Wissahickon

1 Division (Bailey)

2 Division (Farragut)

Brooklyn

Richmond

UNION
CONFEDERATE

29 April Forts St Philip and Jackson (cut off by Union fleet) surrender

Sciota

Iroquois

Kennebec

Pinola

Itasca

Winona

MISSISSIPPI RIVER

3 Division (Bell)

Mortar schooners

2 Division mortar schooners (first position)

To New Orleans

FT ST PHILIP

FT JACKSON

Head of the Passes

Mississippi Delta

0200 hrs, 24 April 1862 Union fleet (Farragut) prepares to move upriver

THE RENDEZVOUS

22

general health were poor, New York state undertook a reexamination of its 47,417 men who had been passed by Union doctors as fit to serve in the army—of these, it sent 5,554 back home on grounds of ill health. It was from New York that the *Star of the West* was sent to supply reinforcements to Fort Sumter, and to New York that the ship returned from her unsuccessful mission.

New York City

Despite its apparent Union affiliations, New York retained strong secessionist sympathies for the duration of the war. Mayor Fernando Wood proposed the secession of the city and Long Island in January 1861, and when this suggestion was rejected, it was suggested that the city should declare itself an independent nation. This extreme measure was also rejected, but nevertheless the city was guided rather by commerce than by politics in its role in the war. The largely Irish immigrant population was terrified at the prospect of freed slaves taking their jobs if they allowed themselves to be drafted into the Union army as per Lincoln's decree, and in July 1863 their unease brought the city very close to revolution.

Norfolk, Virginia

The home of Gosport Navy Yard, the largest shipbuilding facility in the south. Largely manned by Southerners, Gosport was captured for the Confederates on April 18, 1861, by the Virginian Militia led by the ex-governor of Virginia, Henry Wise. Commodore Charles McCauley, in charge of the defense of the captured shipyard, attempted to burn everything of military significance as he evacuated the premises—however, much of the military hardware there was salvaged and turned over to the Confederate war effort.

Confederate forces abandoned Norfolk following Johnston's retreat up the peninsula from the fallen city of Yorktown in May 1862, blowing up everything of tactical importance before they left.

North Carolina

North Carolina, long uncertain in its allegiances, voted against secession on February 28, 1861. However, in April 1861 North Carolina refused to supply troops for the Union war effort, and on May 22 it became the eleventh and last state to leave the Union. Despite its tardy affiliation to the South, North Carolina supplied more troops and suffered more casualties for the Confederate cause than any other Southern state, although by March 1862 it found itself all but sealed off from the sea by Union troops.

North Dakota

North Dakota declared its allegiance to the Union on March 2, 1861. The state saw fighting throughout the summer of 1863, with engagements Big Mound on July 24–25, at Dead Buffalo Lake on July 26, at Stony Lake on July 28 and at Whitestone Hill on September 3–5. The final battle to be fought in North Dakota was that of Killdeer Mountain and Tahkahokuty Mountain on July 28–29, 1864.

Below: Engineers of the 8th New York State Militia, 1861.

Ohio

The Union defined the Department of Ohio on May 3, 1863. Taking in the states of Ohio, Indiana and Illinois, the Department of Ohio was controlled by George Brinton McClellan.

With Southern morale running low in July 1863, Confederate John Hunt Morgan led a raiding party through Kentucky and Indiana into Ohio. His early successes came to an end on July 19, 1863, when his defeat at Bluffington, Ohio, forced him to turn towards Pennsylvania. Skirmishing with Union forces at Rockville and Athens, he was finally run to ground at Salineville, Ohio, on July 26, and surrendered with his 364 remaining men and officers. His raid had been daring and spectacular, but had achieved little of military note.

Ohio River

Running along the Texan border, the Ohio River played an important part in the outcome of the war. The control of its major tributaries, the Cumberland and the Tennessee, were hotly contested throughout the war in the western theater. The Ohio's confluence with the Mississippi at Cairo, Illinois, was one of the North's more jealously defended positions.

Oklahoma

During the opening year of the Civil War, Oklahoma was the site of a series of skirmishes between Confederates and Unionist Seminole and Creek troops under Chief Opothleyahola. The first encounter between the two forces came at Round Mountain on November 19, 1861, and proved inconclusive as the Indians disappeared before they could be pressed to battle—however, two battles later by the end of 1861 the chief had been forced to flee to Kansas. Fighting continued in Oklahoma for the duration of the war. Clashes took place at Chusto-Talasah and Chustenahlah in December 1861, at Old Fort Wayne on October 22, 1862, at Cabin Creek and Honey Springs in July 1863, and at Middle Boggy Depot on February 13, 1864.

Olustee and Natural Bridge, Battles of

In February 1864, Union forces landed in Jacksonville and launched a major expedition westward into the interior of Florida. Union objectives included cutting off Confederate supply lines, locating recruits for black Union regiments, and establishing a pro-Union government in east Florida. The Union expedition was commanded by Brigadier General Truman Seymour. To counter this move, Confederate Brigadier General Joseph Finegan gathered Southern troops sent from north Florida, southern Georgia, and South Carolina.

This was the largest battle fought in Florida, and one of the bloodiest. It ended in a stinging defeat for the Union forces, and helped keep the interior of the state under the South's control. Late in the war, in March 1865, a combined Union army and naval force assembled in the northern Gulf of Mexico off St. Mark's. Almost 1,000 Union troops landed near the St. Mark's lighthouse and moved inland. Following a skirmish at Newport bridge on the St. Mark's River, they moved north by night to Natural Bridge in hopes of crossing the river unopposed. They were observed and Confederate forces were redirected to the area to meet the threat. On March 6, 1865, the Confederates won a minor victory that ensured Tallahassee would remain in Southern hands for the remainder of the war.

Ordnance, Naval

In 1861, the majority of naval ordnance consisted of smoothbore guns, the majority of weapons being based on the Columbiad pattern, which was first introduced in 1811.

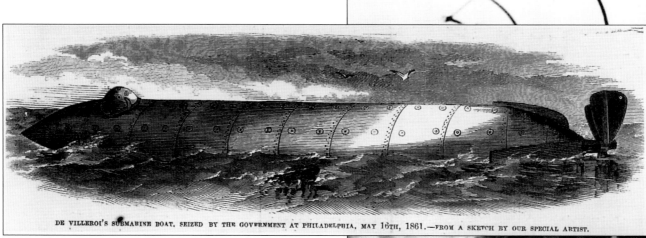

DE VILLEROI'S SUBMARINE BOAT, SEIZED BY THE GOVERNMENT AT PHILADELPHIA, MAY 16TH, 1861.—FROM A SKETCH BY OUR SPECIAL ARTIST.

The ordnance designer Thomas J. Rodman developed an improved version of these guns during the 1840s, and by the start of the Civil War, Rodman Columbiads were in widepread service, while most older guns had been relegated for use in coastal fortifications. These Rodmans offered a greater range and penetration than the weapons they succeeded. Between 1847 and 1855, John A. Dahlgren developed a version of these modified Columbiads which was cast from a solid piece of metal, then bored out, which increased the strength of the barrel. Rodmans and Dahlgrens formed the principal armament of the prewar U.S. Navy, and following the capture of Norfolk Navy Yard in 1861, hundreds of these weapons fell into Confederate hands. The characteristic features of these guns was a heavily reinforced breech, the diameter of the gun increasing steadily from front to rear.

Rifled guns designed by Robert Parrott were patented in early 1861, they were introduced into naval service the following year. They were used in limited numbers, although the eight-inch Parrott rifle proved a popular and effective gun. In the Confederate Navy, the policy was to place a greater emphasis on rifled weapons, so many of the Rodmans and Dahlgrens captured at Norfolk were subsequently rifled. In addition, ordnance designer John M. Brooke developed his own version of the Parrott rifle, and his 6.4-inch and seven-inch Brooke rifles became the principal form of armament for most Confederate ironclads during the war.

Although the Union placed a greater emphasis on smoothbore guns, Dahlgren designed guns of increasing calibre and weight as the war progressed. While nine-inch smoothbores were common at the start of the war, by 1863, Dahlgren's fifteen-inch smoothbores were carried on Union monitors. Similarly, Brooke designed his own ten-inch smoothbore weapons. Although a handful of European guns were employed by the Confederates on European-built cruisers, their own home-produced ordnance proved as effective as anything produced by the Union during the war.

Above: The Confederate Navy relied on ironclads, mines, and even submersibles to counter the overwhelming supremacy of the Union Navy. This is de Villeroi's submarine that was seized by the Federal government at Philadelphia on May 16, 1861.

Right: On this "Canonicus" class monitor—USS *Lehigh*—a Union crew man a twelve-pounder deck howitzer, designed to be used against enemy boarding parties. These guns were rarely used in action.

Pea Ridge, Battle of, 1862

The Battle of Pea Ridge on March 7–8, 1862, was the battle that decided the fate of Missouri. After the Confederates had been pushed southward toward Arkansas by Brigadier General Ryan Curtis' Army of the South West, Major General Earl Van Dorn was given control of the Confederate forces in the area on March 3. These forces consisted of around 16,000 men, split between regular troops under Brigadier General McCulloch, Missouri State Guard under Major General Price and around 800 Cherokees who were fighting for the South. Opposing them Curtis only had 10,250 men. Major General Van Dorn decided on an early Confederate strike to stabilize his position in the state, and so on March 5, he launched a surprise attack around Bentonville, Arkansas. When Curtis realized what was going on, he pulled his outnumbered troops back to a strong defensive position along Pea Ridge. Unwilling to attempt a frontal attack, Van Dorn began a flanking march on the night of the 7th, moving round Curtis' right flank to cut his communications to the north. The Union troops moved north to meet him and there followed two days of hard fighting around Elkhorn Tavern before fierce Union counterattacks, which made clever use of their artillery, and a lack of ammunition forced the Confederates to withdraw for the loss of about 800 men. This battle ensured that the state of Missouri remained under Union control for the rest of the Civil War, though it was plagued by guerilla activity.

Peace Conference at Hampton Roads

Early in 1865, after steadfastly refusing to do so since 1861, President Abraham Lincoln agreed to informal peace talks between Union and Confederate negotiators. By this time, the Confederate States of America had decided to end slavery within its own territory, so the central issue was that of the secession of the eleven Southern states.

The secret peace conference took place on February 3 aboard the steamer *River Queen* anchored in Hampton Roads, Virginia. Lincoln himself attended, accompanied by Secretary of State William Seward. The Confederate side sent Vice President Alexander Stephens, Senator R. M. T. Hunter of Virginia and Assistant Secretary of War J. A. Campbell. Lincoln offered an end to the Civil War if the Confederacy disbanded itself and its army and rejoined the Union. The Southerners insisted on continued sovereignty for the Confederate States of America, and the Hampton Roads Conference ended without a negotiated end to the Civil War.

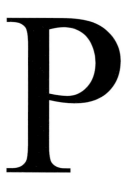

Right: The Battle of Pea Ridge ended Confederate aspirations to conquer Missouri.

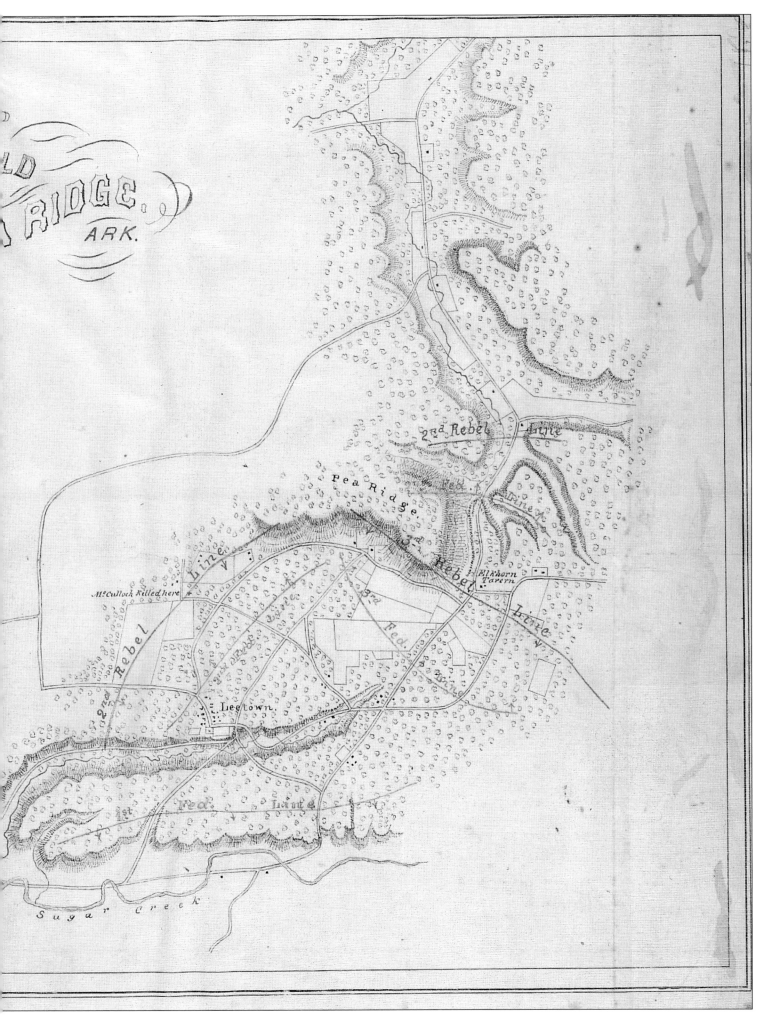

Peachtree Creek, Battle of, 1864

Following General Joseph E. Johnston's withdrawal of the Army of the Tennessee in the face of Sherman's march on Atlanta, the confederate general was removed from his post on July 18, 1864, and replaced with Gen. John B. Hood, a far more aggressive commander. Hood decided to launch an attack on Sherman's forces whilst they were moving into position around Atlanta. On July 20, Hood moved to attack Gen. Thomas' Army of the Cumberland, which was moving on Atlanta from the north. After initial Confederate successes it looked like the Union line might break, however, Thomas' men held and Hood was forced to fall back on Atlanta.

Pemberton, John Clifford (1814–81)

Born in Pennsylvania, Pemberton graduated from the U.S. Military College at West Point in 1837. Although a Northerner, he married a native of Virginia. He served during the Mexican War as a lieutenant—ironically conveying Captain Robert E. Lee's letter of commendation to Lieutenant Ulysses Grant after the capture of Mexico City. He resigned his commission to go South on April 1861 and became a Confederate brigadier general in June 1861. He commanded the Department of South Carolina, Georgia, and Florida and was promoted to major general in January 1862. In October 1862 he became commander of the Department of Mississippi and Louisiana. Ordered to surrender Vicksburg by Johnston, he chose to obey Davis who told him to hold the city. However, he was caught in a siege and forced to surrender in July 1863. Exchanged he resigned his commission, but later became colonel and inspector of artillery. He held this post until war's end and then returned to Pennsylvania, where he died in 1881.

Below: Peachtree Creek was one of several defensive battles fought by the Confederate Army of the Tennessee in defense of Atlanta. Following the repulse of Hood's troops, the Confederates were forced onto the defensive around the city. This is a map of modern Atlanta showing the major engagements.

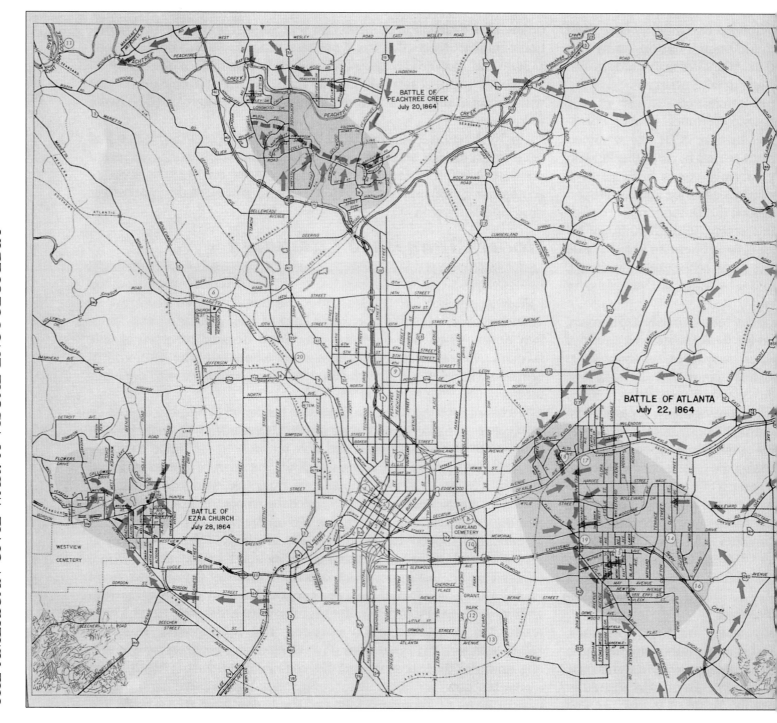

Peninsular Campaign

During the winter of 1861–62, following the disaster at the Battle of First Bull Run, Major General McClellan settled on a plan to move against Richmond in Virginia in the spring. He fixed on a plan that became an obsession to him, to advance on the Confederate capital via the waterways to the east. His theory was sound, in that Richmond could be more easily approached from the east, where the terrain was thought to be less defensible than in northern Virginia, which was crossed by large rivers. Also, an advance along the waterways would allow McClellan to utilize the Northern advantage in sea power, and allow him to establish a line of communication that could not be cut by the

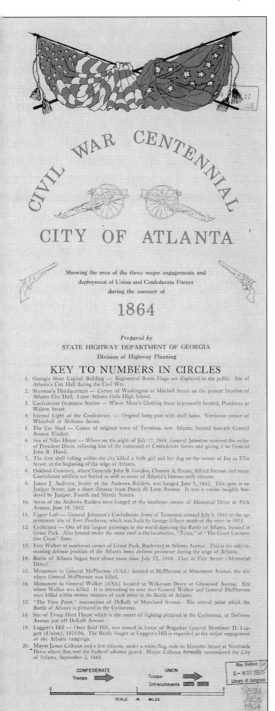

Confederates. This was the theory, but it was far from certain whether the civilian authorities would allow the army to be transported so far from the capital when a Confederate army of 90,000 lay only thirty miles from Washington. McClellan planned first of all to move his force to Urbana, near the mouth of the Rappahannock River, from where he coud seize Richmond before the Confederates had time to react. However, when McClellan unveiled this plan to Lincoln in January 1862 he was met with strong opposition; only when he had agreed to leave a force sufficiently strong to defend Washington was he allowed to proceed. Predicting a move in the spring, Jonhston then moved his army from Manassas to a more defensible position on the Rappahannock. Urbana could clearly no longer be used as a debarkation point, but McClellan clung to his strategy of an approach via the water routes. He decided to land at Fort Monroe on the tip of land between the York and James rivers known as the "Peninsula," the scene of a famous battle for the nation's independence. Some 50,000 men were to be left for the defense of Washington, and Lincoln insisted also that an adequate number of men be left to make Manassas safe.

McClellan marched out from Washington in March with 100,000 men. He had anticipated that it would be a half as strong again, but Lincoln had suspected insufficient strength was being left for the capital and detached McDowell's corps of over 30,000, holding it south of Washington.

This was still superior to the 70,000 Confederates to whom defense of the Peninsula was entrusted. Their commander, Major General John Bankhead Magruder, despite inadequate resources, had a long defensive line constructed with Yorktown serving as its left flank. A secondary line was built some ten miles back from the first, just in front of Williamsburg. Lee, serving in an advisory capacity to President Davis at that time, feared these lines might be outflanked, and on his advice, a third line was constructed about ten miles in front of Richmond, with flanks anchored on the Chickahominy and James rivers. Magruder used his meager resources to their maximum effect, and by bluffing with the forces he had at hand, gave McClellan cause for hesitation in attacking. On April 4, he learned that Fort Monroe, with a 12,000-man Federal garrison, had been taken from his command authority. This, coupled with the knowledge that McDowell's corps would not be joining him on the Peninsula and that a stop had been put to additional Federal recruiting efforts, prompted McClellan to besiege the Confederate positions. During the month that McClellan spent in taking Yorktown,

Johnston concentrated his forces. With Yorktown in Federal hands, McClellan chose to advance along the York River because of the presence of the Confederate ironclad *Merrimac* in the James; on May 5, the Confederate rearguard engaged the Federal advance elements in the battle of Williamsburg, and Johnston successfully pulled back even closer to Richmond.

By late May, McClellan was within a few miles of the Confederate capital. Johnston's belated attack came on May 31 at Fair Oaks, but did little damage to the Federal army and nearly cost him his life. Lee assumed command, and was quick to recognize that his opponent would use his engineering expertise and superior firepower to move slowly forward from one entrenched position to the next until he finally took Richmond. Fortunately for the Confederacy, early June saw heavy rainfall and McClellan's heavy artillery train was immobilized.

After Fair Oaks, McClellan took up positions to the north and south of the Chickahominy, a small stream flowing into the James. Although he could at this point have shifted his base to the James, having neutralized the threat of the *Merrimac*, he chose to maintain a hold on the York to keep connections with McDowell, who was now ordered to march to him from Fredericksburg (see Shenandoah Valley 1862). Lee saw here an opportunity to strike a killing blow, save Richmond, and destroy the Federal army. He proposed to recall Jackson from the Valley, having accomplished his task of preventing McDowell from linking up with McClellan, so boosting his force to 85,000.

The new plan was to leave some 30,000 south of the Chickahominy in their newly constructed entrenchments to hold McClellan's 75,000 on that side of the river, and use the remaining 55,000 Southern troops to crush the 30,000 Federals on the north bank. If Lee were successful in defeating and destroying a large portion of this force, he believed McClellan would retreat along the York, and he would then be able to capture McClellan's supply base and force him out into the open. During June 12–15, J. E. B. Stuart's Southern cavalry rode completely around the Federal army, spreading confusion and confirming the Federal dispositions. Jackson was returning from his Shenandoah Valley Campaign and was due to arrive on June 25. To allow for possible delays, Lee planned the Confederate attack for June 26. There followed a confusing series of battles known as the Seven Days' Battles. Although the series of hammer blows Lee delivered during the Seven Days' achieved its objective of relieving Richmond from McClellan's forces, it was made at a very high cost. The Confederates lost 20,614 casualties compared to Federal losses of 15,849.

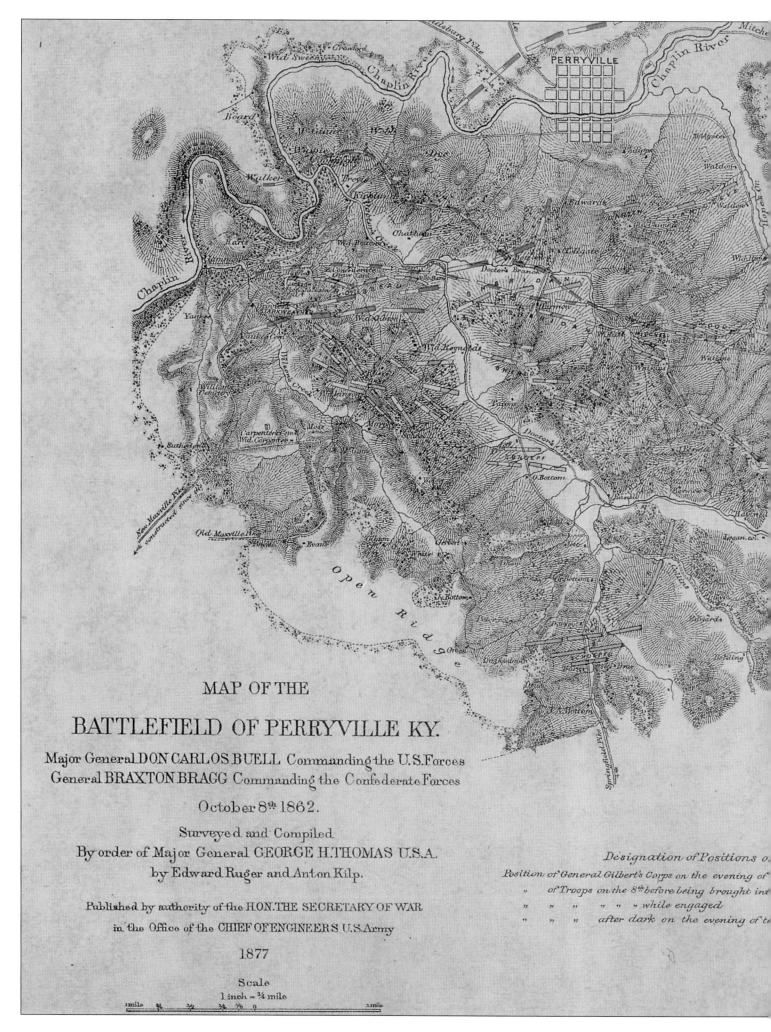

MAP OF THE

BATTLEFIELD OF PERRYVILLE KY.

Major General DON CARLOS BUELL Commanding the U.S. Forces
General BRAXTON BRAGG Commanding the Confederate Forces

October 8th 1862.

Surveyed and Compiled
By order of Major General GEORGE H. THOMAS U.S.A.
by Edward Ruger and Anton Kilp.

Published by authority of the HON. THE SECRETARY OF WAR
in the Office of the CHIEF OF ENGINEERS U.S. Army

1877

Scale
1 inch = ¾ mile

Designation of Positions o.

Position of General Gilbert's Corps on the evening of
" of Troops on the 8th before being brought int
" " " " " " while engaged
" " " after dark on the evening of te

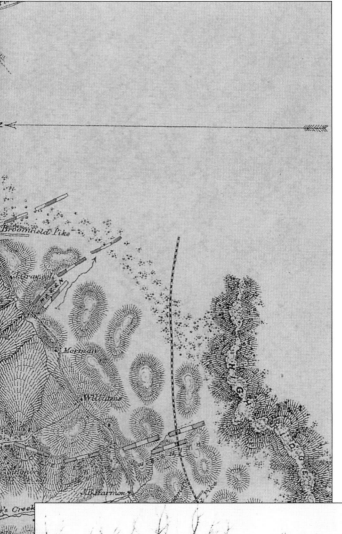

Pennsylvania

Pennsylvania was the site of the battles of Chambersburg and, most significantly, Gettysburg. Chambersburg was pillaged by J. E. B. Stuart's troops on October 11, 1862, and invaded again by the Confederates, this time under McCausland, in July 1864. Gettysburg, meanwhile, was the site of one of the Union's most significant victories on July 3, 1863, following three days of heavy fighting.

Perryville, Kentucky, Battle of, 1862

Although Confederate General Brag's 1862 invasion of Kentucky had initially gone well, Major General Buell's Army of the Ohio confronted him with around 55,000 men. On October 7, the two armies met at the small town of Perryville, Kentucky, and indulged in some desultory skirmishing while awaiting the main strength of the two armies. The following day the battle began in earnest as the Union forces moved up to attack the Confederate line. The battle became very confusing, as new detachments kept arriving and being fed into the battle. A strong Confederate counterattack came very close to breaking the Union left flank, but the line held and the Confederates were forced to retire. During the night of the 8th Bragg, short of men and supplies, withdrew through the Cumberland Gap into East Tennessee.

Left: Although inconclusive, the Battle of Perryville led to the strategic withdrawal of the Confederate army from Kentucky. The battle forced General Braxton Bragg's Army of Tennessee to fall back into northern Tennessee.

Below: Pennsylvania Artillery in firing order, with guns unlimbered.

Petersburg, Virginia

Petersburg was the site of a vital rail junction supplying Richmond. The first assault on Petersburg came on June 15, 1864, when a bungled attack by Major General William Farrar Smith gave Beauregard the chance to reentrench himself. Grant himself launched assaults on June 16 and 18, but, repulsed, he set about tunneling underneath the city. In July 1864, explosives were packed into the completed tunnel and the fuze lit. The Confederate forces were buried in the ensuing blast, but the Union attack was again repulsed when they ran into the blast hole to be decimated by Confederate fire. On April 2, 1865 Grant finally took Petersburg, having stretched the Confederate line to breaking point.

Petersburg, Battle of, 1864

Between May and mid-June of 1864 the Army of the Potomac, under General

Grant's policy of sidestepping Lee's army in Northern Virginia meant that the Army of the Potomac bypassed Richmond. In June 1864 it joined General Butler's forces south of the James River, and advanced on Petersburg, a vital rail junction twenty miles south of the Confederate capital. The siege which followed lasted for nine months, and proved to be one of the most bitter engagements of the war. These scenes are all from around Petersburg.

Ulysses S. Grant, and the Army of Northern Virginia, under General Robert E. Lee, engaged in a series of battles from Fredericksburg down to Richmond, including the Wilderness, Spotsylvania, and Yellow Tavern, where J. E. B. Stuart was mortally wounded. This campaign culminated in the Battle of Cold Harbor on June 3, where Grant tried to force the Confederate lines in front of Richmond with a series of ill-conceived frontal attacks. Three of his corps were destroyed in a convincing defeat for the Union forces and ended Grant's hopes of taking Richmond in a quick assault.

Between June 12 and 16, Grant reorganized his position, pulling his army out of Cold Harbor and crossing the James River heading toward the town of Petersburg. Petersburg was the key supply center for Richmond, without its rail and road network Lee would be forced to withdraw from around the Confederate capital. Between June 15 and 18, 1864 Grant threw the entire weight of his forces against the Petersburg defenses, with the Confederate defenders narrowly averting its loss. Lee finally arrived at the town on June 18 and Grant began a methodical siege operation.

Through a series of maneuvers, Grant continually sought an exposed flank on the right-hand side of Lee's position, thus forcing the Confederate commander to continually stretch both his lines and his resources. Grant made continous thrusts toward Richmond as well; keeping the Army of Northern Virginia stretched to breaking point. By October 1864 Grant had cut off the Weldon Railroad and was west of it tightening the noose around Petersburg. Winter saw a stop to much of the organized fighting; however, there were still large numbers of casualties from sniping and shelling.

By March 1865 Grant was ready to resume operations, and had over 100,000 infantry, 9,000 guns, and 14,700 cavalry compared to Lee's 46,000 infantry, 6,000 cavalry, and 5,000 guns. Grant's plan still remained to outflank Lee to the right and with that intention the Army of the Potomac moved to the left on March 29, with infantry and Sheridan's cavalry trying to outflank the Confederates at Five Forks. Lieutenant General A. P. Hill, realizing the Union intent, attacked Warren's V Corps and forced them back; however, the Union forces rallied and drove Hill's troops back to their trenches. This allowed Sheridan's troops through, but they ran into a combined infantry and cavalry force commanded by Pickett, who drove Sheridan back and forced him to entrench. On April 2, Grant tried attacking the Confederate right again, and this time managed to force the Army of Northern Virginia back, and compelled them to retreat to Petersburg leaving the railway in Union hands. Even the arrival of

Longstreet's corps could do nothing to support the Confederate position. Lee decided to abandon Petersburg and fall back on Lynchburg to join up with Johnston. Grant was determined not to allow Lee the opportunity to slip away.

Photography

The Civil War was one of the first major conflicts of the photographic era, taking place twenty-one years after the

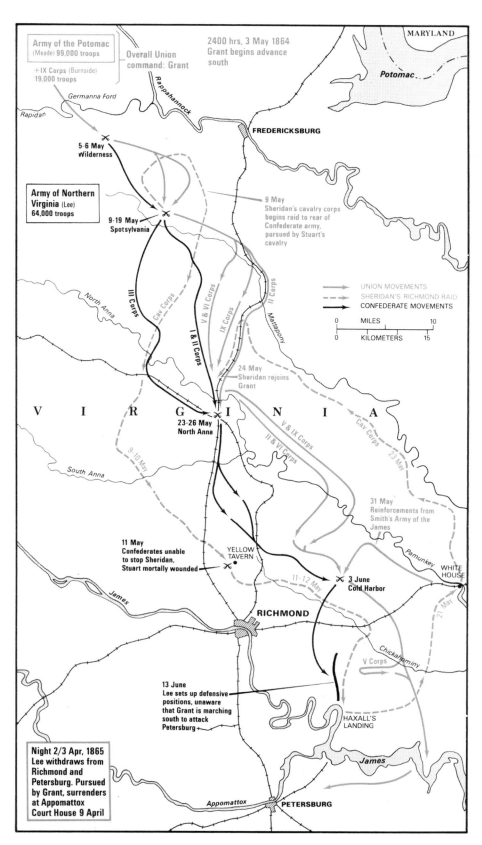

Above: The advance on Petersburg.

Opposite Page, Top Left: The Battle of Petersburg.

Opposite Page, Top Right: The retreat from Petersburg to Five Forks.

Opposite Page, Center and Below: The defenders of Petersburg built an extensive network of trenches and redoubts, and the Union siegeworks facing them were constructed in a similar manner; these were the most extensive use of field fortifications seen before World War I.

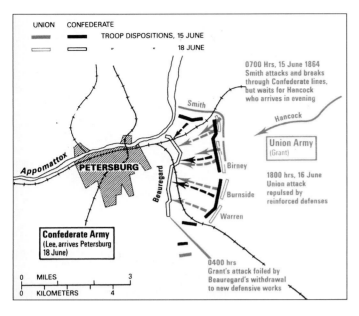

UNION | CONFEDERATE
TROOP DISPOSITIONS, 15 JUNE
18 JUNE

0700 Hrs, 15 June 1864
Smith attacks and breaks
through Confederate lines,
but waits for Hancock
who arrives in evening

Union Army
(Grant)

1800 hrs, 16 June
Union attack repulsed by
reinforced defenses

Confederate Army
(Lee, arrives Petersburg
18 June)

0400 hrs
Grant's attack foiled by
Beauregard's withdrawal
to new defensive works

Smith
Hancock
Birney
Beauregard
Burnside
Warren
PETERSBURG
Appomattox

0 MILES 3
0 KILOMETERS 4

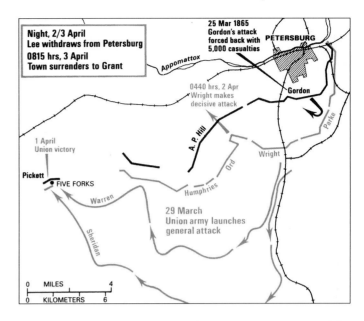

Night, 2/3 April
Lee withdraws from Petersburg
0815 hrs, 3 April
Town surrenders to Grant

25 Mar 1865
Gordon's attack
forced back with
5,000 casualties

PETERSBURG

Appomattox

Gordon

0440 hrs, 2 Apr
Wright makes
decisive attack

A. P. Hill

Wright

Parke

1 April
Union victory

Pickett ● FIVE FORKS

Warren

Humphries

Ord

Sheridan

29 March
Union army launches
general attack

0 MILES 4
0 KILOMETERS 6

THE AMERICAN CIVIL WAR: A VISUAL ENCYCLOPEDIA

introduction of photography to the United States in 1839. Hundreds of thousands of small glass or metal plate portrait images of soldiers were shot by army camp and town photographers, many of new recruits in their uniforms before leaving for the front line or to be mailed home to loved ones. Pictures of generals and other heroes were produced for commercial sale. Also made both for commercial sale and for military use were many pictures taken outdoors depicting battlefields and aspects both army and civilian life during the war. These photographs were taken on glass plate negatives and printed on albumen photographic paper.

Mathew Brady (circa 1823–96) was an established photographer who decided to make a photographic record of the entire war after witnessing and photographing the Union defeat at the battle of Bull Run in July 1861. He employed over twenty photographers, including Timothy O'Sullivan, and spent over $100,000 compiling a unique archive of virtually all the major sites and conflicts of the war. When the government refused to purchase the collection after the war he was forced into bankruptcy.

Timothy O'Sullivan (1840–82) took some of the most famous images of the war while working for Brady, including *Harvest of Death*, a poignant image of scattered corpses in the aftermath of Gettysburg.

Pickett, George E. (1825–75)

A Confederate officer and a graduate of West Point (in the same class at McClellan, who finished second as opposed to Pickett who came last of the class list), he served in Mexico alongside Longstreet, who later commanded him at Gettysburg, when Pickett had command of an all-Virginian division. It was at Gettysburg that Lee, against Longstreet's wishes, sent the Confederate forces in the center on an attack against the Union forces ranged on Cemetery Ridge. This disastrous action on July 2, 1863, called Pickett's Charge, was one of the pivotal points in the battle; Pickett's division itself lost two-thirds of its men. He was one of Lee's commanders in early 1865 when, on April 1, 1865, Sheridan's Union army attacked at Five

Left: Following its evacuation, the ruined Confederate capital of Richmond was occupied by Union troops. This photograph taken from the southern bank of the James River captured the devastated landscape of postwar Richmond.

Forks. At the crucial moment when the assault began, Pickett was absent, and the Confederate forces were defeated, losing some 5,200 men.

Polk, Leonidas (1806–64)

A Confederate general and graduate of West Point, Polk left the army in 1827 to join the church, eventually becoming an Episcopal bishop. Following the secession in 1861, he rejoined the army. Troops under his command entered Kentucky on September 3, 1861, and he captured Columbus. While both sides had invaded the state, the Confederates were perceived as the aggressors and Kentucky decided to join the Union. At Columbus, Polk fortified the heights—nicknamed "Gibraltar of the West." He was later involved in Battle of Perryville on October 8, 1862, under the command of Bragg. However, Polk's forces comprised only 16,000 men and Bragg's forces were defeated. He then commanded the right flank of Bragg's army in Battle of Chickamauga Creek on September 19–20, 1863, but was tardy in effecting his assault with the result that his advance made little headway although the

Confederate forces were ultimately to prove victorious. As a result of his perceived refusal to obey orders, Polk was subsequently suspended by Bragg. Later he served under Johnston during the campaign for Atlanta in the summer of 1864, but was killed by a sniper during the early part of that campaign.

Pollard, Edward Alfred (1831-72)

A Confederate writer and historian, Pollard was the author of several works about political events surrounding secession, such as *The Southern Spy Letters* and *The Rival Administration*. *The Lost Cause* examined the reasons for the Confederate defeat.

Pope, John (1822–92)

Born in 1822, John Pope, who was related to both the Washington and Lincoln families, graduated from the U.S. Military College at West Point in 1842, before serving in Mexico. In June 1861 he became a Brigadier General of Volunteers, commanding the Union Army of the Mississippi. Under his command, this army threatened Columbus in early 1862, before

Above Left: General Pope campaigned in the western theater before being called on to defend Washington. Following his defeat at the hands of Robert E. Lee he was removed from command, and sent to the far west.

Above: General Leonidas Polk was an Episcopal Bishop before the war. The fighting bishop became one of the most prominent corps commanders in the Confederate Army of the Tennessee.

Right: The Southerners were heavily outnumbered by their Northern opponents, and unless the war was brought to a rapid conclusion, the Confederacy was bound to be overwhelmed by sheer weight of numbers.

capturing island No. 10 in the Mississippi (which had been heavily fortified by the Confederate forces after their withdrawal from Columbus) on April 4, 1862, with minimal casualties and captured 7,000. After this victory, he was offered a command in Northern Virginia. This he initially declined but was persuaded by Lincoln, although he was disliked by both friends and foes. His proposed policy of shooting captured guerrillas and seizing rebel property without compensation led him to be

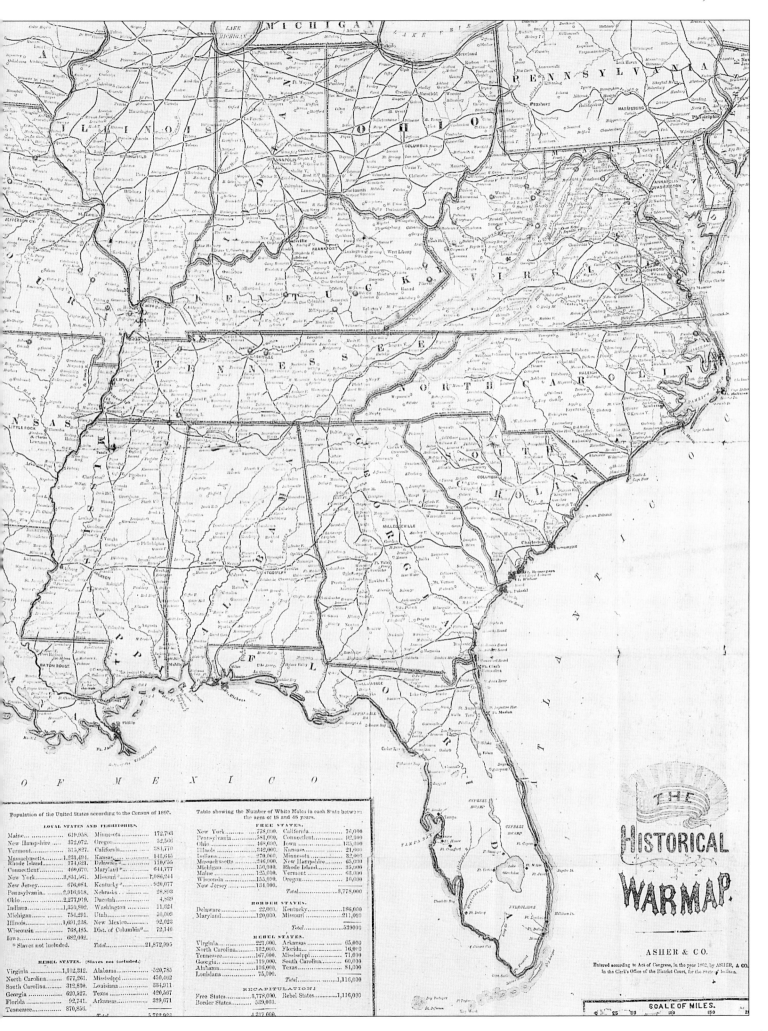

condemned by the Confederate leadership; Lee, for example, referred to him as "miscreant Pope." His fellow Union commanders were also suspicious of his military prowess, doubts which were justified by his failure to counter the Confederate advance towards Washington. He made numerous tactical errors, resulting in the severe defeat at Second Bull Run in August–September 1862. After the battle he was transferred to Minnesota where he had the task of subduing Sioux Indians. Subsequently, he held departmental commands until his retirement in 1886, six years before his death.

Population

At the outset of the Civil War, the total population of the United States, as recorded by the census of 1860, was 31,443,321. Out of this total just under four million were slaves, all of whom, barring a couple of dozen in Utah and Nebraska, lived in the Border States or the South. This was not the only marked difference between North and South. By 1860 only forty percent of the northern population was employed in agriculture, compared with eighty percent in the South. Conversely, twenty-five percent of Northerners lived in urban areas, but only ten percent of Southerners. These figures reflect a relatively slow Southern response to industrialization that was to prove a serious handicap in equipping and financing the war effort.

Port Hudson

Some 240 miles south of Vicksburg, Port Hudson was the site of a Confederate garrison commanding the much-coveted sugar and cotton regions of the Bayou Teche. Soldiers under Nathaniel P. Banks, together with Farragut's warships, had besieged Port Hudson since the last week of May 1864 when, following the surrender of Vicksburg on July 4, Grant decided to send reinforcements to help them take the position. Port Hudson, however, had been holding out in the hope that Johnston's forces would come to its aid after Vicksburg, and with the news of Vicksburg's fall it surrendered on July 9, 1864.

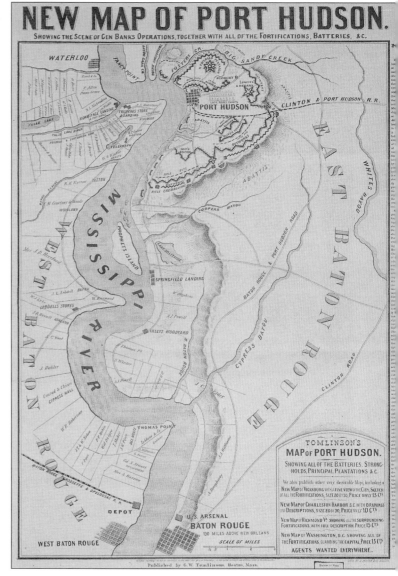

Left and Below Left: The Confederate defenses of Port Hudson were designed to halt a Union drive down the Mississippi River. When it fell the Confederacy was cut in two.

Above: The Battle of Port Royal Sound led to the establishment of a Union naval base on the South Carolina coast. This is the bombardment of Fort Walker.

Below: Rear Admiral David Dixon Porter on the deck of USS *Malvern*—a photograph by Alexander Gardner, January 1865. Note the Dahlgren howitzer on a slide carriage.

Port Royal Sound, Battle of, 1861

By mid-1861, the Union had established blockading squadrons outside all the major Confederate Atlantic ports, but the supply and maintenance of these squadrons was an increasing problem. A secure base was needed on the Confederate seaboard, and Port Royal, South Carolina, offered the greatest potential. An invasion fleet gathered under the command of Admiral Francis DuPont, complete with warships, troopships, engineers, and supplies. On November 4 the fleet arrived off Port Royal and fought off a small Confederate attack. Three days later seventeen Union warships bombarded Fort Walker on nearby Hilton Head into submission, then subdued Fort Beauregard guarding Port Royal Sound. The forts were abandoned, and Union troops landed at Port Royal that evening. Two days later they entered nearby Beaufort. The Union Navy quickly established a coaling and repair yard, making Port Royal a substantial naval base in the heart of South Carolina.

Porter, David Dixon (1813–91)

Born in 1813, he first served as midshipman in the Mexican Navy in 1827. After spending time as a prisoner of war, he joined the U.S. Navy in 1829. He became the commander on USS *Powhatan* in April 1861. He was the commander of mortar boats during capture of New Orleans and became acting rear admiral in autumn 1862 and commander of the Mississippi Squadron. He served during the capture of Vicksburg and was made a full rear admiral. After the failed Red River Campaign, he commanded the North Atlantic Squadron and was involved in capture of Fort Fisher. He became a vice admiral in 1866, being promoted to admiral in 1870.

Potomac River

Dividing the Northern and Southern states of America, the Potomac formed a natural boundary for the duration of the Civil War, north of which the fighting rarely ventured. Jackson's inspirational Shenandoah Valley campaign of May and June 1862 drove Banks' troops back north of the Potomac, in response to a Confederate feint towards Harper's Ferry.

In the September of the same year and exhilarated by victory at Manassas, Lee led his Army of Northern Virginia over the Potomac to Maryland. Lee's bold (but ultimately unsuccessful) move represented a complete change in the nature of the war being waged, as he brought the battle to the North.

Prairie Grove, Arkansas, Battle of, 1862

Following the Battle of Cane Hill, Confederate Major General Thomas C. Hindman, with around 11,000 men, advanced northward to destroy Brigadier General James Blunt's division of around 7,000 before he could be reinforced by Brigadier General Francis Herron's division. Hindman, finding his force positioned between the two Union divisions, left a cavalry screen in front of Blunt and turned on Herron. Hindman routed the Union cavalry and pushed on, encountering the Union infantry who pushed him back. The Union troops assaulted twice and were repulsed. The Confederates then counterattacked, were halted by Union canister, and then moved forward again. Blunt realized that the main action was to his rear and marched around, attacking Hindman in the flank. The Confederates held their position until nightfall and then withdrew to Van Buren.

Press, The

Aided by the telegraph system, which now made possible the rapid transmission of long despatches across the nation, the Press, in the form of daily and weekly newspapers and journals, brought news of the latest battles, victories or defeats from the front lines to cities and towns throughout America. News also of political life in the capitals of Washington and Richmond, of leading personalities, of debates, shifts in strategy, responses to success or adversity. Aspects of life on the home front, or shortages, rising prices, accusations of profiteering and corruption were also a constant theme. Inevitably events were magnified and dramatized in the light of the mood of the day When the progress of the war was going well, every minor victory heralded the final triumph of heroic generals, while in times of retreat every minor setback was a disaster attributable to inept leadership and incompetent strategy. Although there was some effort at censorship on both sides in general

Right: Confederate prisoners-of-war.

Below: The Battle of Prairie Grove fought in northwest Arkansas in December 1862 was the last Union attack on Arkansas for two years.

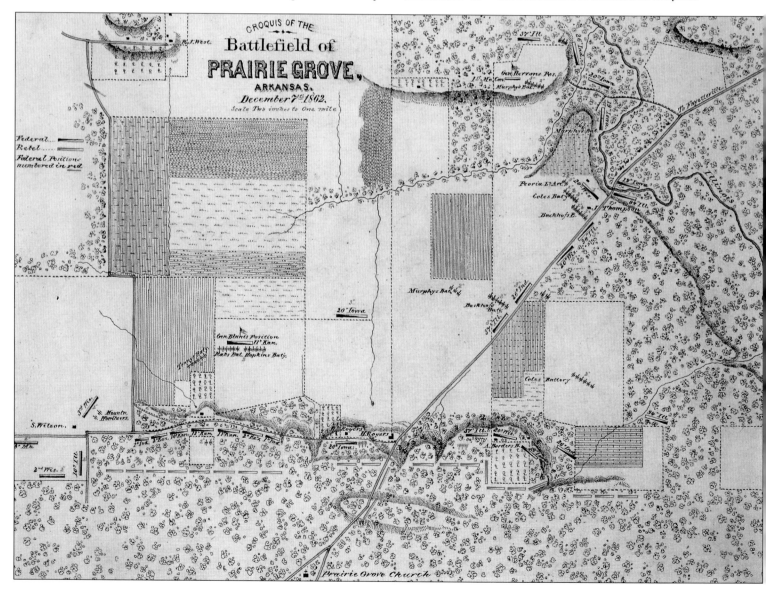

the press was able to comment freely on the course of events, and took the opportunity to advance vigorously both the cause of the Union or Confederacy and the opinions of the editor. The most important editor of the period was Horace Greeley (1811–72) of the *New York Tribune*, an influential backer of Lincoln's nomination and later a powerful voice in favor of emancipation.

Price, Sterling (1809–67)

Having served as a general in the Mexican war, Price was a conditional unionist but events in St. Louis in May 1861 forced him in the secessionist camp. He was appointed by Jackson to run the pro-Southern militia and, despite efforts at a compromise, Missouri was split. Price's forces withdrew from St. Louis to Boonville, where they were defeated on June 17, 1861, and then retreated further south. By this time Price controlled 8,000 men alongside a further 5,000 Confederates under McCulloch; opposing them was Nathaniel Lyon with a numerically smaller force. This engagement resulted in the Confederate victory at Wilson's Creek on August 10, 1861. Price marched northward, now with 18,000 men, and surrounded Lexington, which surrendered on September 20, 1861. The Union commander Frémont, knowing that without

victory his days were numbered, sought, but failed, to engage Price, who had already retreated from Lexington, having realized that he lacked the resources to sustain an occupation of enemy territory. By mid-1862 Price was serving under Bragg and was left, along with Van Dorn, to defend Vicksburg and, having advanced with 15,000 troops into northern Mississippi (taking Iuka on September 14), was then defeated alongside Van Dorn in the Battle of Corinth on October 3–4, 1862. The Union victory put the Confederate forces to flight.

In the spring of 1863 Price was sent to Little Rock in order to bolster the defense of Arkansas, but was unable to stem the two-pronged Union advance through the state during the summer of that year. Little Rock fell on September 10. Price was now to be involved in the shadowy guerrilla war that the Confederates established in the Old Northwest, such as Missouri, through groups such as the "Order of American Knights"; Price was named military commander of this group and, in September 1864, organized a concerted guerrilla invasion of Missouri. This assault proved a failure, resulting in retreat by the end of October and the death of many of the most effective guerrilla leaders (such as "Bloody Bill" Anderson). This was effectively the end of Confederate resistance in Missouri.

Prison camps

Prior to 1863 prisoners were held for short periods in army camps and local jails before being exchanged or paroled and returned to their own side. After the Confederate administration refused to exchange black prisoners, this system broke down and large numbers of prisoners quickly accumulated on both sides. It soon became necessary to construct and manage prison camps to house them. While conditions in Union camps were generally reasonable, with barrack shelters and regular food rations, there was indisputably considerable suffering among prisoners held by the Confederates. The most notorious prison camp was at Andersonville in southwest Georgia, where by August 1864 33,000 men were held prisoner in a twenty-six-acre open stockade. More than a hundred died every day that summer, and in total 13,000 of the 45,000 men held there succumbed to malnutrition, disease, or exposure. The camp became notorious in the northern Press and after the war its commandant, Henry Wirz, was tried and executed for war crimes, in the only trial of its kind. After Secretary of War Stanton called the camp "a deliberate system of savage and brutal treatment," rations for Confederate prisoners were reduced as a

limited response to Press calls for retaliation. Although there clearly were dreadful conditions and acts of brutality, today most historians would attribute the situation to a lack of planning, and to the general inability of the war-ravaged Southern economy to feed its own people adequately, rather than to a deliberate policy.

Prisoners, Exchanges of

At the outset of the war an informal system of prisoner exchanges developed, under which captives from each side were handed back on a local basis after each conflict. Despite some concern that a formal agreement might imply recognition of the rebellion an exchange cartel with the Confederate Army was accepted on July 22, 1862, formalizing this process. Man for man exchanges were agreed for all captives, with ranks weighted up to a general who would be exchanged for sixty privates. Any excess were released on parole, promising not to resume arms until formally exchanged. This system broke down in 1864 when the South refused to exchange any African-American prisoners, and was not renewed until the closing months of the conflict.

Profiteers

While the distinction between a successful businessman and a profiteer is often one of perspective, there is no doubt that large fortunes were made by often dubious means in the course of the war. One of the most notorious incidents came early in the war when the chairman of the Senate Committee on Naval Affairs, John P. Hale, and government naval purchasing agents colluded to sell a number of worthless hulks to the Navy. Trading across the lines in cotton was common from the start, and as the Confederate economy collapsed unscrupulous businessmen took advantage of desperate shortages to smuggle a whole range of goods from the better-supplied North.

Propulsion

Marine steam propulsion was a relatively new invention in 1861. On the Mississippi River and its tributaries, riverboats were usually propelled by high-pressure steam engines, which drove large paddlewheels mounted in the stern of these craft. Elsewhere, side-mounted paddlewheels were more common, particularly with civilian vessels. Many craft of both types were impressed into both the Union and

Right: The huge propeller of USS *Dictator* on the ways at the Delameter Iron Works probably just before she launched on December 26, 1863. *Dictator* would serve with the U.S. Navy until 1883.

Confederate navies and used with some effect as warships. In naval combat, paddlewheels were considered vulnerable to enemy fire, and side-paddlewheels also limited the broadside armament of the vessel. Although some warships (including ironclads) were purposely built using paddlewheel propulsion, the wheel housings were usually armored.

Most warships used low-pressure steam engines, which powered a propeller (screw), as this was less vulnerable to enemy fire. Engines of most of these vessel types used single-cylinder reciprocating systems, although engine configurations varied widely. Boilers used to provide the steam were coal-fired, and were usually mounted horizontally. While most warships had one or two shafts parallel-mounted and boilers, some were far larger. The never-completed Confederate ironclad *Mississippi* was fitted to carry sixteen boilers.

While Union shipyards and industrial facilities ensured that the U.S. Navy's warships were usually fitted with the best available propulsion systems, and that spare parts were never a problem, Confederate engineers were less fortunate. A lack of marine engineering facilities, trained mechanics, and suitable engines made the fitting and supply of propulsion systems a continual problem, and most Confederate ironclads were underpowered, less reliable, and slower than their Union counterparts.

Right: A wide range of marine propulsion systems were used during the war. While screws (propellers) were the major form used at sea, on the Mississippi River and its tributaries paddle-wheels were more common.

Railroads

The Civil War was one of the first major conflicts to be fought since the development of railroads that allowed large quantities of men and supplies to be transported rapidly over vast distances. Both sides recognized that they were of vital strategic importance and key railroad junctions were often the targets of campaign maneuvers. In keeping with its more advanced industrial economy, the Union had at the outset more than twice the density of railroads per square mile as the Confederacy. Moreover, this logistical advantage was backed by a huge superiority in the capacity to produce both locomotives and iron rails. As Union armies moved into the South, they relied on this superiority to maintain increasingly long supply lines. A U.S. Military Rail roads body was established in 1862, which administered over 2,000 miles of track in captured areas of the South. However, these extended supply lines were continually vulnerable to attack, particularly by cavalry raiders who tore up miles of track and burnt engines. Disgruntled locals could also easily block Union lines running through captured rebel territory. Despite this vulnerability, both Confederate and Union forces achieved important strategic goals through

THE AMERICAN CIVIL WAR: A VISUAL ENCYCLOPEDIA

R

Railroads played a vital part in the war, the first major conflict where rail transport was used to move troops and supplies. The photographs on this and the following pages provide an interesting glimpse into the North American railroad system of the period.

Above Right: Destruction of railroad at Manassas, Virginia on Pope's retreat, August 1862.

Right and Far Right: Infantry wait to entrain. Movement by rail eased the logistic nightmares of the past.

Opposite Page, Top: Central Pacific diamond-stack in Bloomer Cut, between Auburn and Newcastle, California. While the Civil War raged, the westbound march of the steam traction continued. This cutting required black powder blasting through a formation of cemented bolders. The line opened east of Newcastle in 1865.

Overleaf:
Inset, Below: The Western & Atlantic Railroad car sheds in Atlanta RR yards. The shed was destroyed by Sherman when he evacuated Atlanta.

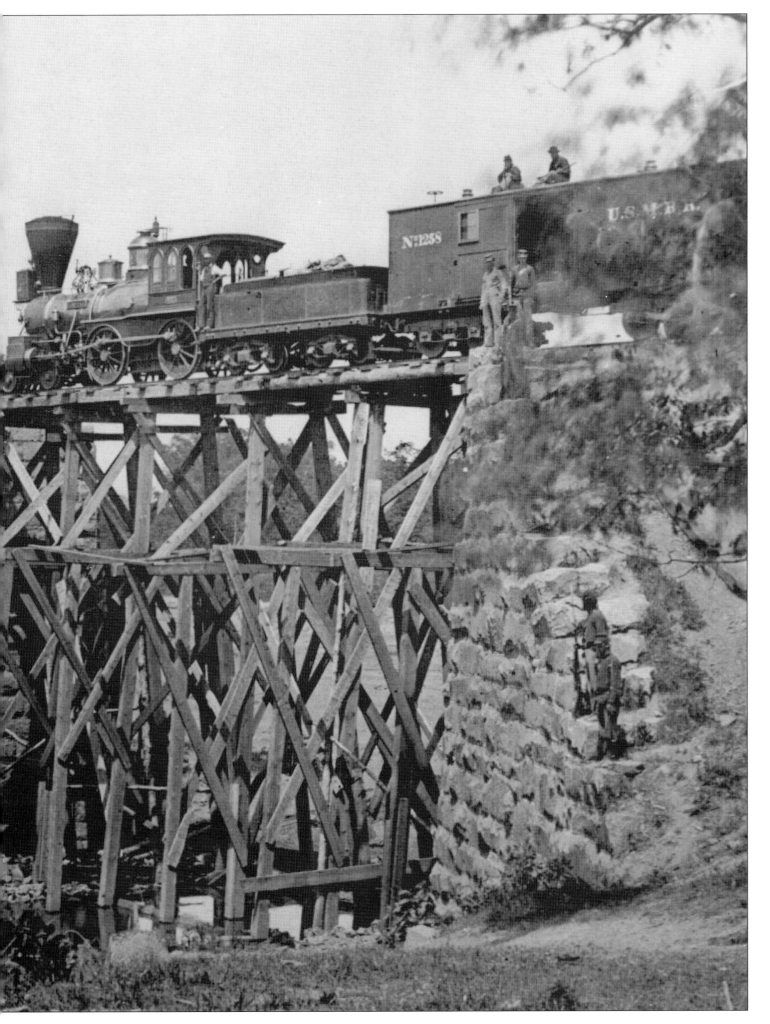

the use of the railroads. In September 1863 Longstreet transported 12,000 men 900 miles through the Carolinas and Georgia in time to reinforce Bragg's Confederate army at the Battle of Chickamauga Creek. After this defeat Union forces relied on railroads to bring up 20,000 more men from the XI and XII corps, with artillery and horses, completing a journey of over 1,200 miles in just eleven days.

Rapidan River

Running between Orange County and Culpeper County, the Rapidan represented the military frontier between North and South for much of 1863. Following Lee's defeat at Gettysburg in July 1863 and his subsequent retreat into Virginia, the fighting alternated between the river lines of the Rappahannock and the Rapidan west of Fredericksburg. Offensives from Lee and the Federal Major General George Meade

The Rapidan and Rappahannock rivers flowed from west to east through northern Virginia. They became crucial defensive barriers for the Confederates.

Left: A battery fords a tributary of the Rappahannock on the day of the Battle of Cedar Mountain, August 1862.

Below: Pontoon bridges spanning the Rappahannock near Fredricksburg, 1862.

led to stalemate by November 7, 1863, and the two forces settled in for the winter with the Rapidan River between them. Meade's men established their base around Culpeper Court House, while the Confederates remained in Orange County on the Rapidan's southern bank.

Rappahannock River

The Rappahannock River was an important fighting front during the American Civil War. The first major battle to be waged across the Rappahannock was that of Fredericksburg on December 13, 1862, as Lee's and Burnside's armies faced one another across the river.

Lee emerged victorious from Fredericksburg, and again used the terrain around the Rappahannock to his advantage in the battle of Chancellorsville on May 1–5, 1863, when he drove surprised Union troops back across the river.

Following the battle of Gettysburg in July 1863, the fighting fronts between North and South alternated between the river lines of the Rapidan and the Rappahannock. This continued until November 7, when Union forces crossed the Rappahannock at two points, driving the Confederates to the far bank of the Rapidan.

Readmission to the Union

The process of "Reconstruction" after the war involved defining the terms under which secessionist states could be readmit-

ted to the Union, and many Republican politicians favored readmission only after these states gave blacks complete equality. Temporary administrations were established in the former states, and some degree of equality introduced. They also introduced crippling taxes, causing widespread resentment. The situation continued until President Grant introduced a general amnesty in 1872, allowing former Confederates to stand for office. One by one regular state administrations were formed in the Southern states, and the states were readmitted to the Union.

Reconstruction

Reconstruction is the name given to the period in the immediate aftermath of the

Civil War during which the United States rebuilt the South, a process that was expected by some to involve a moral and social transformation as much as an economic and political one. Even before the war ended intense debate was raging over questions crucial to the future shape of reconstruction. Was it to be controlled by the President or by Congress? How would states rejoin the Union? Should votes be extended to blacks?

In the event, following Lincoln's assassination neither his Presidential reconstruction decree nor Congress' rival Wade-Davis Act were implemented. The new President, Andrew Johnson, adopted policies widely criticized as far too lenient to the old Southern planter elite, permitting them to pass "black codes" that sought to restrict the rights of freed people and restore land to former owners in defiance of the Federal Freedmen's Bureau. In response to Johnson's veto of Congressional efforts to change course, Republicans passed the Fourteenth Amendment, declaring that persons born in the United States, regardless of color, were U.S. citizens, and restricting state power to limit their rights. Congress took control of the Reconstruction process, passing a series of Reconstruction Acts that limited state powers and set the terms of rebuilding. An attempt to impeach President Jackson prompted by his continued obstruction failed by a single vote. The Fifteenth Amendment, ratified in 1870, widened protection of black voting rights and outlawed discrimination by hotels, theaters, and railroads. Enforcing new rights and gaining economic independence, however, became virtually impossible in the face of widespread and often violent white counterattacks. By the late 1870,s white supremacist Democrats were in control throughout the South and the liberal hopes of Reconstruction radicals long forgotten.

Above: One of the Freedmen's schools built in the South in the Reconstruction era.

Left: The Blue and the Gray at Appomattox after General Lee's surrender, April 9, 1865. Drawn by C. S. Reinhart for *Harper's Weekly*. Following victory the Union worked hard to end the North/South divide. Indeed, President Johnson was accused of being far too lenient.

Red River Campaign

The capture of Port Hudson in July 1863 effectively ended Confederate control of the lower Mississippi River and freed the

forces of the newly created Department of the Gulf for employment elsewhere. Its commander, Major General Nathaniel Prentiss Banks, was in agreement with Grant and Admiral Farragut that an expedition against Mobile, Alabama, would be the most effective means of rendering support to the proposed operations against Bragg at Chattanooga, which they considered the highest priority of the Federal forces in the western theater.

However, the authorities in Washington had a somewhat different view of the situation. Lincoln, motivated by a desire to reestablish a Federal presence in Confederate Texas, directed Banks to move against that territory instead. An attempt to capture the Sabine Pass at the mouth of the Sabine River in September 1863 ended in dismal failure, and after a second expedition to reach the Sabine River by an overland march had to be terminated because of logistical difficulties, Banks resorted to naval operations to reduce the Texas Gulf Coast ports. Between November and December 1863, Brownsville, Corpus Christi, and Fort Esperanza were occupied. By the beginning of 1864, the only major port in Texas still in Confederate hands was Galveston. In early January, Banks began operations against it also.

In early 1864 the Federal authorities began to formulate a plan to capture the cotton-growing sections of Texas, Louisiana, and Arkansas, via an expedition up the Red River. Thus, hardly had the Galveston operations begun than Halleck directed Banks to move against Shreveport, Louisiana. For the operation, Banks was to

Above: General Edmund Kirby Smith commanded the Trans-Mississippi theater with great skill. Under his leadership the Union drive up the Red River into northern Louisiana was thwarted, as were Union drives south into Arkansas from Missouri.

Right: The Union's 96th Pennsylvania Infantry Regiment lined up for inspection at a camp near Washington, 1861. Regiments were the basic building blocks of all army units (see page 376).

receive support from General Frederick Steele's forces in Arkansas, detachments of Sherman's command in Mississippi, and a fleet of gunboats from Farragut under the command of Admiral Porter.

The plan was complicated by a number of factors; first, except for a few rainy weeks in late March and April, the Red River was too shallow to navigate above Alexandria, Louisiana, placing a tight time restriction on the operation, which Banks planned to commence in mid-March. Second, the 10,000-strong force under Sherman, which was to be transported by Porter's gunboats, was to rendezvous with Banks' 17,000 at Alexandria, some 100 miles deep into Confederate-controlled territory. To compound it all, the junction with Steele's 15,000 troops from Arkansas was to occur at Shreveport, a further 150 miles into Confederate-held territory lines. Banks expressed his misgivings, but was unable to convince his superiors of the pitfalls that might lie ahead. As a professional soldier, he resolved to try and carry out his orders to the best of his ability.

His opponent was General Edmund Kirby Smith, Confederate commander for the Trans-Mississippi Theater, with about 25,000 men to oppose the Federal operations. The field commander was Major General Richard Taylor.

Sherman's detachment, transported in Porter's gunboats, occupied Alexandria, Louisiana on March 18, where they joined a week later by Banks' command. On March 27, Banks received new orders from Grant, stating that operations against Shreveport must be concluded by April 25 because of the need for troops for operations against Atlanta and Mobile in early May. This gave Banks cause to consider calling off the campaign, but he reasoned that the Confederates would not be able to concentrate in time or strength, and were likely not to contest the Federal occupation of Shreveport.

By April 3, the Red River had risen enough to allow Banks' transports and thirteen of the smaller gunboats to pass the rapids above Alexandria. On April 8, his advance elements encountered Taylor's army of about 16,000 occupying an advantageous position on the edge of a small clearing about two miles south of Mansfield. In the ensuing battle, known as the Battle of Sabine Crossroads, only the timely arrival of Emory's division saved the Federal forces from complete disaster. Banks withdrew during the night to Pleasant Hill, about nine miles southwest of the Confederates. Taylor, seeking to complete the destruction of the Federal army, put his tired troops on the road in pursuit, but his assault on the hill was repulsed with heavy loss. The following morning found Banks again having retreated. Kirby Smith reached the battlefield and left Taylor with Mouton's division and the cavalry (about 5,200 troops) to continue to harass Banks withdrawal, while taking the remainder to move against Steele in Arkansas, where on April 30, he made an unsuccessful attempt to wipe out Steele's army at the Battle of Jenkin's Ferry, on the Sabine River.

Banks had already abandoned his attempt to capture Shreveport since he could now expect no help from Steele and he must soon

return Sherman's troops. After several skirmishes and minor engagements between Banks' forces, Porter's fleet, and Taylor's pursuing troops, the Federals finally escaped back down the Red River. Sherman's troops were embarked for Vicksburg on May 21-22, and on May 26, the remainder of Banks' command reached Donaldsonville, Louisiana. The Red River Campaign was a complete failure for the Federals. Banks was relieved of command and Kirby Smith fired Taylor as a result of some angry correspondence between the two Confederate commanders.

Regiments, Organization of

In the prewar U.S. Army, each infantry regiment was divided into two or usually three battalions, each containing eight companies. While the regiment was commanded by a colonel, whose staff included quartermasters and a band, each battalion had a small staff, headed by a major, which included medical sections. In total the regiment contained between 2,000 to 2,450 officers and men, while each battalion contained an average of 725 men of all ranks. While nine regular regiments participated in the war on the Union side, the majority of infantry regiments were composed of volunteer units. The organization of the regular infantry regiment served as a model for state volunteer and militia organizations on both sides. The big exception was that, unlike the regular army, volunteer infantry

regiments had no battalions, as each was effectively of battalion strength. Several diffenent regimental organizations existed in the Union army until September 1862, when an authorized regimental establishment was established. Each regiment had a staff of thirteen regimental officers, including a colonel, lieutenant-colonel, three majors, supply officers, surgeons, and sometimes a chaplain. The regiment was divided into ten companies (as opposed to the eight companies of a regular battalion), each of which had an established strength of 101 officers and men. The total regimental strength was 1,024 men, but losses through illness, combat, and desertion meant that this number was never achieved. During the Battle of Gettysburg, some regiments contained over 700 combatants, but others contained fewer than 200 men.

In the Confederate Army, ten-company regiments were also the standard type of formation, but there the similarities ended. Most Confederate regiments lacked the logistical support and medical facilities which were standard parts of the formations of their Northern counterparts. The effective strength of a Confederate regiment laid down in March 1861 was 1,145 men, and this was increased in 1862 to 1,255, increasing the size of the infantry companies from 114 to 139 men.

Another type of formation exclusive to the South was the Legion, which contained both infantry (usually a battalion of about six companies), cavalry, and artillery. By

late 1863, most of these formations had been broken into their constituent parts. Unlike the Union army, Confederate regiments received some replacements, and although numbers dwindled as the war progressed and losses mounted, regiments tended to contain more men than those in the North. This was only a general rule, and relative, as even in 1861, units fielding more than 600 men were uncommon. By 1863, the typical Confederate regiment contained less than 300 men.

In both armies, a regiment was drawn up for battle in a line two men deep, with eight companies usually forming the main line, and two "flank companies" sent forward to form a skirmish screen. While the regimental colors were carried in the center of the line, the regimental staff and all non-combatants took station behind the colors. Similarly, company officers and senior NCOs stood behind their men to ensure their unit maintained its formation.

Republican Party

The Republican Party was formed in 1854 as a coalition bringing together some northern Democrats dissatisfied with their

Right and Below Right: Regiments of volunteers (Right) and Zouaves (Below Right) drilling in their winter camps in northern Virginia.

Below: President Lincoln inspecting sailors and marines, 1861.

party's domination by pro-slavery interests, with the old Whig, Free Soil, and Know Nothing parties. In 1860 Abraham Lincoln was elected to the Presidency as a Republican, successfully balancing the party's radical Abolitionist wing with those who favored a gradualist approach to slavery and were bitterly opposed to any idea of black equality. Republicans led the radical approach to postwar Reconstruction, but by the late1870s, with Democrats in firm control of the South and blacks increasingly disenfranchised, the party moved away from its support for black rights.

Richmond, Virginia

When Richmond was declared the Confederate capital following the outbreak of the Civil War, its population doubled overnight. As capital, Richmond and the surrounding area formed a major target for Union attacks, and bread riots broke out there in April 1863 when Burnside's and

The ruins of Richmond, Virginia, soon after its occupation by Union troops in April 1865. The city was ravaged by fire on the night of April 2, a week before Lee surrendered at Appomattox Court House. The Tredegar Iron Works (Right) survived the worst of the blaze.

THE RUINS OF RICHMOND (*From a photograph made in 1865*)

THE AMERICAN CIVIL WAR: A VISUAL ENCYCLOPEDIA

McClellan's campaigns had devastated the countryside that once supplied Richmond. The Confederate capital moved to Danville on April 2, 1865, following the fall of Petersburg, but when the Confederates left Richmond they left it in flames. Major General Godfrey Weitzel marched into the burning city on April 3, to be followed by Lincoln himself on April 4, 1865.

Roanoake Island, Battle of, 1862

In October 1861 Union forces captured Hatteras Inlet, which gave them access to the Carolina Sounds. Local Confederate forces were gathered on Roanoke Island, so a joint force was gathered to attack the island. Commanded by General Ambrose Burnside contained seventeen wooden gunboats. On February 5, 1862 he approached Roanoke from the south. The island's three fortifications were garrisoned by 3,000 Confederates, commanded by General Henry A. Wise, supported a small "Mosquito Fleet" of gunboats. On February 7, 10,000 Union troops landed on Roanoke under cover of a naval bombardment, and the forts fell to overwhelming numbers of attackers. Underwater obstructions hindered the Union squadron, but once through the outnumbered Confederate flotilla was forced to retreat north to Elizabeth City, where most of the vessels were eventually captured and destroyed. The Union was now firmly in control of almost the entire coastline of North Carolina.

Rogers, John (1812–82)

Captain Rogers participated in the siezure of Port Royal (1862) before commanding a squadron on the Mississippi. He was replaced in August 1861, but he gained further distinction as the captain of the USS *Weehawken* off Charleston in 1863, and as Commodore, he captured the ironclad CSS *Atlanta*.

Rosecrans, William Stark (1819–98)

Born in 1819, William S. Rosecrans graduated from the U.S. Military College at West Point in 1842, although (unlike many of his contemporaries) he did not serve in Mexico. He resigned his commission in 1854. Although a Democrat, he became a Brigadier General of Volunteers in May 1861, first serving in West Virginia where he defeated Lee at Battle of Rich Mountain on July 11, 1861. He then commanded the Army of the Mississippi at Corinth, with battles at Iuka and Corinth. In September 1862 he became Major General of Volunteers and gained command of Army of Cumberland.

He commanded the Union forces at the battles of Murfreesboro and Chickamauga (September 19–20, 1863), although a blunder led to serious defeat at latter. Following this defeat, he was besieged at Chattanooga until relieved by Grant in October 1863. He then commanded the Department of Missouri until December 1864. Relieved of his command, he was on leave until resig-

Above: The first Union gunboats to appear on the Mississippi River were the USS *Lexington*, *Tyler*, and *Conestoga*, all of which were commissioned in the summer of 1861.

Right: The first Union naval commander on the river was Captain John Rogers, who went on to command the monitor USS *Weehawken* in action off Charleston and Savannah.

nation in March 1867. He later served (as a representing of California) in House of Representatives.

Russia during the war, Role of

Russia, perhaps in response to the pro-Confederate leanings of its rival "Great Powers", Britain and France, adopted a policy of diplomatic support for the Union. In particular its diplomats and foreign ministers refused to support any Anglo-French initiates to broker peace deals, which by recognising the de facto division of America, would have constituted a victory for the Confederate States. When Russian fleets wintered in New York and San Francisco harbors in the fall of 1863, this was widely seen as a sign of strong support for the Union, although the Russians had sound strategic reasons for avoiding their own ice-bound ports when conflict with Britain and France was a possibility.

Sabine River, Battle of the, 1863

When Galveston was captured in October 1862, a Confederate counterattack on New Year's Day recaptured the vital. Union losses included the gunboats USS *Harriet Lane* and the USS *Westfield*. The mouth of the Sabine River was considered as an alternative anchorage, but the Confederates constructed Fort Griffin to defend the "Sabine Pass," a pair of bluffs dominating the river. A Union force of eleven wooden warships and 4,000 troops commanded by General Nathaniel Banks attacked the position on September 8, 1863. In less than two hours the two wooden gunboats USS *Sachem* and USS *Clifton* were disabled by gunfire from the fort, then captured by a small Confederate gunboat. The attack was an unmitigated disaster. The debacle was repeated in May 1864, when a second assault was driven off. Fort Griffin eventually surrendered a year later, when news of the Confederacy's capitulation reached Texas.

Savannah, Georgia

The Georgian port of Savannah was the terminal point of Sherman's devastating March to the Sea following the taking of Atlanta. When Sherman's troops arrived in Savannah on December 22, 1864, the city surrendered at once, and Sherman sent a telegram to Lincoln offering him Savannah as a "Christmas present", together with "one hundred and fifty heavy guns and plenty of ammunition, also about twenty-five thousand bales of cotton." An apparently accidental fire seized Savannah as Sherman's troops marched out, destroying much of the city despite the best combined efforts of Union soldiers, Savannah's citizens, and freed slaves to quench the blaze.

Savannah, Defense of

The only major port in Georgia, Savannah, lay on the Savannah River, ten miles from the sea. A series of estuarine channels linked the river with other entrances into the Atlantic, which emptied south of the city. This maze of waterways made it difficult to impose a rigid blockade of the port. Fort Pulaski, built during the 1820s guarded the Savannah River. The defenses were strengthened in late 1861, when secondary batteries and forts ringed the city. In addition, local shipbuilders began constructing a defensive squadron of gunboats and ironclads to ensure the safety of the city. In December 1861, Union forces captured Tybee Island downriver from the fort, then secretly built a series of powerful siege batteries. On April 11, 1862, the fort was subjected to a heavy bombardment, and after thirty hours it surrendered. Any advance up the river was blocked by further batteries upstream. Three ironclads were built to defend the port; the CSS *Atlanta*, commissioned in September 1862, then the CSS *Savannah* and CSS *Georgia*, which both entered service in mid-1863. The *Atlanta* was lost in an engagement with two Union monitors in Wassaw Sound south of Savannah in June 1863, and the *Georgia* proved useless as a warship, so was

BURNING OF THE NAVY YARD AT SAVANNAH BY THE CONFEDERATES, DECEMBER 21ST, 1864.

Above: Major-General Schofield held off the Confederate Army of Tennessee at the Battle of Franklin in 1864.

Above Right: The veteran General Winfield Scott commanded the U.S. Army at the outbreak of the war until his retirement in November 1861.

Top and Left: The destruction of the Confederate naval squadron and ship-yards at Savannah were prompted by the approach of General Sherman's army in December 1864.

relegated to service as a floating battery. These warships combined with local fortifications and the city's garrison were sufficient to deter any Union attack until the city fell to General Sherman following his march from Atlanta to the sea in December 1864.

Schofield, John M. (1831–1906)

Schofield was a Union officer who commanded the 13,000-man Army of the Ohio, following his appointment in March 1864, under Sherman in the campaign against Atlanta in May to September 1864. He led his infantry corps against the Confederate forces in Sherman's victory at the Battle of the Chattahoochee River in mid-July 1864. He then served under Thomas in the campaign in Tennessee, defeating the Confederate forces under Hood at Spring Hill on November 29, 1864 and also at Franklin on the following day. The latter battle cost Hood some 7,000 casualties, including twelve generals and fifty-four regimental commanders.

Scott, Winfield (1786–1866)

Born in 1786 in Virginia and nicknamed "Old Fuss and Feathers," Scott first joined the U.S. Army in 1808. He served during the 1812 war as a brigadier general, being severely wounded at Lundy's Lane. During the Mexican War, Scott—despite the opposition of President Polk (who did not want him to serve in Mexico)—captured Mexico City and forced the Mexicans to make peace. Scott was nominated for the presidency in 1852 (as a Whig—the last time that party contested the presidency), but he was opposed both by the South—being seen as too much under the control of Seward and therefore anti-slavery—and by Northern Protestants, who disliked the fact that his daughters had been educated in a convent. Despite being a Virginian, he remained loyal to the Union. He was, despite his age and infirmities, the initial commander of Union forces and, as such, developed the "Anaconda Plan," which envisaged the South being assaulted from the north, the wes,t and the sea and, thus, gradually squeezed to death (a strategy that was ultimately to be successful as concluded by Grant). However, Scott delayed military action and this led to his dismissal and replacement by McClellan in July 1861. Scott, arguably one of the greatest of all early U.S. soldiers, formally retired in November 1861; he died at West Point in May 1866.

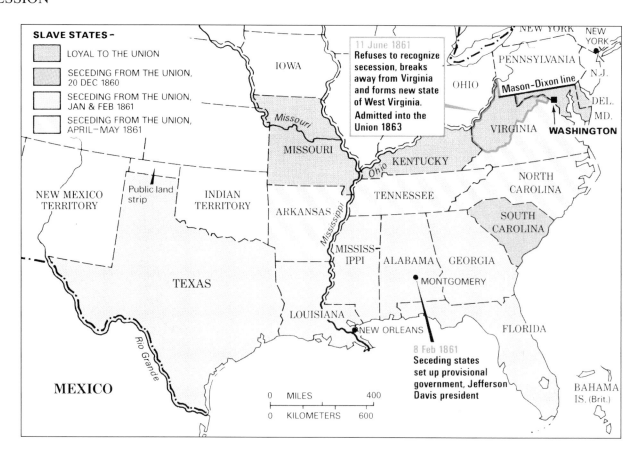

SLAVE STATES -

- LOYAL TO THE UNION
- SECEDING FROM THE UNION, 20 DEC 1860
- SECEDING FROM THE UNION, JAN & FEB 1861
- SECEDING FROM THE UNION, APRIL—MAY 1861

11 June 1861
Refuses to recognize secession, breaks away from Virginia and forms new state of West Virginia. Admitted into the Union 1863

8 Feb 1861
Seceding states set up provisional government, Jefferson Davis president

Secession

Until the victory of Abraham Lincoln on behalf of the Republican Party in the election of 1860, many throughout the South still hoped that further compromises could be found in Congress which would restrict what they regarded as unacceptable interference with their property rights, i.e. their freedom to own and control their slaves, and their ability to enforce these rights throughout the United States. Lincoln's election, with an entirely Northern mandate and an explicitly anti-slavery platform, dashed these unrealistic hopes and pushed many waverers into the secession camp.

By the time of the new President's inauguration in March 1861, seven states—Alabama, South Carolina, Mississippi, Florida, Georgia, Louisiana, and Texas—had already adopted ordinances of secession, and formed the Confederate States of America, with Jefferson Davis as President. In each state, conventions of delegates met and voted for secession, beginning with South Carolina on December 20, 1860.

Each seceding state issued a declaration outlining their grievances with the Union, which centered on, but were not limited to, slavery-related issues. When Lincoln called for troops to put down the rebellion following Southern artillery fire on Fort Sumter on April 12, 1861, four more states—Virginia, Arkansas, North Carolina, and Tennessee—opted to secede. In legal terms, secession was justified by the claim that states had sovereign rights that preceded the formation of the Union, or that each

later qualified as a lawyer. In April 1861 he became the South's Chief of the Lighthouse Bureau. An active believer that maritime forces could determine war, he commanded CSS *Sumter* from New Orleans; despite successes he was forced to abandon her at Gibraltar when she became unseaworthy. From Britain he took command of CSS *Alabama* in August 1862. Following two years of successes, including the sinking of the USS *Hatteras*, Semmes engaged the USS *Kearsage* outside Cherbourg on June 19, 1864, and was defeated. Rescued by a British vessel, he returned to the South, becoming a rear admiral and taking command of the James River Squadron. Eventually the Naval Brigade was placed under the command of Lee and surrendered at Appomattox on April 9 1865.

Seward, William Henry (1801–72)

Born in 1801, Seward was elected Governor of New York State in 1838. A man of strong convictions, he was strongly against Freemasonry and for prison reform. He became Senator for New York and leader of the Northern anti-slavery movement, backing General Winfield Scott in the 1852 Presidential election.

He was expected to get the Republican nomination for the 1860 Presidential election but was perceived as too dangerous with the result that Abraham Lincoln got nominated in his place. Despite his views, he endeavored to keep the South in the Union during the winter of 1860–61 but failed. He was appointed Secretary of State 1861. The Union policy of enforcing a blockade of the southern states meant that he had a major task to keep European powers neutral. He successfully negotiated a treaty with Britain 1862 which effectively ended Atlantic slave trade and published the Emancipation Proclamation following Union victory at Antietam.

Toward the end of the Civil War he was injured following a carriage accident and, while recovering, was the victim of an attack simultaneously with the assassination of Lincoln in 1865. He was, unlike Lincoln, to survive the assassination attempt. In 1867 he negotiated the purchase of Alaska from Russia and forced resulting treaty through Senate. .

Sharpshooters

Two specialist regiments of sharpshooters were raised by the Union Army, and the 1st

---

state possessed a right to rebel in defense of its sovereign liberties.

Seddon, James Alexander (1815–80)

A lawyer and keen advocate of peaceful southern secession, Seddon was a delegate to the Virginia Peace Conference of 1861 which tried to find a means of preventing a war between the states. In November 1862 Seddon became Confederate Secretary of War, a post he retained until February 1865.

Sedgwick, John (1813–64)

Sedgwick was a Union commander. He served under McClellan in the Battle of Antietam (September 17, 1862), where he led an attack against the northern flank of the Confederate force.

Later he fought a crucial role in the Battle of Chancellorsville, on May 2–8, 1863, where he served under Hooker, defeating Lee at Salem Church (May 3–4, 1863) and threatening the rear of the otherwise triumphant Confederate army. Lee's response was rapid and Sedgwick was forced to retreat north over the Rappahannock River.

Semmes, Raphael (1809–77)

Born in 1809, Raphael Semmes was commissioned as a midshipman in the U.S. Navy in 1826. Having served in Mexico, he

and 2nd Sharpshooters formed part of the Army of the Potomac. Usually, companies were detached from their parent unit and operated independently. In late 1864, the two regiments were amalgamated.

Some 2,000 volunteer recruits came from all over the North, and all had to be expert marksmen. These sharpshooters were given distinctive uniforms, and armed with specialist firearms. Initially, these were hunting rifles, but later, Colt revolving rifles and Sharps rifles were issued. Equipped with these effective breech-loading rifles, the sharpshooters proved invaluable on the battlefield.

Riflemen, ATTENTION !

A COMPANY OF ONE HUNDRED MEN to be selected from the

BEST RIFLE SHOTS,

In the State, is to be raised to act as a COMPANY OF SHARP SHOOTERS through the War. Each man will be entitled to

A BOUNTY OF $22,00,

When mustered into the service of the United States, and

100,00 DOLLARS

at the close of the War, in addition to his regular pay.

No man will be accepted or mustered into service who is not an active and able bodied man, and who cannot when firing at a rest at a distance of two hundred yards, put ten consecutive shots into a target the average distance not to exceed five inches from the centre of the bull's eye to the centre of the ball ; and all candidates will have to pass such an examination as to satisfy the recruiting officer of their fitness for enlistment in this corps.

Recruits having Rifles to which they are accustomed are requested to bring them to the place of rendezvous.

Recruits will be received by   JAMES D. FESSENDEN,

Adams Block, No 23, Market Square, PORTLAND, Maine

Sept. 16, 1861.

Opposite Page, Above Left: Recruitment poster for a Maine company to be composed of the "best rifle shots in the state," September 16, 1861.

Opposite Page, Above Right: The Union's Berdan Sharpshooters were issued a special uniform and a knapsack and messkit supplied by Tiffany's.

Opposite Page, Below: Dead Confederate sharpshooter, his rifle and telescopic lens by him.

Above: The most effective sharpshooters were the handful of Confederates equipped with Whitworth rifle—this one is a reenactor.

Left: A reenactor Berdan Sharpshooter with his Sharps rifle.

SHARP SHOOTERS FOR THE WAR.

A Company of Sharp Shooters, to be attached to one of the

MAINE REGIMENTS,

Or to Col. *BERDAN'S* Regiment of Rifle Sharp Shooters, will be raised in this State, under the direction of *JAMES D. FESSENDEN*, Esq.

Recruits will be enlisted at

Bangor by R. R. PARK, at Rockland by JACOB McCLURE,

Augusta by I. J. ROBINSON,

Portland by J. D. FESSENDEN.

As it is important that the Company should be filled at once, applications must be made immediately.

No person will be received who is not an Active Able-Bodied Man, and who cannot, when firing at rest, at a distance of *Two Hundred* Yards, put *Ten Consecutive Shots* in a Target, the average distance not to exceed *Five Inches* from the Centre of the Bull's Eye to the Centre of the ball; and all Candidates will have to pass such examination as to satisfy the Recruiting Officer of their fitness for enlistment in this Corps.

State Bounty, Pay, and U. S. Bounty, will be the same as to U. S. Regiments of Volunteers.

JOHN L. HODSDON Adj. Gen'l.

AUGUSTA, *September 11, 1861*.

Shenandoah Valley

Beginning on March 23, 1862, Thomas J "Stonewall" Jackson's campaign in the Shenandoah Valley was a feat of tactical brilliance. His 17,000 men commanded and immobilized 50,000 Union troops for over two months in the summer of 1862, sweeping through Virginia towards Washington and drawing McClellan's men away from their march on Richmond. Following fighting at Kernstown, Front Royal, Winchester, and Cross Keys, on June 8. 1862 the campaign ended within sight of Washington with the Confederate capture of the Union artillery position at Port Republic.

Shenandoah Valley Campaign 1862

On May 3, in the later stages of the Peninsular Campaign, Lee withdrew from Yorktown toward Richmond. McClellan followed, his army astride the Chickahominy River. Lee learned on May 16 that McDowell and some 40,000 Federal troops would be moving south toward Richmond to reinforce McClellan, whose own force was poised to the east of the Confederate capital, opposed only by Johnston's forces. Johnston could not move to intercept McDowell without exposing Richmond to McClellan. However, if Johnston failed to act McDowell would the city.

The solution to this problem lay in the character of President Abraham Lincoln. He was always particularly concerned about any threat to his capital, and whenever he perceived such a threat Lincoln invariably overreacted. Thus Major General Thomas J. "Stonewall" Jackson was ordered to make an aggressive show in

Above: Another recruitment poster for a Maine company of sharpshooters, this one dated September 11, 1861, at Augusta.

Above Right: Map of the 1862 Shenandoah Valley Campaign.

the Shenandoah Valley that would cause a perceived threat to Washington, D.C.

This sort of independent command made Jackson very happy. After engaging a Federal force at Front Royal on May 23, he then pushed General Nathanial Banks from his supply depot at Winchester on May 25. Besides netting some 3,000 prisoners, 9,000 smallarms and tons of supplies, the

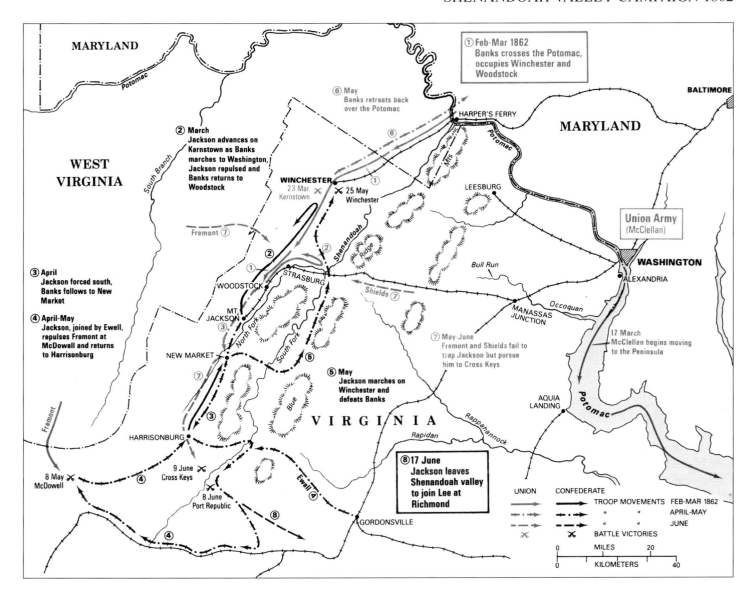

operation had the desired effect of causing Lincoln to order McDowell to halt his advance on Richmond and to try and intercept Jackson. Lincoln may in fact have reacted a little too well, since he saw a chance to trap Jackson and so ordered Frémont's command from the west to take Harrisonburg and close the south end of the Shenandoah Valley.

Jackson, however, did not "rattle" easily. He realized that his present location put him in a dangerous position. He was determined to make good his escape and take all the captured Federal booty with him. Although it was a close race, Jackson broke through the closing jaws of the Federal trap that resulted in a fight at Cross Keys on June 8 and a larger battle at Port Republic on June 9. With only 17,000 men, Jackson had neutralized the threat to Richmond of some 60,000 Federal troops.

Johnston could see that Jackson was performing splendidly. Now all he had to do was defeat the 100,000 or so Federal troops camped outside Richmond. Against this force, Johnston could bring some 70,000 Southern troops. The rain-swollen Chickahominy River offered a possible

opportunity. McClellan, against his better judgment, had been ordered to split his own army across this river. Johnston saw that a rapid attack on the Federal wing on the south side of the river would give the Confederates a local numerical superiority and a good chance for success since Federal reinforcements could be brought in very slowly, at best.

The plan Johnston formulated was a good one, and relatively simple to execute. The divisions of Longstreet, Hill, and Huger would advance east along parallel roads to attack Keyes in front of Seven Pines. However, the rain and mud caused everything that could go wrong to do just that. The march was disorganized and delayed. Men were drowned in crossing White Oak Swamp. At the end of the day, the Confederates could only claim the capture of ten artillery pieces and 6,000 rifles. They had inflicted 5,000 casualties on the Federals, but had suffered 6,000 themselves. It could hardly be called an overwhelming victory. Moreover, Johnston was badly wounded and had to be relieved of command. The man that took his place was none other than Robert E. Lee. Lee

had an uncanny ability to "get into his opponent's head," and in the case of McClellan he saw that he would use his engineering expertise and superior firepower to move slowly forward from one entrenched position to the next until he finally took Richmond. However, before Lee could cope with this, he needed time to improve his own defenses. Fortunately for the Confederacy, the next ten days were continuous rain and McClellan's heavy artillery train was immobilized. The Confederates neutralized any attempt to bring them up by rail by their own thirty-two-pounder artillery piece mounted on a railroad car—the first railroad gun in history. Shovels soon replaced muskets in the troops' hands and the earth was seen flying in the construction of new fortifications.

Lee pulled reinforcements from every quarter until he could muster an effective force of about 85,000 men. The new plan was to leave some 30,000 south of the Chickahominy in the newly constructed intrenchments to hold McClellan's 75,000 on that side of the river and use the remaining 55,000 Southern troops to crush the 30,000 Federals on the north bank. If Lee were successful in defeating and destroying a large portion of this force, he would then capture McClellan's supply base and force him out into the open. During June 12–15, J. E. B. Stuart's Southern cavalry rode completely around the Federal army, spreading confusion and confirming the Federal dispositions. Jackson was returning from his Shenandoah Valley campaign and was due to arrive on June 25. To allow for possible delays, Lee planned the Confederate attack for June 26.

"Stonewall" Jackson's campaign in the Shenandoah Valley in 1862 demonstrated the general's outstanding talents as a soldier.

Shenandoah Valley 1864

The campaign in the Shenandoah Valley between May 1864 and March 1865 aimed at destroying the Confederate position. As a result of the embarrassment of Early's Washington Raid, the Federal authorities set up the Middle Military Division and placed it under Major General Phil Sheridan, who took command on August 7, 1864. Sheridan reorganized the various forces under his command to include a cavalry corps of three divisions. His effective strength was about 48,000 men.

Meanwhile, Early's Army of the Valley, with four infantry divisions and a division of cavalry, was to be reinforced by mid-August with Kershaw's infantry division and Fitz Lee's cavalry division. These

reinforcements, under the command of Richard Anderson, were to support Early's operations east of the Blue Ridge. With these additional troops, Early's strength was about 23,000 infantry and cavalry, although the Federal estimates were that he might have as many as 40,000 men. Therefore, Sheridan was ordered to assume the defensive for the time being.

Nearly five weeks were spent in maneuvering before Sheridan and Early finally met in battle. Because of lack of activity on Sheridan's part, Anderson's forces were ordered to return to Lee. However, Fitz Lee's cavalry remained in the Valley, leaving Early with about 12,000 infantry and 6,500 cavalry.

The return of Anderson to Lee was what Sheridan had been waiting for. This, coupled with overconfidence on the part of Early, led to his defeat at Winchester on September 19. Early fell back to Fishers Hill where Sheridan again defeated the Confederates on September 22. The demoralized Southerners reached Browns Gap where they were again reinforced by Kershaw's division. Sheridan reorganized his cavalry with Brigadier General George Custer and Colonel William Powell as division commanders following the dismissal of Averell for lack of aggressiveness and Wilson's transfer to Sherman.

Sheridan believed he had ridded the Valley of any threat by Early, and was in the process of transferring troops to reinforce Grant. These troops had to be recalled when Sheridan learned that Early was still in the area.

In a brilliant dawn surprise attack, Early's numerically inferior forces struck the Federals in camp at Cedar Creek on October 19. Despite initial success in driving the Federals from their positions, Sheridan arrived on the scene and helped rally his men to counterattack and rout Early's command. This was the last major action in the Valley.

Sheridan detached most of his infantry to rejoin Grant and Sherman, but kept his excellent cavalry corps in the divisions of Custer and Devin (about 10,000 troopers). Meanwhile, Early was left with only two brigades under Wharton (about 2,000 men) and two artillery battalions. Sheridan decided to eliminate this remaining Confederate force. At Waynesboro on March 2, 1865, Custer's division overran and annihilated these remaining troops. Early managed to escape with several others, but his military career was ended.

Sheppard, William Ludwell (1833–1911)

In the decades that followed the Civil War, pictorial depictions of the conflict that showed the human, personal side of the action were popular in both the North and the South. Of the artists who painted such images, William Ludwell Sheppard of Virginia was of particular note because he had actually served in combat. Sheppard served in the Confederate Army of Northern Virginia, painted some of his earliest war art in 1861, and studied in Paris after the war. His work is perhaps best recalled for its accurate depictions of Confederate uniforms. This is of particular value to scholars and reenactors because Confederate uniforms were anything but uniform, and there were many variations from the standard-issue gray. Among his most notable Civil War works are "News from Home," which portrays a Confederate soldier reading

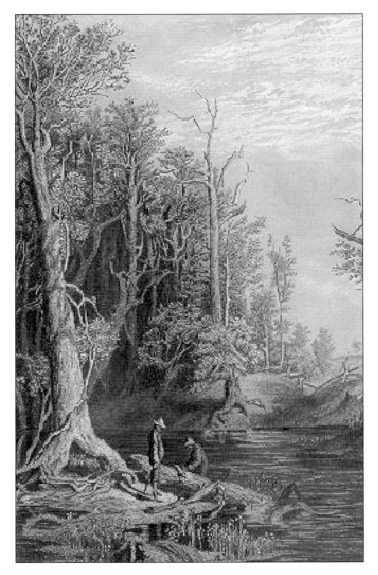

Above Left: Custer with Generals Sheridan, Merritt, Devin, and Forsyth, 1865.

Left: One of Sheppard's engravings, this one showing the Chickahominy River.

Opposite Page, Above: The cavalry charge at Winchester, Virginia, September 19, 1864.

Opposite Page, Below: The 34th Massachusetts on parade in 1862.

a letter, and "Angels of the Battlefield" depicting nurses at a field hospital.

Primarily noted as a watercolorist, Sheppard also worked as an engraver and as an illustrator with *Harper's Weekly* in the late 1860s, where he depicted scenes of life in the South, such as African Americans bringing tobacco to market, circa 1830, and African American emigrants seeking homes in the North after the war.

In 1891, he painted what is considered by some to be the definitive portrait of Pocahontas, the Native American princess who figures prominently in seventeenth century Virginia history. Late in his career, Sheppard turned to sculpture. In this genre, he executed the bronze statue of Governor William Smith, which was unveiled in 1906 on the north side of Capitol Square in Richmond, Virginia.

Sheridan, Philip Henry (1831–88)

Born in 1831, Sheridan formally graduated from the U.S. Military Academy in 1853; he actually concluded his studies in 1852, but a fight with a fellow student resulted in a one-year suspension. On graduation, he joined the 4th Infantry, Grant's old regiment, and by 1861 had become quartermaster of the regiment. He served a similar role for Halleck near Corinth before achieving a transfer away from staff work to

become colonel of the 2nd Michigan Cavalry in May 1862. He was promoted to Brigadier General of Volunteers in September 1862, following his success at Booneville, Mississippi, on July 1, 1862 when he had defeated the Confederate force led by Chalmers. Again promoted in March 1863, as a result of his involvement at Perryville, Kentucky (October 8, 1862), and Murfreesboro, Tennessee (December 30, 1862, to January 3, 1863), where he served under Buell and Rosecrans respectively. Commanding XX Corps, he then saw action at Chickamauga (September 19, 1863) and Missionary Ridge (October 1863), where he was noted by Grant. He was given command of the Army of the Potomac when Grant took command in the eastern theater.

He was sent by Grant to attack the Shenandoah Valley, Lee's supply route, in mid-1864; after completion Sheridan commented that if a crow needed to cross the

valley he would have to carry rations. This resulted in Lee being entrenched at Petersburg but cut-off from supplies. One of the commanders at Petersburg and Richmond in the spring of 1865, Sheridan's forces attacked Lee's flanks. Lee was forced to retreat but was caught in pincer movement with Grant to the rear and Sheridan to the front, surrendering at Appomattox on April 9, 1865.

He continued in army service after 1865, and was quoted as saying "the only good Indians I ever saw were dead." This did not stop him being made a general in 1888 shortly before his death in Massachusetts on August 5.

Sherman, William Tecumseh (1820–91)

Born in Ohio in 1820, Sherman graduated from the U.S. Military Academy in 1840—having been sent there by his foster-father Senator Thomas Ewing (Sherman's natural father, an Ohio supreme court justice, had died in 1829). He served in the U.S. Army from then until 1855. After resigning his commission, he became a banker in California before holding a number of other positions in Louisiana prior to its secession.

He was recalled to the army on the outbreak of the Civil War and became commander of the 13th U.S. Infantry Regiment in May 1861. He was one of the Union commanders at the First Bull Run and, despite the Union defeat, achieved enough to merit being despatched as the new Union commander to Kentucky, with instructions to hold the state. However, it would appear that he suffered from the stresses of this command and had to be replaced by Buell. He returned to action in Tennessee where the troops under his command at Shiloh were among the first to be attacked on April 6–7, 1862. Despite poor preparations, however, he held out until reinforcements arrived. He became a major general the following month. He was defeated by Smith at Chickasaw Bluffs, Mississippi, on December 27–29, 1862. As commander of XV Corps he was involved with the assault on Vicksburg during April to July 1863 and in September 1863 went to Chattanooga to reinforce Grant's army prior to his corps serving at Missionary Ridge, part of the Battle of Chattanooga (November 23–25, 1863).

By this stage, Sherman was effectively deputy to Grant and succeeded him as commander in the western theater during March 1864. Following this promotion, his most famous action was the invasion of Georgia during the summer of 1864. On August 12, 1864, Sherman was promoted to be a regular army major general. For much of the early part of the campaign in Georgia the Confederate forces, led by Joe Johnston, had managed a skillful retreat—despite defeats at Rocky Face Ridge on

May 5–11 and at Resaca on May 13–16, a victory at Kenesaw Mountain on June 27 and a final defeat at Chattahoochee River on July 5—but Johnston was replaced by John B. Hood, who was less successful, suffering defeats at Peachtree Creek (July 20) and Ezra Church (July 28) and victories at Utoy Creek (August 5–6) and Lovejoy (September 2–6). On September 1, 1864, Sherman's forces captured Atlanta, Georgia. The success of the invasion of Georgia was followed in November and

Above: If General Grant was the architect of Union victory, General Sherman was his able lieutenant, who led Grant's former troops to victory in the West.

Right: Following Sherman's capture of Atlanta his men cut a swathe through Georgia from Atlanta to Savannah, cutting the South in two and leaving destruction in their wake.

December by the "March to the Sea" of 300 miles with 60,000 men toward Savannah, which drove a wedge through the South. Encouraged to pillage and destroy, Sherman's troops left a path of destruction (partly the destruction wrought on South Carolina was seen as punishment for a state that had been the first to secede and was therefore perceived as the progenitor of the Civil War); victories during this campaign included Sandersville on November 26, 1864. Having reached the coast, Sherman headed north to rejoin Grant, having defeated Johnston for a final time at Bentonville, North Carolina, on March 19–21, 1865, during his northward march. Sherman accepted surrender of last Confederate forces on April 26, 1865. From 1869 until 1884 Sherman was Commander in Chief of U.S. Army. He died in 1891 in New York City.

Sherman's "March to the Sea"

During 1864, the eastern campaigns were paralleled by outstanding achievements in Georgia, which Sherman invaded on May 5. Marching through Georgia at the head of 100,000 men Sherman steadily pushed Johnston's 60,000-strong Army of Tennessee southward along the Western and Atlantic Railway, fighting many battles (Resaca May 13-16; New Hope Church, May 25-28; Pine Mountain, June 14; Kenesaw Mountain, June 27; and Peach Tree Creek, July 20) en-route. He crossed the Chattahoochee River, only eight miles from Atlanta on July 17, and took this important rail center on September 2. The loss of Atlanta was a major blow to public morale in the deep South. President Davis made a hurried trip to Georgia and Alabama and made earnest efforts to rally the country's flagging zeal, but to little avail, as the pall of defeat was by now settling heavily over the land.

Entrusting pursuit of Hood's Army of the Tennessee to Thomas, and leaving Atlanta smouldering in his wake, Sherman put a force of 60,000 in three armies on his famous march to Savannah on the Atlantic seaboard on November 16, 1864. Tracing a line of march between Macon and Augusta, he carved a sixty-mile wide swath of destruction in the Confederacy's heartland. The field order of November 9 which specified conditions of the march directed the army to "forage liberally," and although forbidding trespass and indiscriminate molestation of property, this order was frequently violated by stragglers. The only forces the Confederacy could bring to oppose him were Wheeler's cavalry and a motley collection of militia, young boys, and old men totaling perhaps 14,000 troops; certainly no match for Sherman's 62,000 Union veterans.

His army marched in two large columns under the command of Howard and Slocum. With only token opposition, Sherman reached Savannah on December 10. The Confederate garrison could not hope to prevent its capture, so evacuated the city with 10,000 troops via a pontoon bridge and federal forces occupied the city eleven days later. After entering the town, Sherman cabled Lincoln, "I beg to present you as a Christmas gift the city of Savannah with 150 heavy guns and plenty of ammunition and also about 25,000 bales of cotton."

After the unsuccessful peace conference at Hampton Roads, the South began to take desperate measures to stave off the defeat that many felt inevitable. Too late, Lee was

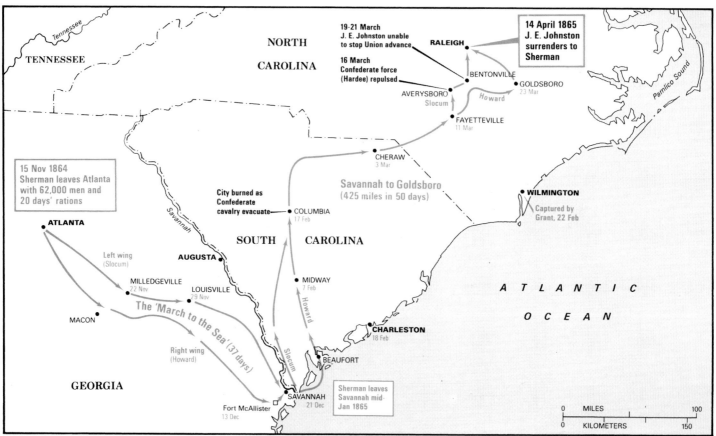

19-21 March
J. E. Johnston unable
to stop Union advance

14 April 1865
J. E. Johnston
surrenders to
Sherman

NORTH

CAROLINA

RALEIGH

16 March
Confederate force
(Hardee) repulsed

BENTONVILLE

GOLDSBORO
23 Mar

TENNESSEE

AVERYSBORO
Slocum

Howard

Pamlico Sound

FAYETTEVILLE
11 Mar

CHERAW
3 Mar

15 Nov 1864
Sherman leaves Atlanta
with 62,000 men and
20 days' rations

Savannah to Goldsboro
(425 miles in 50 days)

WILMINGTON

Captured by
Grant, 22 Feb

City burned as
Confederate
cavalry evacuate

COLUMBIA
17 Feb

ATLANTA

SOUTH   CAROLINA

Left wing
(Slocum)

AUGUSTA

MILLEDGEVILLE
22 Nov

LOUISVILLE
29 Nov

MIDWAY
7 Feb

ATLANTIC

MACON

The 'March to the Sea' (37 days)

Howard

OCEAN

CHARLESTON
18 Feb

Right wing
(Howard)

Slocum

BEAUFORT

GEORGIA

Sherman leaves
Savannah mid-
Jan 1865

Fort McAllister
13 Dec

SAVANNAH
21 Dec

MILES   0   100

KILOMETERS   0   150

appointed commander of all the Confederate forces on February 6, and the Confederate Congress made provision on March 16 for the recruitment of slaves to replenish forces depleted by death and desertion. But these measures were to little avail, for Sherman did not linger long at Savannah, and despite the miserable winter weather was soon on the march again, this time northward.

Shiloh Campaign

At the end of the first year of war, the Confederate victory at First Bull Run (Manassas) had brought a temporary stalemate in the eastern theater. West Kentucky, which had attempted to remain neutral, had been occupied by troops from both camps by the end of 1861. During the winter of 1861–62 the stalemate was broken by General Grant's Federal forces pushing southward from St. Louis and capturing Forts Henry and Donelson on the Tennessee and Cumberland rivers. This action forced General Johnston to abandon southern Kentucky and much of west and middle Tennessee. After withdrawing further south, he established a new line covering the Memphis and Charleston Railroad, the only all-weather link between Richmond and Memphis. Johnston, under pressure from both Confederate Press and politicians, carefully rallied his scattered forces at Corinth, in the northeastern corner of Mississippi, in an attempt to halt Grant's advance and take the offensive. With troops brought from as far away as the Gulf of Mexico, Johnston had near 40,000 men under his command by the end of March.

While Johnston reinforced, Halleck, the Union department commander, ordered Grant's troops southward along the Tennessee River to make a reconnaissance. They encamped at Pittsburgh Landing to await the arrival of Buell, with 37,000 troops to add to the 40,000 of Grant's Army of the Tennessee. With General Don Carlos Buell's Army of the Ohio en-route from Nashville, Johnston recognized that he needed to strike quickly to avoid being overwhelmed by a force near twice his own in number. Such deficiency in numbers dogged the Confederacy throughout the conflict.

On April 2, 1862, Johnston began his march from Corinth. Meanwhile, at the Union camp at Shiloh, the Federal troops spent a day drilling and merry-making. Grant wired his superior General H. W. Halleck, "I have scarcely the faintest idea of attack." Halleck told Grant to "sit tight at Shiloh and wait for Buell to arrive." Brigadier General Sherman, division commander, was quoted saying to reporters, "Take your regiment to Ohio. No enemy is nearer than Corinth."

By the night of April 5, the powerful Army of the Mississippi was just out of sight of the Union camp, poised to strike. They fell upon the Union camp the following day, and achieved complete surprise. Only the arrival of Don Carlos Buell's forces saved the day for the Union. On the morning of the 7th, Buell's fresh troops pushed the Confederates back over the ground that they had fought so hard to win the day before. The Southerners were forced back to Corinth. The final number of dead or missing was 13,000 on the Union side and 10,500 on the Confederate side. (It is worth noting that there were as many people killed at Shiloh as there were at Waterloo.)

Shiloh was one of the most important campaigns of the war, both in terms of its strategic influence and the effect it had on the population. A victory for the South might have given succor against the recent territorial losses in Kentucky and Ohio. Instead, Johnston's defeat at the hands of a force twice his in number opened a path into the Mississippi Valley. Memphis and Vicksburg were now vulnerable to Union attack, and after Corinth few doubted that those cities would be the next targets.

Moreover, the campaign and the battle came as a great shock to the people of the North and the South, who were shocked to learn that some twenty-five percent of the troops engaged had been lost. Grant and his men were rid of their overconfidence by the Battle of Shiloh. They now knew that hopes for an easy victory over the South were

Above Left: Winter quarters for Sherman's troops during the "March to the Sea."

Below Left: Map showing Sherman's "March to the Sea."

Below: Grant's first real test came at Shiloh, where his Army of the Tennessee held off a larger Confederate army until reinforcements arrived.

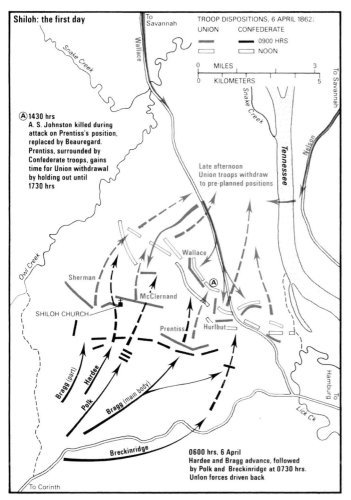

Shiloh: the first day

TROOP DISPOSITIONS, 6 APRIL 1862:
UNION   CONFEDERATE
            0900 HRS
NOON

A 1430 hrs
A. S. Johnston killed during
attack on Prentiss's position,
replaced by Beauregard.
Prentiss, surrounded by
Confederate troops, gains
time for Union withdrawal
by holding out until
1730 hrs

Late afternoon
Union troops withdraw
to pre-planned positions

0600 hrs, 6 April
Hardee and Bragg advance, followed
by Polk and Breckinridge at 0730 hrs.
Union forces driven back

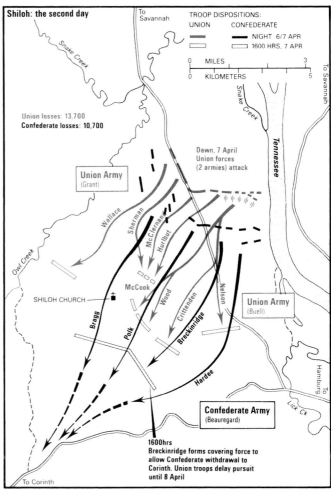

Shiloh: the second day

TROOP DISPOSITIONS:
UNION   CONFEDERATE
            NIGHT 6/7 APR
            1600 HRS, 7 APR

Union losses: 13,700
Confederate losses: 10,700

Dawn, 7 April
Union forces
(2 armies) attack

1600hrs
Breckinridge forms covering force to
allow Confederate withdrawal to
Corinth. Union troops delay pursuit
until 8 April

Above: The fighting at Shiloh, April 6 and 7, 1862.

**Left and Below Left: The Battle of Shiloh was
fought in dense woodland, and at the time was the
bloodiest battle ever fought on American soil.**

ill-founded. Grant realized that the war was
going to be, in the words of a Union
Soldier, "A very bloody affair."

THE BATTLE

The Battle of Shiloh, April 6–7, 1862, was
the first major battle in the Western Theater
of the American Civil War. General
Johnston had withdrawn his forces into
Tennessee following the loss of Fort Henry
and Fort Donelson to Grant. Here, along
with his second in command General
Beauregard, he concentrated around 55,000
men around Corinth in the newly named
Army of the Mississippi. Grant concentrated
his 42,000 men of the Army of the
Tennessee twenty miles to the north,
around Pittsburgh Landing and Shiloh
Church while he awaited the arrival of
Buell's Army of the Ohio so that he could
continue his offensive. Realizing that Grant
lay in an exposed position, and wishing to
attack him before Buell arrived with reinforcements, Johnston advanced on April 3,
with his main strength of 42,000 men divided
into four corps commanded by Polk, Bragg,
Hard, and Breckinridge. Arriving just

outside Grant's positions at dawn on April
6, 1862, Johnston caught the Union forces
completely by surprise. The Confederate
forces charged forward and found that the
Union troops had not bothered to fortify
their positions. Spearheaded by Hard and
Bragg, with Breckinridge sent to the right,
the Confederate forces fell upon Sherman
and Brigadier General Prentiss' divisions
amongst their tent lines. By 9:00am the
Confederate assault had routed most of
Prentiss' division and severely battered
Sherman's division, which was forced to
retire, but retained its unity and engaged the
Confederates in savage fighting around
Shiloh Church.

While the Union right was holding
Prentiss' division had reformed and was
holding a heavily wooded position known
as the Hornet's Nest on the left flank of the
Union line, preventing any Confederate
breakthrough. This gave Grant time to
establish a fall-back position for the Union
forces, covering the area around Pittsburgh
Landing.

During the course of the afternoon, a
stray bullet killed General Johnston, rob-
bing the Confederate forces of their leader
at a time when they most needed direction.
Beauregard took control of the army.

By nightfall the Union position at the
Hornet's Nest had been eliminated, and
Beauregard tried one last attempt to drive
Grant into the river. However, this failed

and the positions stabilized for the night.
Overnight, Grant received substantial reinforcements from Buell's Army of the Ohio
and his own Reserve Division and decided
to launch a fierce counteroffensive the
following morning.

Taken by surprise, Beauregard's forces
were pushed back, but he managed to rally
around 30,000 men and conducted a stiff
defense of his positions. However, the
weight of numbers told and Grant's 25,000
fresh men swung the day. The Confederates
were steadily pushed back and around
3:30pm Beauregard gave the order to
retreat from the field and fell back to
Corinth.

The Battle of Shiloh was the bloodiest
battle yet fought on American soil, with
over 13,000 casualties on the Union side
and 10,000 for the Confederates, nearly
thirty percent of their forces. The battle
inevitably led to the loss of Corinth for the
Confederacy, but also almost ended Grant's
career; he was only spared through
Lincoln's intervention when he noted "I
can't spare this man, he fights."

Shipbuilding

The war came at a time of transition, when
wooden warships were being replaced by
ironclads. As ship designs became increasingly complex, industrial capacity and the
transportation of raw materials became an

important part of warship production. For the Union, the Navy Yards in Washington, Boston, Portsmouth (Maine), and Brooklyn (New York), as well as commercial yards, were developed to take advantage of the latest mass-production techniques, and both ironclads and wooden gunboats were produced with skill and rapidity. Of these, Brooklyn was the most extensive and productive of these Union shipyards. On the Mississippi River, commercial shipbuilding facilities were adapted for naval use at riverside towns such as Mound City, Cincinnati, and St. Louis. Nearly 150 warships of all types were produced in these Midwestern yards.

By 1864, positional defenses were commonly used by the outnumbered Confederates in Georgia and Virginia. During the siege of Petersburg (1864–65) Confederate trenches (Below) were subjected to a nine-month bombardment by Union siege guns, such as this eleven-inch smoothbore piece (Above Right) and smaller artillery pieces.

In the Confederacy, shipyards were concentrated in the major ports (Norfolk, Wilmington, Charleston, Savannah, Mobile, and New Orleans), while several river cities also had small shipyards. These centers lacked the scale of Northern shipyards, and warship production was further limited by a lack of materials, a poor transport network, and the Union blockade. When New Orleans was captured in April 1862, the loss of the Mississippi port was a severe blow to the Confederacy. This ability to create shipbuilding facilities from virtually nothing was repeated elsewhere in the South. The ironclad CSS *Albermarle* was built in a cornfield in North Carolina, while the completion of the CSS *Arkansas* on the Yazoo River was an incredible achievement given the lack of available infrastructure.

Siege weapons

Siege is one of the oldest and well-established military strategies; there are epic accounts of sieges in the Old Testament and Greek classical literature, and the Romans elevated it to the level of a science. At the time of the Civil War, siege warfare was still generally considered to be an effective means of dislodging an enemy from a fortified position; most of the general officers were schooled in the art, and they employed a number of well-established siege tactics during the war's course, of which mining and bombardment were the most common and effective.

Siege warfare has prompted military engineers to develop specialized siege weapons, a tradition that was maintained during the Civil War. The most important was the artillery piece—rifled cannon, smoothbore cannons, mortars, and howitzers. The newly developed rifled cannon was particularly effective in knocking down fortifications, and after it became available in 1862 played decisive roles at the sieges of Vicksburg and Atlanta. The most common types of rifled guns were the three-inch Ordnance and ten-pounder

Parrott rifles, both of them considerable more accurate and with a longer range—up to about 2,300 yards—than their smoothbore counterparts. These could be safely positioned a considerable distance from the enemy defenses and to a large extent made the fortress obsolete. In April 1862, Union forces used rifled cannon to bombard the eleven-foot-thick solid brick walls of Fort Pulaski, near Savannah, to such effect that the Confederate garrison were forced to surrender, thus proving the ineffectiveness of masonry fortress against the new weapon.

Although breech-loading rifled cannon were available, almost all Civil War cannon were muzzle-loading; those breech-loading models that were used, such as the British twelve-pounder rifled Armstrong and Whitworth cannons, were generally unreliable and awkward.

Smoothbore artillery, including naval and siege cannons, was still much in evidence. Dahlgrens and Rodman smoothbores were among the heaviest and most powerful of them.

Howitzers and mortars, which were used for plunging fire, were used in every major siege and also in defense, in calibers up to eight and ten inches. Again, they were muzzle-loaded. The largest of the siege howitzers had ranges of over 2,000 yards and could fire forty-five and ninety-pound shells. Against fortifications, the artillery used solid shot and shell ammunition, each of which came in any of the nine common artillery calibers.

The sheer size of some of these weapons made them awkward to handle by comparison with the lighter field guns. The mountings had to be carefully prepared, and once in position they were difficult to move. During a siege smaller mortars and howitzers were positioned in specially constructed trenches opposite the enemy works. All of these weapons were commonly mounted on the decks of naval vessels, which could be easily moved into new positions, and in least one instance, a heavy siege gun was attached on a railway carriage—the first railway gun in history.

Sigel, Franz (1824–1902)

Foreign-born, Sigel was one of a number of those from the minority populations made commanders by Lincoln in order to ensure the support of these communities for the Union. He served under Lyon at Wilson's Creek on August 10, 1861, when he was despatched with 1,200 men to help form a pincer on the Confederate camp. However, confusion ultimately led to Union defeat. He commanded a regiment of German-Americans from Missouri and Illinois at the Battle of Pea Ridge on March 7, 1862. This was a one-sided Union victory. However, the German-American force—the "Dutch" Corps—had a poor reputation, not helped by their role at the Battle of Second Bull Run, when, again, they were commanded by Sigel. He then led forces during the drive south through the Shenandoah Valley in May 1864. Having captured Staunton, he was stopped by cadets from Virginia Military Institute and other Confederate forces, under the command of John C. Breckinridge, at New Market, Virginia, on May 15 and forced to retreat. By now, Halleck and Grant were convinced that Sigel's primary military skill lay in retreat and so convinced Lincoln to have him relieved of his command; he was replaced by Major General David Hunter.

Above and Far Left: The siege of Petersburg—two views of Union artillery in June 1864.

Left: General Sigel led the ill-fated Union invasion of the Shenandoh Valley in early 1864.

Slavery

Slavery, and more specifically disputes over the right of slave-holders to recover fugitives and to extend slavery into newly established states, was the main issue over which Confederate states seceded from the Union. Over the preceding 150 years, a slave-based plantation economy had developed in the South that was increasingly unacceptable to important sectors of opinion in the North. In turn, Northern interference and obstruction became unacceptable throughout the South. Rebellion and war followed.

By around 1680 settlers in the American colonies were increasingly turning to African slavers rather than European indentured servants to meet the labor requirements of the growing communities. Slave codes were enacted that severely restricted the rights of Africans and their descendants in the interests of the increasingly slave-owning white elite. Large plantations with substantial slave labor forces were developed in South Carolina and Georgia, smaller groups on the tobacco farms of Virginia and Maryland. Slaves worked in ones and twos as servants, craftsmen, and laborers in the towns and cities across the colonies, and as farmhands in parts of the North where large estates were rare.

Although conditions were often harsh, the intense exploitation and high death rates typical of Caribbean plantations were rare on the mainland, allowing the black population to rise by natural increase from a comparatively small number of direct imports. The number of persons of African descent rose from under 7,000 in 1680 to 1,377,080 in 1810 and in excess of four million by 1860. The key to this dramatic growth was the rapid expansion of cotton growing in the South following the invention of the cotton gin in 1793. In the early nineteenth century around a million slaves were

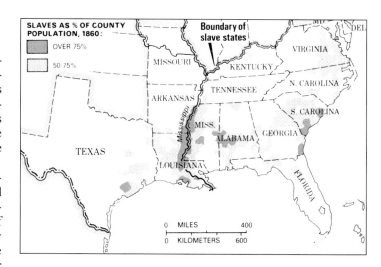

forcibly moved through an internal slave trade to supply new cotton-growing regions in the west. The two decades before Congress banned the importation of slaves in 1807 saw the peak of American involvement in the horrors of trans-Atlantic slaving. Despite the paternalistic self-image of Southern slaveholders, slaves were subject to brutal exploitation, had no rights, and could be whipped, sold away from their families, or even killed on the whim of their masters.

In the aftermath of the Revolution, the incompatibility of slavery with the ideals of the Founding Fathers became apparent to many in the North, where slavery was in any event economically of little importance. Graduated emancipation acts were passed, which in concert with voluntary manumission by many Northern slave

PICKING AND SORTING THE LEAVES FOR FILLERS.

THE SPINNING PROCESS FOR WORKING INTO PLUG.

Above Left: Map showing slavery as a percentage of country population, 1860.

Left and Above: The institution of slavery was the underlying cause for the war. Slaves were used primarily for picking cotton or tobacco, as seen here.

owners meant that virtually all Northern blacks were free by the early decades of the nineteenth century. In the upper South more half-hearted easing of restrictions on manumission increased the proportion of free blacks. Abolitionist sentiments became widespread, particularly in New England. Southern apologists for their "peculiar institution" became increasingly defensive. Runaways found refuge and assistance with sympathizers who organized safe escape routes (the "Underground Railroad") and thwarted efforts by slaveholders to recapture escapees using powers granted by the Fugitive Slave Acts of 1793 and 1850. In the South vigilante groups harassed anti-slavery activists and free blacks. In Congress disputes raged each time the admission of new states threatened to upset the increasingly bitter stalemate between slave and free states. Once war broke out the need to transform the whole basis of Southern economy and society became apparent. The Emancipation Proclamation of January 1, 1863, heralded the abolition of slavery throughout the United States that was finally achieved with the passage of the Thirteenth Amendment in 1865.

Smalls, Robert (1839–1915)

A slave from South Carolina, Robert Smalls achieved fame when, in May 1862, he took over a small despatch vessel in Charleston harbor and used it to escape to join up with the Union forces blockading the harbor. He was subsequently a pilot in the U.S. Navy.

Soldiers' Rest Convalescence Camp

The forerunners of today's USO, "soldiers' rest" camps provided dormitories, food, books, baths, and laundry facilities for Union soldiers traveling along the major routes to and from the fighting. Established by the United States Sanitary Commission, these camps were provided as a free service supported by the surrounding communities and by donated food and services. Over the duration of the war, they were used by 800,000 soldiers, who between them consumed 4,500,000 meals and slept 1,000,000 nights.

South Carolina

South Carolina cast in its lot with the Confederacy with its secession on April 3, 1861, and witnessed the first shots of the Civil War when Edmund Ruffin opened fire on Fort Sumter on April 12, 1861. By March 1862, all of South Carolina's major

harbors had been sealed or blockaded by Union troops.

In February 1864 South Carolina became the target of Sherman's "total war" campaign, as, having taken Atlanta and Savannah and laid waste to the countryside in between, he marched on Columbia.

South Mountain, Battle of, 1862

Realizing that Major General McClellan had learned of the division of the Army of Northern Virginia, General Robert E. Lee, sent Longstreet's corps to support D. H. Hill's division that was guarding the passes over South Mountain. On September 14, McClellan ordered Franklin's VI Corps to take Crampton's Gap; Reno's IX Corps to take Fox's Gap and Hooker's I Corps to assault Turner's Gap. These three engagements are collectively known as the Battle of South Mountain. By nightfall, the Confederate defenders had been driven back in all three locations, but the delay imposed by these actions, plus McClellan's own aptitude for inaction, led to Lee being able to concentrate his forces at Sharpsburg in anticipation of the Battle of Antietam.

Spies

Both sides made use of espionage during the war, and extensive spy networks were developed and run by government agencies. In the North, Allan Pinkerton ran the Federal Secret Service, although the bureau's effectiveness was erratic. In the Confederacy, Major William Norris of the Signal Bureau managed another network, and often achieved spectacular results. Some of the best agents were women, such as the Confederate spy Belle Boyd, or Elizabeth Van Lew, an Abolitionist who spied for the Union. If caught, spies were liable to execution by firing squad or hanging, although female operatives were usually punished less severely.

Spotsylvania, Battle of, 1864

After Grant had been bested at the Battle of the Wilderness on May 5, 1864, he turned his Army of the Potomac toward Richmond, hoping to cut the line of communication between Lee and Richmond at Spotsylvania. Lee had realized that this would be Grant's objective and had ordered Major General Richard Anderson to lead a column on a parallel march to the Union forces, aiming to arrive at Spotsylvania Court House on May 8. During the course of May 8, both armies took up their positions. One Confederate corps, Ewell's, was entrenched in a salient projecting out from the Confederate lines and called the "Mule Shoe."

On May 9 and 10 Grant attempted to find a weakness in Lee's position, but to no avail. Following an imaginative attempt to reduce the "Mule Shoe" with twelve regiments on May 10, Grant tried again on the 12th with two corps. This attack reduced the salient in the end, but only after some attritional fighting.

Although the Confederate salient had been reduced, Lee's line still remained firm and there was very little that Grant could do to break it. He tried pushing troops in other directions, and even attempted an attack by Hancock at the base of the salient on May 18; however, these all proved unsuccessful. On May 20, 1864, Grant sent Hancock south, attempting to bypass Lee's position, and the rest of the Army of the Potomac followed on the 21st. Lee reacted by moving his army southward as well, so as to remain between the Union forces and the Confederate capital of Richmond.

Stanton, Edwin McMasters (1814–69)

Appointed Secretary of War in 1861 by Lincoln, Stanton had previously been Attorney General as a Democrat. Like a

The celebrated Confederate spy Belle Boyd was nicknamed "La Belle Rebelle," and despite arrest and imprisonment, she still found ways to pass on information to her contacts. Her actions were celebrated in music halls for years.

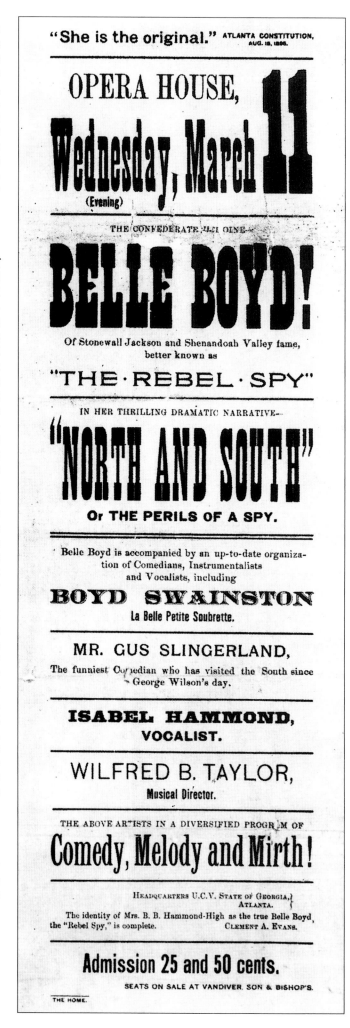

number of erstwhile Northern Democrats, he was to become Republican during the course of the war. Among other policies, he created a network of provost marshals who roamed the country arresting and jailing, without trial, draft dodgers, anti-war protesters, and others (including three judges and five newspaper editors). In February 1862 he established the U.S. Military Rail Roads under Daniel McCallum; this was a reflection of the importance of railway transport in the war. By 1862 he was vigorously demanding that Lincoln sack McClellan. However, after his victory at Antietam, McClellan sought to turn the tables and endeavored to get Stanton sacked. In 1863 he sent Charles A. Dana to investigate Grant and the Army of Tennessee; Dana's positive reaction ensured that Grant kept his command. Stanton was present at the bedside of Lincoln on April 15, 1865, after the President had been fatally wounded by John Wilkes Booth, and commented "Now he belongs to the ages" when the President died.

State Militia

In most states, a state militia system already existed before the war began, and along the Atlantic seaboard many of these units could trace their origins back to the earliest days of Colonial America. In addition, "volunteer state militia" regiments were raised during the conflict to augment the existing militia organization. Militia companies were unusually organized on a county basis, with one or more companies raised in each county, then grouped together into regional militia regiments. At the start of the war, it was extremely unusual for any of these units to have any experience of operating on a regimental level.

On April 6, 1861, the army laid down a system of brigade organizations for these militia units, and a mixture of experienced regular officers and regional political appointees were appointed to command these larger formations. In this manner, units from the same state were frequently brigaded together by both sides. State militia regiments were numbered in order of their foundation, and after the first year of the war, almost any difference between state militia and volunteer state militia had disappeared. In the Confederacy, differences between various state militias were minimal, but in the North, many retained their own distinctive organizations and uniforms for much of the war. In addition to these established units, additional regiments were sometimes formed when the home state was threatened by invasion. This occurred during the Confederate invasion of Pennsylvania in 1863, and in response to Confederate cavalry raids in Ohio and Indiana.

States, Role in the war

Ostensibly, the Civil War was fought over the rights of individual states to govern themselves. In 1819 a balance between Northern "free" states and Southern "slave" states, meant the two groups had equal representation in the Senate. The addition of new states into the Union—such as Maine or Missouri—threatened to upset this parity, as did the adoption of California as a state (1850). During the 1850s, Kansas and Nebraska were allowed to determine their own attitude towards slavery, causing extensive acrimony and increasing the hostility between both blocks of states.

Stephens, Alexander Hamilton (1812–83)

Stephens—who served in Congress as a Whig from his native state of Georgia and who later became a Democrat when the Whig party disintegrated—was elected Vice President of Southern States in 1861, although he had previously opposed secession. However, he had also opposed Abolition, saying in 1849 the he would "hold no connection with a party that did not disconnect itself from those aggressive abolition movements." Stephens was floor manager in Congress for the 1850 Compromise and wrote after it was passed, "I feel as if the Mission of my life was performed." From the start of the war he believed in the use of cotton as an economic weapon to try and force Britain and France to recognize independence by ceasing to export this vital raw material. By 1863 he thought that the time was right to try to negotiate peace and, on July 3, 1863, started to travel to Washington to do this. However, the expected Confederate victory at Gettysburg—which would have opened up Washington to the Confederate forces

Above Left: Confederate agent Jacob Thompson. A former U.S. Congressman and former U.S. cabinet officer, he was sent to Canada in 1864 as a Confederate secret agent.

Above: Officers of the First Battalion, 1st Regiment Capital Guards, Kentucky State Guards. The Kentucky State government reestablished the State Guards late in the war to combat guerrilla activities. Several battalions of men enlisted for service within the state. This organization replaced the earlier, largely pro-Confederate, State Guard.

under Lee—failed to materialize and Lincoln refused him free transit. He regarded Confederate President Jefferson Davis as "weak and vacillating, timid, petulant, peevish, obstinate, but not firm" and also as "my poor old blind and deaf dog."

Stevens, Congressman Thaddeus (1792–1838)

A native of Pennsylvania, he entered the House of Representatives in 1849 as a radical anti-slavery Whig (later Republican). He became leader of the Republicans in the House after 1861 and was also Chairman of the House Ways and Means Committee. In January 1863, arguing that rebel states had, by their actions, ceased to exist as legal entities and therefore ought to be treated as conquered provinces subject to the will of the victor (which was a view not widely

accepted by the rest of the party) he said: "We have the right to treat them as we would any other provinces that we might conquer." An industrialist, he owned an ironworks near Chambersburg which was destroyed by Confederate forces during summer of 1863. Later he was accused with Charles Sumner of plotting against Johnson. As part of the postwar settlement he proposed land redistribution for blacks, but these proposals were too radical and never progressed. He was described by one foreign observer as the "Robespierre, Danton, and Marat" of the postwar settlement.

Stonewall Brigade

Initially known as the 1st Virginia Brigade, this unit was named after its first commander, General Thomas "Stonewall" Jackson.

At Bull Run (July 21, 1861) the brigade consisted of five Virginia regiments (2nd, 4th, 5th, 27th, and 33rd) and an artillery battery (Pendleton's). The brigade established its reputation during the battle, but after participating in "Stonewall" Jackson's Shenandoah Campaign (1862) it became the most celebrated unit in the Confederate Army. Following Jackson, five other brigadiers commanded this elite unit, leading it through almost every major engagement in the eastern theater until its surrender at Appomattox in April 1865.

Stuart, James Ewell Brown (1833–64)

Born in 1833 and nicknamed "Jeb," Stuart graduated from the U.S. Military Academy in 1854. Post-graduation he served in the cavalry, being seriously wounded in action against the Indians. He served with Lee, as a lieutenant, at Harper's Ferry on October 17, 1860, when the militias from Maryland and Virginia sought to dislodge an anti-slavery raid. In 1861 he became a colonel in the Confederate cavalry.

He commanded the Virginian Cavalry at First Bull Run on July 21, 1861, when his force—St. Virginia Cavalry—attacked the 11th New York (Fire Zouaves). Following the Confederate defeat at Antietam, Stuart led his forces on October 9, 1862, on a raid north to Chambersburg in Pennsylvania and, three days later, defeated a Union force under Pleasanton at Monocacy in Maryland. Stuart was to achieve a further victory, at Kelly's Ford, Virginia, on March 17, 1863, when he defeated a Union force under Averell. At the Battle of Chancellorsville, May 1–3, 1863, Stuart assumed command of "Stonewall" Jackson's corps when the latter was mortally wounded on the 2nd. Following the Confederate success at Chancellorsville, Stuart again proved triumphant at Middleburg, Virginia, on June 17, 1863, when a Union force under Duffie was vanquished; this triumph was, however, to be shortlived as a second battle at Middleburg, two days later, saw Stuart's fortunes changes as a Union force under Gregg proved too great an obstacle. Ten days later, however, Stuart returned to his winning ways, with victory over Knight at Westminster, Maryland, on June 29, 1863. However, once again, this success was soon

Right: J. E. B. Stuart was the best-known cavalry commander of the war, and commanded the cavalry arm of the Army of Northern Virginia from the start of the war until his death.

overturned, with defeat on the following day by Kilpatrick at Hanover, Pennsylvania. Further engagements later in 1863 brought two victories—against Buford at Rappahannock Station, Virginia, on August 1–3 and against Kilpatrick at Buckland Mills, Virginia, on October 19— alongside one defeat, against Owen at Catlett's station, Virginia, on October 14.

Stuart was notorious for not being particularly reliable (although a dashing figure who was rapidly promoted) and Lee failed to keep up him under strict control. At a crucial moment, for example, in the build-up to Gettysburg, Stuart's cavalry was away on a raid without Lee being precisely aware of their location (Stuart was endeavoring to repeat his success of riding around the Union forces that had proved successful against McClellan in June 1862). Following Gettysburg, where he had sought to deflect criticism by placing the blame elsewhere in official reports that were disingenuous in the extreme, Stuart was promoted lieutenant general. He was killed at Yellow Tavern on May 11, 1864.

To contemporaries Stuart was a complex commander; immature in many respects, yet a good leader and a shrewd tactician. He had the fortune to be able to fight in many engagements against poorly trained and ill-organized Union forces; however, luck is an attribute that many leaders need in their commanders and Stuart certainly possessed more than his fair share.

Submarines

Unable to defeat the Union blockade by conventional means, the Confederates examined other solutions. Charleston designer Theodore Stoney devised a semi-sumbersible craft powered by steam and fitted with a spar torpedo (mine). The ves- sel was named the *David*. In October 1863 the *David* attacked the USS *New Ironsides* off Charleston, but failed to sink her. The submersible *Pioneer* was built in New Orleans as a privateer, but was never used in action. A *Pioneer II* was built in Mobile, but foundered in February 1863. Around the same time the Mobile-built *Hunley* arrived in Charleston. Although successful in her attack on the USS *Housatonic* in February 1864, the submarine was lost in the attempt Although no further Confederate submersibles were built,

Below: The Confederate *Manassas*.

Union designers produced an experimental submarine named the "Intelligent Whale," but when an improved version, the USS *Alligator*, was lost during trials in 1862, the submarine program was abandoned.

Sumner, Charles (1811–74)

Born in 1811, Sumner was a noted Republican orator from Massachusetts. He was elected to the Senate in succession to Daniel Webster (died 1852) as a result of split Democratic vote and was subsequently reelected. A strong opponent of slavery, in 1856 he made an abusive speech in the Senate on "the crime against Kansas"—over delays in admitting the non-slave-owning state of Kansas to the Union—which outraged Preston Brooks, a Representative from South Carolina. The aggrieved Brooks attacked Sumner, nearly killing him, resulting in the orator becoming nicknamed "Bleeding Sumner." Later, he was accused, along with Thadeus Stevens, of plotting against President Johnson.

Supreme Court

In contrast to its relative inaction during the war years, the Supreme Court took a number of major decisions in the pre- and postwar period that had an important impact on events. In his key ruling in the "Dred Scott" case of 1856, the Chief Justice, Roger Taney, declared that Congress did not have the power to forbid slavery in the territories and that the Missouri Compromise of 1820 was unconstitutional. After the war the Supreme Court, in a series of rulings that became known as the Slaughterhouse Cases acted to reassert state rights over those of citizens in interpreting the Fourteenth Amendment.

Swords

Swords were issued to both naval and land forces in large quantities, but were mostly used by cavalry units. Others receiving them included staff and regimental officers, non-commissioned officers, musicians, and foot and horse artillery units. However, they were not particularly popular items of equipment with many of these groups, although officers used them as a symbol of authority. The use of swords as an offensive tool in battle, particularly among foot troops, became a rare event.

Swords came in a variety of styles, chiefly straight or slightly curved, had a length of around thirty-six inches, and a width of between one and one and a quarter inches wide. In the North, brass hilts were common, and the grips were constructed from wood, which was wrapped in black leather over which was wound twisted brass wire. Southern swords were, more often than not, somewhat crude copies of the North's. Oil cloth rather than leather and untwisted copper wire were commonly used on the grip, and the brass hilts often had a decidedly red tinge due to excessive amounts of copper used. Scabbards were usually made from either metal or leather and often had brass fittings. (See also pages 161–63.)

Left: The semi-submersible, spar-torpedo boat CSS *David* in Charleston. Powered by a steam engine and armed with a torpedo (mine) extending beyond her bow, the craft attacked the USS *New Ironsides* off Charleston in October 1863. Although not a true submarine, the vessel shared many qualities with submersibles such as the CSS *Hunley*.

Tactics

The American Civil War was, in many senses, the last of the old-fashioned wars, in which massed ranks of troops marched into battle in tight regimented formations, often through walls of grapeshot and canister. In other senses it was the first of the modern wars, in which new weapons were used and others—such as the hand grenade, the land mine, and the observation balloon—were revived. Tactics both new and old were employed, and for the first time the telegraph and railroad became intsruments of warfare.

Infantry tactics at the time were based on the use of the smoothbore musket, a weapon of limited range and accuracy. Firing lines that were much more than a hundred yards apart could not inflict very much damage on each other, and so troops massed together for an attack, elbow to elbow, and then charged for the opposing lines; if there were enough of them, and they ran fast enough, the defensive line could not hurt them seriously, and when they got to close quarters the advantage of numbers and the use of the bayonet would settle things.

These tactics underwent a profound change during the war, due to the introduction firstly of the muzzle-loading rifle and gradually the breech-loading rifle. Before the war the use of rifles in battle was considered impractical and largely limited to corps of elite marksmen. Expensive, tightfitting projectiles had to be jammed into the grooves of the rifle's muzzle, a time-consuming process. However, in 1848 a French army officer perfected a hollow-based bullet that could be quickly and easily rammed into the bore, expanding when the weapon was fired to catch in rifling and be shot spinning out of the barrel. That spin made the Minié ball, like other, more expensive and unwieldy rifle bullets, a highly precise and far-traveling projectile. They could reach a half-mile or more, and an average soldier could easily hit a target 250 yards away. By 1855, Harper's Ferry armory worker James H. Burton had honed an even cheaper version of the Minié ball, which, along with the rifle itself, soon became widely used in the U.S. Army. It was the standard bullet for both sides in the Civil War, although neither anticipated the enormous difference this would make on the battlefield. Against a defensive line using musket fire—requiring a twenty-five-second reloading period and accurate to only fifty feet or less—a frontal infantry charge was likely to be successful if the assaulting force moved quickly enough.

The greater accuracy and a far longer range of the muzzle-loading rifle completely changed the conditions under which soldiers fought. An advancing line could be brought under killing fire at a distance of

At the start of the war, the regular army was trained to fight in close formations, and to form squares as a defense against cavalry attack (Opposite Page, Below). Tactics soon changed to take account of the latest changes in the effectiveness of weaponry. By 1864, entrenchments (Right and Opposite Page, Above) were frequently used to offset enemy superiority in numbers, and to reduce the slaughter caused by close-range fire.

THE AMERICAN CIVIL WAR: A VISUAL ENCYCLOPEDIA

half a mile, now, and the massed charge of Napoleonic tradition was miserably out of date.

When a defensive line occupied field entrenchments, a direct frontal assault became almost impossible. The hideous casualty lists of Civil War battles owed much of their size to the fact that soldiers were fighting with rifles but were using tactics suited to smoothbores. It took the generals a long time to recognize that a new approach was needed. The widespread use of the Minié bullet had shifted the balance greatly to the defense's favor, yet Civil War generals continued ordering suicidal frontal attacks, learning only after hard and bloody battlefield experience—from the assault on Marye's Heights at Fredericksburg to Pickett's Charge at Gettysburg—that their strategy would have to be altered.

ARTILLERY

Much the same development was taking place in the artillery, although the full effect was not yet evident. The Civil War cannon, almost without exception, was a muzzle-loader, and although the rifled gun was coming into service, the old smooth-bore—a brass gun of 4.62-inch caliber, firing a twelve-pound spherical shot—remained popular to the end of the war; in the wooded, hilly country, where so many Civil War battles were fought, its range of slightly less than a mile was about all that was needed, and for close-range work against infantry the smoothbore was better than the rifle. For such work the artillerist fired canisters—tin cans full of iron balls, with a propellant at one end and a wooden disk at the other—and the can disintegrated when the gun was fired, letting the iron balls be sprayed all over the landscape. In effect, the cannon became a huge sawed-off shotgun, and at ranges of 250 yards or less it was murderous. When employed in support of an infantry advance, artillery was used in a supporting role to reduce enemy positions.

CAVALRY

Cavalry was used most effectively for scouting and for raiding, where its high speed and maneuverability could be used to maximum advantage. Stuart and Early both demonstrated how a relatively small, fast-moving cavalry force could wreak havoc behind enemy lines. On the march, cavalry forces were sent ahead and to the flanks to check against any surprise movement by the enemy.

Left: A Union cavalry regiment deployed in line, and grouped into squadrons of two companies apiece. European-style cavalry charges were soon abandoned in favor of dismounted tactics, and cavalry became little more than highly mobile infantry.

THE AMERICAN CIVIL WAR: A VISUAL ENCYCLOPEDIA

Cavalry more than any other arm underwent a radical transformation in tactical doctrine. Although cavalry were sometimes used to attack on horseback (Left), the horses and men were extremely vulnerable to enemy fire, and were usually unable to attack formed infantry (Below Left). While infantry tactics emphasized the use of skirmish formations (Right), there was often little alternative to full-blown attacks by infantry in line formation. These dense infantry formations made excellent targets for artillery batteries (Below).

Tactics, Naval

For the naval officers of both sides serving during the Civil War, there was no tactical manual whose advice they could draw on. The revolution which naval warfare had undergone was too dramatic, as in the space of two decades before the war, steam-propulsion, rifled artillery, and shell-firing guns had altered the face of naval combat. These officers were at the forefront of this revolution, which was further complicated by the introduction of ironclads, the surprising ineffectiveness of conventional coastal fortifications, and the development of new "infernal machines" such as torpedoes (mines) and submarines.

The design of Confederate ironclads necessitated the firing of the vessel's broadside at the enemy, which also presented the largest possible target to them. By contrast, Union monitors could fire their guns in virtually any direction, introducing problems of fire control which had never existed before. The effectiveness of the ironclad over unarmored wooden warships was demonstrated by the ease with which the CSS *Virginia* destroyed two wooden steam warships during the Battle of Hampton Roads. Combat between ironclads was relatively ineffective. The Confederates added rams to many of their warships, rediscovering one of the main naval tactics of antiquity. Ramming was a principal tactic during several of the battles on the Mississippi River, and was one of the few options open to the captains of the Union's wooden warships who fought the CSS *Tennessee* at the Battle of Mobile Bay in August 1864. Naval strategists closely studied tactical lessons learned during the war.

Tallahatchie River

Flowing into the Yazoo River north of Vicksburg, the Tallahatchie River saw sporadic skirmishing from June 1862 until the August of 1864. The river's most important role in the war came during the two Union attempts on Vicksburg via the Yazoo Pass. In December 1862, Sherman's advance on the city via the pass was halted by a sunken steamer, the *New Moon*, positioned by the Confederacy to block the route through the Tallahatchie. Grant's assault of March 1863 meanwhile succeeded in moving up the Tallahatchie, but was soon halted by news of new Union fortifications on the Yazoo itself.

Above Left: A Union squadron attacking Fort Walker on Hilton Head Island in November 1861.

Left: The battle between the ironclads USS *Monitor* and the CSS *Virginia* off Hampton Roads on March 9, 1862, revolutionized naval warfare.

Right: Bird's eye view of the Tennessee River.

Taxes

The Union government relied heavily on taxation to finance the war effort, in contrast to the Confederate administration, which printed vast quantities of treasury notes and suffered the consequences of disastrous inflation. The Internal Revenue Act of 1862 put direct taxes on luxuries, liquor, tobacco, and numerous other goods, taxed dividends, corporate receipts, manufactured goods, inheritances, and numerous other transactions, It also set up the Bureau of Internal Revenue and introduced an income tax for the first time in American history. Unpopular though these measures were they raised over twenty percent of government war finances, compared with around five percent in the South.

Tennessee

The people of Tennessee rejected secession in February 1861, but political manipulations soon brought the state into the Confederacy: when the Union issued its call to arms on April 16, 1861, the governor of the state refused and applied to the South for protection. Tennessee finally seceded on May 6, 1861, together with Arkansas, and was officially admitted to the Confederacy on May 15. Strong pro-Unionist pockets remained in eastern Tennessee for the duration of the war, and the state was lost to the Confederacy for all practical purposes by March 1862. Following the loss of Atlanta, Hood set out on the disastrous Tennessee Campaign that would cost him his army and his position. Key battles of the western theater, including Franklin, Murfreesboro, Nashville, Pittsburgh Landing, Savannah, Shiloh, Memphis, and Chattanooga were fought out in Tennessee.

Tennessee River

Running directly through the heart of Kentucky, Tennessee, and Alabama, control of the Tennessee River was crucial to the control of the western theater of the war.

Albert Sidney Johnston, the man originally charged with holding the western theater for the Confederacy, built Fort Henry to defend the Tennessee. This fort soon fell to Grant, who correctly identified it as a week point in Johnston's line of defense. Important battles waged along the banks of the Tennessee included the then-unprecedented bloodbath of Shiloh and the Union victory at Chattanooga, which finally put an end to the Confederate threat west of the Allegheny mountains.

Texas

Texas was admitted to the United States as a slave state in 1845, and at the outbreak of war, Governor Sam Houston resisted secession. In February 1861 the state seceded without him and he resigned.

The port of Galveston was one of the most heatedly contested positions in Texas—taken by the Union in October 1862, it was retaken by the Confederacy in January 1863 and did not surrender until June 1865.

In March 1863, General Nathaniel Banks' launched his ill-fated Red River Campaign, intended to rob Texas of its cotton resources—however, following a series of embarrassing rebuffs and misfortunes, Banks was forced to withdraw in May 1863. The Confederate loss of the Mississippi in late 1863 severed Texas from the rest of the south.

Theaters of battle

Historians of the war have traditionally referred to these as the eastern theater, the western theater, the Trans-Mississippi theater and so on. Although the armies ranged far and wide across the North American continent, the war was fought predominantly in the eastern theater; the capitals Washington, D.C, and Richmond quickly became centers of troop concentration, and Virginia proved the main battleground, since both governments showed such overt concern for their capital that they tended to neglect the forces and the objectives in the west. The Confederacy in particular suffered from overemphasis in the east.

Thomas, George Henry 1816–70

The "Rock of Chickamauga" was a Union general who did much to forge Federal victories in the western campaigns. His stubborn defense of Chickamauga prevented a Confederate rout and allowed an orderly Union withdrawal. At Nashville, in December 1864, Thomas stopped the attack of John B Hood's army and preserved Federal communication lines. Born in 1816, Thomas served as artillery officer in Mexican War. Although Virginian, he remained loyal to the Union and was to reach high rank in the Union army as a result of his undoubted skill. In January 19, 1862, his force was attacked by a Confederate force under Zillicoffer at Logan's Cross Roads (Mill Springs), Kentucky, but repulsed the assault. He was subsequently one of a large number of Union commanders and future commanders that were involved with the River War of 1862 and the assault on Corinth in October of that year. His stubborn defense saved the Union Army of Cumberland at Chickamauga in September 1863 and he then replaced Rosecrans as commander of that army in the following month. He served with his Army of Cumberland at the Battle of Atlanta in July 1864 before defeating the Confederate forces under Hood at the Battle of Nashville on 15/16 December 1864 during Sherman's "March to the Sea."

Torpedoes and Mines

With limited resources, the Confederates were forced to find new ways of countering the numerical superiority of the U.S. Navy. One of their most effective solutions was the development of torpedoes (mines) as part of their static defenses guarding the principal ports and rivers of the Confederacy. In theory, a small explosive charge in a submerged chamber could destroy a powerful enemy warship. In July 1861, Union sailors recovered a crude torpedo off Washington Navy Yard. This crude device was the forerunner of

THE AMERICAN CIVIL WAR: A VISUAL ENCYCLOPEDIA

Above Left: **Minelaying off Charleston harbor.**

Below Left: **General Thomas distinguished himself during the Battle of Chicamauga in 1863.**

Right: **The Confederates made extensive use of trenches at Fredericksburg in 1862 and during the siege of Petersburg.**

Below Right: **The Union ironclad USS *Casco* was a failed monitor converted to carry a spar torpedo.**

thousands of torpedoes used by the Confederacy during the war. The principal method of detonating a torpedo was by contact, where the hull of an enemy vessel struck a contact detonator on the device. A more unusual variant was the electric torpedo, which was detonated by an operator on the shore with a detonating switch, connected to the mine by a cable. An electrical torpedo of this type almost destroyed the USS *New Ironsides* off Charleston in April 1863, but the cable had been severed by accident. The Torpedo Bureau in Richmond was responsible for developing ever more deadly devices, including sunken glass demijohns, drifting contact torpedoes and the numerous "keg" torpedoes, the forerunners of the contact mines used in both World Wars. In addition, torpedoes fastened to the end of spars were fitted to several Confederate warships, but the most spectacular spar torpedo attack was conducted by the Union, when a steam launch fitted with one sank the CSS *Albermarle* in October 1864.

Uncle Tom's Cabin

Uncle Tom's Cabin by Harriet Beecher Stowe simplified and sentimentalized the issues of slavery and Abolition in a way that captured the mood of the time and in the process proved a hugely influential propaganda coup for the Abolition movement. The novel, published in 1852, sold more than two million copies in the United States alone in the following decade. Lincoln is said to have read Stowe's later volume *A Key to Uncle Tom's Cabin* when agonizing over the issue of slavery in the summer of 1862 and to have greeted the author, "So you're the little woman who wrote the book that made this great war."

Underground Railroad

The Underground Railroad was an informal network of anti-slavery activists in the North who assisted fugitive slaves, concealing them from slave hunters and bounty seeking officials and conducting them towards safety in Canada. Between the 1790s and 1860 many thousands were assisted to escape and each success provided useful publicity in aid of the Abolition cause. One of the best known activists of the "railroad" was Harriet Tubman (c.1820–1913) who escaped from slavery in Maryland in 1849, then made nineteen journeys back to assist some 300 others to freedom, including her own parents.

Above Right: Runaway slaves on their route north along the "underground railroad."

Right: Harriet Beecher Stowe's home.

Opposite Page, Above and Below: At the start of the war, many uniforms were elaborate, but by 1863, most superfluous decoration was abandoned in favor of a more practical form of uniform.

THE AMERICAN CIVIL WAR: A VISUAL ENCYCLOPEDIA

Uniforms

At the outbreak of war there was enormous variety in the style and color of the uniform dress of the Union and Confederate armies, and attempts were made to standardize the soldiers' clothing. Generally speaking, Confederate uniforms were light gray, and later, butternut brown in color. The Union troops wore dark blue and sky blue, corresponding to the colors of the prewar U.S. Army uniform.

Both armies adopted uniform trim to distinguish different ranks, trades, and specializations—an infantryman wore light blue trim, a cavalryman wore yellow, and an artilleryman wore red. Gold-colored braid, stars, and stripes on his uniform told the soldier's rank. In early 1863 the Union Army went further and started using badges to represent the different army corps. Twenty-three badges were adopted. The corps badge was worn on the uniform, usually on top of the hat.

UNION UNIFORM

The most notable feature of the U.S Army uniform coat was its dark blue color, the traditional hue of the American army since the Revolutionary War. The notion of a soldier wearing a uniform that served to camouflage him would have been very foreign to the thinking of military officers, who held firm to the belief that their men should be easily distinguished on the battlefield. In fact, it was not until the Spanish-American War that the Army adopted uniforms of a khaki color that had some camouflage value.

Similarly the uniform was made of wool and no effort was made to produce a uniform that would be comfortable in warm climates. It was not unusual for soldiers to dress more casually while on campaign, but the standards of the day were unforgiving. Heat stroke was a common occurrence while on the march in hot weather,

Certain uniform items were light blue. This material was much less expensive to purchase during the period. The quartermaster enjoyed the cost savings of the light blue pants and overcoats and they also provided a contrast in color. The Invalid (Veteran Reserve) Corps, established during the war to return wounded men to limited service, wore a totally sky blue uniform.

Another notable feature of the Union uniform is the use of the eagle motif, which was officially adopted as the central element of the seal of the United States. Eagles were used to pin the side of the hat up, as the motif on many of the buttons, on the cartridge box cross-belt plate and on the sword-belt plate. The abbreviation U.S. appeared on the oval belt buckle and cartridge box plate.

The Union uniform took its familiar form from an 1851 directive, which prescribed

for the commissioned officers a thigh-length frock coat of dark-blue cloth, single-breasted for captains and lieutenants, double-breasted for all other grades. For enlisted men the uniform coat was a single-breasted frock of dark-blue cloth, The uniform trousers for officers and enlisted men were of cloth of sky blue mixture. For enlisted mounted men they were reinforced in the seat. The general officers and the general staff wore dark-blue cloth.

The cap for all officers and enlisted men was of dark-blue cloth, higher in front than back, with a horizontal visor. It was fastened by a chin strap of strong black leather and a yellow metal buckle. Generals and general staff officers' hats had an embroidered wreath in front encircling the letters "U. S." in old English letters in silver; the artillery had crossed cannon; the infantry, the bugle; and for officers of dragoon (cavalry), crossed sabers. For enlisted men, at the bottom of the cap bands of scarlet, light blue and orange-colored cloth were used for the artillery, infantry, and dragoons, respectively. The decorative pompon for general officers was an embroidered acorn and for all other officers and enlisted men, a worsted spherical acorn in the colors adopted for the department and the arms of the service. The color of the infantry feather was Saxon blue. Brass shoulder knots instead of the worsted were prescribed for the dragoons and artillery.

For all mounted officers and for mounted enlisted men, yellow metal spurs were prescribed. There were also prescribed styles for sword belts, and many other items; epaulettes were to be worn by all officers as badges to distinguish rank, and a shoulder strap was to be worn in lieu of epaulettes. Interestingly, this order stated that

"mustaches are not to be worn, except by cavalry regiments, by officers or men under any pretense whatever."

Although there were some amendments this style is remarkably consistent with the uniform of the Union armies during the Civil War. The coat remained practically the same for officers, as mentioned and for officers and enlisted men the trousers were of dark-blue cloth, except for companies of light artillery, which were of sky blue. The enlisted men of the cavalry and light artillery were allowed a uniform jacket of dark-blue cloth with standing collar, and a sack coat of dark blue flannel for fatigue purposes. It was not until 1863 that a change was made in the uniform trousers of

the regimental officers and enlisted men, as follows: "The cloth to be of sky blue mixture, the welt for officers and stripes for non-commissioned officers of infantry to be of dark blue." Epaulettes were retained, as were the shoulder-knots and chevrons. The overcoat for officers was of dark blue, and for enlisted men of sky-blue cloth.

The soldiers were also issued a knapsack, haversack, and canteens. The orders of this time prescribed "the hair to be short; the beard to be worn at the pleasure of the individual; but when worn, to be kept short and neatly trimmed."

Army chaplains, medical cadets, non-commissioned officers, and the invalid corps had their own variation on these dress codes.

CONFEDERATE UNIFORMS

Confederate policy on uniform was conditioned by circumstance. Lacking the material resources of their northern enemy, the Confederacy adopted a rather more relaxed approach to uniform dress. Confederate officers were expected to provide their own uniforms, and while they were certainly better dressed than most of their enlisted men, their clothing was equally non-uniform. Although the standards set by the War Department in 1861 for military officer attire were generally observed, they were subject to the tastes and circumstances of the individual.

Coats were of many different cuts and materials, but after the first year of the war, they were usually a shade of gray. As with the Union uniform, wool was used. Officers' coats—whether tunics, frock coats, or shell jackets—featured standing collars and were double-breasted, with rows of seven brass buttons down the front. Generals could be distinguished from other officers by the eagles on their buttons, which were distinctively spaced in pairs. The regulations made no distinctions among the uniforms of different grades of generals, but some major generals adopted the Federal custom of spacing their buttons in groups of three. The rank insignia for generals was found on the collar; for all grades it consisted of three stars encircled by a wreath. Cuffs, collars, edging, and sash of a buff color also denoted the rank of a general. Officers had gold braiding on their sleeves. Generals' uniforms had four strands of the braiding; lesser ranks had fewer strands. Dark blue trousers trimmed in buff were standard for Confederate generals. Soldiers in all ranks wore a wide variety of hats, with no particular distinction for generals.

Confederate Generals "Prince" John Magruder, cavalry commander "Jeb" Stuart, and P. G. T. Beauregard were noted for their splendid uniforms. In contrast, "Stonewall" Jackson was known for

his drab, threadbare uniform and the old Virginia Military Institute forage cap he wore down over his eyes. Lee's appearance was always neat but his usual uniform bore the collar insignia of a mere colonel.

In the west most Confederate units wore civilian clothes. Headgear consisted of slouch hats, sombreros, and various military hats. A number of captured Union supply depots yielded current issue and earlier military uniforms. Those who entered service directly from the military, or who were veterans, often brought their old uniforms with them. When surplus or captured U.S. uniforms were used, it was common practice to turn the belt buckle upside down and turn the coat inside-out to reduce the chances of being shot at by friendly troops. Despite the heat, wool was used as linen or cotton could not offer the same protection against the sun, rain, and sudden drops in temperature. Cavalrymen's pants were reinforced with buckskin, and moccasins were preferred to boots while traveling through deep snows during cold weather. Large neckerchiefs were used by the experienced westerner, for everything from keeping one's hat on in the wind to serving as a dust mask or bandage. Some military units even adopted certain colors and patterns. Union overcoats were certainly present and were on occasion used as part of a disguise.

NAVAL UNIFORMS

The Union naval officer's uniform—a navy blue frock coat with two rows of gilt buttons, navy blue trousers, and cap—was a practical reflection of wartime conditions. Blockade conditions and operations in the hot southern climates created the need for appropriate garments to allow comfort in the heat. Straw hats and white coats were authorized.

In the U.S. Navy, there was also increased standardization in enlisted clothing and the beginnings of rate and specialty distinction. The dramatic growth in the number of naval personnel and ships necessitated further distinctions in uniform appearance. In 1862, master-at-arms, yeoman, stewards, and paymaster stewards, were authorized the wear of the double-breasted officer-type coat. Other enlisted men were dressed in jumper/bell-bottom uniform. It was practical, easy to work in, resisted soilage and provided protection against the elements. It should be noted that the scope of wartime procurement permitted many small deviations from a standard appearance, and a government fighting for its survival was not about to argue details.

United States of America

It was from the United States that the Confederate States of America seceded, thus starting the Civil War. Throughout the war, the principal goal of the United States war effort was to "end the

rebellion" and compel the eleven Southern states to disband the Confederacy and rejoin the United States, which often referred to itself as "the Union."

The United States recognizes its beginning as having occurred on July 4, 1776, although all of the signatories would not have completed the signing of the Declaration of Independence for nearly a month. Under this Declaration, the Continental Congress officially declared thirteen British North American colonies to be independent of Great Britain. The thirteen colonies (that would become the first thirteen states) were (from north to south) New Hampshire, Massachusetts, Rhode Island, Connecticut, New York, New Jersey and Pennsylvania, Delaware, Maryland, Virginia, North Carolina, South Carolina, and Georgia. The latter four would become part of the Confederacy in 1861.

Having declared independence, the United States was obliged to fight the War of Independence that lasted until October 1781, when Lord Cornwallis surrendered his army to General George Washington after the Battle of Yorktown. Subsequent negotiations continued until November 1782, when the two sides finally agreed on terms of an agreement, although the formal treaty was not signed until September 3, 1783. On that date, Great Britain recognized the independence of the United States as declared on July 4, 1776, and agreed to withdraw all its armies, fleets, and garrisons.

The United States continued to grow in size. Vermont joined the Union in 1791, and Kentucky (which was part of Virginia but later formed into a separate state) in 1792. Tennessee was formed out of North Carolina in 1796. After the admission of Mississippi in 1817, Illinois, Alabama, Maine, Missouri, Arkansas, Michigan, Florida, and Texas were admitted through May 1846, bringing the total number of states to twenty-eight. Six more states— Iowa, Wisconsin, California, Minnesota, Oregon, and Kansas—were admitted into the Union from the beginning of the Mexican War to 1861. When the Civil War started, there were thirty-four states with a population of 31,443,321 (by the 1860 census).

In six weeks, beginning late in December 1860, seven states seceded from the Union: Alabama, Florida, Georgia, Louisiana, Mississippi, South Carolina, and Texas. In April 1861, Arkansas, North Carolina, Tennessee, and Virginia also withdrew. This reduced the population of the United States to 22,339,989 (based on the 1860 census). However, the western counties of Virginia subsequently seceded from that state and joined the Union as the state of West Virginia in 1863.

Though it was reduced in population, the United States retained a better than two to

one advantage over the Confederacy in manpower available for military service. It was reduced in size, but the United States greatly exceeded the Confederate States of America in industrial strength and transportation infrastructure. Of the 31,000 miles of railroad in the prewar United States, only 9,000 miles were located in the South.

Though it was never totally effective, the United States' naval blockade of Confederate seaports reduced the South's ability operate a viable ocean-going commerce. Meanwhile, Northern seaports, which were already much larger and more commercially important than the Southern ports, operated virtually as normal throughout the Civil War. Before the war, only ten percent of United States foreign trade had been via Southern ports. During the war, traffic at these ports diminished while it expanded in the North.

The North retained a better than five to one ratio in total manufacturing capacity, and a thirty to one superiority in arms production. Most of the prewar United States' coal, copper, iron, and steel production was centered in the North. Even the Southern textile industry was a mere seven percent of

that of the North in terms of the value of its output. The North also retained virtually all of the prewar United States financial and commercial resources. It is also worth pointing out that the United States had a governmental and military infrastructure in place and operating, and the Confederacy had to build these institutions from scratch.

Though the Confederacy did extremely well militarily during most of the Civil War, the economic superiority and larger population of the U.S. was clearly the dominant factor in the outcome. The Confederate States of America ceased to exist in 1865, and by 1870, after a period of military occupation, all eleven secessionist states had been readmitted to the U.S.

Left and Below Left: By the last years of the war, Union soldiers such as this collection of staff officers adopted a relaxed attitude to uniform regulations, and wore what they considered practical. For the Confederates, they wore whatever clothes were available. The navies of both sides wore similar styles of uniform, and although attempts were made to introduce Confederate gray naval uniforms, many Southern officers continued to wear their old U.S. Naval uniforms of navy blue.

Below: Union infantry and artillery uniforms.

Above Right: Map of the campaign and siege of Vicksburg.

Vermont

Despite being the least-prepared of all the Northern states when Civil War broke out in 1861, Vermont soon mustered forces that would make a significant impact on the war. At the outbreak of war, Vermont's ill-organized militia consisted of four skeleton regiments, many of whom were without guns and suitable equipment to take on campaign.

Although no major battles of the Civil War took place in Vermont, when pro-Union scandal-mongers claimed that Confederate agents were carrying out raids against civilian establishments and banks in Canada, one of the most notable of these alleged raids was that carried out at St. Albans, Vermont by Lt. Bennett H. Young and nineteen Confederates. Republican campaigners claimed that this and other alleged incidents were irretrievably harming Anglo-American relationships, and used this as a factor in their favor in the 1864 presidential elections.

Vicksburg, Mississippi

Vicksburg, the so-called "Gibraltar of the West", was almost impregnably located in a hairpin bend of the Mississippi. Grant, under Halleck, recognized the strategic importance of the town, but the Confederates were equally aware of the necessity of maintaining control of Vicksburg. The first Union assault on Vicksburg was to be tandem operation between Grant and Sherman—however, Grant's forces were restrained by rebel troops and the attempt failed. Subsequent doomed attempts included full frontal assaults, routes via canal, the Louisiana swamps, Steele's Bayou and the Yazoo Pass—eventually, the besieged city's defenses collapsed on July 4, 1863. With the fall of Vicksburg, the Mississippi fell into Union hands and the Confederate will was all but broken.

Vicksburg Campaign

In an address to civil and military leaders, President Abraham Lincoln underlined the importance of Vicksburg thus: "See what a lot of land these fellows hold, of which Vicksburg is the key! The war can never be brought to a close until that key is in our pocket . . . We can take all the northern ports of the Confederacy, and they can defy us from Vicksburg . . . I am acquainted with that region and know what I am talking about, and as valuable as New Orleans will be to us, Vicksburg will be more so."

Vicksburg controlled the middle stretch of the Mississippi River, itself the single most important economic feature of the continent at the time of the Civil War. Upon the secession of the Southern states, Confederate forces had closed the river to navigation, which threatened to strangle northern commercial interests. It was considered imperative, therefore, for the administration in Washington to regain control of the lower Mississippi River, thereby opening that important avenue of commerce enabling the rich agricultural produce of the northwest to reach world markets.

The capture of Vicksburg would also split the South in two, sever a vital Confederate supply line, achieve a major objective of the Anaconda Plan, and effectively seal the doom of Richmond. In the spring of 1863, Major General Ulysses S. Grant launched his Union Army of the Tennessee on a campaign to pocket Vicksburg and provide Lincoln with the key to victory.

Vicksburg was situated on high, unscalable bluffs from which its heavy artillery could control the river below. It was also very difficult to approach overland. Directly to the north was the vast Yazoo Delta, impassable to any large body of troops. Federal gunboats could not sail past Vicksburg without risking destruction. One hundred miles downstream at Port Hudson, Louisiana, a second Confederate river fortress prevented Union naval forces from moving upstream.

Grant initially planned a two-pronged advance on Vicksburg. Sherman would move down the Mississippi River, turn the Federal fleet up the Yazoo River and attempt to land troops to the north of Vicksburg. In the meantime, Grant would move south down the railroad through Grenada, hopefully forcing Lieutenant General Pemberton's Confederate forces to move to try and intercept him. The plan was a failure, largely due to the harassing raids by Forrest's and Van Dorn's cavalry during December. The second raid led by Van Dorn, destroyed Grant's large supply depot at Holly Springs, Mississippi. With his supplies destroyed, and thanks to Forrest, no way of bringing in more, Grant was forced to retreat to Memphis. Sherman likewise had no success in attempting to land troops at Chickasaw Bluffs and was repulsed with severe losses. However, Grant did not lose sight of his objective. He would eventually make five more attempts and suffer five more failures before he achieved his final objective.

The first was an ambitious engineering project to construct a canal across the tongue of land in front of Vicksburg to divert the river channel and bypass the city's artillery batteries, but this was abandoned when a dam collapsed and flooded the Federal camps. The next attempt, to move the fleet via a circuitous route through Lake Providence, about fifty miles north of Vicksburg, and then through several bayous before rejoining the Mississippi River by way of the Red River a few miles

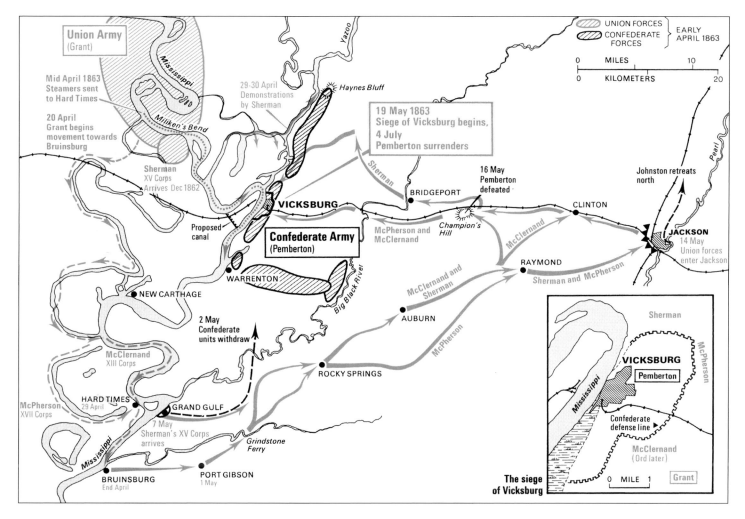

above Port Hudson, failed when it the bayous were found to be too blocked by cypress trees and flotsam .

A third waterborne project also aimed at exploiting the complex river system around Vicksburg, this time via a bayou called the Yazoo Pass, just south of Helena, Arkansas. However, after initial success in moving into the Tallahatchie River system, a Confederate fort blocked further attempts and the Union fleet was forced back. The fourth attempt was made to reach the Yazoo River above Haines Bluff through the maze of weed-choked bayous in the region, but the waterways proved impassable to the fleet's paddle wheels. Finally Grant's engineers tried to construct a second canal just below Duckport that would allow the passage of light draft vessels, but falling river levels made this attempt impractical also.

In April 1863, after forestalling efforts of Major General John McClernand to take over direction of operations against Vicksburg, Grant marched his army down the western bank of the Mississippi River to a point south of the city where Rear Admiral David Porter's fleet, which had successfully run the Vicksburg batteries on the night of April 16-17, lay at anchor. Grant ordered diversionary moves by Sherman at Haines Bluff and a cavalry raid by Colonel R. H. Grierson, and had his expedition ferried across to the eastern

bank of the river to Bruinsburg on April 30. Admiral Farragut had also run two Federal gunboats past the batteries at Port Hudson and could now control the Mississippi below Vicksburg.

Due to confusion caused by Grant's diversions resulting in a dispersion of the Confederate army, Pemberton was unable to rapidly field substantial forces to contain Grant's bridgehead. A Confederate task force under Brigadier General John Bowen met Grant's advance elements at Port Gibson on May 1, but was forced to retreat when no reinforcements were available.

Grant now took it upon himself to implement a bold new operational strategy. Correctly informed that Johnston was assembling an army in central Mississippi to come to Pemberton's support, Grant moved inland with 20,000 men in order to split the two Confederate forces, abandoning his river-based line of communications as he did so. Pemberton, meanwhile, despite urgings by Johnston to immediately concentrate his own forces and move against Grant's bridgehead, pulled the Confederate defenders back into the vicinity of Vicksburg. On May 12, Grant's force met and defeated a small task force under Brigadier General John Gregg at Raymond and two days later captured Jackson, the Mississippi state capital. The Confederates abandoned the important railhead and supply depot and escaped to the north.

Delaying until May 15, Pemberton finally assembled three of his five divisions and marched out of Vicksburg with the intention of cutting Grant's now non-existent supply line. On May 16, Pemberton had a change of heart and decided to obey Johnston's initial order, to link up with him at Brownsville by countermarching his field force back through Edwards Depot. He was too late to prevent Grant from splitting his Federal troops between the Confederate armies, and was defeated first at Champion Hill and then at Big Black River, on May 16 and 17 respectively.

After the stand at the Big Black River, the Confederates retired into the Vicksburg defenses, allowing Grant to reestablish contact with the Federal fleet on the Yazoo River on May 18. He ordered assaults on the Vicksburg defenses on May 19, and again on May 22, but these were repelled with heavy losses. With an army now numbering 40,000, Grant settled down to a siege to starve the garrison into submission. In the meantime, Johnston was rapidly accumulating additional troops to attempt to relieve the siege.

On June 15 Johnston notified the Confederate authorities that he considered saving Vicksburg hopeless. By the end of June, the constant pressure and lack of food was beginning to tell on the Vicksburg defenders. On July 4, Pemberton formally surrendered his army of 2,166 officers and

27,230 enlisted men, 172 cannon, and 60,000 small arms. Five days later another 7,000 Confederate troops would surrender to Major General Nathanial Banks at Port Hudson, Louisiana. The Mississippi River was once again open to sea and the Confederacy was effectively split in half. Grant's persistence and bold strategy had finally paid dividends.

Vicksburg, Siege of, 1863

Vicksburg, known as the "Gibraltar of the West" was the key to the Mississippi River and the battle was to prove decisive to the course of the war. General Ulysses S. Grant aimed to split the confederacy in half by taking Vicksburg and Port Hudson, the only two strong Confederate outposts on the river. At the end of October 1862, he was given command of the Army of the Tennessee and permission to attack the Confederates wherever he saw fit.

Initially Grant attempted to take Vicksburg by the overland route, marching straight southward by way of the Mississippi Central Railroad. To that end Major General Sherman was sent in transports down the Mississippi with 32,000 men while Grant himself followed the railroad with 40,000. Grant was stopped by Van Dorn's cavalry capturing his cavalry, while Sherman was defeated by Confederate general John C. Pemberton at the Battle of Chickasaw Bluffs.

Following these setbacks there followed four other failed attempts by Grant: he attempted to build a canal past the Vicksburg defenses, but this failed due to high water; he attempted to build another canal to enter the Mississippi twenty miles below Vicksburg, but this failed due to low water levels; he then attempted to force a route through from Lake Providence, but this proved too slow; he also attempted to force a route through the Yazoo pass—however, the Confederates set up gun positions at Fort Pemberton and denied him access.

The final campaign against Vicksburg was waged from March 29 to July 4. At the end of March Grant sent McLernand on a reconnaissance expedition to find a route along the banks of the Mississippi south of Vicksburg, such a place was found at New Carthage. Next Admiral Porter's transports and gunboats were sent down the river under the guns of Vicksburg itself. On the night of April 16, Porter managed this for the loss of only one ship and on April 30, and Grant crossed the Mississippi at Bruinsburg. Having been ordered to await reinforcements form Banks, Grant now decided to operate on his own. Against all orders from his superiors, he decided to march on Jackson to disrupt the Confederate forces assembling there for the defense of Vicksburg. On May 14, 1863, Grant routed Johnston's forces at Jackson, before turning to the west and defeating Pemberton at the Battle of Champion's Hill on May 16, who then withdrew to Vicksburg. On May 19 Grant assaulted the Vicksburg defenses, but with no success, a similar pattern established itself when Grant attempted another frontal assault on

May 22, and he decided to settle down and the starve the city into submission. The Confederate defenders were slowly reduced in numbers by disease and wounds, nearly 10,000 men became casualties. Finally, on July 3, 1863, Pemberton asked for terms for surrender. Grant demanded unconditional surrender, but Pemberton hoped that by surrendering on July 4 he would obtain better terms. He did and Grant allowed parole for the Confederate troops.

CSS *Virginia*

The CSS *Virginia* was converted from the remains of the wooden screw frigate USS *Merrimac*, and consequently the ironclad was often referred to by this earlier name. Her designers were able to use the machinery and lower hull of the frigate in its construction. Her design centered around an armored casemate built on top of the *Merrimac*'s hull, and the vessel served as a prototype for most of the twenty-one Confederate ironclads which followed. The *Virginia*'s action off Hampton Roads against the USS *Monitor* on March 9, 1862, was considered a turning point in history; the first clash between two ironclads. When Norfolk was abandoned in May 1862, the *Virginia* drew too much water to retire up the James River to Richmond. Instead, her crew destroyed her on May 11.

Dimensions: 263 feet x 51 feet x 22 feet
Armor: Four-inch iron, with wood backing
Armament: Six smoothbore guns, four rifled guns
Commissioned: March 1862

Above: The ironclad USS *Indianola* running the batteries at Vicksburg to join the USS *Queen of the West* on February 13, 1863.

Left: A shanty town of soldiers huts erected behind Union lines during the siege of Vicksburg.

Left: The interior of the casemate of the CSS *Virginia* during its battle with the USS *Monitor*. The engagement between the two ironclads ushered in a new era in naval warfare.

Below Left: Another view of the historic battle.

Right: The batteries of Captains Rodgers, Jones, and Aurilla at Petersburg. Part of the outer line of Confederate fortifications, they were captured by XVIII Corps on June 15, 1864. The campaign became a series of battles which centered around Union attacks on fortified Confederate positions.

Virginia Campaign 1864-65

Petersburg and Richmond were two of the jewels in the Confederate crown; the former city a key railhub (railroads from all over the Confederacy led into Petersburg, with one railroad linking Petersburg to Richmond), port, and supply station, the latter the capital of the Confederacy itself. During the Virginia Campaign of 1864-65 that ended the war, Petersburg was the scene of many famous battles. The siege of the city itself began on June 12, 1864 and ended on April 3, 1865, lasting a total of 292 days. All of the more famous sieges—Vicksburg, Atlanta, and Richmond—were inferior to it in terms of the number of battles fought and of lives lost in its defense.

When General McClellan, in the summer of 1862, was forced to abandon his advance upon Richmond by way of the Peninsula and fall back on Harrsion's Landing, he proposed to cross to the south side of the James River and operate against Richmond by that side, seizing Petersburg and the railways leading to that city and Richmond from the south. His request for reinforcements for this venture was turned down by Halleck, Commander-in-Chief of the Army, who ordered the Army of the Potomac to withdraw from the Peninsula. Thereafter, no further effort was made to advance south of the James until May 1864.

Then, in cooperation with the campaign beginning in the Wilderness, Grant ordered Butler, commanding the Army of the James, to cross to the south side of the river and, moving close along its bank, press for Richmond. Butler was held at Drewry's Bluff, and again at Bermuda Hundred. On June 9, Butler ordered Generals Gilmore and Kautz to take Petersburg and destroy the railroad bridge over the Appomattox. Their effort failed, as did Grant's costly effort to reach Richmond from the north

through the Wilderness. The Union commander then decided to transfer his army to the south of the James River and conduct operations against Petersburg and Richmond similar to those first proposed by McClellan two years previously. Halleck disapproved, favoring another advance from the north, but Grant adhered to his own plan and sent Sherman on a mission to destroy the railroad to the north and west. On June 12, he began to withdraw from his positions in front of Lee at Cold Harbor, then crossed the Chickahominy and then the James, at and near to Wilcox's Landing, so the entire Army of the Potomac was south of the river, in the rear of Bermuda Hundred, at midnight of June 16.

Before all the army was across, Grant had already ordered the first advance on Petersburg. General W. F. Smith breached the line of entrenchments that evening, but confusion between Generals Meade, Hancock, and Smith meant that there was a delay in bringing up reinforcements and the chance to take Petersburg that same night was lost. Instead, Lee was able to bring his army into the line between the Federals and Petersburg, and when daylight came the attackers found a new line of earthworks before the city, manned by the best of Lee's veterans. During the next three days some 10,000 Federal troops were lost in attempts to carry Petersburg. Thereafter Grant decided that a siege was necessary, and ordered communications with the city to be destroyed. On June 22 General Wilson marched to destroy the Petersburg and Weldon Railroad and the Southside Railroad, which they accomplished. In the south Kautz's and Wilson's cavalry cut the southern railinks.

During the next month both armies were comparatively quiet, intrenching and throwing up redoubts, but there was incessant skirmishing all along the lines with

severe losses. On July 23, the Federals attempted to break the deadlock using the famous Petersburg mine, an effort that ended, in Grant's words in "… stupendous failure".

On July 30 the armies of the Potomac and the James investing Petersburg and Richmond numbered about 59,000 effective infantry and 12,000 cavalry. Lee had about 38,000 effective infantry and 8,300 cavalry. The Army of the Potomac undertook the investment of Petersburg, while the Army of the James held Bermuda Hundred and all the ground north of the James River. Grant had sent one corps to Washington to oppose Early, and in order to prevent Lee from sending reinforcements, Grant ordered a movement against Richmond on August 12 that succeeded in capturing the Weldon Railroad. For a full month after, quiet again settled over the lines, until on September 28, acting on information that the Confederate lines north of the James were now poorly defended, Grant launched a sudden attack on Richmond, hoping to carry the city before Lee could respond. The key Confederate strongholds at Spring Hill and Fort Harrison were taken and the two sides then retreated to their relative positions to the north of the James River for the duration of the ensuing siege. In cooperation with the movement north of the James, Federal Generals Warren and Parke moved on September 30 to extend the intrenched line beyond the Weldon Railroad, but the movement was checked at Poplar Spring Church. During October, both sides fought piecemeal actions to secure tactical objectives; at the end of the month another movement toward Richmond by the Federals was repulsed, and on December 6 Federal cavalrymen launched a raid that destroyed the Weldon Railroad as far as Hicksford, about forty miles south of Petersburg.

As an unusually severe winter set in, Lee's poorly clothed and under-fed men strengthened the Confederate works. Grant could with some satisfaction reflect upon the fact that his army held Lee tightly to his defences, while elsewhere the Federal forces were carrying out his own comprehensive plans. At the beginning of February, Grant captured Hatcher's Run, an important fording point across the James, and with Sherman now approaching from the south Lee was forced to contemplate the evacuation of Richmond and Petersburg. He determined to evacuate both in early March, as soon as the roads were passable, and to rendezvous at Danville with Johnston and from there attack Sherman. Meanwhile he proposed an attack on the right of the line held by the Army of the Potomac, which he hoped would postpone the necessity of abandoning Richmond and Petersburg until the weather was more favourable. On March 25, an assault was launched at Fort Stedman, which if successful would have cut the Federal army in two and opened an escape route for Lee. Although initially successful, the Confederate troops were driven back.

Grant now made the move that heralded the beginning of the end of the war. His army swelled to nearly 116,000 by the arrival of Sherman's command, twice that of Lee, Grant moved the Army of the James secretly on the night of the 27th to the left of the Army of the Potomac, and attacked Lee's right. After the battles at Dinwiddie Court House and White Oak Road on the 30th and 31st, the decisive battle at Five Forks was carried by the Federals. Suspecting that the Confederate intrenchments around Petersburg had been emptied of men to meet the assault, Grant attacked on April 2 with 63,000 men, against the lines before which he had been held for 10 months. They were opposed by less than 20,000 men, and despite desperate resistance the line was broken and Lee ordered a retreat. When Grant ordered a fresh assault on the morning of the 3rd, it was discovered that Lee had abandoned his lines. Petersburg was thus seized, and later that same day Richmond was surrendered to General Weitzel, who had entered it from north of the James.

Virginia

In January 1861 Virginia upheld hopes of finding peaceable solutions to Northern and Southern differences, but its bid to retain peace failed and on May 23, 1861, Virginia voted in favor of secession. Pro-Union feeling in the western mountains remained strong, however, and this region soon broke away to form the Union state of Western Virginia. The poverty of Virginian resources in 1863 led to bread riots in Richmond, and formed part of Lee's motivation in trying to win the richer state of Maryland for the Confederacy.

The first significant battle of the war was fought at Big Bethel, Virginia on June 10, 1861. Subsequent fighting in Virginia included that at Appomattox, Fredericksburg, Harper's Ferry, Shenandoah, Richmond, Yorktown and Petersburg.

Virginia Military Institute

The Virginia Military Institute was the training ground for many of the leading fig-

Right: Confederate quarters at Manassas, Virginia.

Below Right: The approaches to Culpeper, Virginia, seen earlier in the war, August 1862.

Below: Government Wharves, Alexandria, Virginia.

ures in the Confederate Army; including General Thomas J. "Stonewall" Jackson who served on the VMI Faculty as a controversial Professor of Philosophy & Instructor of Artillery from August 1851 until the beginning of the Civil War in April 1861. At the small battle of New Market on May 15, 1864, a charge by 247 Virginia Military Institute cadets aged between fifteen and seventeen helped the Confederates to victory and won them a permanent place in southern history.

Volck, Adalbert

A memorable pro-Confederate political cartoonist and illustrator, Adalbert Volck was born in Augsburg, Germany in 1828, but emigrated to the United States at the time of the 1848 German Revolution. He settled initially in St. Louis, but later relocated to Baltimore, where he gave up a dental practice to take on work as a printmaker. By the time of the 1860 election, Volck was publishing satirical cartoons of Abraham Lincoln. These cartoons, pub-

lished in secret because of the mood of the city at the time, lampooned Lincoln as a Don Quixote figure on the quest of an impossible dream. Volck continued to work as an illustrator during the Civil War, but became a portrait painter in his later years. He died in 1912.

Volunteers

Before the Civil War, the United States had a volunteer militia system in almost every State, a system which existed well before the American Revolution. At the outbreak of the war, President Lincoln called for 90-day volunteers to augment the regular army, as he predicted a quick end to the war. . After the Union defeat at the Battle of Bull Run (July 21, 1861), it became apparent that the war would last a lot longer than three months. The three month period of service was therefore extended to three years. These established volunteer units were augmented by regiments or companies raised by individuals, often drawing on a local wealthy sponsors to subsidise the

enterprise. These volunteer units were frequently given titles and uniforms at the whim of their founders, and officered by men selected by their regional peers. In time, the exotic uniforms were replaced with more conventional ones, and the inexperienced soldiers were trained through exposure to combat. The majority of regiments raised by the Union were volunteer units, organised by the home State of the volunteers. Early in the war, once a unit was formed, no further recruits were added to its roster. Instead, a new volunteer regiment was raised. After the initial enthusiasm for the Union cause subsided, volunteer regiments depleted by heavy casualties were sometimes augmented by draftees. In all it has been estimated that 1,550 volunteer regiments were formed during the war, the majority being raised during the first year of the war.

Below and Right: In both North and South, thousands of volunteers answered the call to arms, encouraged by bounties for new recruits. Once in the field, they joined what were effectively armies.

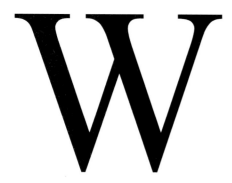

W

Washington D.C.

Washington DC was the Federal capital, and unlike the Confederate capital of Richmond it remained relatively untouched by the ravages of war. Shortly after Lincoln's inauguration in Washington in March 1861, the city found itself all but cut off from the rest of the continent when Baltimoreans severed rail and communication links through their city.

No serious Confederate attack was launched on Washington, although in March 1863 it was feared that Lee would attack, and eighteen and nineteen-year-olds rallied to defend their capital. In July 1864 Early's troops reached Washington's outskirts, but their commander knew better than to attempt to take the city.

Following his assassination in 1865, Lincoln was buried in Washington on April 19.

Waud, Alfred R. (1828–91)

Alfred Waud and his brother William were two of the better known sketch artists of the period. Before the reproduction of photographs in journals became common, newspapers and periodicals sent artists into the field in order to produce drawings for reproduction as line-cuts. Alfred and William produced artwork that was reproduced in two Northern journals, *Harper's Weekly* and *New York Illustrated News*.

Welles, Gideon (1802–78)

Born in 1802, Gideon Welles was Congressman for Connecticut prior to the Civil War. On Lincoln's election he was appointed Secretary of the Navy, a post that he held during the Civil War. He was nicknamed Father Neptune by Lincoln on account of his beard. He had the major task of trying to develop and enforce the blockade of the South at a time when the Union navy was small. At the time Secession occurred, over two-thirds of the potential force at the disposal of the Union was spread widely over the globe with only a dozen or so vessels capable of enforcing the blockade in home waters. Welles was noted as an able administrator, although he was strongly assisted by his dynamic Assistant Secretary (Gustavus V. Fox), who masterminded the raid on Fort Sumter. Despite personal reluctance, authorised work to counter the Confederate's ironclad programme, resulting in construction of the USS *Monitor*. Welles died in 1878.

West Point

West Point provided the army training and the grounding in classical military tactics to many of the leading generals and numerous other officers of both armies. Some historians have argued that the high casualties of the early years of the conflict are in part attributable to a reliance on close order

Far Right: One of the forts protecting Washington during the Civil War. Fort Corcoran was named after the commander, Colonel Michael Corcoran (standing on the parapet) of the 69th New York Regiment. Howitzers, mounted on wooden carriages, were installed in the spring of 1861, shortly after the outbreak of the war. Grapeshot, piled in the foreground, was prepared for an expected Confederate attack on Washington which never happened.

Right: Crowds watching a parade of VI Corps. The view is down Pennsylvania Avenue toward the Capitol building, May 1865..

infantry assaults that was outmoded in the face of rifle fire. Among the major figures to have trained at West Point were Robert E. Lee, Ulysses S. Grant, Stonewall Jackson, William Sherman and Phillip Sheridan.

West Virginia, part played in the war

Western Virginia became a state in its own right on June 20, 1863, when it was admitted to the Union. Made up of the mountainous regions of Virginia that had most opposed the state's secession in 1861, Western Virginia was effectively won for the Union by Major General George B. McClellan's early victories there—most notably that at Phillipi. The war came as a liberating force to such western regions as Western Virginia, giving them an opportunity to declare their own identities and allegiances.

Wheeler, Joseph (1836–1906)

Joseph Wheeler was a Confederate commander. He commanded the Cavalry Corps as part of the Army of Tennessee prior to reorganization of November 1862. In the build-up to the Battle of Murfreesboro in December 1862, Wheeler had success against Rosecrans's reserve forces on December 29, 1862. Later he suffered a number of defeats during Sherman's March to the Sea: at Dalton, Georgia, on August

14–16, 1864; at Lovejoy, Georgia, on November 16, 1864; at Griswoldville, Georgia, on November 21–22, 1864; at Sandersville, Georgia, on November 26, 1864; and at Waynesboro, Georgia, on November 29, 1864. After these defeats, Wheeler and his cavalry formed part of the defence of Virginia, but was unable to resist the relentless march of the victorious Union forces under Grant. Wheeler continued in a military role after peace; serving as a major general during the Cuban campaign of 1898.

Whitman, Walt (1819-92)

Born on Long Island, New York, Whitman was to become one of the foremost U.S. poets of the nineteenth century. His background, however, was not one that led automatically to this as he started his working life as an office boy before moving on to become an itinerant teacher in country schools. His first novel was published in 1842 and from this started a career in journalism. As editor of *The Brooklyn Eagle* he was a staunch supporter of aggressive U.S. expansion. In 1848 he and his brothers briefly visited New Orleans, before returning to Brooklyn where he continued to write In 1862, one of his brothers was injured at the Battle of Fredericksburg and Whitman was called to help look after him. He then spent the remainder of the war helping in the army hospitals of

Washington. The strain significantly impaired his health and, after working as a government clerk from 1865 until 1873, he retired following a stroke to New Jersey, where he lived until his death supported financially by his many literary admirers.

Wigfall, Louis Treservant (1816–74)

Hailing from Texas, Louis T. Wigfall was a Democrat politician who strongly supported Secession. He advocated attacking Fort Sumter in order to support the secessionists in Virginia—the belief that secession would fail in the border states unless positive action was taken. Having served briefly under Johnston as a general in Virginia, he was elected Senator for Texas in 1862. Advocating conscription in the Senate on March 28, 1862, he said "No man has any rights, which come into conflict with the welfare of the country." The motion allowing for conscription was passed. He became a strong critic of Jefferson Davis in 1863, regarding the Confederate president as being pig-headed and perverse, believing that the confusing command structure had resulted in the Confederate forces' defeat in the West. However, he ardently opposed the policy of drafting and arming the black population, despite the fact that this would have allowed the Confederate forces to be considerably strengthened.

Wilderness, Battle of the, 1864

Having spent much of April, 1864, engaged in formulating his plans, Lieutenant General Ulysses S. Grant instructed Meade's Army of the Potomac, with around 120,000 men, to strike at General Robert E. Lee's Army of Northern Virginia, wich was 63,000 strong. To this end The Army of the Potomac crossed the Rapidan River on May 4, 1864, passing across the front of the Confederate army moving towards their right wing.

Lee quickly realized the Union plan and immediately ordered his forces to march east and strike their opponents in territory known as the Wilderness, an area of tangled vegetation fourteen miles long by ten miles wide. Lee hoped that Grant's superior numbers would be ineffective in the dense undergrowth. Ewell moved via the Orange Turnpike and Hill utilized the parallel Orange Plank Road to the south. Longstreet's Corps had a far longer journey to make, so Lee advised Ewell and Hill not to get involved in a general engagement until he arrived.

On the morning of May 5, Meade's advance regiments encountered Ewell's position and the Battle of the Wilderness was underway. While Ewell's troops were encountering the Union advance, A. P. Hills divisions were pressing through the Wilderness aiming for the Brock Road, the main north-south, if they managed to hold this they would isolate Hancock's corps from the rest of the Army of the Potomac. Grant realized the danger and rushed one of Sedgewick's Divisions to the crossroads, where they were able to hold Hill and eventually drive him back until nightfall. Hill then made no attempt to fortify his position as he assumed Longstreet would relieve him. However, Longstreet was running late and the next morning Hill faced a major Union assault from an unfortified position and was completely overwhelmed. Fortunately, Longstreet arrived with his corps in time to reinforce Hill's position and drive back Hancock's advance. Taking advantage of this shift in the fortunes of the battle, Longstreet fed four brigades around the Union left flank and began to roll it up. Unfortunately, at this point Longstreet was seriously wounded and could take no further part in the battle and the attack lost its momentum with Hancock able to restore his lines.

This Page and Opposite, Above: In the Battle of the Wilderness fought in the dense woods south of the Rappahannock River, Lee's army was outnumbered two to one. There were over 30,000 casualties, including 7,000 Confederates. Many of the dead were lost as uncontrolled fires scoured the battlefield.

Opposite Page, Below: The bombardment of Fort Fisherin January 1865 led to the capture of the fort and the fall of Wilmington.

THE BATTLE OF THE WILDERNESS VA. MAY 5TH & 6TH 1864.

This was one of the most desperate Battles of modern times, and was fought between the gallant "Army of the Potomac" under the immediate command of that great Hero, Lieut. Genl. U.S. Grant; and the "Rebel Army of Virginia" under Lee and others. — On Wednesday May 4th the "Army of the Potomac" crossed the Rapidan, and on the 5th attacked the Rebels with great fury, and after two days of desperate fighting, in which the losses on both sides were immense, the Rebel hordes were compelled to give way, and Saturday (the 7th) were glad to save themselves in flight to the South.

To the north, Sedgewick and Warren had failed to penetrate Ewell's lines and, late on May 6, Gordon assaulted Grant's unprotected right flank. This attack routed the troops on that side, but due to the lateness of the hour the Confederates were unable to exploit their advantages and the Union troops reformed overnight.

On May 7 there was little further fighting and both sides entrenched. During the night of 7–8 the Army of the Potomac disengaged and both armies began the maneuvering that was to lead to the Battle of Spotsylvania on May 9.

Wilmington, Defence of

The principal port of North Carolina, Wilmington lying near the mouth of the Cape Fear River was guarded by Fort Fisher, the strongest coastal fortification in the South. Although a Union blockading force was stationed off the port, local conditions made it difficult to maintain an effective blockade. Consequently, Wilmington remained a popular blockade-running port throughout the war.

Two "Richmond class" ironclads were built at the port; the CSS *North Carolina*, commissioned in December 1863, and the CSS *Raleigh*, in service from April 1864. A month later the *Raleigh* sortied to attack the blockading squadron, but was wrecked on Wilmington bar. The *North Carolina* was poorly built, and eventually sank at her moorings in September 1864. As the Union blockade tightened, blockade-running all but ceased. The port's defence centerd around Fort Fisher, and when it was captured on January 15, 1865, the port capitulated a week later.

Wilson's Creek, Battle of, 1861

The Battle of Wilson's Creek, fought on August 10, 1861, was the first major engagement west of the Mississippi River. Brigadier General Nathaniel Lyon's Army of the West attacked Confederate troops under the command of Brigadier General Ben McCulloch. Advancing in two columns Lyon attacked the Confederate cavalry, who fell back down the hill. The Confederate infantry then moved forward and stabilized the position. Three times the Confederate forces tried to breach the Union line but were each time driven back. However, they did manage to kill Brigadier General Lyon, who was replaced by Major Samuel D. Sturgis. Following the third attack, which ended at 11:00am, the Confederates withdrew. Sturgis declined to pursue due to a shortage of ammunition and the tiredness of his men.

Winchester, Battle of, 1862

After skirmishing with Major General Nathaniel P. Banks's retreating army at Middletown and Newtown on May 24, Major General T. J. Jackson's division continued north on the Valley Pike toward Winchester. There, Banks was attempting to reorganize his army to defend the town. Ewell's division converged on Winchester from the southeast using the Front Royal Pike.

On May 25, Ewell attacked Camp Hill, while the Louisiana Brigade of Jackson's division outflanked and overran the Union position on Bowers Hill. Panic spread through the Federal ranks, and many fled through Winchester. Banks's army was soundly defeated and withdrew north across the Potomac River.

Winchester, Battle of, 1864

On September 19, 1864, Sheridan advanced toward Winchester along the Berryville Pike in an attempt to crush the forces of Jubal Early, which were scattered in the vicinity of Winchester. The Union advance was delayed long enough for Early to concentrate his forces to meet the main assault, which continued for several hours. The Confederate line was gradually driven back toward the town. In the mid-afternoon, Crook's VIII Corps and the cavalry turned the Confederate left flank and Early ordered a general retreat. The battle cost the Confederates around 4,000 casualties and Sheridan around 5,000

Yazoo River

Emptying into the Mississippi from the east twenty miles south of Vicksburg, the Yazoo River was utilized in two unsuccessful Union attempts on the city.

On December 27, 1862, 32,000 men under Sherman attempted to approach Vicksburg via the Yazoo, but were routed by a Confederate advance guard. Later, in the March of 1863, the roundabout route via the "Yazoo Pass" became the focus of Grant's third attempt to take Vicksburg, but he was forced to abandon his plan when the Confederates built a fort blocking the pass ninety miles north of the city.

Yorktown, Battle of, 1862

Following his invasion of the Yorktown Peninsula in 1862, Major General George B. McClellan's army encountered Major General John B. Magruder's small Confederate army at Yorktown behind the Warwick River. Magruder made a great show of marching his troops up and done behind his fortifications and ordered the construction of wooden guns, known as "quaker" guns after the pacifist sect. Fooled by this bravado into believing Magruder had many more men than he did, McClellan settled down for a siege, giving time for General Joseph E. Johnston to reinforce Magruder. A Union reconnaissance in force on April 16 found a weakness that could have rolled up the entire Confederate line, but McClellan refused to exploit it. By the time he was ready to attack on May 4, the entire Confederate force had slipped away.

Above Left and Left: In the first significant engagement of his Peninsular Campaign in 1862, General McClellan's Army of the Potomac laid formal siege to the Confederate positions at Yorktown, Virginia, which is the purpose of Battery 4 and its thirteen-inch mortars outside Yorktown in May 1862, and the Union encampment (Left).

Zouaves

The performance of French "Zouave" units (French African troops) during the Franco-Austrian War of 1859 prompted many volunteer regiment s on both sides of the Civil War to ape the appearance of these elite French troops. One appeal for this fad was the exotic uniforms worn by the Zouaves, characterised by baggy pants, short jackets and turbans. Although a handful of Southern units such as the Louisiana Tigers retained their Zouave appearance, shortages forced most such Confederate units to adopted regular uniforms within a few months.

In the North, fifteen Zouave regiments were formed, the majority in New York.

Above Right and Right: Zouaves were uniformed in the style of contemporary French colonial troops, and were considered elite soldiers. The photograph at right is a well-known shot by Mathew Brady.

Credits

The publisher wishes to thank the following for kindly supplying the photographs in this book:

Via Bill Yenne for front cover photograph, and pages 30, 41 (top), 43 (top right), 43 (middle right), 43 (bottom right), 66 (top), 84, 86 (top), 117, 118-119 (top), 118 (bottom), 123 (top), 125 (bottom), 138 (top), 164, 181 (top), 201 (top), 206-207, 220, 293 (bottom), 294 (top), 294 (bottom), 296-297, 330 (left), 358 (bottom), 368 (inset top left), 368-369 (main), 370 (top), 370 (bottom), 391 (bottom), 392-3 (main), 411, 425 (bottom), 442 and 443 (bottom);

Hulton|Archive for pages 2, 5, 6 (top right), 6 (bottom right), 146 (bottom), 147 (top), 147 (bottom), 158 (top), 245, 373 (inset top right), 374-375 (main), 377 (top), 424 (top) and 424 (bottom);

Via Chrysalis Images for pages 6 (bottom left), 7 (bottom), 8, 10, 16 (top), 16 (bottom), 21, 22 (top), 25 (top), 25 (bottom), 29 (top), 29 (middle), 29 (bottom), 32-33, 34 (near left), 38-39, 40 (bottom), 41 (bottom left), 41 (bottom right), 42 (top left), 42-43 (main), 44-45 (bottom), 46-47, 48, 53 (bottom), 56 (bottom), 57 (bottom), 58 (bottom left), 60, 68, 69, 73, 75 (top), 75 (bottom), 77 (top left), 77 (top right), 78 (left), 79 (top), 83 (bottom), 85 (top), 86 (bottom), 89 (top), 91, 92, 98 (bottom), 99, 105, 106 (top left), 106 (top right), 106 (bottom), 108, 109 (top), 112 (top), 113 (top), 113 (bottom), 114, 115 (top), 116 (top), 123 (middle), 123 (bottom), 132, 133 (top), 133 (bottom), 138 (bottom), 139, 143, 144, 148-149 (main), 148 (top, inset), 154 (top left), 154-155 (main), 160-161, 162 (top), 162 (bottom), 168, 170-171, 175 (bottom right), 182 (top), 183 (top), 183 (bottom), 184 (top left), 186 (top), 187, 188-189, 195, 196 (top), 196 (bottom), 197 (bottom), 198 (top), 210-211 (top), 210-211 (bottom), 214 (top), 217 (top), 222-223 (bottom), 225 (top), 225 (bottom), 226, 228, 230, 231 (top), 231 (bottom), 234, 238, 242-243, 244, 250 (top), 251, 255 (bottom), 260, 260-261 (bottom), 263 (top), 263 (bottom), 267, 269 (right), 270 (bottom), 277, 278 (left), 278-279 (main), 282, 283 (left), 283 (right), 291, 293 (top), 295, 301 (top), 302-303, 304, 310, 314, 315, 317, 318-319, 320-321, 322-323, 338, 339 (bottom), 349 (right), 350 (bottom left), 353 (middle), 353 (bottom), 356 (left), 356 (right), 357, 359 (top), 361, 364-365, 366 (bottom left), 366-367 (top left), 367 (top right), 367 (bottom right), 371 (top), 371 (bottom), 372-373 (main), 374 (top left), 376, 378 (bottom), 381, 383 (top left), 383 (bottom), 384 (bottom), 390 (top), 392 (top left), 397, 400, 401 (top), 403 (bottom), 404 (bottom), 405, 409, 412-413, 415 (top), 418 (top), 418 (bottom), 419 (top), 420, 420 (bottom), 421, 422 (top), 423 (top), 423 (bottom), 425 (top), 426 (top), 430 (bottom left), 433, 434, 435 (top), 435 (bottom), 440 (top) and 444 (top);

Courtesy of the Library of Congress for pages 7 (top), 13, 14 (top), 17 (bottom), 26, 31 (top), 50, 72, 77 (bottom), 83 (top), 85 (top), 90, 93, 105 (top), 128-129, 134-135 (top left), 145, 152 (left), 174-175 (bottom left), 176 (bottom), 184-185 (main), 212-213, 216, 250 (bottom), 254, 273 (bottom), 274-275, 280 (inset left), 334-335 (main), 354-355, 368 (inset bottom left), 382, 385, 386 (bottom), 395, 398 (top), 398 (bottom), 416-417, 419 (bottom), 438, 440 (bottom), 441 (top) and 443 (top);

U.S. Navy Photograph: page 9 (top);

U.S. National Archives for pages 9 (bottom), 15 (bottom), 17 (top), 18 (top), 23, 31 (bottom), 44-45 (top), 52, 74 (bottom left), 80-81, 88, 107, 116 (bottom), 122 (top), 124 (bottom), 125 (top), 125 (middle), 126-127 (top), 176-177 (top), 184 (bottom left), 190-191, 192-193 (main), 197 (top), 201 (bottom), 214 (bottom), 215, 219 (bottom), 246-247, 350-351 (top right), 351 (bottom), 378-379 (top), 379 (bottom), 396 (top), 410, 439, 441 (bottom) and 444 (bottom);

Library of Congress/U.S. National Archives for pages 11, 153 (top), 175 (top), 194, 203, 208, 218-219 (top), 271, 285 (top), 285 (bottom), 286 (left), 306 (bottom), 311, 312-313, 325, 336, 344-345, 346-347, 348-349 (main), 358 (top) and 360;

U.S. Naval History Center Photographs: pages 12, 34 (top far left), 57 (top), 192 (inset), 236-237 (main), 255 (top), 258-259 (top), 268-269 (main), 273 (top), 300, 301 (bottom), 305 (top), 327 (top), 333 (bottom), 342 (left), 380, 383 (top right), 394, 408, 422 (top), 430-431 (main) and 432 (top);

Copyright 2001 Richard Natkiel for pages 15 (top), 53 (top), 62, 82 (top), 82 (bottom), 87, 94, 122 (bottom right), 124 (top), 146 (top), 165 (top left), 165 (top right), 165 (bottom), 217 (bottom), 227, 307, 339 (top), 352, 353 (top left), 353 (top right), 384 (top), 389, 396 (bottom), 399, 404 (top) and 429;

Official U.S. Navy Photographs: pages 19, 54 (drawing in the Lowe Collection), 55 (top), 63 (bottom), 151, 237 (bottom), 256 (inset bottom), 258-259 (bottom), 262, 308-309, 332 (bottom), 333 (top), 335 (inset), 342-343 (main) and 432 (bottom);

TRH Pictures/U.S. National Archives for pages 20, 28 (left), 28 (right), 34-35, 36-37, 55 (bottom), 58-59 (main), 61, 66 (bottom), 70 (inset left), 76, 78 (right), 95 (top), 95 (bottom), 110 (bottom), 111 (bottom), 127 (bottom right), 130 (bottom left), 130-131 (top), 131 (bottom right), 13 (top right), 136 (bottom left), 137 (bottom right), 140, 141 (bottom), 153 (bottom), 156 (top), 156 (bottom), 157 (top), 157 (bottom), 158 (bottom), 166, 172, 178 (inset left), 181 (bottom), 182 (bottom), 186 (bottom), 198 (bottom), 199 (top), 199 (bottom), 200, 202, 204-205 (main), 205 (top), 239, 265, 272, 284 (left), 286-287 (main), 288-289, 298 (inset left), 340-341 (bottom), 386 (top left), 388, 401 (bottom), 402-403 (top), 426 (bottom), 437 (top), 437 (bottom) and back cover photograph;

From the collection of Dale S. Snair for page 22 (bottom);

Chicago Historical Society for pages 24 (top), 63 (top), 253 (right) and 280-281 (main);

TRH Pictures/National Maritime Museum for page 27;

G.A. Department of Archives and History for pages 49 (top), 337 and 414;

Minnesota Historical Society for pages 64-65;

Courtesy of Little Bighorn National Monument for pages 70-71 (main), 150 (top), 150 (bottom) and 391 (top);

TRH Pictures for pages 79 (bottom), 89 (bottom), 110 (top), 111 (top), 120-121, 141 (top), 235 (top), 235 (bottom), 284 (right), 298-299 (main), 306 (top) and 427;

TRH Pictures/U.S. Navy for pages 96-97, 178-179 (main), 224, 256-257 (main), 257 (inset bottom), 305 (bottom), 330-331 (main), 332 (top) and 359 (bottom);

Hans Halberstadt for pages 98 (top), 101 (top), 101 (bottom), 102-103, 229, 232-233, 386 (top right), 387 (top) and 387 (bottom);

Massachusetts Commandery Military Order of the Loyal Legion and the US Army Military History Institute for page 109 (bottom); US Army Military History Institute for page 112 (bottom);

Courtesy of the National Library of Medicine for page 115 (bottom);

The Illustrated London News Picture Library for page 119 (bottom);

U.S. Army Photographs: pages 135 (bottom) – reference no. SC105692; 126 (bottom left) - reference no. SC113748; 180 - reference no. SC113748; 67; 18 (bottom) - reference no. B384; 252 (left) - reference no. B665; 159 - reference no. B754; 292 (top) - reference no. BA1932; 40 (top) - reference no. BA19849; 24 (bottom) - reference no. SC107371; 104 - reference no. SC107402; 122 (bottom left) - reference no. SC113751; and 436 - reference no. SC320471;

TRH Pictures/US Signal Corps (Brady Collection) in the National Archives for pages 136-137 (top) – reference no. 111-B-158; and 173 (bottom) – reference no. 111-B-276;

Museum of the Confederacy for pages 152 (right) and 248-249;

© Bettmann Archive/CORBIS for page 167;

TRH Pictures/DoD National Archives for pages 169 and 402 (bottom);

Via Hans Halberstadt for pages 173 (top) and 377 (bottom);

Courtesy of the Collection of the New-York Historical Society (negative number 56756) for page 209;

Mrs Howard Branson for page 218 (bottom);

TRH Pictures/National Portrait Gallery, Washington D.C. for page 221;

Missouri Historical Society for pages 223 (top), 248 (inset, top) and 266;

U.S. Signal Corps Photographs (Brady Collection) in the National Archives for pages 264 – reference no. 111-B-1782; 49 (bottom) – reference no. 111-BA-1673; 56 (top) – reference no. 111-BA-5005; 292 (bottom) – reference no. 111-BA-5867; 415 (bottom) – reference no. B-244; 240-241 – reference no. B-326; and 14 (bottom) – reference no. B-7199;

Kentucky Historical Society/Kentucky Military History Museum for page 270 (top);

TRH Pictures/Library of Congress for pages 276 and 328-329;

Collection of Michael J. McAfee for page 290;

Smithsonian Institution for pages 326 and 327 (bottom);

TRH Pictures/Mariners' Museum, Newport for pages 362-363;

MOLLUS— Massachusetts Collection, U.S. Army Military History Research Collection for page 390 (bottom);

The Library of Virginia for pages 406 (left) and 407.

All reasonable efforts have been made to contact the relevant copyright holders of the images contained within this book, at the time of going to press. If we were unable to reach you, please contact PRC Publishing Limited at the address on page 4.

THE AMERICAN CIVIL WAR: A VISUAL ENCYCLOPEDIA